Public Sector Reform

Public Sector Reform

Rationale, Trends and Problems

edited by Jan-Erik Lane

SAGE Publications
London • Thousand Oaks • New Delhi

This book owes its origins to an ECPR research session in
Heidelberg in September 1996

Editorial selection, Introduction, Chapters 7, 12 and 13
© Jan-Erik Lane 1997
Chapter 1 © John Halligan 1997
Chapter 2 © Evert A. Lindquist 1997
Chapter 3 © Ira Denkhaus and Volker Schneider 1997
Chapter 4 © Joachim Jens Hesse 1997
Chapter 5 © Michael J. Goldsmith and Edward C. Page 1997
Chapter 6 © Walter J.M. Kickert 1997
Chapter 8 © Thierry Postif 1997
Chapter 9 © Gerry Stoker 1997
Chapter 10 © Bernard Steunenberg and Nico Mol 1997
Chapter 11 © Carles Boix 1997

First published 1997

 SAGE Publications Ltd
6 Bonhill Street
London EC2A 4PU

SAGE Publications Inc.
2455 Teller Road
Thousand Oaks, California 91320

SAGE Publications India Pvt Ltd
32, M-Block Market
Greater Kailash – I
New Delhi 110 048

British Library Cataloguing in Publication data

A catalogue record for this book is available
from the British Library

ISBN 0 7619 5366 3
ISBN 0 7619 5367 1 (pbk)

Library of Congress catalog number 97–062135

Typeset by Mayhew Typesetting, Rhayader, Powys
Printed in Great Britain by Redwood Books, Trowbridge, Wiltshire

Contents

Contributors

Carles Boix is Assistant Professor in the Departments of Political Science and Economics at Ohio State University. He is author of a number of articles in the *American Journal of Political Science* and the *British Journal of Political Science* and *Political Parties, Growth and Equality* (Cambridge University Press, forthcoming).

Ira Denkhaus is a PhD student at the Max Planck Institute for the Study of Societies, Cologne and was masters student of political science, information science and social psychology at the University of Saarbrücken. She has published a work on advanced transport telematics as a major policy initiative in Germany and her current research interest is railway reform in the 1990s.

Michael J. Goldsmith is Professor of Politics at the University of Salford. He is currently Visiting Professor at the University of Rennes. His main research interests are in comparative local government and urban politics, and public policy. He has published an edited book on European integration and local government and is now working on two further projects: one on local government chief executive officers, and a second on innovation policy and regional economic development.

John Halligan is Professor of Public Administration at the Centre for Research in Public Sector Management at the University of Canberra. He has edited *Public Administration under Scrutiny: Essays in Honour of Roger Wettenhall* (Royal Institute of Public Administration Australia and University of Canberra, 1996) and co-authored (with John Power) *Political Management in the 1990s* (Oxford University Press, 1992) and *Local Government under Challenge* (Allen and Unwin, forthcoming 1998).

Joachim Jens Hesse has been Ford-Monnet Professor of European Institutions and Comparative Government in the University of Oxford and since 1997 has acted as Executive Director of the European Centre of Comparative Government and Public Policy in Berlin. His most recent publications include, *Constitutional Policy and Change in Europe* (Oxford, 1995), *Federalising Europe?* (Oxford, 1996), *Das Regierungssystem der Bundesrepublik Deutschland* (8th edn, Wiesbaden, 1997), *Rebuilding the State. Public Sector Reform in Central and Eastern Europe* (Baden-Baden, 1997), and *The European Yearbook of Comparative Government and Public Administration*, Vol. II (Baden-Baden/Boulder, CO, 1997).

Walter J.M. Kickert is Professor of Public Management at the Department of Public Administration at Erasmus University, Rotterdam and a former counsellor at the Ministry of Education and Sciences. He has published on government planning, public management and organization. His current research interests are public management and governance in complexity. He has edited *Public Management and Administrative Reform in Western Europe* (Edward Elgar, 1997) and was co-editor of *Public Policy and Administrative Sciences in The Netherlands* (Harvester Wheatsheaf, 1995).

Jan-Erik Lane is Professor of Comparative Politics in the Department of Political Science at the University of Geneva. He has published widely in comparative politics and public policy including *The Public Sector* (2nd edn, Sage, 1995) and, with Svante O. Ersson, *European Politics* (Sage, 1996) and *Politics and Society in Western Europe* (4th edn, Sage, 1998).

Evert A. Lindquist is Associate Professor in the Department of Political Science at the University of Toronto and former Visiting Fellow of the Treasury Board of Canada. He has published widely on the budget process, government restructuring, alternative delivery issues, consultative processes, transitions, Canadian think tanks, and policy communities. He is currently editing a volume for the Institute of Public Administration of Canada entitled *Government Restructuring and Career Public Service in Canada*.

Nico P. Mol is Professor of Public Financial Management at the Royal Military Academy, Breda, and Associate Professor of Public Finance at the University of Twente. He has published widely on budgeting and efficiency improvement in government organizations.

Edward C. Page is Professor of Politics at the University of Hull. His research interests are in the field of comparative public administration and public policy. Recent publications include (edited with J.E.S. Hayward) *Governing The New Europe* (Polity Press, 1995) and *People who Run Europe* (Oxford University Press, 1997).

Thierry Postif is a legal adviser at the Legal Department of the French gas utility, Gaz de France, master of conferences at the Institute of Political Education, Paris and former lecturer at the University of Paris.

Volker Schneider is Professor of Political Science at the University of Konstanz. He has published widely on the politics of technological development, policy networks and the evolution of governance structures. His current research interests are the role of long-term historical evolution of public policies, and the role of private actors in policy-making at the national, European and global level.

Bernard Steunenberg is Associate Professor in the Faculty of Public Administration and Public Policy at the University of Twente and Coordinator of The Netherlands Institute of Government. His main research interest is institutional rational choice and collective decision-making. He is co-editor (with Frans van Vught) of *Political Institutions and Public Policy: Perspectives on European Decision Making* (Kluwer Academic, 1997).

Gerry Stoker is Professor of Politics at the University of Strathclyde and was Programme Director of the five-year ESRC Local Governance Research Programme 1992–7. He has lectured in applied social sciences and public administration at Leicester Polytechnic, at Inlogov, the University of Birmingham and at the Department of Government, University of Essex. He was Visiting Professor, CULMA, at Wayne State University during 1990–1. He is author or editor of more than ten books and was a member of The Commission for Local Democracy.

Introduction

Public Sector Reform: Only Deregulation, Privatization and Marketization?

Jan-Erik Lane

The DPM framework

It is time to make an assessment of the outcomes of the public sector reform drive that has been going on for at least 10 years. Such an evaluation would be a kind of half-way statement of both ambitions and realities, as we may expect that it will not end for at least another decade. Public sector reform ideas are one thing, as discussed in the mass media as well as in scholarly journals. Public sector reform realities may be a quite different matter, as there tends to be a huge distance between lofty theory and down-to-earth practice.

A comparative approach seems to be the most suitable in this assessment, as countries differ substantially in their policy ambitions as well as in the policy outcomes that they have actually achieved. By comparing a couple of key countries one is in a better position to understand the logic of public sector reform, as one would be confronted with the actual variation in the scope and the orientation of policies as well as in the outcomes. One would thus be less prone to accept the ready-made blueprints of public sector reform that figure so prominently in the debate. We will look at a few of the industralized countries: Western Europe, Australia and Eastern Europe.

On the one hand, there is the ideology of public sector reform, as hammered out in the newspapers, in conferences and colloquia, and in politics. The standard ideas about public sector reform have been most influentially shaped by the teachings of Chicago School economics, focusing on deregulation (D) and privatization (P), as well as by the *Reinventing Government* message, arguing in favour of marketization (M). On the other hand, we have the realities of public sector reform, which are far more diverse than the DPM message. This tension between the simplistic notions about public sector reform and the complexities in actual reality is the theme of this volume, which examines both country experiences of and key issues in government reform.

The DPM framework can be seen as a three-stage rocket launched against the huge public sectors in the advanced capitalist countries adhering to the democratic regime. Once deregulation has been enacted, one proceeds to the questioning of the existence of large public enterprises, which ought to be incorporated and sold out. After deregulation and privatization it is time to proceed to the marketization of public sector core activities, the bureaux. Thus, external privatization would be followed by the creation of *internal markets* within government. Is the DPM framework feasible? And is it the only relevant approach to public sector reform?

Background

The public sector reform drive was initiated during the 1980s in the advanced capitalist democracies as a response to the public sector expansion process that had been such a dominant feature of the OECD countries after the Second World War. In the early 1980s there was a realization that the public sector had a profound problem in relation to how well its various programmes were operating, given the fact that the public sector had grown from below 25% to over 45% of GDP in a couple of decades as an OECD average. The public sector performance problem called for reform strategies; however, these could vary considerably in scope, orientation and accomplishments.

To some the search for improved public sector performance was simply the task of making the public sector work better by shaping it up. But to others, it was the starting point for a complete questioning of the welfare state. Actually, the public sector reform drive has taken place at the same time as the welfare state crisis has emerged, but these two processes are not identical although they are linked. The search for improved performance has been directed to all kinds of public expenditures or programmes, not only those making up the welfare state.

The public sector encompasses all the various programmes that governments at different levels run by means of taxation in a broad sense, including social security schemes. The public sector deals mainly with three functions: public resource allocation, income redistribution and public regulation. In all these branches of government there are today reform attempts. The DPM approach – deregulation, privatization and marketization – argues that the public sector needs to be reformed in a fundamental fashion, touching all three fundamental government functions: allocation, redistribution and regulation. From where comes the DPM framework?

Chicago School economics: deregulation and privatization

In the teachings of the scholars connected with the Economics Department at the University of Chicago there is always a strong preference for the private sector as against the public sector. Societies are less dependent upon governmental intervention in the market economy than has been traditionally believed in, for instance, the theory of market failure. Actually, the

public sector may face serious difficulties in policy-making and implementation, which in the public choice school are called 'government failure'.
The implication is that the public sector ought to reduce its commitments,
as markets work better than governments (Friedman, 1962).

The Chicago School message concerning public sector reform is very
much focused on deregulation and its implications for the role of government in the economy. If public regulation, as George Stigler argued, is
unnecessary, then numerous public sector programmes regulating the
economy could be done away with, including the agencies that were implementing these public regulatory schemes.

Extensive deregulation could hardly take place without altering the
position of the many and often very large public enterprises. What would be
the role of public monopolies in a world without entry regulation? 'Privatization' was the answer from scholars adhering to the Chicago School
(Friedman and Friedman, 1980; Posner, 1992). Thus, considerable portions
of the economy would first be deregulated and then the public enterprises
operating in these sectors would be made into joint-stock companies and
sold out to private investors (Stigler, 1975).

No doubt the combination of deregulation and privatization appeared
logical, but in actual practice things were not that clear cut. Neither
deregulation nor privatization was accomplished in a straightforward
manner, except in a few cases. As soon as deregulation was attempted, it
was often realized that other forms of regulation became necessary
(Majone, 1994). And governments turned out to be reluctant to privatize
their chief public enterprises, instead choosing to transform them into public
joint stock companies, largely owned by government. Theory does not
match reality when it comes to the Chicago School recommendations,
which attracted so much attention that one almost forgot another major
source of ideas about public sector reform, namely public management.

One may also question whether the internal logic in the Chicago School
interpretation of public sector reform was always stringent. Deregulation
was called for because competition, if allowed to rule without restrictions,
would bring about efficient solutions in the allocation of resources. But how
could one be assured that the playing field had been levelled for all potential
participants? Anti-trust policy-making could offer such effective competition
rules, yet Harold Demsetz (1990; 1991) rejected the whole notion of
government regulation enhancing competition.

In the new public management ideology, government should use competition as one of its chief tools for the provision of services. Thus, one
often observes governments engaging in new and more daring schemes for
anti-trust policy-making, such as for instance the European Union with its
competition framework, covering not only the market institutions but also
public sector procurement. There is a kind of contradiction in the Chicago
School message for public sector reform, rejecting both government regulation of markets and government creation of competition. Governments do
two things: they restructure their traditional public enterprises, turning them

into public joint stock companies operating in a market environment, and they sharpen the institutions of competition and free entry in order to level the playing field. The drive for anti-trust policy-making and implementation is both domestic and international, as deregulation can only work if the rules enhancing contestability are transparent and enforced by the state or an international body.

When governments in the advanced capitalist economies have engaged in extensive deregulation of infrastructure, they have also made institutional reforms of their own business, that is by changing their public enterprises into public joint stock companies or into privatized firms. Why is it attractive to have public joint stock companies instead of public enterprises or bureaux? Ian Thynne (1994) has called attention to the major trend towards *incorporation* in the public sector. In such a world of public–private competition for contracts it is absolutely essential that fair rules of competition are in place, meaning that there must be anti-trust policy-making. In a public sector that has been extensively incorporated, where public joint stock companies operate in a Stigler world of competition, the Demsetz rejection of anti-trust measures cannot be upheld.

Marketization: tendering/bidding

In their *Reinventing Government* (1993) David Osborne and Ted Gaebler summarized most of the reform proposals within that branch of public administration which goes under the label of 'public management'. Instead of looking at the public sector as a system of rules for governing in an impartial manner in order to meet the requirements of equity and the rule of law (the public administration perspective), public management has emphasized goals and the achievement of objectives. Thus, we find in Osborne and Gaebler a number of traditional ideas such as: catalytic government: steering rather than rowing; mission-driven government: transforming rule-driven organizations; results-oriented government: funding outcomes, not inputs; customer-driven government; meeting the needs of the customer, not the bureaucracy; anticipatory government; prevention rather than cure; as well as decentralized government, moving from hierarchy to participation and teamwork; and community-owned government, empowering rather than serving.

However, these ideas about public sector reform were hardly new, as they had surfaced time and again since the early 1960s. It is wrong to believe that nothing had been done about public sector reform before the mid 1980s. On the contrary, numerous ideas about budgetary reform and implementation, for example, were launched at the end of the 1960s and during the 1970s (Wildavsky, 1979; 1988). Thus, management by objectives has attracted lots of interest for a long time.

What was new in the *Reinventing Government* message was the role that was given to market forces, not in the Chicago sense of reducing government in order to increase the private sector, but in the sense of employing the mechanisms of markets within government. The introduction of so-called internal markets within the public sector is what Osborne and Gaebler had in mind, calling for: competitive government, injecting competition into service delivery; enterprising government, earning rather than spending; and market-oriented government, leveraging change through the market.

The public sector seems very much anchored in the use of authority and hierarchical organization, whereas the market employs voluntary exchange as its mode of operation. Yet, the *Reinventing Government* message was that short-term contracting could play a far larger role in the provision of services than realized within traditional public management theory. However, again realities do not match theory, as the so-called purchaser–provider model has turned out to be more a complement to authority or hierarchy in the Williamson (1975) sense than a substitute.

Managerialism in the public sector has to be combined with the traditional concerns of public administration, that is the rule of law. Thus, when governments have attempted to implement the *Reinventing Government* scheme, they have been conscious of the trade-offs that have to be made between goal achievement and procedural accountability in the public sector. Thus, governments have tried to distinguish the business activity of government, to be financed by user fees, from the service activity, to be paid for by taxation. The *Reinventing Government* message is far more appropriate to the business sector of government than to the service sector, where not only does efficiency meet other concerns but also it is the case that the accomplishment of effectiveness requires an understanding of how government agencies operate (Wilson, 1989).

The quest for internal marketization of the public sector amounts to a new form of managerialism, much more radical than has been witnessed before, as described by Gerald Caiden in *Administrative Reform Comes of Age* (1991). The British compulsory competitive tendering (CCT) scheme is appropriate in relation to certain services where the Walras conditions for competition hold, but can it really be extended to all kinds of public sector activities? The case for hierarchy in lowering transaction costs, as stated in the Williamson (1996) governance model, seems as relevant today as when Weber argued the case for bureaucracy. Lower production costs in CCT versus higher transaction costs: only an analysis of the outcomes of public sector reform can allow us to judge what the benefits and the costs will be.

The double concerns of public sector reform

Although Chicago School economics and the *Reinventing Government* framework offered the attractive DPM blueprint for public sector reform, they did not identify, individually or in combination, all the ongoing concerns in relation to reforming the public sector. In order to grasp both the comprehensiveness and the depth of public sector reform in the 1990s we need to cast our nets in a much wider fashion. Examining what has been accomplished rather than listening to simplistic messages, we note that public sector reforms are driven by two entirely distinct considerations, playing different roles in various country developments. The DPM framework only identifies one of these concerns, namely efficiency, and this it does in a partial manner.

Efficiency has no doubt been a major concern for those countries with an advanced economy and a large public sector founded upon a constitutional democracy. The efficiency search has meant that public sector growth had to be halted, that public programmes often needed to find new service delivery mechanisms or alternative sources of funding, and that, generally speaking, public expenditures should be pruned or public sector commitments rolled back. The drive for efficiency has been a most general one, dealing with macro and micro aspects as well as with both sides of efficiency, that is internal efficiency or productivity and external efficiency or effectiveness.

At the same time, however, it must be pointed out there has been another public sector reform drive that has called for more state action or other and new forms of public intervention in society, namely the search for better public accountability and the promotion of individual or group justice in the form of fairness. The most conspicuous expression of the accountability search is the increased attention paid to key phrases such as 'human rights', 'due process' and 'transparency of rules'. And the demand for these reforms has not been confined only to the public sector, but has included also private sector reforms such as the promotion of human rights or collective group rights in the market economy: 'equal protection' – something entirely left out in the DPM scheme.

Nowhere has the search for accountability been more characteristic than in Eastern Europe in the early 1990s, when the former communist countries established a *Rechtsstaat*. But the ambition to broaden and more firmly implement civil and political rights has been typical also of Western Europe and the other advanced capitalist countries, certainly the Anglo-Saxon countries overseas, where the principles of the rule of law have been given new content, calling for the protection of the rights of many minorities or a majority group such as women, especially but far from only in multicultural societies.

One should analyse the public sector reform drive in a comprehensive fashion, more specifically as a search for either economic efficiency or public accountability or both. The former we will call 'proportionality', that is between public sector costs and benefits, and the latter we will refer to as 'impartiality' in law, which not only relates to the public sector but concerns also the private sector, where efficiency usually makes consideration of the rights of certain individuals or collectivities marginal.

The degree of comprehensiveness of state reform varies from one country to another just as the focus of orientation shifts towards either efficiency or justice. This is hardly surprising considering that we are talking about a phenomenon of the size of the state in societies with a mixed economy. Whatever the measuring rod – money, employees or laws – the states in the advanced capitalist countries are large as they practise in one form or another a mixed economy. This is not denying that the size of the public sectors differs in a profound manner among the advanced capitalist countries. But the search for public sector reform has been a vital concern both in the welfare states and in the welfare societies.

Although much attention in public sector reform has focused on efficiency, this is too simplistic a picture, because at the same time there is a renewed emphasis on citizens' rights in relation to both the public and the private sectors. Let us discuss briefly the two chief objectives in public sector reform. First, what, more specifically, are the concerns of economic efficiency in relation to the public sector, that is the allocative, redistributive and regulative branches of government?

Economic efficiency: proportionality

Countries with a large public sector, as in the advanced capitalist countries, face the profound problem of relating the income side of the public household to the expenditure side. The relationship between demand for and supply of public programmes involves the interaction between the citizens (the tax payers) and the politicians and the officials (the spenders). One approach to modelling this relationship between the income and expenditure sides is to focus on how a quid pro quo is established between taxes and charges on the one hand and the provision of goods and services on the other. This is the micro approach to efficiency in the public sector.

Micro efficiency

The quid pro quo model was first launched by Knut Wicksell (1967) in an attempt to create a rational foundation for the public sector. The model underlines the basic reciprocity in the public sector between the population and the officials/managers of the state and its institutions: how are decisions to be made such that what the public sector delivers is worth what the citizens have to pay for it? The model is as relevant today as when it was first presented around 1900. It entails questions about institutional performance which are highly relevant for public sector reform in the 1990s, although the labels are new or have a new meaning: 'privatization', 'internal markets', 'compulsory competitive tendering', 'public joint stock companies', 'user fees', 'benefit taxation' etc.

The quid pro quo model may not only be used to analyse the strong market drive that has already had heavy consequences for the public sector in many countries. It may also be employed for the interpretation of the reform attempts within the public sector, that is measures which aim not to undo public administration but to improve upon it. Efficiency in the public sector between the demand side and the supply side refers basically to proportionality or the quid pro quo equating of taxation and user fees on the one hand and the reception of services and goods on the other hand, meaning value for money in each programme.

On the one hand, the delivery of services must be such that the taxpayers feel that quantity and quality in service provision are proportional to taxes and charges. Why would citizens put up so much money for a public sector if they felt that the service provided is not worth the costs they have to carry? The question of proportionality can be tackled in various ways, as there is a choice between alternative institutions structuring the economic interaction between the electorate and the politicians. The question of proportionality requires deliberations about not only the total size of the public sector but also the use of alternative mechanisms for the provision of various services. Public sector reform is as much about the containment of public sector expansion as about the pros and cons of new institutions for service delivery as well as funding.

Public expenditures must make economic sense. There is in the 1990s a realization that the huge tax state may suffer from inefficiencies, where the occurrence of waste undermines the legitimacy of the entire public household. The critical question is then how to design mechanisms that will promote efficiency in public expenditures. Economic efficiency in the public household refers most often to allocative expenditures. And it may be tackled by means of spectacular reform efforts such as hiving off, competitive tendering and the introduction of public joint stock companies. Or economic efficiency may be enhanced by down-to-earth budgetary reforms such as the introduction of performance evaluation.

Economic decision theory suggests that choice in demand and competition in supply enhance economic efficiency in equating the willingness to pay and the minimization of costs: proportionality, as it were. But how do governments increase choice and competition without accepting a straightforward market regime where the public household would be restricted to classical public goods provision?

The objective of economic efficiency is to be accomplished in the context of a mixed economy, which means that citizens will compare what they get from government with what they could achieve in the market. Transaction costs will lead them to choose public provision of many services, especially if there are also opportunities for free riding. But citizens will be concerned about the production costs in public provision, as minimizing transaction costs is not the sole concern. The market is a real challenge to politicians and officials, as citizens may demand that government be scaled down when value is not proportional to cost. Often public sector reform responds to the market challenge by the adoption of market metaphors without hiving off.

The public household operates at different levels of government including sub-national government units having various degrees of discretion from the national government, including taxation powers as well as budgetary autonomy. Much of the European welfare state is concentrated in the local governments, either the communes or the county councils. Whereas public sector reform aiming at economic efficiency has focused mainly on the national government, proportionality at the regional and local level remains a very relevant concern. The difficulty is that local governments attempt to achieve the objectives of both democratic responsiveness and economic efficiency. This double objective function has certainly strained the local governments, because democratically elected councils are simply not the same institutions as firms producing outputs. At the local government level one may observe numerous reforms attempting to get to grips with economic efficiency, including incorporation, internal markets and hiving off. The problem of efficiency becomes complicated when the public sector is structured at various levels of governments. Decentralization has been a major reform strategy for handling complexity in the public sector. Do unitary and federal states differ here?

The call for improved performance in the public sector has been made in all key public sector operations: allocation, redistribution and regulation. And there is a search for new institutions in the public sector which result in improved state performance guided by new institutional economies (Alchian, 1977). This is one major side of state reform in Europe.

Allocative efficiency, meaning effectiveness or that benefits equal costs, as well as X-efficiency in the Leibenstein sense of minimizing average costs or productivity, has been promoted by the employment of various strategies, including incorporation, bidding/tendering and benchmarking:

1 decentralization and devolution of tasks and competences through institutional autonomy and managerial independence as well as free agencies and multi-year budgets
2 performance assessment, and reviews of efficiency and effectiveness
3 user choice through greater freedom of choice for citizens, and user voice through management boards with user representation
4 separation between provider and producer, and contract steering via tendering and contracting out of services
5 transformation of public enterprises into joint stock companies owned by the state, or the sell-out of a few of these
6 competition between public and private organizations and public–private cooperation, blurring the traditional borders between the public and the private sectors.

'Privatization' and 'deregulation' have been words very often used as banners by politicians who engage in an encompassing public sector reform strategy. What these phrases mean in actual practice may differ from country to country, meaning that one needs to take a close look at the reform strategies, at what they entail as well as what their actual consequences are in different countries. They relate mostly to the allocative and regulative branches of government. The overall trend is towards the insertion of market type decision mechanisms into the public sector without resorting to privatization proper. The key phrases include 'value for money', 'choice', 'discretion to manage in return for better outcomes', 'better service at less cost'. Contract steering is employed more and more. In Europe the implementation of European Union economic principles concerning public sector tendering further strengthens the tendencies towards marketization, which does not necessarily mean hiving off to the private sector.

Efficiency considerations have also loomed large in public redistribution, which refers to the other side of the coin: macro efficiency. Yet efficiency considerations raised in relation to the redistributive branch of government come under the label of 'incentive compatibility', focusing on the effects of huge transfer programmes on economic motivation and its role in the economy, especially for taxation.

Macro efficiency

In the Wicksell approach the focus was clearly on each public programme and how it could be funded in such a way that those that benefited from it also paid the cost for it. However, Wicksell was very much aware of the problem of income distribution as groups of people could for various reasons lack a level of purchasing power that would allow them to enter the market economy or demand public programmes. Thus, social justice required public intervention in the form of the redistribution of income and wealth.

In the advanced capitalist states, the size of the redistributive expenditures has grown immensely during the last decade. And the rise in transfer payments of various kinds involves a tremendous challenge for governments to both find equitable programmes and fund them in a manner that does not hurt the economy. Transfer programmes have been attacked owing to their consequences for incentives in the economy. Thus, it is argued that tax financed income redistribution involves a heavy excess burden. Questions about the consequences for the economy of tax wedges of various kinds, in taxation or in subsidies, naturally concern the entire public sector, but they tend to be most acute in relation to the huge social security contributions as well as the transfer payments.

Governments have tried to control the growth mechanisms in the transfer payments by a number of public sector reforms. Since transfer programmes are pay-as-you-go systems in most countries, governments have attempted two things. One is to reduce the generosity built into the programmes, reflecting the many individual promises often made during elections which taken as whole are difficult to keep. The other is to introduce new schemes of funding, which in a Wicksellian spirit tie the benefits more closely to the costs. Thus, transfer programmes have been trimmed and at the same time connected to individual contributions according to the principles of insurance systems.

The search for macro efficiency has had implications for the making and conduct of macroeconomic policies. The awareness of excess burden problems has made governments less receptive to a Keynesian macro-economic regime and more prone to accept some form of monetarist regime, favouring low inflation ahead of selective government demand management and undoing tax wedges.

Now managerialism, with its emphasis on micro efficiency in performance and on macro efficiency in reforms to the transfer state with its pay-as-you-go system, is not the sole concern of parliamentarians and executives in Europe. They also face an increasingly strong demand for more accountability and ethos in state operations as well as in the private sector. Let us turn now to the second major concern of public sector reform.

Accountability: impartiality

Accountability stands for impartiality and the equal protection of all with regard to human rights. In a democratic state with a market economy, impartiality is a highly relevant concern. This is the other side of the public sector reform movement. In the last decade we have seen a number of reforms attempting to increase accountability in the public sector. They range from measures designed to increase democratic legitimacy, through for instance participatory democracy or new forms of representative democracy, to the introduction of more human rights and new institutions for the implementation of these rights. Due process and civil and political rights have been underlined not only in the new democracies but also in the established ones. Legality is a prominent feature in the constitutional democracies. Which strategies have been promoted in various countries in order to increase public accountability?

There is a strong demand for more accountability of public officials, and strong voices are raised for the protection of minority rights by means of public sector programmes. Legality is emphasized by groups who seek to protect collective rights by means of public policy. In a few countries, corruption and the fight against it are given much attention. The notion of human rights is given an increasingly prominent place in both policy and the legal order in several West European countries, partly as a response to demands for minority protection. And the conception of judicial review in one form or another has been given much more attention at both the national and international levels: the judicialization of politics. A number of reforms that have figured prominently recently include:

1 more political accountability by devolving power and influence
2 bolstering the role of parliamentarians in checking government
3 establishment of citizen tribunals
4 introduction of a constitutional court
5 more scope for judicial review
6 codification of comprehensive human rights
7 increased recognition of the European Court of Justice
8 strengthening of the control of administrative processes

9   more power to ombudsmen/women
10 increasing relevance of the rights of individuals or groups in the private
    sector.

What the call for more legality and the rule of law in both the public and
the private sectors may lead to is the judicialization of politics. This could
entail that the balance in the *trias politica* is tipped in favour of the judicial
branch of the state at the expense of the executive and legislative branches.

One may find strong currents towards the judicialization of politics at the
national level and on the intergovernmental level in the European setting.
Thus, the European Convention on Human Rights of the Council of
Europe plays an increasing role in codifying what residents in Europe may
expect in terms of civil and political rights. And the EU Court has begun to
take decisions with implications for human rights.

Demands for and supply of public sector reform

The extensive as well as intensive search for new governance mechanisms in
the public sector is driven by a true ambition to accomplish social objectives
such as proportionality and impartiality, but on the other hand one cannot
bypass the role of opportunistic behaviour in these reform attempts.

Public sector reform has become one of those things that no government
can do without. Since all governments attempt it, each and every government must engage in it. There is policy diffusion going on, as left-wing
governments feel tempted to try the things that right-wing governments
have done, even if outcomes are mixed.

On the demand side, there is within the electorate an uneasy feeling that
the public sector is neither efficient nor impartial, although there is no call
for a complete dismantling of the welfare state: see *The Scope of Government* (Borre and Scarborough, 1995) for an analysis of citizen attitudes
towards the welfare state. Thus, politicians are pressed to do something
but not question the entire public sector. There is a clear risk here of the
occurrence of garbage-can processes, where reforms are initiated and
implemented without clear objectives, reliable means and standard operating procedures for evaluation and further correction. Clearly, a majority
in the electorate favours the principle of proportionality in relation to the
public sector, getting value for money, but there are also sizeable groups
who fear the consequences of the implementation of the DPM framework.
Thus, on the demand side, in some countries there is considerable political
conflict over the use of the DPM format, even intense confrontation,
whereas in others the silent majority has prevailed.

Public sector reform can become a myth that politicians feed with various
proposals, more or less taken out of the blue, in order to maintain the
legitimacy of their concerns, without any belief in substantive results and
final accomplishments. Public sector reform may develop into a public
pathology, where people talk about what is going on without really

knowing why things are going on and how the outcomes are related to the efforts. If the public sector reform drive takes this turn towards symbolic policy-making, then the major goal of enhancing efficiency will be hurt.

The tendency towards a garbage-can process is reinforced by the competition among politicians for offering various proposals for public sector reform. The fear of not being seen as progressive and the danger that one's opponents come first is fuelled by myopia and opportunism. Offering public sector reform policies may pay off heavily in the short run. At the same time, when public sector reform processes enter a garbage-can stage, the risks for the participating politicians are considerably increased, as the electorate will ask questions about the outcomes, at least in the long run.

On the supply side, public sector reform proposals are often suggested by the bureaux and the public enterprises themselves. There is a kind of managerial revolution in the bureaux and the public enterprises, where reform is sought for reasons of efficiency but where one cannot rule out a strong wish for larger managerial discretion. Perhaps these two goals coincide when managers offer reform proposals to politicians or the public, often backed by experts or the mass media.

Managers have found ample opportunities to refer to the new DPM framework in order to push for reforms which strengthen their position. The most conspicuous expression of this is the attempt to transform public enterprises into joint stock companies, controlled by the state or local governments by means of their ownership of shares. The drive for incorporation is one of the most pronounced aspects of public sector reform, which is not confined to the often huge public enterprises but has been attempted also in relation to ordinary public agencies.

On the supply side, one may observe that the DPM framework seems to be more attractive than the alternative approach to the public sector, that is the theories within public policy and public administration that underline complexity (Kaufman et al., 1986; McKevitt and Lawton, 1994; March and Olsen, 1995). And simplicity is maximized by institutions such as incorporation, internal markets and tender bidding. It almost seems as if the forces on the supply side want to alter the conception of the citizen in relation to public administration into the role of consumer of goods and services, somehow with an arrangement under market-like forms but with participation by political authorities. Ordinary people are no longer *Bürger* but *Kunden* in the public sector. Again, the simultaneous quest for impartiality is a strong antidote to the DPM excesses on the supply side.

Conclusion

The seminal process of public sector expansion since the Second World War has left politicians with a huge set of tasks and promises to be fulfilled by means of various programmes. There is increasingly a realization that a big public sector not only offers a set of tools for solving social problems but has efficiency problems of its own. Besides the search for more efficiency in the public sector there is the call for more accountability and rule of law in society. Here there is a focus on justice and the ethos of governments. The standard DPM framework for public sector reform seems highly limited in its concerns when one takes into account the variety of public sector reform in the advanced capitalist countries.

Economic efficiency and political accountability may not go together, meaning that goal conflicts may occur. Clearly, both objectives – efficiency and accountability – have played a major role in the efforts at public sector reform, but can they be accomplished at the same time without trade-offs? The political accountability of the public household involves difficult questions about democracy and administrative legality. Any evaluation of the public sector reforms that have also figured prominently in the 1980s and early 1990s must focus on public accountability. The economic side of the coin may have been more spectacular than the legal side, but both exist not only in Eastern Europe but also in Western Europe where governments both pursue market strategies and introduce rights and mechanisms for their protection. Is there a contradiction here? Market strategies are supposed to cut costs but the rights legislation will probably increase costs. Yet, there is a trade-off only if these two types of strategy are commensurable, which indeed they may not be because they respond to different needs.

There may be a tension between these two values: performance or effectiveness of government operations, and justice as the rule of law in the state. Efficiency is not the same as accountability. On the contrary, it may come into conflict with the requirements of due process and legality. Efficiency and the rule of law are extremely valid values. As objectives they are entirely different, one being on the economic or technological side and the other on the legal side.

The basic purpose of this volume is twofold. First, it argues the limitations of the DPM framework in both the analysis and the practice of public sector reform, as it fails to give an understanding of the complexities of the search for proportionality and impartiality. Public sector reform is much more than DPM. It is not only that the drive for more impartiality in public sector reform is entirely neglected by the DPM approach. It is also that the efficiency drive stemming from the search for proportionality between costs and benefits in the public sector involves much more than simply deregulation, privatization and marketization (Eliassen and Koiman, 1993; Olsen and Peters, 1996). Secondly, it shows that the country experiences with public sector reform differ widely in terms of how radical the implementation of the DPM framework has been up to now. The two polar cases are Australia and New Zealand on the one hand, where it has been put into practice with determination and completeness, and Scandinavia on the other hand, where simplicity has hardly replaced complexity and where the DPM framework has entered into a symbiosis with big government.

This volume includes both analyses of country experiences and examination of analytical issues. Thus, it covers the following countries: the UK,

Australia, New Zealand, Canada, Germany, France, Spain, The Netherlands, the core East European countries and the Nordic countries. Each chapter has, however, its own approach to public sector reforms, focusing specifically on some reform policies and their outcomes. Moreover, the volume contains four special analytical chapters dealing with the status of local governments, the question of decentralization, the search for economic competitiveness by policy measures, and the status of the public joint stock company.

Public sector reform in the advanced economies with a democratic regime results from two policy ambitions. On the one hand, there is the search for efficiency and impartiality in the public sector with implications for the private sector. On the other hand, there are attempts at a reduction of the commitments of the welfare state (Peters and Savoie, 1995). In the well-known case of New Zealand these two developments coincide in an almost drastic manner, but countries may move along only one of these tracks (Kelsey, 1995; Boston et al., 1996). What follows is an examination of both these major trends in the 1990s.

Public sector reform activates political conflict in the advanced capitalist democracies. The DPM framework is the programme of the marketers – a Ricardian conception of changing the public sector towards more choice and competition. When public sector reform involves cut back management then distributional conflicts surface, especially when politicians attempt to reduce already made commitments in transfer payments towards citizens.

D = deregulation meets with broad approval. Opening up markets to free entry and eliminating licenses seem everywhere to have the same effect: more production and lower prices. Traditional economic regulation creating legal monopolies does not work, all concerned parties agree. A number of sectors have been deregulated: communication, infrastructure, bank and insurance, energy and water, etc. The process of mondialization no doubt further promotes the pressures for deregulation. P = privatization as a strategy for public sector reform gives rise to political confrontation, as political parties and trade unions accept incorporation of public enterprises but not their hiving off to the private sector. The huge state monopolies are in a process of change, but there are alternatives other than full scale privatization. Some countries maintain some of their public enterprises, whereas others incorporate them and sell out some of the equity on the bourse. It is generally argued that D implies some form of P, meaning that in a deregulated market public enterprises have to be joint stock companies, at least partially listed on the stock exchange. M = marketization, or the creation of internal markets by tendering/bidding, is the most conflictual kind of public sector reform. It raises critical questions about the status of public employees in relation to public law as well as calls for the introduction of a public competition policy implemented by means of court procedures. Sometimes it is argued that M entails P, as government must be strictly neutral when it handles processes of tendering/bidding, meaning that many of its own bureaux should also be incorporated and treated as independent players bidding in fair competition.

The call for public sector reform as more proportionality and impartiality is accepted also among groups who reject the DPM framework, especially P and M. Public enterprises and bureaux may improve their manner of operating by less spectacular and more down-to-earth reforms, such as performance evaluation and decentralization. The demand for more transparency and rights comes to a considerable degree from egalitarians, who wish to see more equal treatment not only within government but also in the private sector, i.e. in markets. Fairness is not only narrowly about competition, but raises many questions about impartiality in both the public and the private sectors. Justice as the reason for public sector reform is a call for more government regulation against corrupt practices wherever they may appear.

References

Alchian, A.A. (1977) *Economic Forces at Work*. Indianapolis: Liberty Press.

Borre, O. and Scarborough, E. (eds) (1995) *The Scope of Government*. Oxford: Oxford University Press.

Boston, J., Martin, J., Pallot, J. and Walsch, P. (1996) *Public Management. The New Zealand Model*. Aukland: Oxford University Press.

Caiden, G.E. (1991) *Administrative Reform Comes of Age*. Berlin: de Gruyter.

Demsetz, H. (1990) *Ownership, Control and the Firm*. Oxford: Blackwell.

Demsetz, H. (1991) *Efficiency, Competition and Policy*. Oxford: Blackwell.

Eliassen, K. and Koiman, J. (1993) *Managing Public Organization: Lessons from Contemporary European Experience*. London: Sage.

Friedman, M. (1969) *Capitalism and Freedom*. Chicago: University of Chicago Press.

Friedman, M. and Friedman, R. (1980) *Free to Choose*. New York: Harcourt Brace Jovanovich.

Kaufman, F.X., Majone, G. and Ostrom, V. (eds) (1986) *Guidance, Control and Evaluation in the Public Sector*. Berlin: de Gruyter.

Kelsey, J. (1995) *Economic Fundamentalism*. London: Pluto Press.

Majone, G. (1994) 'The rise of the regulatory state in Europe', *West European Politics*, 17: 77–101.

March, J. and Olsen, J.P. (1995) *Democratic Governance*. New York: Free Press.

McKevitt, D. and Lawton, A. (eds) (1994) *Public Sector Management*. London; Sage.

Olsen, J.P. and Peters, B.G. (1996) (eds) *Lessons from Experience*. Oslo: Universitetsferlaget.

Osborne, D. and Gaebler, T. (1993) *Reinventing Government*. New York: Plume.

Peters, B.G. and Savoie, D.J. (eds) (1995) *Governance in a Changing Environment*. Montreal and Kingston: McGill-Queen University Press.

Posner, R.A. (1992) *Economic Analysis of Law*. Boston: Little, Brown.

Stigler, G. (1975) *Citizen and the State: Essays on Regulation*. Chicago: University of Chicago Press.

Thynne, I. (1994) 'The incorporated company as an instrument of government: a quest for a comparative understanding', *Governance*, 7: 59–82.

Wicksell, K. (1967) 'A new principle of just taxation', in R.A. Musgrave and A.T. Peacock (eds), *Classics in the Theory of Public Finance*. New York: St. Martin's Press. pp. 72–118.

Wildavsky, A. (1979) *Speaking Truth to Power*. Boston: Little, Brown & Co.

Wildavsky, A. (1988) *The New Politics of the Budgetary Process*. Boston: Little, Brown & Co.

Williamson, O. (1975) *Markets and Hierarchies*. New York: Free Press.

Williamson, O. (1996) *Governance*. Oxford: Oxford University Press.

Wilson, J.Q. (1989) *Bureaucracy*. New York: Basic Books.

1

New Public Sector Models: Reform in Australia and New Zealand

John Halligan

Australia and New Zealand have attracted international attention for their public sector reforms. New Zealand in particular has been hailed as an exemplar of reform, providing a model that displays many unique features, which have been widely emulated. Australia is sufficiently similar to be readily comparable for many purposes while otherwise offering a distinctive approach to reform. In both countries, the last 20 years have been remarkable for the level of public sector change. Four features have been important: the magnitude of the reform, the breadth of the reforms, the longevity of the process and the importance of the changes.

The Australian and New Zealand experiences have been characterized by a wave of reform which surfaced in the early to mid 1980s. There have been two periods of intensive change in their histories since the foundation of their governments in the mid nineteenth century. A major period of modernization occurred between the 1880s and the 1920s; the second period has been in the 1980s and 1990s. Both periods are characterized by intensive change, experimentation and attention to system design, and have been identified with social experiments and antipodean laboratories of change.

Both countries emerged in the 1980s from a long period characterized by heavily regulated economies and a commitment to using the public sector for providing the services of a welfare state. Increasingly both countries turned to the private sector and the use of market principles within the public sector, which have been linked to broader programmes of economic reform. They have responded to economic pressures with distinctive models of reform which share similarities. In both cases fiscal difficulties played a significant part, and financial deregulation of both economies produced intensified pressures for public sector reform. For New Zealand the crisis was most acute with a budget deficit, a balance of payments deficit and structural imbalances. In the Australian case a package of reforms was promoted by a new government with a mandate and determination to launch a reform programme. With mounting economic demands the programme was extended and enlarged.

A second common feature was that reform was rapid, systemic and comprehensive in two senses: specific reforms were applied across the public service/sector and a full range of measures was introduced which left no area untouched. Thirdly, reform has been sustained over a long period – since 1983 for Australia, and 1984 for New Zealand. Finally, what differentiated the 1980s from the 1970s was the rejection of traditional ways – identified with administration – and their replacement by a package of reforms based on management and market. However, despite these similarities between the two countries, major differences have existed with regard to the framework, the institutional design and the reform process, the most significant being in the realm of ideas with institutional economics exercising great influence in New Zealand.

In a short review, it is possible neither to cover fully the range of reforms in both countries, nor to develop comparisons between them.[1] This chapter addresses questions about analysing reform, before focusing on the results and consequences of key reforms in the two countries.

Analysing reform options and objectives

Evaluating reform

The relationship between reform objectives and outcomes can be difficult to establish where reform has been comprehensive and ongoing. Under a comprehensive programme, a specific initiative is part of a series of reforms, and isolating individual reforms can be problematic. The transience of public service systems is also problematic, one challenge being how to monitor the results of reforms when the pace of change is rapid and performance criteria continue to evolve and performance boundaries keep expanding. In both countries retrospective rationalizing has been apparent, leading to adaptations and refinements designed to validate the design decisions. The reform programme stretched across several stages: the long-term impact depended upon review, refinements, additions and consolidation.

In the case of Australia, an official and authoritative source on reform is not readily discerned. New Zealand is more straightforward, with an original document, a coherent but complex model, and an explicit legislative basis. Yet still observers have noted the difficulties in acquiring sound evaluation of the model: the lack of good empirical evidence, and the difficulties with making comparisons over time and isolating the impact of reforms from broader economic factors (Kelsey, 1995; OECD, 1996a; Boston et al., 1996a).

Goals may be ambiguously expressed, and may change as reforms are implemented and experience suggests modifications (Olsen and Peters, 1996). There may be a lack of clarity in objectives. A reform may have multiple objectives, which apply at several levels. There are few reformers who do not invoke efficiency, and more usually accountability appears in some guise, but political rhetoric does not necessarily provide a firm basis for subsequent analysis. In seeking to link reform objectives to the results, there is therefore a range of difficulties. Nevertheless, results can be related

Table 1.1 *Reform options*

	Public sector	
Focus	Core	Outer/margins
Intrasector	Public service reforms	Corporatization
Intersector	Intergovernmental (decentralization)	Privatization

in a general way to the objectives of reformers and the extent to which they have been accomplished, with reference to efficiency and accountability.

Reform options

There are three basic components in the public sector: the core (often identified with the public or civil service), the outer (or off-budget) sector, and the sub-national sphere. Reform that involves movements between any of these, and possibly the private sector, produces the options in Table 1.1, the three main ones being corporatization, privatization and intergovernmental reform, the last involving the sub-national components of government. Within the core itself a range of options is available including commercialization, reorganization and various financial and human resource management reforms.

A second approach is to address the application of specific market principles to the core. It is here that some of the more radical dimensions of the New Zealand system come into play, but both countries have become increasingly the subject of contractualism, competition and contestability as marketization has been accepted as having general application to all parts of the public sector. The use of these principles has to some extent been specific to policy sectors, and involves separating out roles in delivery from other responsibilities. Associated with this focus on non-commercial functions is contraction of the scope of the sector, and the greater reliance on non-government agencies.

A third consideration is the use of a management framework for guiding and giving coherence to reforms. To this end the question of the level of reform needs clarification. It is clear that change varies according to magnitude and significance and that some recognition of these variations is helpful. These may be differentiated according to whether they are first-, second- or third-order changes (Hall, 1993). At the most basic level we find adaptation and fine tuning of accepted practices. The second order extends to the adoption of techniques. The third level is concerned with sets of ideas which comprise the overall goals, the framework guiding action. Since Australia and New Zealand claim to have been working within some form of framework, its contribution to the development, coherence and long-term impact of their reform programmes is clearly important.

Reform strategies

The reform sequence in the two countries covered similar ground but in different ways. In New Zealand's case the process was fairly explicit and largely sequential. Corporatization was followed by privatization plus reform of the core public service. Intergovernmental reform (focusing on local government) and financial management reform were next, and subsequently attention centred on the 'non-commercial' welfare state. The legislative basis was established by three Acts which also reflected stages in reform: the State-Owned Enterprises Act 1986, the State Sector Act 1988 and the Public Finance Act 1989. They respectively laid the basis for corporatization (and subsequently privatization), departmental and public service reforms, and financial management changes. An extension of this agenda was the Employment Contracts Act 1991 and the Fiscal Responsibility Act 1994, produced by a different government, and further significant management refinements in the 1990s.

For Australia, the process was somewhat different. Australian attitudes were influenced *inter alia* by the failure of management in specific agencies. A bipartisan view emerged that the management skills of the senior public service were both deficient and undervalued relative to their policy and administrative work. Over time a shift from emphasizing management skills to a new management framework occurred (Halligan, 1996). The sequence differed from New Zealand in that the development of initiatives was more protracted. The main elements of the reform programme focused initially on the core public service (including commercialization, decentralization and the senior public service) and improving financial management, followed by corporatization and later privatization. The flagging reform momentum in the mid 1980s produced new directions which were linked to the emerging microeconomic reform agenda, the most significant element being the major reorganization of the machinery of government. Australia concentrated much more on the core public service reform because the need for corporatization was less pronounced than in New Zealand, and privatization was resisted more. The legislative basis was apparent for some purposes (such as the Public Service Reform Act 1994).

A new stage in reform became apparent in both countries in the 1990s. For New Zealand, the foundations were laid by the principles that were adopted in the 1980s. What occurred seemed like a natural extension of these principles, including the move towards separating out delivery roles in specific sectors such as health, although the augmentation of the management focus was highly significant. For Australia's part, its disinclination to grasp some principles emphatically and its tendency to rely on gradualism meant that it finally had to shift in the mid 1990s. Prior to the 1996 election, Australia had already moved into a further phase of reform that is placing greater emphasis on the market and contractual relationships.

In Australia, it was also necessary for the nationalization of reform to occur. The federal system had been important for the introduction, testing and diffusion of reforms among the state and national governments (Halligan, 1996). However, it had also acted as a barrier to national reform to the public sector. Intergovernmental (or Commonwealth–state) reform was pretty well ignored during the 1980s because it represented the most intractable option as a result of the states' constitutionally established autonomy. This option was only addressed in the 1990s after other reform options had seemingly been exhausted.

In examining developments, we can observe two processes: the move towards a framework that would break with the past and offer something workable for the future, and the search for machinery and principles that would serve the framework. These processes were not as clear to the participants as they became with hindsight; moreover, a framework did not emerge full-blown in a single flourish but took several years. There is no doubt though that the vision first expressed in the mid 1980s by the New Zealand Treasury, in conjunction with key politicians, laid the foundation for the New Zealand programme of reform, and that it worked within a framework that emerged early and was implemented quickly. For Australia, the development of its management framework took longer and was a product of balancing principle and pragmatism and combining a strategic focus with experimentation (Halligan, 1996).

In the realm of ideas, a number of theories were drawn upon. Public choice theory exercised greater influence in New Zealand than in Australia, as seen by the separation of policy and administration and the rise of ministerial staff. The latter occurred earlier in Australia, but was rationalized in terms of political ideas about the constitutional roles of the political executive and the need for it to provide policy direction. Agency theory and transaction cost economics have been significant in New Zealand. Managerialism has been significant in both countries. Both systems produced significant reports in late 1996 which will influence the future character of their public sectors (Reith, 1996; Schick, 1996).

Results in New Zealand

The New Zealand model combines standard management reforms pursued in other OECD countries with some distinctive, often unique features. The special element was supplied by the ideas derived from public choice and institutional economics, and which addressed *inter alia* the questions of agency and transaction costs.

A number of objectives underlie the new model including improving allocative and productive efficiency, enhancing the effectiveness of programmes, improving accountability of public organizations and of the political executive to Parliament, and reducing government expenditure and the core public sector. Some of the main principles and specific policies that have been applied are as follows (Boston et al., 1996a: 4–5):

1 As a general rule, activities that can be performed better by the private
   sector and NGOs should not be retained in the public sector.
2 Any commercial activities left in the public sector should be organized
   similarly to companies in the private sector.
3 The objectives of all types of government organizations should be
   explicitly stated.
4 The separation of responsibilities should occur where there are conflicts
   (for example, commercial and non-commercial functions), where the
   roles are distinctive (such as ministers and chief executives of
   departments), and where different functions are involved (for example,
   purchaser and provider; policy advice and regulation).
5 Public services should be subject to the principle of contestability and
   competitive tendering.
6 The organization of government administration should be designed to
   minimize agency and transaction costs.

The policies included a reliance on incentives for enhancing performance,
written contracts for a range of activities, simplicity in accountability relationships, and decentralization of decision-making on operational matters
(1996a: 5).

Corporatization and privatization

Turning to the application of these principles, the first component addressed
was the group of government trading bodies which accounted for 12% of
GDP in the mid 1980s and whose performance was regarded as poor (OECD,
1996a: 96). A number of trading functions – such as coal, electricity, forestry
and telecommunications – were still within ministerial departments. The
State-Owned Enterprises Act 1986 established the legislative framework for
enabling trading departments to become corporatized. It defined objectives,
incentives and a new operating environment for state-owned enterprises
(SOEs). They were to operate like a business and demonstrate comparable
performance in terms of efficiency and profitability. A number of government
department and trading activities were converted into enterprises. Increases,
some significant, in the productivity of state-owned enterprises were later
recorded as pricing policies and products changed, staff were reduced and a
more commercial and competitive approach was adopted.

Corporatization eventually became seen as a step towards privatization by
which public assets were transferred to the private sector. The main reasons
appeared to be fiscal (for example, reducing public debt) and efficiency. Over
20 public organizations (or major assets in some cases) were privatized (Table
1.2), including the national airline, a tourist hotel corporation, telephone
services, shipping services, an insurance company, and the development,
trading and savings banks (Mascarenhas, 1991; Boston et al., 1996a: 65–7).

In evaluating the impact of corporatization and privatization, there are
problems with isolating the results of reforms from other economic influences and changes (such as regulation and technology) and with making

Table 1.2 *Privatization: assets sold by New Zealand government since 1985*

Asset	Year of sale	Sale price ($NZ million)
New Zealand Steel Limited	1988	327
Petrocorp	1988	801
Development Finance Corporation	1988	111
Post Office Bank Limited	1989	678
Shipping Corporation of New Zealand	1990	32
Air New Zealand	1989	660
Landcorp financial instruments	1989–90	77
Rural Bank	1989–92	688
Government Printing Office	1989–93	39
State Insurance Office	1990	735
Tourist Hotel Corporation	1990	72
New Zealand Liquid Fuel Investment	1990	(203)
Maui Gas	1990	254
Telecom Corporation	1990	4,250
Forestry cutting rights	1990	1,027
Export Guarantee Limited	1990–93	20
Synfuels stocks and current assets	1990–95	206
Housing Corporation mortgages	1991–95	13,165
Taranaki Petroleum mining licences	1992–93	118
New Zealand Timberlands Limited	1992	366
Bank of New Zealand	1992	850
New Zealand Rail Limited	1993	328
Fletcher Challenge shares	1993	418
Government Computing Services Limited	1994	47

Excludes sales under $NZ5 million.

Sources: New Zealand Government Asset Sales as at 31 December 1995; OECD, 1996a: Table 17

comparisons with pre-corporatized businesses that were not explicit about their objectives (OECD, 1996a: 98–9). Evaluation of the impact on efficiency is also hampered by the lack of empirical studies. An OECD report claims that general evidence suggests that 'corporatisation and deregulation have had positive effects on the efficiency of government businesses in performing commercial services, while empirical findings as to their influence on the achievement of social goals are generally unavailable' (1996a: 97–8). Significant drops in employment, real price cuts and improved profitability have been recorded. Receipts from privatization have, as a proportion of GDP, been considerably higher than those in Britain and Australia.[2]

Core public service

The core public service was also subjected to the application of new principles in reformulating the departmental structure, the two most important being the separation of responsibilities for policy and delivery, and the identification of specific functions with specialized organizations. In addition to the three central agencies (Prime Minister and Cabinet, State Services Commission and Treasury), there were now 17 policy ministries, 11 delivery departments, and three which combined both. There are some qualifications to this neat picture: some ministries are small and focus on policy, while others have not been entirely stripped of other functions. The division between operations and policy is more pronounced in some fields such as housing and transport. It is only in a few fields (most notably health) that the purchaser/provider functions have been differentiated. The so-called functional model (as opposed to the sectoral model or vertical integration, which has received stronger support in Australia) has a number of advantages, including providing for greater contestability of services (Boston et al., 1996a: 91).

The State Sector Act 1988 produced changes that had constitutional implications. It was concerned with the efficiency and effectiveness of management and provided for improved autonomy and greater accountability of managers, but it also redefined the relationship between ministers and department heads.

A range of financial management reforms was introduced under the State Sector Act and the Public Finance Act. Two distinctions should be noted: that between inputs, outputs and outcomes (with the emphasis now being on outputs), and the definition of government's role as either the purchaser of outputs from agencies (whether public or private) or the owner of agencies with an interest in the return on its investment.

Of particular significance has been the increasing reliance on contracting out the delivery of services to private and voluntary sector providers. The new contractualism has been prevalent in health and welfare sectors, but its applications can also be seen in other areas of government activity where there are relationships between two or more parties (Boston, 1995).

Also central was the redefinition of the relationship between ministers and departmental chief executives (CEs). One of the most startling innovations is the separation of political and managerial roles through the association of outcomes with ministers and outputs with chief executives. The minister selects the outcomes, and purchases the outputs from the chief executive who selects the necessary inputs. This arrangement is meant to allow the CE to be held accountable by the minister for departmental results. The relationship is seen as being contractually based: the government purchases outputs from departments, while at the same time is defined as the owner.

The renamed chief executive, whose predecessors were permanent officials, hold contract appointments based on performance agreements. There are annual performance reviews of chief executives. The chief executives' extensive responsibilities include the appointment of departmental staff, a process which is meant to be thereby insulated from political influence in order to maintain the tradition of the non-partisan public service. A Senior Executive Service (SES) was created, but it has a more restricted membership than comparable systems elsewhere, being confined to the level below chief executives. Senior executives are appointed on contracts of up to five years. The SES was meant to produce a unified set of career professionals, but this objective has not been realized.

The financial management reforms were designed to obtain greater value from public expenditure, to improve efficiency and accountability. The changes are similar to Australia's FMIP (and the UK's FMI), but there are significant differences including the contractual relationship between ministers and chief executives already referred to, the distinction between purchase and ownership, and the distinction between outputs and outcomes (Scott et al., 1990: 155–6). The new system of financial management was also regarded as unprecedented because it provided for the introduction of accrual accounting to core departments to assist with monitoring government's ownership.

The strategic capacity of government was a neglected element in the NZ model, producing a short-term policy focus and inattention to the collective side of government. The Logan (1991) Report addressed the issue, leading to planning for the medium and long term and the introduction of strategic result areas (SRAs) and key result areas (KRAs) for specifying government priorities and focusing performance.

Another recent innovation, the Fiscal Responsibility Act 1994, seeks to make budget accounting more transparent (and has influenced the proposed Australian Charter of Budget Honesty). A number of benefits have been reported including the credibility of the fiscal policy process, the focusing of politicians on efficiency and cost overrun questions, and pressure on the Treasury to improve its performance because the legislation specifies transparency and accountability (National Commission of Audit, 1996: 389).

Decentralization

Decentralization has been an important element as in other OECD countries that have been moving towards a managerialist approach, but its broader application has been fairly limited. It has been applied to the human resource functions of the central personnel agency (State Services Commission) in favour of line departments, and also within departments.

The local government system was restructured, reducing the number of local authorities from around 700 to 73 (a figure which excludes sub-municipal community councils and 12 regional councils). Local government's modes of operation, function and culture have also been subjected to other changes, notably the greater use of business units and external providers for the delivery of services. At the margins there was some adjustment in functions but hardly sufficient to change the centralist New Zealand state. Local government in New Zealand, as in Australia, has never been a prominent part of government, and only accounts for around 10% of public sector expenditure. The position in this sphere was seemingly disclosed by a Labour minister who declared that the operating principle was that local government should not receive any responsibilities that could be performed better elsewhere. But the commitment to reducing government and contracting out meant a reluctance to enhance its responsibilities (Boston et al., 1996a: 183).

Reforms in the two key sectors of education and health have yet to be noticeably decentralizing. In the education sector, centralized practices remain significant, central government accounts for 80% of education expenditure, and the reforms have strengthened the centre's formal control (OECD, 1996a: 116, 136).

Contractualism, competition and markets

The new wave of reforms in the 1990s, which developed the functional separation of roles further, came in the health sector. The aims of major changes announced in 1991 and implemented in 1993 included encouraging 'efficiency, flexibility and innovation in the delivery of health care' and reducing 'the politicisation of decisions about resource allocation'. The reforms have been producing a 'contract system' of health care, similar to that of the United Kingdom. Regional health authorities contract with crown health enterprises and other providers to supply services (OECD, 1996a: 115).

Judged in terms of their stated objectives the reforms have been wanting. The health reforms are regarded by key figures in the reform process as highly problematic. Real competition between providers has not been achieved in most service areas, nor has decision-making about the services of government-owned hospitals been depoliticized. At the same time the complexities of accountability have not been resolved by compartmentalization of roles (Boston et al., 1996a: 174–7; OECD, 1996a: 120). The OECD's judgement is that 'hospitals are facing a challenging task to restructure services in a way appropriate for the new competitive environment and also to develop the necessary costing and information systems to manage demand effectively and equitably' (1996a: 136).

Competitive tendering and contracting (CTC) have not been surveyed as in Australia (Boston, 1996; Domberger and Hall, 1996), but contractualism permeates the public sector and the reliance on market testing is extensive. Contracting out is well developed at the local level and extends to welfare services.

Overall judgement

The New Zealand model has won international admiration as a unique case of public sector reform. The framework is widely acknowledged to be the most sophisticated and coherent: 'a carefully crafted, integrated, and mutually reinforcing agenda', which has been upheld for 'its conceptual rigour and coherence' (Boston et al., 1996a: 3; Hood, 1990). However, two of the most experienced doubters observe that the extension of some of the key principles into the restructuring of the core of government is considerably more controversial. Reference to separating ownership and purchasing interests, contestability, public choice, principal/agency theory, new institutional economics has impressed many because of the clear intellectual framework that evolved. At the same time . . . it seemed to lose sight of the multitude of factors which underpin sound strategic policymaking. (Holmes and Shand, 1995: 570)

This question of the capacity of government to direct centrally became a key issue in the 1990s. A departmental head reports 'that something . . . was lost in the shift to strong vertical lines of accountability between ministers and chief executives and away from collective discipline and strong central management' (Laking, 1995: 100). The inadequacies of strategic capacity were 'a serious flaw in the original design . . . derived from the strong emphasis on operational efficiency and accountability', which produced the distinction between political and managerial accountability (Schick, 1996: 53). The recent review found that strategic result areas (SRAs) and key result areas (KRAs) were working effectively and that they attracted more positive comment from ministers and senior public servants than most reforms: 'The SRAs and KRAs have been so rapidly and fully integrated into the reformed public sector that it is easy to forget that they were added only a few years ago' (1996: 54).

Accountability has been inclined to focus on managerial rather than political accountability. A major theme of the reforms has been about clarifying the responsibilities of ministers and public servants, and while the reassertion of ministerial authority has occurred, it is less clear for what purposes. The distinction between outputs and outcomes, and their respective identification with public servants and ministers, has been widely questioned. The detractors argue that public servants need to consider outcomes, but that the definition of the relationship unduly complicates this (Holmes and Shand, 1995: 109). The government has continued to have difficulties with identifying outcomes, monitoring progress and evaluating programmes against specific outcomes (Schick, 1996: 8). The government needs 'better systems for evaluating policies empirically. Indeed, it has often not attempted to assess the likely effects of programs, nor to monitor public satisfaction with the outcomes' (OECD, 1996a: 129).

Nevertheless, Graham Scott (1996a: 103), an architect of the New Zealand model and the former Treasury Secretary, asks whether an accountable management system can be run by departments unless they have control. Outcomes are subject to too many influences, a number of which cannot be readily controlled. Whereas, outputs are the 'linchpin of the New Zealand accountability system . . . because they provide a reliable basis for enforcing managerial accountability . . . the supply of outputs can be directly attributed to the performance of chief executives and their departments' (Schick, 1996: 74).

This drive to achieve full accountability for results has produced the most distinctive features of the system's reform: 'the performance and purchase agreements, appropriation by output classes, the split between funds voted to Ministers and money provided to departments, and accounting and budgeting on an accrual basis' (Schick, 1996: 73). There is, however, a price for 'the contractual model goes further than managerial reform in demanding accountability in the public sector. But . . . it exacts a substantial cost for achieving efficiency in output production.' The demands of accountability overload departments with substantial costs which have escalated as the requirements increased. The operation of the accountability system requires far more resources than was necessary five years ago (1996: 26, 83–4). Schick's praise is nevertheless fulsome in his claim that a major important contribution to public management has been New Zealand's development of new modes of accountability: 'The accountability relationship of purchasers and providers has stimulated the invention of new forms of contracting for and assessing performance . . . No other country has accomplished what New Zealand has in building accountability into the framework of government' (1996: 84).

According to the recent official assessment, difficulties arise with the roles of ministers, chief executives and senior managers in terms of ownership: 'the purchase and ownership roles of the Responsible Minister pull the departments in opposite directions. The purchase role has dominated to this point, as demonstrated by the annual purchase agreement, and now it is important that the ownership role be given greater scope' (1996: 2).

The accountability procedures for contractual relationships have been questioned because it is not necessarily clear who is accountable where functions have been separated between purchaser and provider. Some reforms have in effect 'depoliticized' government activity, and detached ministers from being held responsible for public actions. Managerial accountability has been developed while the political responsibility of ministers has become more tenuous (Martin, 1995: 37–42; Boston et al., 1996a: 359, 360). Parliamentary scrutiny has been ineffectual despite improved reporting requirements (Laking, 1994: 313). However, the system has been responding:

> concerns that the output orientation might place too much emphasis on managerial accountability at the expense of accountability to Parliament and the public at large are beginning to be addressed through developments in whole-of-government budgeting and reporting, strengthened committee processes, and work on linking SRAs and KRAs. The assumption is that greater transparency will result in more informed public debate and reduce political risk. (Boston et al., 1996a: 359)

The gaps in the system's capacity to learn from experience have been recognized, in particular the ability to make 'systematic, empirical evaluations of policies a matter of routine'. The OECD (1996a: 112) advocates institutionalizing the process because these assessments sometimes embarrass agencies or politicians, and commends the experiences of countries such as Australia, France, Canada and the United States in designing an evaluation policy.

Table 1.3 *New Zealand public service staff, 1984–96*

Year	Number
1984	85,738
1985	85,423
1986	88,507
1987	72,417
1988	60,940
1989	58,830
1990	55,016
1991	46,337
1992	44,371
1993	36,156
1994	34,675
1995	33,263
1996	32,917

Sources: Laking, 1995; State Services Commission

The rise of the new contractualism has prompted debate as it permeated the system of government in various forms (Boston, 1995). The OECD is cautious in its judgement of the 'system's reliance on output contracting between ministers and agencies as a mechanism for enhancing efficiency. The introduction of contracting has probably been helpful' (1996a: 112). Yet the overall consequences of the 'contractual model of reform' have also been problematic in some areas: the failure of the Senior Executive Service, the lack of progress on specifying outcomes, and the difficulties with identifying the ownership interest of the government (Schick, 1996: 26).

The efficiency objective of the reforms has been linked to the country's economic performance, which improved towards the mid 1990s (growth rates up and unemployment declining), although without consistent trend data there is difficulty in showing the extent of the reforms' contribution (Boston et al., 1996a: 359; Scott, 1996c: 80). The New Zealand economy recovered in the 1990s and outperformed most countries in the OECD. In late 1996 it recorded relatively low unemployment (6.2%), inflation of 2.1%, and a budget surplus of 2.6% of GDP (Kelly, 1996: 7). Figures for international competitiveness placed New Zealand eleventh on the Institute for Management Development's ranking, and third on the World Economic Forum list (*The Economist*, 1 June 1996). According to the 1995 *World Competitiveness Report*, respondents to its survey gave the government a positive rating for 'transparency and communicat[ing] its intentions successfully' (ninth out of 48, up from twentieth out of 45 for 1994).

The size of the public service declined by 60% in the first decade of reform (in large part because of corporatization and privatization), and has continued to drop (Table 1.3). The proportion of public expenditure accounted for by GDP fell from 40% to 35% during the 1990s. Departmental expenditure on administration is also claimed to be significantly down (Boston et al., 1996a: 359; OECD, 1996a: 136–7; Schick, 1996).

The evidence of efficiency and productivity is strongest for the results of corporatization and privatization, which have delivered profits, reduced prices, introduced market mechanisms, improved the measurement of costs, and led to dividends being declared for fields that had previously recorded losses. Privatization accounted for receipts of $NZ14 billion with direct implications for the public debt (Scott, 1996c: 78). The *World Competitiveness Report* for 1994 claims that on the basis of its survey of businesses, the privatized NZ Telecom is ranked second, and that other infrastructure services (whether corporatized or privatized) ranked well. The scope of government activities was reduced (Scott et al., 1990: 148). In general, 'the reforms have led to a much leaner and more efficient government business sector, which now employs only about a quarter of the workforce it occupied in the late 1980s' (OECD, 1996a: 98–9). The final judgement from the OECD is positive but qualified: 'Empirical evidence, though limited, generally suggests that the initiatives have increased incentives and enhanced efficiency. Nonetheless, there is still unfinished business' (1996a: 135–6).

While management practice and discourse have been transformed, the perennial questions of public administration remain as challenges which cannot be defined out of consideration by principles which separate roles or seek to leave matters to the market (for example, relations between politicians and bureaucrats). The condition of the public service has been commented on: the need to re-emphasize 'the professional ethic of public service' (Laking, 1995: 100); and the 'risk of an unduly short-term focus and a possible loss in "civil service culture"' (OECD, 1996a: 113). Several observers have noted unfinished and outstanding questions, including senior executives, incentives and performance measurement, and strategic management under coalition governments (Boston et al., 1996a: 361–2; Scott, 1996b).

The New Zealand model has been subjected to an official evaluation (Schick, 1996), which examined the main components and produced a sophisticated report. It is a testament to the credentials of the model that it has been subjected to such an external review which, while pronouncing it to be sound and successful, criticizes some of the closely cherished economic principles that have accounted for the system's uniqueness. Schick recognizes that the adoption of SRAs and KRAs provides 'evidence of the malleability of the reforms and their capacity to adapt to fresh ideas and reconsideration of old ones' (1996: 54). Recent reviews report positive reactions. The management and accounting reforms generally receive widespread, if qualified, support from politicians and senior executives (OECD, 1996a: 109). Moreover, 'there is near universal agreement that New Zealand government is much better managed now than before' (Schick, 1996: 7). The reforms are put in perspective by the observation that although they 'have been more comprehensive and rigorous than those introduced in other countries, they have been neither complete nor perfect'. There is further need 'to debug' the less successful elements, and to make modifications that will allow further development (1996: 1, 3, 54).

Results in Australia

In Australia, the reform programme initially consisted essentially of two broad agendas – political and managerial – each of which comprised a set of reforms. In order to accomplish change the political executive had to secure control over the bureaucracy. This was eventually accomplished by relying on a shift from administering to managing within the bureaucracy (Halligan and Power, 1992).

Australia has worked hard at developing and implementing a new management philosophy over the past decade. This was designed to replace the traditional administrative approach, which emphasized inputs and processes, by a focus on results. Unlike the New Zealand approach, Australia's central focus has been on evolving a management framework (new public management principles such as devolution, flexibility, accountability, outputs) pragmatically while applying them across the public service.

Core public service

The political agenda was the first priority of the new Labor government which saw the need to re-establish ministerial control and greater responsiveness to government policies and priorities. This was part of a political framework which promised to increase 'democracy' by allowing the minister to have greater influence (and by expanding the accessibility and diversity of the public service) and diminishing the roles of the public servant (Wilenski, 1986). The reform programme was driven, at least in the early stages, by this concern of Labor with political control, both as an end in itself and as a means to implementing party policy. To achieve this required a redistribution of power between the bureaucracy and the politicians. Other reforms were not ignored; they either conformed with the political objectives (such as top-down, centrally directed budgeting and management) or were simply subservient to them.

A number of measures were introduced that were designed to reduce the permanency of the public servants, the public service's monopoly on advice to ministers and its independence (Halligan and Power, 1992).

A reformulation of the senior public service was a central component of the Australian reform programme. In 1984, the senior public service was recast as the Senior Executive Service (SES). Following the existing schemes in the United States and the state of Victoria, the basic principles were the concept of a service-wide executive group that was to be internally mobile and increasingly invigorated by the recruitment of persons externally, more emphasis on the development of managerial skills, and more flexibility for department heads in the allocation and use of senior staff resources.

The government's microeconomic reform agenda was a primary consideration in the major reorganization of the machinery of government in 1987. The restructuring focused on line departments with an important economic role, plus other rationalizations. The most interesting changes were the major mergers that produced the new 'mega' departments of Foreign Affairs and Trade; Education, Employment and Training; and Transport and Communications. The overall departmental system was changed as 28 portfolio departments became 18 which covered all areas of government. The changes were highly significant because they provided a new structure for the conduct of government administration. They were designed to improve overall management of the public service by reducing the number of departments while enabling them to be represented in Cabinet; to provide a framework within which the internal structure of departments could be rationalized and decisions made concerning the reappointment of senior officials; and to enhance the quality and coherence of both policy advice and programme delivery. There were no significant departures from the structure established in 1987 until 1994.

The Financial Management Improvement Program (FMIP) dominated the reforms of the 1980s as an initiative that was designed to produce more efficient use of resources. Corporate management established overall direction for organizational management. The implementation of FMIP occurred through three broad spheres of activity: changing the budgetary and regulatory environment; improving management systems (which centred on the 'managing for results' components of corporate management, programme management, organization design, management information and evaluation); and emphasizing standards and practices (such as training in management skills) (Keating and Holmes, 1990; Campbell and Halligan, 1992).

The centre-piece of FMIP was programme budgeting. Its purpose was to assist participants in the public expenditure process in assessing how well programmes had been developed and implemented relative to their objectives. The term 'programme management and budgeting' was adopted to promote the emphasis on improving departmental corporate management and assisting managers to focus more clearly on outcomes and results. Three other elements were the forward estimates and running cost systems and efficiency dividends. Running costs provided managers with greater flexibility in managing administrative costs and permitted carry-overs to the next financial year. Efficiency dividends or annual savings (of say 1%) on running costs have applied for the last decade.

Evaluation tied the loop in the management cycle. The Department of Finance pronounced it to be the 'crucial element' in managing for results, performing the essential function of linking policy development and programme implementation. All programmes had to be reviewed at least once every five years and evaluation plans produced annually for central scrutiny by the Department of Finance.

Another major reform strand was the adoption of 'commercial' practices. Agencies were expected to use techniques based on private sector practices which were meant to reflect the similarities between management in the private and public sectors. The list of practices has covered commercialization, cash management, asset management, purchasing reforms, risk management and user charging. Commercialization has been closely associated with the transition of a department or agency to a user-pays or fee-for-service operation, together with the implementation of new accounting and auditing arrangements. A simple example was the Australian Bureau of Statistics, which from 1988 began charging for all publications and information, eventually effecting a shift in the culture and operation of the organization, and changing the pattern of demand for its services.

Business units – entities operating on separate accounts based on commercial practice – were established within the structure of nine departments of state, but with management and operational systems comparable to a business, and a commercial approach. Commercialization and the development of business units were most closely identified with the Department of Administrative Services, which until recently was operating 14 such units, including Australian Construction Services, the Land Information Group and DASFLEET. The general purpose of the reforms was to introduce a more business-like approach. Most programmes moved to charging on a full cost-recovery basis for services, while others operated as self-funding business undertakings.

Corporatization and privatization

The debate about the role of state enterprises centred on the form of the relationship with government, what sort of guidelines promoted its objectives, and whether some enterprises should remain within the public sector. The question of greater ministerial control versus more business-like operations featured prominently. The desire to improve the efficiency of government business enterprises (GBEs) was central to the government's programme of microeconomic reform. Reform packages were devised for various enterprises, the most important being for the eight major enterprises in the Transport and Communication portfolio. New GBEs were also created from parts of departments. The government was to focus on strategic directions with agreed objectives negotiated with the minister, but did not relinquish control over certain types of activities, and the scope for external intervention remained. Consequently these reforms did not go as far as the New Zealand experiment with corporatization.

The government gradually moved its enterprises towards private sector models. The company form of incorporation was chosen for a number of enterprises. But for the first decade of reform the government was inclined to preserve enterprises within the public sector, while promoting greater competition.

A programme of major asset sales was finally launched in the late 1980s by the former Labor government, the main rationale being reductions to the budget deficit. The pace of activity continued to be constrained by party

Table 1.4   *Privatization: assets sold by Australian government since 1985*

Asset	Year of Sale	Revenue ($A million)
Belconnen Mall (Canberra)	1986	87
Williamstown Naval Dockyard	1987	100
Commonwealth Catering and Accommodation Services Ltd	1988	15
Defence Service Homes Corporation mortgage portfolio	1988–90	1,516
Tokyo Embassy	1988–90	666
Avalon Airfield (lease sold)	1990	70
Defence Force Home Loan Assistance Scheme (franchise)	1991	42
Commonwealth Housing Loan Assistance Schemes in ACT	1991	47
Australian Airlines*	1992	400
Qantas Airline	1992–95	2,116
Commonwealth Serum Laboratories	1993–94	299
Commonwealth Bank	1993–97	6,700
Moomba–Sydney Pipeline	1994	534
Telstra[†]	1997–98	10,000

Excludes minor asset sales.

* Sold to Qantas.

[†] Upper estimate of revenue from the first tranche for one-third of Telstra.

Source: Department of Finance, *Annual Reports*, 1987–8 to 1995–6

policy which forbade privatization, and the exceptions had to receive party conference ratification. The government eventually acted to privatize some major authorities with partial sell-offs providing an intermediate stage in this process. The net result has been the gradual attrition of the number of Commonwealth business enterprises of any substance as the list of assets sold has mounted over time (Table 1.4). Few significant GBEs are left, with the notable exception of the Australia Postal Corporation. Several such as the Australian National Line, the National Rail Corporation and the Federal Airports Corporation are on the market, and there are moves under the coalition government towards extending the privatization of tele-communications (Telstra Corporation) and disposing of the shipping line.[3]

Decentralization

The microeconomic reform agenda which first emerged in the mid 1980s focused on reform to various sectors of the economy, but by the mid 1990s was concentrating firmly on the national rationalization of utilities and the benchmarking of performance nationally (such as for hospitals). The national focus on improving competitiveness and the emergence of a Council of Australian Governments made the difference. The nationaliza-tion of reform in Australia finally appeared to be occurring.

An agenda for rationalizing and decentralizing the delivery of health and community services has been identified but progress continued to be hesitant because of the need to obtain broad agreement among a number of units of government. Significant decentralization continued to be rare and

Australia, while decentralized federally, is centralized at the sub-national level, with local government accounting for around 6% of the public sector expenditure.

One official report which has yet to receive government support recommends radical rationalization of the responsibilities of levels of government (National Commission of Audit, 1996). How far this will be decentralizing within government is unclear, for marketization is also an ingredient.

Contractualism, competition and markets

The first phase of reform produced commercialization and gradually competitive elements entered specific areas of the public service (for example, legal work and the business units referred to above). Contracting out of work has become standard practice over the last decade with all departments to varying extents engaging in it, the rapid increase being at the expense of in-house staff (Howard, 1996; Industry Commission, 1996).

The second phase received its greatest impetus from the Hilmer Report on *National Competition Policy* (National Competition Policy Review, 1993). Australia has since acquired a competition fixation, with *National Competition Policy* providing an agenda-setting role nationally for the public and private sectors. The Commonwealth and the states reached agreement in 1995 to implement the recommendations of the Hilmer Report, two being competitive neutrality between the government and the business sector, and the structural reform of public monopolies to allow competition.

The first clear statement from the government since its election in 1996, a Discussion Paper from the minister responsible for the public service (Reith, 1996), foreshadows its thinking without making final detailed commitments. The elements include a deregulated personnel system that is more comparable to the private sector; a public service that contributes to policy development, implements legislation and provides oversight of service delivery; and contestability of delivery of services with greater use being made of private and voluntary sectors.

Overall judgement

The Australian experience has attracted international interest and study (for example, Gore, 1993; Byrne et al., 1995). After a decade of intensive change, Australia undertook possibly the first extensive evaluation of the new wave of reforms in one country (TFMI, 1993). Yet, despite the setting of new goals to be pursued in sustaining and building on reforms (Keating, 1994), there was a listlessness about the programme, and by 1995 there were divisions about directions (as expressed by departmental secretaries in Halligan et al., 1996) pending formal clarification. An agenda that had not received priority earlier could no longer be ignored. By late 1966, an overall judgement of Australian reforms was affected by the actions of the new government in propelling the system into another phase of extensive change that will again transform the public sector.

An examination of the extent to which objectives were attained has to take into account the nature of the reforms, described by the Task Force on Management Improvement as 'a combination of broad policy objectives, long-term strategies and specific one-off or ongoing changes acted upon in all parts of the APS' (TFMI, 1993: 6). Nevertheless, broad directions can be discerned and the early objectives were explicit and substantially achieved: strengthening of the political executive, improved efficiency and management change (TFMI, 1993; Halligan and Power, 1992).[4]

The emphasis in the 1980s on corporate government and strategic management achieved considerable success in focusing government on microeconomic agendas. The greater directive capacity of the political executive had been made possible by a policy-active Cabinet and measures to strengthen the roles of ministers. Policy coordination was enhanced by the major reorganization of government machinery, including improved policy coherence within departments, better external relationships with other agencies, and greater attention to coordination of processes and outcomes (Campbell and Halligan, 1992; Craswell and Davis, 1993).

The management framework was developed, but over time. This led to difficulties in characterizing the reforms, for the Task Force found that 'it was not clear which . . . items formed the totality of the APS reforms' (TFMI, 1993: 48). The official version of the management framework was subsequently articulated more clearly: Cabinet is responsible for strategic directions and objectives, which are grounded in financial planning through the forward estimates system; ministers and the public service have acquired management flexibility for meeting the objectives, and the incentives to improve management performance; and public servants are accountable to ministers for their work and achieving objectives. This framework was argued to have a 'consistent, logical and integrated structure, whether it be in relation to financial management, industrial relations or people management' (Sedgwick, 1994: 341).

There was therefore considerable success in reinforcing political accountability, and there was no doubt that accountability within the public service (particularly at senior levels) was conceived in hierarchical terms (Campbell and Halligan, 1992). The emphasis on management by results was also well regarded. Performance-based management stressed accountability by results in return for 'devolution' of responsibilities and greater flexibility for managers. The range of mechanisms for management reporting has increased the potential for greater accountability, and while parliamentary committees have made greater use of the opportunities than in New Zealand, there remains concern about the effectiveness of accountability. The increasing complexity of the issues arising from cross-portfolio, client focus and service delivery questions means that the simple tradition model will be replaced by one that recognizes multiple lines of responsibility and accountability (Trosa, 1996: 19).

A distinctive aspect of the Australian reforms was the commitment to evaluation, where, unlike New Zealand, it became mandatory. According to two key reformers, the 'Australian experience has been that evaluation has been the most controversial element of PMB/FMIP', and was 'the most difficult element of a "managing for results" approach', the problems reflecting 'its multiple, but linked objectives – improving program perform-ance, assisting government decision-making, and as a quid pro quo for the devolution of authority to managers, thus contributing to accountability' (Keating and Holmes, 1990: 174). The Task Force reported that the amount of evaluation activity had increased in number and quality but varied among portfolios, and was costly. However, most members of the Senior Executive Service were not making much use of evaluation information in their work: 'ironically, there may be a tendency to focus on satisfying the requirement for evaluation . . . rather than learning to use evaluation to improve program outcomes' (TFMI, 1993: 378–9).

The long-term results of the Senior Executive Service have been reason-ably successful (arguably more so than comparable schemes in NZ and the US), with some mobility, steady infusions of outsiders, a degree of corpor-ate identity, and regular use of performance appraisal and (more problem-atically) performance pay. Departmental secretaries were divided in their attitudes towards performance pay, many doubting the importance of remuneration as a motivating force, and most having a negative view of the implementation of performance pay for senior staff (because the process was mismanaged: Halligan et al., 1996). The combination of political and market pressures is pointing towards fixed-term contracts for all SES members, and leading to renewed concern about the system's capacity to maintain professional independent advice to politicians.

A number of parliamentary and official inquiries have reported that productivity and efficiency have grown in the public service and in the business enterprises of the broader public sector (for example, TFMI, 1993; SCNPMGTE, 1995). The efficiency dividend was later claimed to be saving $60 million annually (HRSCFPA, 1990: 119). Commercialization and corporatization have produced significant improvements in the efficiency and effectiveness of the provision of goods and services by agencies, according to the Joint Committee of Public Accounts:

> Improvements in the financial performance of commercialised agencies have been impressive, with deficits being reversed and healthy returns made to the Govern-ment. Even commercialised areas that continue to lose money are now recording smaller losses. At the same time, prices charged to the customer have generally risen at a rate lower than the CPI and in some cases have fallen. Non-financial indicators of performance have also shown improvements. (1995: xxvii)

However, there is wide variation between parts of the system, and with greater acceptance of the need to benchmark internationally the perform-ance of enterprises in specific fields, the criteria for judging are becoming much more demanding (National Commission of Audit, 1996; Productivity Commission, 1996). The current emphasis under *National Competition*

Table 1.5   *Expenditure for selected OECD countries (% of GDP)*

	Current expenditure on goods and services (1994)	Current disbursements (1993)	Total government outlay (1994 est.)
Australia	17.5	36.9	38
Canada	20.2	49.0	48
France	19.6	51.5	55
Germany	17.7	45.6	49
Japan	9.8	26.9	35
The Netherlands	14.2	55.4	55
New Zealand	14.7	–	–
Sweden	27.3	67.3	67
United Kingdom	21.6	42.7	43
United States	16.4	35.8	34

Current disbursements = current expenditure on goods and services plus current transfers and payments of property income. Outlay = current outlay plus net capital outlays.

Sources: OECD, 1995; 1996a

Policy will ensure that improving productivity and performance through deregulation and increasing competitiveness will continue to dominate.

The Australian economy's performance has been credible over the last two and a half decades: 'real GDP per head increased by over 1/3 between 1972 and 1995 and this performance put us somewhere in the top 10 in the OECD growth league. Over the last five years Australia's per capita growth performance ranks among the top five' (Argy, 1996: 2). In international terms, figures for international competitiveness place Australia at 21 in the Institute for Management Development's ranking and 12 on the World Economic Forum list, in both cases lower than the New Zealand rankings (*The Economist*, 1 June 1996).

Australia ranks as one of the smallest public sectors relative to GDP in the OECD (Table 1.5), largely because income transfers are lower. The projected reductions in government outlays (including state and local) will give Australia a ratio of 33%, the lowest of any OECD country (OECD, 1996b: 61). The size of the public service has declined over the last decade (Table 1.6) and will drop substantially further once the cuts of around 10,000 in 1996 show up fully in the statistics. The coalition government is reducing the size of the public sector and is seeking to cut the size of the deficit.

The Australian government reported in 1993 on the progress of its reform programme and the directions for the future following the first comprehensive official analysis and evaluation of 10 years of reform. The exercise was indicative of the Australian concern with systematic review and performance: a commitment to evaluate had been a feature of the reform programme. The review, however, was not externally based (although partly inspired by a parliamentary committee) but undertaken by the Task Force

Table 1.6   *Australian public service staff, 1983–95*

Year	Number
1983	162,200
1984	169,517
1985	173,664
1986	180,893
1987	177,677
1988	171,912
1989	165,883
1990	161,833
1991	163,220
1992	164,332
1993	166,062
1994	160,513
1995	146,165
1996	143,305

Source: Department of Finance and Public Service Board/Commission Statistical Bulletins

on Management Improvement, a quasi-independent group of public servants subject to central mentors (TFMI, 1993).

According to two experienced reformers, Australia's

> reform program attempted more than any other to balance the relationship between the centre and its accompanying parts, between policymaking and implementation and between strategic policymaking and the service-wide systems that support it (notably for budgeting and personnel management). It is the need for balance in these elements which is crucial if the 'multitude of factors that need to be balanced at the level of strategic decision making' are to be adequately addressed. The results are not as wonderful as [they] might be . . . but it is because of the search for balance, the core principles and the pragmatism of the Australian efforts that they are worthy of study. (Holmes and Shand, 1995: 569–70)

The development of the new management framework was a precondition for long-term reform but was insufficient as a comprehensive solution to complex pressures on the public service. The 1990s were seen as a time for implementation and consolidation. New objectives were articulated – benchmarking, continuous improvement, service quality and aspects of human resource management – but the ongoing agenda lacked the sharp edge and urgency of the 1980s that was provided by economic pressure. The pressure to incorporate market principles in the core government proved to be irresistible. Australia is consequently more a system in transition than New Zealand (Halligan et al., 1996; Trosa, 1996), as new reform directions emerge from the new government (Reith, 1996). The future is likely to see a substantially contracted core, contestability of service delivery, accrual accounting as standard practice throughout the public sector and performance-based charters. The changes will push the Australian system closer to that of New Zealand.

Other outcomes and costs

Unintended outcomes

Improved economic performance has been a primary objective in both countries, with considerable success in the 1990s. But major costs have also been incurred: three significant unintended outcomes for politics and society can be mentioned.

The social costs have been high in both countries, but more acute in New Zealand. Major increases in unemployment, poverty, crime and social conflict have been experienced. In New Zealand, unemployment peaked at over 11% in 1992, as a result of the first major phase of reform. Corporatization is credited with increasing unemployment and causing serious problems for small communities that had depended on the operations of government enterprises (and stimulated opposition to the then Labour government, which lost office in 1990). Unemployment was down to 7.5% in 1995 (and lower in 1996), but 'official jobless' was reported to be higher at 9.7% (and the 1995 figures for Maori and Pacific Islander unemployment were respectively 16.1% and 19% (Kelsey, 1995: 260–2; OECD, 1996a: 99).

The highest unemployment in Australia (11.2%) was also recorded in 1992, and declined to 8.2% in July 1995. More generally, 'relative to the more reformist Anglo-Saxon countries, although not relative to continental Europe, Australia has performed poorly on unemployment over the last two decades' (Argy, 1996: 2). The increases in GDP per head reported earlier provide only a 'crude measure of economic welfare: we also need to take account of associated changes in income security, quality of life, the natural environment, and inter-personal and inter-generational distribution. When this is done the story is less rosy' (1996: 2).

Economic inequality has increased in both countries (Raskall, 1993). New Zealand was described as being 'a deeply divided society' whose 'social structure was severely stressed' (Kelsey, 1995: 271). The proportion of those below the poverty line was around 16–17% (depending on the measure). There was now discussion of two nations and the developing underclass (1995: 275, 296).

The relationship to the state was now different. Much of it was gone, and replaced in some cases by foreign ownership (an increasingly sensitive issue where major utilities were involved). The universal welfare state was being replaced by targeted welfare and the limited safety net. The conception of the relationship was changing fundamentally: people's dealings with the state were increasingly viewed in terms of the market and being a customer (Kelsey, 1995).

A third area concerns political responsibility and integrity. Major reform has been accomplished in part through what is widely regarded in the media and public debate as electoral deception. The failure to obtain electoral mandates and support for radical change in New Zealand has led to great cynicism about politicians and alienation from the system of government. An attitudinal profile of 1993 voters indicated:

> strong endorsement of the notion of a universalist rather than a residualist welfare state, including support for more taxes (although not necessarily a willingness to pay more tax personally), as well as an underlying conviction that politicians are out of touch and unworthy of the voter's trust. The National Government's commitment to a more residual welfare state is not shared by the voting public. Indeed implicit in the response is a high level of public concern that the government's policies are tearing apart the essential fabric of the New Zealand welfare state. (Vowles et al., 1995: 97)

The new coalition government in Australia lost the previous (1993) election because it declared in advance its intention to introduce radical economic reform (including a form of value-added tax). It had learnt the art of the minimalist manifesto by the 1996 election and of ignoring its own policies on the public sector once in office (but note that the previous Labor government also failed to submit to the electorate plans for major asset sales). Possible medium-term effects of leadership cynicism are not yet apparent (although the voter unwillingness to accord the government an upper house majority has ensured some legislative compromises).

The New Zealand response to their politicians has been a voter revolt and rejection of the political system. The most fundamental retaliation for the paradigm change was to counter it with a new electoral system, which was believed to be more sympathetic to voter expectations. However, there were already indications that the post-war consensus in New Zealand was breaking down, two indicators being declining support for the two main political parties through membership and voting, and a drop in the high turnouts traditionally recorded for elections (Vowles et al., 1995). Having experienced 'elite-driven agendas of change', the backlash came emphatically: Labour lost the 1990 election, and then National's large majority evaporated at the 1993 election. Debate came to centre on whether the electoral system should be changed, and the belief that mixed member proportional (MMP) representation would promote greater political consensus: 'MMP became a catchword for more democratic and accountable government' (1995: xii, 8). The outcome of the referendum held in conjunction with the 1993 election was the rejection of the first-past-the-post system in favour of MMP.

Much now depended on the extent to which the voters, having changed the system, would seek recognition of their policy preferences. A 1993 survey indicated that a majority of voters favoured universal free health and education, and support for the welfare state was strong. Most respondents supported increased government spending on health, education and unemployment, even if an increase in income tax was necessary (1995: 97). New Zealand's first election (October 1996) based on the new system of proportional representation produced no immediate government, but the protracted post-election negotiations over policy produced a coalition government based on National and a minor party. Whether deals on welfare state expenditure will lead to significant modifications to, or compromises with, the operation of the New Zealand model is unclear (although pre-election analysis suggested that major departures were not expected: Boston et al., 1996b). The coalition agreement indicates retention of the model, while discontinuing the privatization of assets programme, modifying health commercialization and expanding health and education expenditure. The potential for instability in the coalition is reportedly high, with the minor partner opposing aspects of the NZ model.

Government and society

The historical experience of both countries saw a significant role for the state as the developer in the face of a weak private sector and the need for major infrastructure. This role was increasingly overtaken by the welfare state (even if it was not as extensive as in other OECD countries). The structural adjustments in Australia and New Zealand have reversed the process of extending and maintaining the role of the state.

The contraction of the state is evident overall, and has continued through several stages, most apparent in New Zealand. First it was explicit in commercial areas and activities which were most readily transferred to the private sector. Next non-commercial areas became vulnerable – health, housing and government research – either because universalism had been terminated, or because private means had been found for services, or because the state had simply withdrawn from activities, such as social services. Thirdly, various functions have been increasingly opened up to private provision: these have ranged from specialist management and technical support, through service delivery, to policy advice (Kelsey, 1995; Boston et al., 1996a: 356).[5]

Australia has not travelled as far down this track as New Zealand but there are strong indications that its movement was accelerating in 1996. First, the debate about deregulation and the primacy of the economic agenda erupted in the early 1990s with critiques of the rise of economic rationalism and the prominence of rationalists within the senior public service (Pusey, 1991).

Secondly, Australia now has the first neo-conservative government to be elected at the national level during the current reform period, which has focused on reducing the budget deficit by cutting the number of public servants heavily.[6] Australia's standing in the OECD as having a small public sector meant little to a new government bent on having its belated turn at reshaping the state. The result is the largest downsizing ever attempted through a multi-faceted process of shedding more public service jobs and pruning programmes. In contrast institutional reforms (Lane, 1994), such as privatization and devolving responsibilities to the states, are expected in the future. The government's National Commission of Audit

(1996) has included in its evaluation of the public sector the core question of whether there is a role for government in all publicly funded activities.

Reform unlimited?

The conventional wisdom about reform once centred on the difficulty of accomplishing it. The lessons of Australia and New Zealand are that success in major reform is possible, but that it does not bring an easy resolution. While management practice and discourse have been transformed, the perennial questions of public administration remain.

In Australia's case, managerialism has supplanted traditional administration as the core of a new framework. However, approaching 15 years of reform have not produced relief from change, but merely laid the foundation for more. Prior to the last election, Australia had already moved into a new phase of reform that was likely to see greater emphasis on the market, contractual relationships, and principles such as purchaser/provider. In part this reflected the limitations of Australia's pragmatic approach which had largely ignored some dimensions of change significant in the UK and NZ. The extent to which Australia's managerialist mix of principle and pragmatism will survive the current push towards market-based approaches is unclear at this stage.

For New Zealand the officially sponsored interpretation by Schick (1996) documents the two strands: the path breaking and unique reliance on institutional economics, and the management dimension which increasingly came to prominence in the 1990s. Of the former he argues that

> the government could have implemented major changes in managerial practice without introducing these novel features. This is not to say that the contractual reforms do not add value; rather, it is to make the point that not all that New Zealand has accomplished is dependent on theories of opportunism, capture, agent–principal problems, transaction costs, and the like . . . a major portion of what has been accomplished has been due to conventional management ideas – freeing managers in exchange for holding them accountable for results – rather than to institutional economics. (1996: 19)

The Schick Report indicates the need for recognizing the strengths of, while making modifications to, the NZ model. This emphasis on the value of good management alerts us to the commonalities between Australia and New Zealand (Mulgan, 1996).

Australia and New Zealand stand in the highest ranks of successful public sector reformers. New Zealand, in particular, has attracted universal admiration and interest for its handling of the economy and the radical nature and coherence of the reform programme.[7] What is apparent, however, is that this admiration does not necessarily extend to emulation of the model as a whole, although specific reforms have been influential in many systems. Few countries are willing to be as bold as New Zealand, some preferring to learn from the Australian approach as a good compromise.

Australia and New Zealand are emerging from the political transitions of 1996 and are awaiting the resolution of uncertainties associated with the programmes of new governments. The former is extending rapidly its commitment to competition and contestability; the latter is reassessing the value of management. Both systems can expect to experience further change and possibly greater convergence in the years ahead.

Notes

1 For example, the extensive sub-national reforms in Australia are ignored. (For a comparative analysis of state government reform up to the early 1990s see Halligan and Power, 1992.) A comparison of the two experiments, in some respects already dated, is Castles et al. (1996).

2 The New Zealand receipts were 3.5% of the average GDP figures for 1988–92, compared with proportions of 1.0% for Britain and 0.5% for Australia (*The Economist*, 19 June 1993: 112; quoted in Schwartz, 1994: 528).

3 The extensive privatizations at the state government level include state banks, ports, insurance companies and an electricity distribution system (plus experiments with private sector control of water supply and prisons).

4 The government's equity objectives were inclined to be overridden by efficiency goals, although equal employment opportunity has survived. For a full treatment of the reforms, see TFMI (1993).

5 Despite the commitment to withdraw, the government has been obliged to intervene in some cases (such as electricity, where the government breached its own corporatization rules: Kelsey, 1995: 124).

6 This was despite some recent evidence that taxpayers support unit levels of public expenditure – although preferring some changes to its composition – and public sector delivery (Withers et al., 1994: 41).

7 New Zealand is also rated as the least corrupt country in the world to do business in, according to Transparency International. Australia was in seventh place for 1996.

References

Argy, Fred (1996) *The Balance between Equity and Efficiency in Australian Public Policy*. Public Policy Program Discussion Paper 49, Australian National University, Canberra.

Boston, Jonathan (1995) 'Inherently governmental functions and the limits of contracting out', in Jonathan Boston (ed.), *The State Under Contract*. Wellington: Bridget Williams Books.

Boston, Jonathan (1996) 'The use of contracting out in the public sector: recent New Zealand experience', *Australian Journal of Public Administration*, 55(3): 105–10.

Boston, Jonathan, Martin, John, Pallot, June and Walsh, Pat (1996a) *Public Management: the New Zealand Model*. Auckland: Oxford University Press.

Boston, Jonathan, Levine, Stephen, McLeay, Elizabeth and Roberts, Nigel S. (1996b) *New Zealand under MMP: a New Politics?* Auckland: Auckland University Press with Bridget William Books.

Byrne, Denis et al. (1995) 'Strategic management in the Irish civil service', *Administration*, 43(2): 4–153.

Campbell, Colin and Halligan, John (1992) *Political Leadership in an Age of Constraint: Bureaucratic Politics under Hawke and Keating*. Pittsburgh: University of Pittsburgh Press.

Castles, Francis, Gerritsen, Rolf and Vowles, Jack (eds) (1996) *The Great Experiment: Labour Parties and Public Transformation in Australia and New Zealand*. Sydney: Allen and Unwin.

Craswell, E. and Davis, G. (1993) 'Does the amalgamation of government agencies produce better policy co-ordination?', in Patrick Weller, John Foster and Glyn Davis (eds), *Reforming the Public Service: Lessons from Recent Experience*. South Melbourne: Macmillan.

Domberger, Simon and Hall, Christine (1996) 'Contracting for public services: a review of antipodean experience', *Public Administration*, 74 (Spring): 129–47.

Gore, A. (1993) *From Red Tape to Results: Creating a Government that Works Better and Costs Less. Report of the National Performance Review*. Washington, DC: Government Printing Office.

Hall, P.A. (1993) 'Policy paradigms, social learning, and the state: the case of economic policymaking in Britain', *Comparative Politics*, 25(3): 275–96.

Halligan, John (1996) 'Learning from experience in Australian reform: balancing principle and pragmatism', in J.P. Olsen and B.G. Peters (eds), *Lessons from Experience: Experiential Learning in Administrative Reforms in Eight Democracies*. Oslo: Scandinavian University Press. pp. 71–112.

Halligan, John, Mackintosh, Ian and Watson, Hugh (1996) (compilers) *The Australian Public Service: the View from the Top*. Coopers and Lybrand and University of Canberra.

Halligan, J. and Power, J. (1992) *Political Management in the 1990s*. Melbourne: Oxford University press.

Holmes, Malcolm and Shand, David (1995) 'Management reform: some practitioner perspectives on the past ten years', *Governance*, 8(4): 551–78.

Hood, Christopher (1990) 'De-Sir Humphreyfying the Westminster model of bureaucracy: a new style of governance?', *Governance*, 3(2): 205–14.

Howard, Michael (1996) 'A sea change in staffing mode? Commonwealth departmental spending on external consultants and in-house employees, 1988–89 to 1993–94', *Canberra Bulletin of Public Administration*, no. 80: 75–83.

HRSCFPA (1990) *Not for Dollars Alone*. House of Representatives Standing Committee on Finance and Public Administration. Canberra: Australian Government Publishing Service.

Industry Commission (1996) *Competitive Tendering and Contracting Out by Public Sector Agencies*. Canberra: Australian Government Publishing Service.

Joint Committee of Public Accounts (1995) *Public Business in the Public Interest: an Inquiry into Commercialisation in the Commonwealth Public Sector*. Report 336. Canberra: Australian Government Publishing Service.

Keating, M. (1994) 'A MAB/MIAC perspective', in *Public Service Reform: Volume 1*. Report from the Senate Standing Committee on Finance and Public Administration, Department of the Senate.

Keating, M. and Holmes, M. (1990) 'Australia's budgetary and financial management reforms', *Governance*, 3(2): 168–85.

Kelly, Paul (1996) 'New Zealand applies brakes to economic reform', *Weekend Australian*, 14–15 December: 7.

Kelsey, Jane (1995) *Economic Fundamentalism: the New Zealand Experiment – a World Model for Structural Adjustment?* London: Pluto.

Laking, R.G. (1994) 'The New Zealand management reforms', *Australian Journal of Public Administration*, 53(3): 313–24.

Laking, R.G. (1995) 'Changing ideas of public service in New Zealand', *Asian Journal of Political Science*, 3(1): 93–103.

Lane, Jan-Erik (1994) 'Ends and means of public sector reform', *Staatswissenschaften und Staatspraxis*, Heft 4, 5 Jahrgang: 459–73.

Logan, B. (1991) *Review of State Sector Reforms*. Report of Steering Group for Review of State Sector Reforms in New Zealand, State Services Commission, Wellington.

Martin, John (1995) 'Contracting and accountability', in Jonathan Boston (ed.), *The State Under Contract*. Wellington: Bridget Williams Books.

Mascarenhas, R.C. (1991) 'State-owned enterprises', in Jonathan Boston, John Martin, June Pallot and Pat Walsh (eds) *Reshaping the State: New Zealand's Bureaucratic Revolution*. Auckland: Oxford University Press. pp. 27–51.

Mulgan, Richard (1996) *Comparing Public Sector Reforms in the Australian Commonwealth and*

New Zealand Governments. Discussion Paper for Institute of Policy Studies, Wellington, 5 November.

National Commission of Audit (1996) *Report to the Commonwealth Government.* Canberra: Australian Government Publishing Service.

National Competition Policy Review (1993) *National Competition Policy.* Chairman F.G. Hilmer, Canberra: Australian Government Publishing Service.

OECD (1995) *Governance in Transition: Public Management Reforms in OECD Countries.* Paris: Organisation for Economic Co-operation and Development.

OECD (1996a) *OECD Economic Surveys 1995-1996: New Zealand.* Paris: Organisation for Economic Co-operation and Development.

OECD (1996b) *OECD Economic Surveys 1996-1997: Australia.* Paris: Organisation for Economic Co-operation and Development.

Olsen, Johan P. and Peters, B. Guy (eds) (1996) *Lessons from Experience: Experiential Learning in Administrative Reforms in Eight Democracies.* Oslo: Scandinavian University Press.

Productivity Commission (1996) *Stocktake of Progress in Microeconomic Reform.* Canberra: Commonwealth of Australia.

Pusey, Michael (1991) *Economic Rationalism in Canberra: a Nation Building State Changes its Mind.* Cambridge: Cambridge University Press.

Raskall, Phil (1993) 'Widening economic disparities in Australia', in Stuart Rees, Gordon Rodley and Frank Stilwell (eds), *Beyond the Market: Alternatives to Economic Rationalism.* Leichardt: Pluto. pp. 38–52.

Reith, Peter (1996) *Towards a Best Practice Australian Public Service.* Discussion Paper, Australian Government Publishing Service, Canberra, November.

Schick, Allen (1996) *The Spirit of Reform: Managing the New Zealand State Sector in a Time of Change.* Report prepared for the State Services Commission and the Treasury, Wellington.

Schwartz, Herman (1994) 'Small states in big trouble: state reorganization in Australia, Denmark, New Zealand, and Sweden in the 1980s', *World Politics,* 46 (July): 527–55.

SCNPMGTE (1995) *Government Trading Enterprises Performance Indicators 1989-90 to 1993-94. Volume 1: Overview.* Melbourne: Steering Committee on National Performance Monitoring of Government Trading Enterprises.

Scott, Graham (1996a) 'The use of contracting in the public sector', *Australian Journal of Public Administration,* 55(3): 97–104.

Scott, Graham (1996b) 'The New Zealand Experience of Reform', in Conference on Challenges and Opportunities: the Next Phase of Public Sector Reform, Department of Finance, 3 September.

Scott, Graham (1996c) *Government Reform in New Zealand.* International Monetary Fund Occasional Paper 140, Washington, DC, October.

Scott, Graham, Bushnell, Peter and Sallee, Nikitin (1990) 'Reform of the core public sector: New Zealand experience', *Governance,* 3(2): 138–67.

Sedgwick, S.T. (1994) 'Evaluation of management reforms in the Australian public service', *Australian Journal of Public Administration,* 53(3): 341–7.

TFMI (1993) *The Australian Public Service Reformed: an Evaluation of a Decade of Management Reform.* Task Force on Management Improvement. Canberra: Australian Government Publishing Service for the Management Advisory Board.

Trosa, Sylvie (1996) *The Changing Role of the Australian Public Service: the Trends and Issues for the Future.* Public Sector Papers 1/96, Centre for Research in Public Sector Management, University of Canberra.

Vowles, Jack, Aimer, Peter, Catt, Hemena, Lamare, Jim and Miller, Raymond (1995) *Towards Consensus: the 1993 Election in New Zealand and the Transition to Proportional Representation.* Auckland: University Press.

Wilenski, Peter (1986) *Public Power and Public Administration.* Sydney: Hale and Iremonger.

Withers, Glenn, Throsby, David and Johnston, Kaye (1994) *Public Expenditure in Australia* Paper 3, Australian Government Publishing Service for Economic Planning Advisory Commission, Canberra.

2

The Bewildering Pace of Public Sector Reform in Canada

Evert A. Lindquist

Canada is in the midst of a wholesale realignment of governance responsibilities, ranging from jurisdictional issues to experimenting with alternative ways to deliver a great variety of policies and programmes. Much of this realignment has been driven by the brute fiscal facts of growing deficits and debt obligations – and the brute political facts of tax fatigue and public cyncism about government – that all federal and provincial governments, regardless of political ideology, could not ignore. Not surprisingly, the goals of increased efficiency and effectiveness have been the commonly repeated mantras of government leaders as they reviewed the menu of alternatives for delivering and financing existing and new programmes.

In his introductory chapter, Jan-Erik Lane suggests that the current round of administrative reforms, arguably much deeper than those associated with the managerialism of the 1980s, cannot be evaluated solely in terms of efficiency and effectiveness, even if those values are of crucial importance. He suggests that broader considerations, such as transparency and public accountability, must be factored into any assessment, however preliminary, of the public sector reforms now in train. I would take this argument an important step further: it is essential that we venture assessments about the impact of reform on civil society and on the quality of public discourse about governance.

Canada presents an interesting case for exploring all of these matters because public sector reform is proceeding apace at all levels of government. The worry and perplexity of public servants and citizens about these changes are palpable; they are equalled only by the cavalier claims about the scope for change or the complete political and public disinterest in the subject. Considerable public sector reform has occurred, but, beyond pointing to the bottom line, Canadian governments seem unable to convey the extent and meaning of change to date. The federal government in particular seems incapable of arguing the positive case for state involvement, whether limited or not; nor has it succeeded in developing a national view on the status and impact of these reforms.

The result is, in my view, a potentially dangerous intellectual vacuum: on the one hand, Canadians seem unaware of their collective capacity for change; and on the other hand, there seems to be an appetite for radical change (or at least an unwillingness to question the need for such change) that may be counterproductive for the longer-term interests of citizens and communities. We are collectively incapable of developing a context for evaluating the progress made to date, except in the crudest terms. I argue that the gap in discourse and public comprehension is not solely due to the ineptness of the current government, but reflects a series of missed opportunities during the last two decades. This gap is particularly worrisome in the context of the ongoing debate over how to restructure the federation and, indeed, the very fate of the country.

In order to address these issues, this chapter begins with a review of public sector reforms in Canada during the 1980s, which can broadly be characterized as 'managerialist' in nature. I then take a closer look at the era of government restructuring associated with the early and mid 1990s, when Canadian governments acted in a variety of more concerted ways to bring deficits and debt under control. I concluded by exploring the effectiveness of these reforms, and express some worry about the state and public discourse on these issues and whether the costs of reform and the stock of social capital are sufficient to sustain the new governance regimes for the longer term.

Canadian governments and managerialism in the 1980s

The challenge of reforming government in Canada may be high on the public agenda during the 1990s, but unlike in other countries, it was not a central priority of most federal and provincial governments during the 1980s, even if worry began to build on the part of ministers and senior officials. There were efforts to control costs and overhaul government operations, but these actions were not boldly advocated by most political leaders, and were typically designed to minimize the political consequences and to ensure that pain fell as lightly as possible on programmes and public servants.

The decade began with the difficult economic recession of the early 1980s, which wreaked havoc with government budgets and further contributed to the impotence of governments in the face of the stagflation of the 1970s. It was during this time that the federal government, led by Liberal Prime Minister Pierre Trudeau, launched two major policy interventions as part of the October 1980 and the November 1981 budgets, the National Energy Program and a major tax reform initiative respectively. The infamous National Energy Program was a unilateral and massive attempt to restructure and Canadianize the oil and gas industry, particularly with respect to exploration and ownership, one that greatly angered the Alberta government and its citizens (Desveaux, 1995; Doern and Toner, 1985). The tax reform budget was a dramatic political failure; launched with little forewarning, it was subjected to withering criticism on content and process, and many measures were quickly dropped or delayed. The final major initiative was that of the federal government to patriate the Canadian constitution from the United Kingdom and to include a Charter of Rights and Freedoms. It led to conflict and intense negotiations with the provinces; Quebec citizens were particularly incensed and isolated, but the new constitution was proclaimed in April 1982 (Russell, 1993).

These three initiatives may seem unrelated to the subject of public sector reform, but they were crucial in establishing the context in which a Progressive Conservative government, led by Prime Minister Brian Mulroney, took power in autumn 1984. There was increasing worry about the state of federal–provincial relations, and the state of national finances since the deficit had ballooned following the recession and the collapse of world energy prices. The new Prime Minister came to Ottawa promising that his government would give 15,000 public servants 'pink slips and running shoes' (out of roughly 244,000 employees), and also announced four across-the-board cuts to operating budgets (as opposed to programme funding) in November 1984, May and November 1985, and February 1986 – the last including a cap on future increases in operating budgets. During this time, the Task Force on Program Review was appointed by the Prime Minister, and was led by the Deputy Prime Minister, Erik Nielsen. The Task Force consisted of teams of public sector and private sector representatives that reviewed over 1,000 federal programmes (Wilson, 1988).

The fate of the Nielsen Task Force is important to examine because it points to larger constraints on more fundamental public sector reform during the 1980s. The Task Force took 19 months to issue its final report, which was submitted in March 1986. As Vince Wilson has observed, many Canadians were, on the one hand, against irresponsible government spending in the abstract but, on the other hand, were not inclined to cut funds for specific programmes. Various Task Force teams floated ideas for programme elimination or restructuring, but the government and its ministers adopted a defensive posture, in part because of strident outcries by affected interests, and in part because ministers had moved through the transition phase and had already identified strategic priorities. Many of the ideas generated by the Task Force were ignored or downplayed by the government, and the Deputy Prime Minister became increasingly isolated. In a very different policy arena, a similar dynamic was at play: the plan of the government to de-index public pensions came to a screeching halt when a senior citizen – Solange Denis – berated the Prime Minister in a very personal and public moment for breaking his vow that social programmes would be a 'sacred trust'. The incident shook the confidence of the government on social policy and, as a result, a swathe of programmes were taken off the table as objects of public sector reform.

None of the above should be constructed as concluding that the Mulroney government was inactive on all policy fronts. Indeed, three major initiatives were launched, each with important ramifications for public sector reform, as follows:

Constitutional reform   A high priority of the Prime Minister was to ensure that the province of Quebec, whose leaders objected to the 1982 constitution and whose government had invoked its 'notwithstanding' clause, could agree to amendments that would enable its leaders and citizens to positively embrace a modified constitution. The Prime Minister had made this promise a key part of his election platform to Quebec citizens, who gave strong support to his party. Discussions were initiated with the provinces, which culminated in the Meech Lake Accord in April 1987 between the Prime Minister and provincial premiers. However, ratification was delayed when two provinces withheld support, in part because of growing public concern about the closed process of negotiation and the terms of the agreement. Following the 1988 federal election, the Mulroney government initiated a more open process that led to the Charlottetown Accord, but the agreement was rejected in a national referendum in 1992.

Tax reform   The government proceeded with tax reform, in large measure responding to developments in the United States where the Congress approved legislation to simplify tax reporting, reduce tax levels, and broaden the tax base. The Canadian government began by announcing reforms in June 1987 on the personal income tax side, but for our purposes, the most controversial and consequential initiative was the adoption of the goods and services tax (GST). The GST is a value-added tax that replaced the previously hidden manufacturers' sales tax (at 13%), but it applied to a broader range of goods and services at a lower rate of 7%. Its very transparency led to a groundswell of resentment by citizens and business owners alike about the GST in particular, and tax levels in general, every time they purchased a good or service.

Free trade negotiations   Although the Progressive Conservative Party had not campaigned on a free trade platform, the Mulroney government embraced the recommendations of the Royal (Macdonald) Commission on the Economic Union and Development Prospects to initiate negotiations with the United States in order to retain access to a huge market and support the export market. The initiative touched off an enormous debate that revolved around whether Canada could retain its autonomy and distinctiveness as a country, and how more permeable borders and less scope for protectionist measures might accelerate the process of economic restructuring, and combined with tax fatigue, put pressure on long-standing federal and provincial programmes. The government ran on the issue in the 1988 federal election and, with a second majority government, soon concluded an agreement with the United States.

The point of this discussion is not to provide a detailed review of the Mulroney government policy initiatives, but rather to show that it did have an ambitious policy agenda, albeit one that did not make public sector reform a centrepiece in the manner of the governments of Australia, New Zealand, and the United Kingdom during the 1980s (Aucoin, 1996; Savoie, 1994). Nevertheless, the policy agenda did create a new political topography for public sector reform by the end of the 1980s: the public began evincing its resistance to increased taxation; both federal and provincial governments began preparing for how free trade would necessitate policy and administrative reforms in numerous sectors; and conversely, increasingly prickly federal–provincial relations and reduced federal spending power made deeper programme restructuring a political challenge.

Although public sector reform may not have been a central political priority of the Mulroney government, it did launch several reform initiatives. In 1986, the government proceeded with the Increased Ministerial Authority and Accountability initiative dedicated to increasing flexibilities and reporting burdens for operating departments and to negotiating agreements with certain departments for further flexibilities in exchange for better accountability regimes. In 1990, the Prime Minister announced the Public Service 2000 exercise, a series of deputy ministerial task forces that were to improve the management of the financial and human resources of federal public service and introduce service quality precepts. Swept up and given higher profile in the process were two important pilot projects: the adoption of single operating budgets, which granted more budget flexibility for managers so they could shift resources between salaries, minor capital needs, and other non-capital expenditure categories; and the creation of special operating agencies (SOAs), a Canadian twist on the executive agency concept, one that granted increased management and financial flexibilities (such as revolving funds) to agencies or programmes that provided services on a cost-recovery basis, but still reported directly to a deputy minister, and thus did not have the independence of British agency heads (Veilleux and Savoie, 1988; Savoie, 1990; Clark, 1994; Swimmer et al., 1994).

In retrospect, it is clear that although the Mulroney government supported these initiatives, they were viewed as little more than administrative plumbing and best left to senior public servants to oversee. On the budget front, the government and the Department of Finance continually relied on optimistic forecasts, and underestimated the flow of tax revenues and the cost of interest payments on the debt due to a sluggish economy and high interest rates. Even though the government had operating surpluses during this time, it simply could not make progress on reducing the size of the deficit, since a quarter of outlays went to interest payments. Moreover, even though the government did reduce the size of the federal public service, the number of employees began to increase once more (Lee and Hobbs, 1996).

Up to this point, I have focused on the federal government and not on the experience of provincial governments during the 1980s. With the exceptions of British Columbia and of Saskatchewan – where conservative governments did launch significant restructuring, downsizing, contracting out, and privatization of provincial programmes and bureaucracies – the nature of provincial reforms is best depicted as being consistent with managerialism, repetitive budgeting, and growing deficits. That few provincial governments embarked on more significant restructuring was, in part, due to the fact that the federal government had not pressed forward with reductions in transfers to the provinces, and the westernmost provinces benefited from increased resource revenues owing to increasingly favourable international markets (Dupré, 1996; Maslove and Moore, 1996).

In short, Canadian governments generally did not adopt radical approaches to public sector reform; a growing economy during most of the 1980s (despite the recessionary bookends of the decade) diverted public attention from the disturbing underlying trends in public sector finances. Governments recognized these trends, but were unwilling to leap ahead of public opinion when it came to restructuring or cutting programmes. Generally, they drew the line at securing operating efficiencies and limiting increases in compensation. Restructuring the public sector could not compete with the acrimonious national debates over free trade, amending the constitution, and tax reform – although the outcomes of these debates created a cranky electorate and increased public cynicism about the quality of governance at the political and bureaucratic levels. Governments had talked a good deal about the need to control taxes and expenditures but, by the end of the 1980s, it was clear they had failed. In a surprising turn-around, governments found themselves well behind the increasing concern of the public and of the markets about the fiscal health of the country and its provinces, and for elected leaders the challenge of the 1990s would be how to catch up with different yardsticks for measuring political performance.

Canadian governments and public sector restructuring in the 1990s

For many Canadian governments, the 1990s presented an entirely different political landscape. It began with a sharp recession and jobless recovery, which hit particularly hard the wealthiest province, Ontario. The size of provincial and federal deficits became increasingly newsworthy because a higher proportion of Canadian public debt was held by international bondholders, and the views of foreign analysts began to dramatically influence credit ratings and the cost of servicing the debt. Finally, political leaders understood that citizens would not countenance further increases in tax levels.

The federal government was placed in an increasingly untenable situation; its attention and political capital were sapped by its constitutional struggles, but political leaders and senior officials began to realize that decremental, indirect strategies focused on reducing 'overheads', as opposed to eliminating or restructuring programmes, would not produce the needed change. They also realized that since programme restructuring and deficit reduction would dominate the political agenda for some time, and therefore

Cabinet decision-making and bureaucratic structures needed to be put on a different footing. In January 1992 the Prime Minister asked one of his ministers, Robert de Cotret, and a small circle of former and current officials, for advice on how to create a smaller Cabinet and new set of ministerial portfolios and departments. The report was submitted in autumn 1992, but the Prime Minister declined to act immediately, deciding instead to leave final decisions and implementation to his successor, Kim Campbell, when she appointed her new Cabinet. It was on 25 June 1993 that the new Prime Minister unveiled a radically smaller Cabinet with 25 ministers (down from almost 40), the consolidation and the restructuring of several departments into larger entities, and the demotion of several deputy ministers and assistant deputy ministers.

Budget realities also pointed to future pressures. By the early 1990s, more than a quarter of all federal outlays went to servicing the debt, and almost another quarter were transfers to individuals (that is, elderly, veterans, and unemployment benefits); the latter, for the most part, were politically untouchable. This left a major category of outlays to the provinces for equalization payments, Established Programs Financing for health and postsecondary education, and the Canada Assistance Plan for welfare assistance. In the early 1990s, the federal government put a cap on the Canada Assistance Plan – a plan whereby the federal government had paid 50% of the provincial costs incurred for providing social assistance – for the wealthiest provinces (Alberta, Ontario and British Columbia); this deeply affected those provinces, which were severely hit by the recession. Many provincial and territorial governments, anticipating further declines in future federal funding, began to attack their own deficits and launched into serious restructuring of provincial programmes and of the larger public sector, including education, health, social services, and municipal governance. In many cases, provincial actions – such as Cabinet and public service restructuring, delayering and other means for achieving efficiencies, compensation rollbacks, and programme reviews – predated the increasingly more dramatic actions of the federal government (Lindquist and Murray, 1994).

Canadian governments began to mobilize public support for deficit reduction and programme restructuring in a manner that would have been unthinkable just a few years earlier. Two new premiers of Alberta and Saskatchewan (respectively leading Progressive Conservative and New Democratic governments) appointed commissions to quickly investigate and to issue public reports on the state of the provincial finances. In this way, the 'truth' about difficult budgetary situations was received by those governments from independent actors. A second innovation was that several federal and provincial governments launched public consultations on budget priorities and deficit reduction strategies in advance of introducing their budgets, a clear departure with traditional practice (Lindquist, 1994b). Governments hosted round tables, conferences, and legislative hearings that relied more heavily on the input of 'ordinary' citizens; interest groups were not ignored, but often their input was channelled by having them contend with the demands of other groups, experts and citizens, as opposed to elected leaders and officials listening to a series of in camera demands from experts and interest groups. These arrangements had the effect of casting deficit reduction as a strategy directed towards furthering the common good and muting demands of interest groups. These initiatives had spillover effects: the efforts of one government were widely reported and created expectations for other governments.

Political leaders searched for ways to remedy the widespread distrust of governments, and one approach was to clearly state commitments and act on them. Following several budget round tables, Premier Ralph Klein of Alberta introduced a budget in May 1993 and later a deficit reduction plan, and then called a provincial election. His political agenda consisted of the budget which had yet to receive approval; it was later reintroduced and became law. The federal Liberal Party, led by Jean Chrétien, produced an extensive Red Book of commitments as part of its campaign strategy for the October 1993 election; the Progressive Conservatives produced a Blue Book at short notice, but it was widely perceived as an opportunistic and cynical ploy. Later, Ontario's Progressive Conservatives developed a document outlining the principles and the commitments of its 'common sense revolution' well in advance of the 1995 provincial election, a radical plan to downsize and restructure government programmes; this document, and the collapse of the Liberal Party campaign, led the party to victory. Canadian voters began to reward political parties that clearly outlined commitments and governments that honoured them. In this connection, it is worth noting that several prime ministers and premiers alike have reduced the size of cabinets and streamlined decision-making processes in order to focus the attention of ministers on meeting the fiscal imperative and furthering strategic priorities (Lindquist and White, 1997).

However, although the Red Book was an important launching pad for the new Liberal government led by Premier Jean Chrétien, signalling a new era in transparency and political commitment, it did not prepare ministers for the challenges of designing and implementing a significant programme of public sector restructuring. Not long after the transfer of power, the government initiated several policy reviews, and most importantly a program review process as part of the February 1994 budget. The Minister of Finance circulated 'notional' targets for each minister and department to accompany their reviews which had to respond to six test questions. The process culminated several months later when department plans and proposals were vetted first by a committee of senior deputy ministers, and then by a programme review committee of Cabinet ministers. These decisions informed the February 1995 budget, which announced the government's intention to proceed with major spending reductions, alternative delivery decisions, and significant public service downsizing (the figure touted was 45,000 employees from a base of 225,000 employees). Also announced were significant reductions to provincial governments for funding of education, health, and welfare: the Canada Assistance Plan and Established Programs Financing were converted into the Canada Health and Social Transfer programme which reduced federal outlays over time but granted provinces increased flexibilities in allocating funds. This was a major shift in strategy for the Liberals, but inevitable if the government was to live up to commitments to reduce the debt-to-GDP ratio and not to increase levels of taxation (Armit and Bourgault, 1996; Greenspon and Wilson-Smith, 1996).

I do not want to make too much of the federal government actions, since many provincial governments had already initiated significant deficit reduction and restructuring plans, and many observers viewed federal actions as little more than offloading tough decisions onto the provinces (Lindquist and Murray, 1994). In addition to the Canada Health and Social Transfer initiative, the federal government proceeded with its efficiency of the federation agreements (a series of bilateral agreements to reduce overlap and duplication with provinces) and a federal infrastructure programme, which levered federal, provincial, and municipal funding for local projects. It is fair to say that these initiatives did not capture the imagination of the public, and progress on this front was highly constrained by the sensitivities before the Quebec referendum in late October 1995 and its aftermath. For example, it has taken a considerable time for the federal government to announce and then negotiate the devolution of responsibilities for active labour market training programmes to the provinces.

However, for many Canadians, the real impact of the restraint and deficit reduction plans of federal and provincial governments is connected to the restructuring of public services that are associated with the larger public sector (Lindquist and Murray, 1994). By the larger public sector I mean the provincially funded or regulated education, health, municipal, and social service sectors. There is a consistent pattern in many provinces of consolidating school boards, refocusing the curricula of schools, and allowing universities to raise tuition fees. In the health sector, there has been an impetus to close or amalgamate hospitals and to reallocate liberated resources to community-based care, and to delegate the responsibility for identifying priorities and implementation to regional health boards and authorities, but retaining financial discipline by defining funding envelopes. Provincial governments have been involved in tough negotiations with physicians and other health professionals over billing schedules, and over the inflow of younger physicians and where they may be allowed to practice, and some provinces have argued that the federal government should permit a larger proportion of health services to be delivered on a private basis. Provincial governments have sought to make welfare assistance less attractive to current and would-be recipients by lowering benefits, improving training programmes, and removing barriers to lower-income families to take up employment, such as the loss of income or benefits. Several provincial governments have sought to make municipal governance more efficient by means of amalgamation, and through overhauling of property tax regimes. Owing to these and other pressures, there has been considerable restructuring and experimenting with the delivery of municipal services (McDavid and Clemens, 1995; Sancton, 1996). Finally, during the early 1990s, many provincial governments legislated that employers in the wider public sector, and not just provincial public servants, bear their share of compensation freezes or reductions as part of broader deficit reduction strategies.

Even more fundamental governance reforms are proceeding outside the provinces, in Canada's northern territories (Cameron and White, 1995). Territorial governments, which have traditionally been outposts of the federal Department of Indian and Northern Affairs, have increasingly received devolved authorities and province-like status in their dealings with the federal government, even though territories do not have constitutional status as provinces. Particularly interesting is the fact that, while territorial governments rely heavily on parliamentary principles for decision-making, they have developed unique and more open styles of governance, reflecting the linguistic and ethnic diversity of constituent communities, and the huge land mass that must be governed (Lindquist and White, 1997). But as territorial governments are receiving more authority and responsibilities, they are also contending with several enormous challenges: the federal government is reducing transfer payments and other programme support as part of its larger programme of expenditure reduction; the Northwest Territories will soon be divided into two new territories (Nunavut and the Western Northwest Territories); and the settlement of land claims is leading to negotiation of a host of bilateral agreements with First Nations and territorial governments. All of these developments will have significant repercussions for public servants, many of whom are currently working for the federal or territorial governments, and who may soon serve communities in the territories in very different arrangements.

The general political lesson learned by all Canadian governments, as well as opposition parties and leaders aspiring to power, was that considerable political mileage could be made out of commitments to reduce deficits and debt. The public appetite for the enunciation of longer-term goals and fiscal plans not only imposed financial discipline and new standards for evaluating demands for new programmes, but also served as an important line of defence when announcing expenditure reductions or programme elimination. Although it is not clear that there was ever an undue amount of overlap and duplication across governments, or across departments or ministries in a given government, the drive for increased efficiencies and the need to meet expenditure reduction targets, as well as demands to better serve citizens, generated incentives to look very closely at how to reallocate responsibilities and improve coordination across and within governments. As provincial governments and local governments were put under increasing pressure to reduce expenditures owing to lower transfers from more senior governments, they demanded more flexibility and autonomy.

The discipline of long-term fiscal targets and expenditure reduction plans, and the demise of sizeable policy reserves, have led to increasing interest by governments in 'thinking the unthinkable' with respect to deregulation, contracting out, privatization, or public–private partnerships. Currently, such exploration is proceeding under the umbrella concept of 'alternative delivery' of government programmes (Lindquist and Sica, 1996; Ford and Zussman, 1997), though it must be acknowledged that many of the 'alternatives' are not new, with the exception of special operating agencies, more competitive regimes for delivering services, innovative use of information technologies, and the drive to provide single-window service for citizens and business organizations, which require more horizontal coordination across ministries and departments within and sometimes across jurisdictions. These circumstances – ministers and citizens alike willing to countenance alternatives to reliance on the core public service to deliver programmes – would seem opportune for more fiscally conservative governments to push forward with privatization and contracting out, but even those governments have not acted rashly. The tempering twist is that alternative delivery options must make good fiscal sense in the short term and the long term, and it is essential to provide governments and citizens alike with sufficient reporting and redress mechanisms for ensuring accountability.

There has been a drive across the country for more transparent and more accountable government. The federal government and many provincial governments have embraced new strategic planning, reporting, and accountability regimes which generally fall under the label of 'business planning'. Their cabinets and central agencies require departments and ministries to identify key 'lines of business' (formerly called programmes), major adjustment and restructuring challenges, anticipated resource flows for usually about three fiscal years, key client groups, and performance indicators (Lindquist, 1996a; Lindquist, 1997). A goal of some of these governments is not simply to ensure that ministers and central agencies can better monitor the performance of departments and programme managers, whether they work as part of or outside the public service, but also to encourage more meaningful scrutiny by the elected representatives in legislatures, concerned interests, and the broader public (Harder and Lindquist, 1997). Remaining an open question is whether or not business planning documents and performance indicators has led to increased transparency and accountability; a key factor is whether outsiders have sufficient background information to evaluate and contest the plans developed by departments (Lindquist, 1996b). Moreover, it does not appear that business plans yet function as the basis for performance of deputy ministers in Canada according to an *ex ante* contract, as they do for the chief executive officers of the British executive agencies and the New Zealand state-owned enterprises (Aucoin, 1996).

If the managerialism of the 1980s was demoralizing to Canadian public servants, then the public sector restructuring of the 1990s has fundamentally changed their expectations and, in many cases, their career trajectories. The conventional understandings of 'career public service' have been torn asunder, with public servants no longer believing that steady and even exemplary performance will necessarily be rewarded with promotions or salary increases (Lindquist, forthcoming). Public servants now take up training, development and promotion opportunities less with an eye towards furthering careers in a public service, and more towards maximizing career prospects in the private or non-profit sectors. The litany of reorganizations, downsizing, adoption of new technologies, and exploration of alternative delivery possibilities has exacted a real toll on public servants. Workplaces have been decimated when governments offer early retirement or buyout packages because often the most mobile and talented public servants have been the first to leave. One now hears not just of demoralized workers, but also of burnout and health problems as the public servants who remain are asked to cover for a broader range of responsibilities. There has generally been very little intake of younger public servants, but in public services where such hiring has occurred the youngest staff are often the first to leave since they were hired on limited-term contracts or bumped by colleagues with greater seniority.

Beyond efficiency and effectiveness: engaging citizens and communities

This chapter has provided only a general account of developments in Canada, but I hope it successfully conveys a sense of the extent, scope and pace of public sector reform. Such reform, when coupled with the separatist threat from Quebec and the emerging imperatives of the new information economy, generates considerable uncertainty and pessimism about the future. It is no wonder that citizens and public servants find such multi-faceted change bewildering.

There can be little doubt that the actions of governments have been efficient and effective in the most global sense. All provinces and the federal government have made progress on reducing deficits, and recently many governments have significantly reduced exposure to the whims of inter-national debt markets. Some jurisdictions, such as Alberta and the federal government, have more than met their targets, so the quandary for their elected leaders has been whether to restore funding to some programmes or to support new policies, or to channel all surpluses to deficit and debt reductions. And perhaps most importantly for the leaders of many govern-ments, these more radical reforms have enabled them to meet the crucial political tests of re-election.

A less easy determination to make is whether public sector reforms have generally been more efficient and effective with respect to the quality of services and governance provided to citizens. A definitive answer could only emerge from detailed analyses on a case by case basis, and through com-parisons of practices in different jurisdictions. However, one can venture the observation that much has been accomplished by means of bridging strategies in the short term. Arguably employees in core public services and the larger public sector have been providing citizens and ministers with the same level of services with significantly less resources, but the incidences of burnout and low morale are legion, and many talented public servants have left owing to better opportunities in the non-profit and private sectors. In other words, it is not clear that the current arrangements can be sustained in the longer term, particularly since the impact of restructuring and previously announced cutbacks has yet to be fully felt by citizens.

Although it is difficult to gauge such impacts, it does seem clear that the loss of federal 'spending power' is redefining the role of the federal government. Increasingly, federal ministers will be less able to 'buy' provincial support for national programmes, and instead will have to rely on genuinely good policy ideas, moral suasion, public support, and a cooperative approach. In some quarters, it is believed that the provinces, as opposed to the federal government, will take responsibility for proposing, designing and implementing national social programmes since they have jurisdiction and may have sufficient incentives to agree on national standards and conditions for approving the flow of people, services, and goods. This does not mean that the federal government will be completely 'hollowed out', but rather that its roles will be clarified and its influence exercised more in proportion to its spending and constitutional authorities.

An important theme of this chapter is that when one takes an aggregate view of public sector reform in Canada, it is hard not to say that the country is in great turmoil, having entered into an era of experimentation, for better or for worse, that involves all levels of governance: federal, provincial, regional, local and aboriginal. However, the great irony is that the Canadian federation has been trapped in constitutional gridlock, born of a reluctance on the part of many political leaders and citizens to experiment with new governing arrangements. For some reason, however bewildered by the extent of government restructuring, Canadians seem far more willing to countenance more radical change in the administrative domain, change likely to have a far more profound influence on their lives than agreement to be more flexible on points of constitutional principle.

A premise underlying the enthusiasm of more supporters of smaller government and more radical public sector reforms is that citizens and communities, and non-profit and for-profit organizations will absorb more responsibility for providing public and quasi-public goods. Advocates rarely make persuasive arguments about the extent of social capital and the state of civil society in Canada (Putnam, 1993), and yet the flip side of an aggressive and permanent use of alternative programme delivery and financing regimes should be a dramatic shift in the political cultures of Canada and its regions, with greater emphasis on corporate and individual philanthropy and volunteerism. It is too early to predict whether progress can be made in this regard, but suffice it to say that Canadians are not noted for generous giving, perhaps due to a more interventionist state (Lindquist, 1992). Moreover it is not yet clear that Canadians are willing to embrace subsidiarity fully as a guiding principle: first determine if you or your community can provide a public good, and failing that, turn to increasingly higher orders of government to accomplish such objectives (Paquet and Pigeon, forth-coming). Even more sobering is the fact that Canadian governments, although often arguing that citizens and communities should take on more responsibilities, have not provided sustained moral exhortation to do so, although the federal government may increase tax incentives to stimulate more giving.

More generally, there have been few attempts by governments to develop positive visions of what Canadian government and society might look like in the future. To be sure, there have been some scenario-building exercises undertaken by outside groups and sponsored by government agencies (see, for example, Rosell, 1995). The vision offered by most governments, to date, consists of meeting deficit targets and debt-to-GDP ratios; images of what a 'just society' might look like in the information age are in terribly short supply. The political party most likely to offer a social vision, the New Democratic Party, with the exception of the Saskatchewan government, seems to be in retreat; its leaders have yet to find new rhetoric and arguments that stir the social conscience of Canadians and prod them to move beyond worrying about tax levels and disposable income. Perhaps there will be more debate on these matters during the next few years, since political and economic pundits have already started to argue that 'the light is at the end of the tunnel', that deficit reduction strategies are well on track, that baby boomer generations occupying positions of authority will be retiring, and that the problem soon to confront all governments will be how to spend fiscal dividends. The possibilities are stark: should surplus tax revenues go towards further reducing the deficit and debt, granting further tax relief, rewarding public servants with compensation increases, or restoring programmes cut during the last decade? So, although there is generalized public support for public sector restructuring and deficit reduction, as specific needs move higher on the public agenda – such as health care, homelessness, unemploy-ment, and education – there should be lively political debate about future priorities.

I continue to worry, however, about the quality of public debate over these matters. In part my pessimism derives from the failure of Canadian governments to adequately convey the financial, human and other costs of restructuring, as well as the longer-term consequences of cutbacks and downsizing. It is not clear that the public sector reforms described above have necessarily led Canadians to become better informed about what governments do, and how well services are delivered by governments. There continues to be a surprisingly cavalier attitude in many quarters about the effectiveness and worth of government activities. I believe that Canadian citizens have lost a sense of proportion about the economic and social value received for tax dollars spent as well as the responsibilities owed to other citizens and society, a problem exacerbated by the fact that they are objectively receiving less value for tax dollars as debt payments remain significant. Some responsibility for the current state of affairs must fall to governments rather than citizens: political leaders have failed to defend, reward and celebrate the contributions of the public sector employees for some time. Even if significant restructuring of the welfare state was inevitable, our leaders have pandered to public opinion, pointing to public sector institutions and public servants as the problem.

How do we collectively regain that sense of proportion, without necessarily making an argument for bigger government or previous ways of delivering public goods? My pessimistic response hinges on the notion that the current malaise in public and indeed elite discourse on what and how public goods should be delivered is a product of many years of neglect, and therefore cannot be remedied quickly. Rather, it seems more likely that we will learn the hard way; the current working generations of Canadians are experiencing their own Great Depression, which, though driven by different social and economic forces, will similarly define political expectations for the foreseeable future. The gaps in incomes between skilled and non-skilled workers, between employed and non-employed citizens, and between the rich and the poor, are currently widening, and yet it is unclear that those more favoured in these times are developing any renewed sense of obligation to those less favoured. Perhaps the gaps will have to get much worse before better-off citizens come to believe that the plight of those less favoured directly impinges on their own interests.

The most important mitigating factor is that good discussion of public sector reform issues can only proceed if they hold meaning for citizens. While the fiscal crisis of the traditional welfare state is undeniable, large bureaucracies did redistribute wealth and deliver services with a degree of efficiency and effectiveness previously unimagined. At the same time, the welfare state depersonalized the sense of obligation, reduced the popular grasp of how tax dollars were spent, and created new dependencies and a reflex to turn to governments rather than communities to solve problems. It is not surprising that, at the time of writing, many of the most vital debates in Canada are occurring in the northern territories, and in the provinces at the local and community levels as governments have amalgamated local governments, closed hospitals, and created new governance structures for managing the delivery of education and health services. If federal and provincial leaders are interested in promoting engaged and responsible government, regardless of their views on whether the government should be larger or smaller, they should investigate more closely the reasons why citizens and communities care to get more involved in those debates.

References

Armit, Amelita and Bourgault, Jacques (eds) (1996) *Hard Choices or No Choice? Assessing Program Review.* Toronto: Institute of Public Administration of Canada.

Aucoin, Peter (1996) *The New Public Management: Canada in Comparative Perspective.* Montreal: Institute for Research on Public Policy.

Cameron, Kirk and White, Graham (1995) *Northern Governments in Transition: Political and*

Constitutional Development in the Yukon, Nunavut and the Western Northwest Territories. Montreal: Institute for Research on Public Policy.

Clark, Ian D. (1994) 'Restraint, renewal, and the Treasury Board Secretariat', *Canadian Public Administration*, 37(2): 209–48.

Desveaux, James A. (1995) *Designing Bureaucracies: Institutional Capacity and Large-Scale Problem Solving.* Stanford: Stanford University Press.

Doern, G.B. and Toner, Glen (1985) *The Politics of Energy: the Development and Implementation of the NEP.* Toronto: Methuen.

Dunn, Christopher (ed.) (1996) *Provinces: Canadian Provincial Politics.* Peterborough: Broadview Press.

Dupré, J. Stefan (1996) 'Taming the monster: debt, budgets, and federal-provincial fiscal relations at the *fin de siècle*', in Christopher Dunn (ed.) *Provinces: Canadian Provincial Politics.* Peterborough: Broadview Press. pp. 379–97.

Ford, Robin and Zussman, David (1997) *Alternative Service Delivery: Sharing Governance in Canada.* Toronto: KPMG Centre for Government Foundation and the Institute of Public Administration of Canada.

Greenspon, Edward and Wilson-Smith, Anthony (1996) *Double Vision: the Inside Story of the Liberals in Power.* Toronto: Doubleday.

Harder, Peter and Lindquist, Evert A. (1997) 'Expenditure management and reporting in the government of Canada: recent developments and background', in Jacques Bourgault, Maurice Demers and Cynthia Williams (eds), *Public Administration and Public Management: Experiences in Canada.* Québec: Publications du Québec.

Lee, Ian and Hobbs, Clem (1996) 'Pink slips and running shoes: the Liberal government's downsizing of the public service', in Gene Swimmer (ed.), *How Ottawa Spends 1996–97: Life under the Knife.* Ottawa: Carleton University Press. pp. 337–78.

Lindquist, Evert A. (1992) 'From crisis to opportunity: moving beyond *laissez-faire* philanthropy', *The Philanthropist*, 11(2): 11–34.

Lindquist, Evert A. (1994a) 'Administrative reform as decentralization: who is spreading what around to whom and why?', *Canadian Public Administration*, 37(3): 416–30.

Lindquist, Evert A. (1994b) 'Citizens, experts and budgets: evaluating Ottawa's emerging budget process', in Susan D. Phillips (ed.), *How Ottawa Spends 1994–95: Making Change.* Ottawa: Carleton University Press. pp. 91–128.

Lindquist, Evert A. (1996a) 'On the cutting edge: program review, government restructuring and the Treasury Board of Canada', in Gene Swimmer (ed.), *How Ottawa Spends 1996–97: Life under the Knife.* Ottawa: Carleton University Press. pp. 205–52.

Lindquist, Evert A. (1996b) 'Information, Parliament, and the new public management', *Canadian Parliamentary Review*, 19(1): 12–15.

Lindquist, Evert A. (1997) 'Critical issues in department "business" planning', for the *Critical Management Issues in Program Review Project.* Ottawa: Canadian Centre for Management Development (17 May 1997).

Lindquist, Evert A. (ed.) (forthcoming) *Government Restructuring and Career Public Service in Canada.* Toronto: Institute of Public Administration of Canada.

Lindquist, Evert A. and Murray, Karen (1994) 'A reconaissance of Canadian administrative reform during the early 1990s', *Canadian Public Administration*, 37(3): 468–89.

Lindquist, Evert A. and Sica, Tammy (1996) *Canadian Governments and the Search for Alternative Program Delivery and Financing: a Preliminary Survey.* Toronto: KPMG Centre for Government Foundation and Institute of Public Administration of Canada.

Lindquist, Evert and White, Graham (1997) 'Analyzing Canadian Cabinets: past present and future', in Mohammed Charih (ed.), *New Public Management and Public Administration in Canada.* Toronto: Institute of Public Administration of Canada.

McDavid, James C. and Clemens, Eric G. (1995) 'Contracting out local government services: the B.C. experience', *Canadian Public Administration*, 38(2): 177–93.

Maslove, Allan M. and Moore, Kevin D. (1996) 'Provincial Budgeting', in Christopher Dunn (ed.), *Provinces: Canadian Provincial Politics.* Peterborough: Broadview Press. pp. 321–50.

Paquet, Gilles and Pigeon, Lise (forthcoming) 'In search of a new social covenant', in Evert A.

Lindquist (ed.), *Government Restructuring and Career Public Service in Canada*. Toronto: Institute of Public Administration of Canada.

Peters, Guy and Savoie, Donald (eds) (1995) *Governance in a Changing Environment*. Kingston and Montreal: McGill-Queen's University Press.

Putnam, Robert D. (1993) *Making Democracy Work: Civil Traditions in Modern Italy*. Princeton: Princeton University Press.

Rosell, Steven A. (1995) *Changing Maps: Governing in a World of Rapid Change*. Ottawa: Carleton University Press.

Russell, Peter H. (1993) *Constitutional Odyssey: Can Canadians Become a Sovereign People?*, 2nd edn. Toronto: University of Toronto Press.

Sancton, Andrew (1996) 'Reducing costs of consolidating municipalities: New Brunswick, Nova Scotia and Ontario', *Canadian Public Administration*, 39(3): 267–89.

Savoie, Donald (1990) *The Politics of Public Spending in Canada*. Toronto: University of Toronto Press.

Savoie, Donald J. (1994) *Thatcher, Reagan, Mulroney: in Search of a New Bureaucracy*. Toronto: University of Toronto Press.

Swimmer, Gene (ed.) (1996) *How Ottawa Spends 1996–97: Life under the Knife*. Ottawa: Carleton University Press.

Swimmer, Gene, Hicks, Michael and Milne, Terry (1994) 'Public service 2000: dead or alive?', in Susan D. Phillips (ed.), *How Ottawa Spends 1994–95: Making Change*. Ottawa: Carleton University Press. pp. 165–204.

Veilleux, Gérard and Savoie, Donald J. (1988) 'Kafka's castle: the Treasury Board of Canada revisited', *Canadian Public Administration*, 31(4): 517–38.

Wilson, V. Seymour (1988) 'What legacy? The Nielsen Task Force Program Review', in Katherine A. Graham (ed.), *How Ottawa Spends 1988–89: the Conservatives Heading into the Stretch*. Ottawa: Carleton University Press. pp. 23–47.

3

The Privatization of Infrastructures in Germany

Ira Denkhaus and Volker Schneider

Privatization and public sector reform as an international phenomenon

After a continuous expansion of governmental involvement in all kinds of social activities since the beginning of this century, the last two decades have been characterized by a drastic cutback of state intervention through the reduction of public welfare programmes and the deregulation, liberalization and privatization of economic activities. Virtually all of the industrialized as well as most of the developing countries have launched some kind of fundamental restructuring programme in their public sectors, and in some cases these reform projects have targeted areas which even economic liberals have taken for granted to be core functions of the state. Adam Smith, for instance, listed the provision of infrastructural facilities such as highways, bridges, canals, schools and post offices amongst his three basic duties of a government, and it is striking that he termed these 'publick Works and publick Institutions'.[1]

In Germany, most of the public sector reform measures during the 1980s are related to the conservative Kohl government that came into power in 1982. As in other countries these reforms are clearly challenging the welfare state. But since the public sector seems to be more deeply entrenched and the unions are much better organized in Germany than in Britain or the USA, the government has been much more careful to attack the welfare state as a normative ideal and to suggest conflict-generating proposals like the privatization of core welfare programmes (Olsen, 1992: 278–9). Most of the privatization initiatives, however, have also been linked to progressing European integration since the mid 1980s, stimulated by the European internal market programme and the subsequent Maastricht Treaty. However, as just said, the German approach to public sector reform can be seen as relatively moderate. In fact, German reform policy can be depicted as a middle course between, on the one hand, liberalization and cutting back the state, and, on the other hand, the enforcement of control by the state combined with moderate decentralization tendencies characteristic of the French approach to public sector reform (Hesse and Benz, 1988: 80).

As in most public sector reforms world-wide, basic objectives in Germany have been 'decentralization', 'breaking up' and 'rationalization'. But the demand for institutional renovation has been relatively restricted from the very beginning. Furthermore, the breaking-up and decentralization questions in particular entail lengthy negotiations between different levels of government, which usually end by comprehensive compromises – one of the reasons why recent reform measures have been relatively modest. Recent German privatizations include the selling of government shares in enterprises in competitive markets,[2] different forms of administrative reforms aiming at the introduction of more commercial principles in public sector management and, last but not least, the privatization of some major utilities and infrastructures.

The various privatization measures in the transport and communications sectors, and their similarities and differences, are the topic of this chapter. In the first section we will give a short conceptual introduction to the theme, which will then be followed by a detailed description of the different privatization processes. In the last section, it will be questioned why such institutional changes in property forms and market structures have occurred at all, and why the outcomes of these transformation processes have differed. By a comparative analysis of these similarities and differences in the governance of infrastructural sectors, the chapter aims to achieve a better understanding of the various causes and conditions of this type of institutional transformation.

Privatization of infrastructure supply: conceptual considerations

Theoretical approaches to the privatization of infrastructures presuppose a theory on the differentiation between private and public spheres in modern society. For instance, they have to explain why a given set of social and economic activities is governed by individualistic market relations instead of administrative hierarchies and other political coordination and decision-making mechanisms. In contrast to instrumentalist approaches conceiving institutional forms as a direct reflection of individual or collective preferences (of a ruling class, a dominating elite or the population as a whole), structural theories seem to be more convincing: institutional differentiation is not a result of conscious decisions, but chiefly a non-intentional effect of the interplay between individual and collective action, and the structural properties of specific action goals and action areas.

Amongst the various theories which are guided by this very general orientation, there are a growing number of studies on 'governance' which have gained popularity during the last decade.[3] Within the frame of these theories, a privatization process has to be seen as a transformation of governance structures – in most cases from public hierarchies to private markets. Based on a structural model of explanation, we assume that the causes of these transformations are largely related to some changes in the structural characteristics of social action areas that will be analysed in this chapter, that is the provision of certain infrastructural services to the society at large.

Infrastructure

The term 'infrastructure' refers to a variety of general support systems in industrial society on which most of the other social, economic, cultural and political activities are dependent. The term is borrowed from the French, in which it designates the material foundation of a building or construction complex.[4] The *Basis* versus *Überbau* opposition of Karl Marx's theory of society, for instance, appears in French as *infrastructure* versus *superstructure*. In a similar sense, the term is also used in military language and refers to all the buildings, facilities, transport and communication networks that are necessary to ensure troops' supplies (McKay, 1989: 21).

In the context of this chapter the term 'infrastructure' is used in a rather restricted sense not covering, for instance, energy supply or educational or legal infrastructures. It is applied to the area of transport and communications, that is a cluster of socio-economic activities enabling and facilitating the transport of physical as well as informational objects. Since most – if not all – of these 'performance structures' (Mayntz and Scharpf, 1995) involve large technical inputs and a high degree of 'systemness', they can also be conceived as 'large technical systems' (Mayntz, 1995).

Infrastructures are preconditions for a wide range of activities and therefore a core prerequisite for social and economic development. Alongside their direct effects on the operation of communications and transport services themselves, those infrastructures also cause a variety of broader economic and social benefits such as increases in employment, spatial ordering, increases in demand and support for supply.

Technical and economic characteristics of infrastructures Infrastructures do have technical and economic as well as political characteristics that are frequently quoted as arguments for public intervention. One major example is the *market imperfection* or *market failure* argument that in our case is often related to natural monopolies and network effects.

Natural monopoly is defined 'as an industry in which least cost provision of a good (or service) requires that no more than one firm be in production' (Domberger, 1986: 270). The sufficient condition for a natural monopoly is the sub-additivity of the cost function which is often referred to as 'economies of scale' (decreasing long-term average costs with increasing enterprise size), 'economies of scope' (benefits from the joint production of two or more goods or services arising from the more efficient use of the indivisible production factors) and 'economies of density' (decreasing short-term average costs with increasing capacity use of a section within a network) (Ewers, 1994: 185–6). Further pressures towards monopoly are present when network externalities are involved (the larger a network is, the more valuable it is for its users).[5] Most if not all of the major infrastructure sectors have these structural properties and therefore show market imperfections which will usually generate public interventions.

Governmental control, however, is not the only way to solve the natural monopoly problem. As Baumol (1985) maintains, there are some conditions under which a natural monopolist will act as if operating in a competitive market, since he has to fear potential market entries when realizing monopoly profits. Such contestability requirements are: complete information of the participants in the market, non-existence of sunk costs, and price-making behaviour by the market participants where the price set by the established supplier is taken as given and serves as a decision basis for the potential entrants to it (Blankart and Knieps, 1992: 75–6).

As Rothengatter points out: 'Sub-additivity and irreversibility provide the basis for a natural monopoly' (1990: 54). It is easy to see that sunk costs play an important role in the infrastructure sectors since the physical infrastructure parts can only be moved to another location with considerable difficulties, and in most cases they are also not useful for other than their original production purpose. So the 'markets for infrastructure' cannot be seen as contestable natural monopolies and therefore require some form of public intervention.

A further argument which is frequently used for the legitimization of political intervention into the provision of infrastructures is their 'public good' character. Generally, 'public goods' (or collective goods) are defined by two properties. The first is non-exclusiveness, which means that if the good is available to one individual then it is automatically available to all other individuals. The second is non-rivalry (or jointness of supply), which is that given a level of production, the consumption by one individual does not thereby diminish the supply of the good being potentially available for consumption by other individuals (Buchanan, 1965: 3; Musgrave and Musgrave, 1976: 50–3). Figure 3.1 illustrates the two dimensions in the specification of public goods.[6]

Non-control over exclusion can be defined as the marginal costs of exclusion MC_{exclus} ranging from zero to infinity (and therefore from perfect control to complete non-control over exclusion of individuals from consumption). The level of MC_{exclus} depends partly upon the physical properties of the good itself. But, it is the social context of that good (that is the structure of society, political systems, and property rights) that is much more important for the degree of control over exclusion. MC_{ext} refers to the marginal costs of extending the consumption of a good, that is enhancing its non-rivalry (or decreasing its rivalry). The ideal-type public good is defined by $MC_{ext} = 0$ and $MC_{exclus} = \infty$, whereas pure private goods are defined as $MC_{ext} = \infty$ and $MC_{exclus} = 0$. The marginal costs of production MC_{prod} refer to the point where more practical definitions can be implemented: private provision of goods will occur where MC_{ext} exceeds MC_{prod} but MC_{exclus} is lower than MC_{prod}. Public provision is the only possibility in cases where MC_{exclus} exceeds MC_{prod} but MC_{ext} is lower than MC_{prod}. No

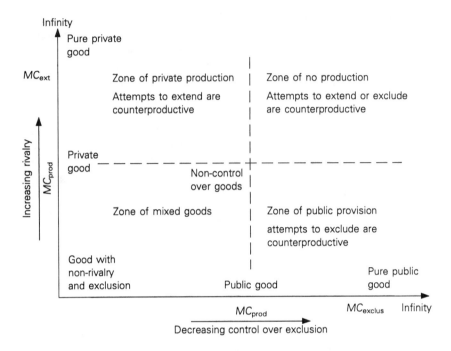

Figure 3.1   *Typology of goods. MC, marginal costs; prod, of production; ext, of extension; exclus, of exclusion. Source: Snidal, 1979: 543*

production of goods will take place when both MC_{ext} and MC_{exclus} exceed MC_{prod}. This is the area of free goods, meaning that the supply of goods in this area will only occur by virtue of natural supply. The term 'mixed goods', refers to a category in which varying degrees of private and public good properties are to be found (Snidal, 1979; 542–4). Infrastructures are usually defined as mixed goods because of their nature.

Snidal emphasizes that non-rivalry is conceptionally distinct from free goods, decreasing costs, excess capacity, jointness in production and 'lumpiness' (indivisibility). Since infrastructures are characterized by a high degree of 'lumpiness' involving sub-additivity of the cost function, the question of where to locate lumpy goods in Figure 3.1 is crucial. In the case of lumpiness, the marginal costs of production MC_{prod} will appear low as long as there is excess capacity, but very high once this excess is exhausted. Therefore the discontinuous nature of MC_{prod} connected with the property of lumpiness renders inappropriate a goods categorization without reference to the level of capacity utilization (Snidal, 1979: 544).

One of the basic findings of the theory of collective action is that within a society of utility maximizing individuals, public goods will be in short supply (Olson, 1965). In view of the good characteristics of infrastructures, this situation is likely to occur, bringing about another cause for public intervention. Snidal thus introduces the notion of a quasi-public good, which depicts a case in which 'an erstwhile public good has had payment and exclusion mechanisms attached to it by a central authority structure' (Snidal, 1979: 558–9). He views political organization as a way to achieve control over exclusion of a good without deleteriously affecting its inherent jointness and conceives this role as one of the main functions of states.[7] According to this conception of infrastructures as quasi-public goods, various forms of public intervention or provision can be justified.

Last but not least, infrastructures are also associated with either positive or negative externalities of economic action. The term 'externalities', refers to a divergence between private and social marginal utility (cost) functions. In the case of a positive externality, the private marginal utility is less than the social marginal utility, whereas in the case of a negative externality, the private marginal utility cost is less than the social marginal utility cost (Lane, 1985: 30). Although both kinds of externalities can occur where infrastructures are concerned, positive externalities are predominant in communication infrastructures, whereas the extent of negative externalities of transport infrastructures increasingly becomes a matter for public discussion as well as political problem-solving strategies.[8]

In sum, it can be stated that already, at the economic level, infrastructures have particular properties which render them different from 'ordinary', competitive markets and therefore create specific problems when the question of privatization is raised.

Political characteristics of infrastructures　In many cases, infrastructures are also of political relevance. From a purely historical perspective, infrastructures have always had considerable impact upon the military capacities and economic welfare of nation states, and also currently have an impact on transport, regional, structural, research and development aspects of public policy. Before this, they were widely recognized as being merit goods.[9] The political obligations connected with this characteristic mostly have a negative influence on their productive and allocative efficiency, since infrastructural capacities have often been created by politicians or bureaucrats without any considerations of economic rentability.

Private involvement in infrastructure provision　With regard to the issue of privatization or increasing private involvement in the provision of infrastructures, it is important to differentiate whether or not the construction (financing) or the operation of an infrastructural system (or both) are transferred to the private sector. The simple cross-tabulation in Table 3.1 illustrates this point. There are basically four possible combinations with respect to the modes of financing and operation of an infrastructural system.

BOT stands for 'build, operate, transfer' and describes the practice of private infrastructure financing and operation with the transfer of the property rights from the private to the public sector after a contractually agreed period (Nijkamp and Rienstra, 1995: 233). The difference between the BOT model and a purely private infrastructure is that supply is based on

Table 3.1 *Financing and operation of infrastructure*

| | | Financing | |
		Private	Public
Operation	Private	BOT model; fully private infrastructure	Separation of infrastructure and transport; operation as introduced by some railway reforms
	Public	Leasing; franchising	Traditional model of public infrastructures

Source: Nijkamp and Rienstra, 1995: 228; Horn, 1994; 28

the property status. With respect to private financing, infrastructures do again show some special characteristics which pose difficulties for a private involvement. Those features are:

1 long amortization periods
2 long periods between the start of capital formation and the beginning of financial returns
3 sunk costs
4 high political influence upon planning and construction, posing extra risks to the investors
5 high capital intensity combined with the usual low return on capital (Klatt, 1990: 209; Rothengatter, 1990: 84).

Privatization

Concepts and types In a very general sense, the term 'privatization' refers to any reduction in the scale or scope of governmental involvement in societal activities. In a more specific sense, privatization involves the transfer of ownership of assets and production of goods and services from the public to the private sector where that which is transferred may be ownership as well as management, management alone, or several other functions involved in producing the service or good (Starr, 1990: 27).

Basically, property rights theory argues that the tradability of well-defined property rights tends to lead to a situation where the person who guarantees for the highest productivity of an enterprise's resource actually attains the right of disposal. This is because the individual with the highest future profit expectations will pay the highest price for the property rights of the production entity. A major economic argument for privatization, therefore, is that the mere transfer of property rights from the public to the private sphere increases efficiency. A further argument is that the stronger private property rights are, the closer the relationship is between the welfare of the owners and the economic or social consequences of their decisions (Alessi, 1987: 26). A related economic argument in favour of privatization is

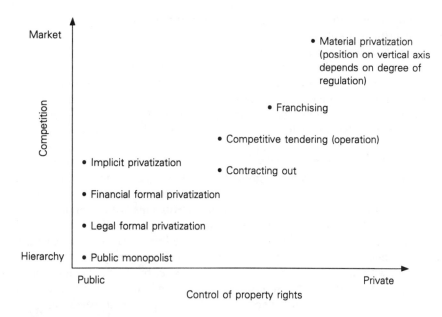

Figure 3.2   *Privatization of infrastructure – a two-dimensional typology*

that in most cases higher efficiency is caused not only by the shift in property, but also by an increase of potential and actual competition (Yarrow, 1986: 325).

Privatization provides a change in governance structures, an institutional transformation along several dimensions, which – for the sake of simplicity – in our chapter will be reduced to two. This two-dimensional outline of privatization strategies is depicted in Figure 3.2. In the typology:

Material privatization simply means the transfer from public to private ownership.

Franchising refers to the case where the production of a certain good or the operation of an infrastructural system is licensed to a private company financing the production or operation output through charges levied from the consumers. In contrast to competitive tendering, the franchising of operational functions sees the financial responsibility transferred from the public to the private sector. Within this rough sketch, different forms of franchising and competitive tendering (such as long-time lease of assets or infrastructure) are possible.

Contracting out reduces vertical integration (production depth) of public enterprises: goods and services which were previously produced by the public enterprise are now tendered and contracted out to private suppliers.

Implicit privatization designates the practice of introducing competition into sectors that are dominated by state-owned monopolists. Without changing the organizational and legal structure of a public enterprise enjoying a monopoly position, the private market access is facilitated by a number of things (for example deregulation).

Financial formal privatization refers to the mere private financing of public responsibilities with all other functions remaining in the public sector.

Legal formal privatization describes the transfer of a state-owned enterprise from public to private legal form, for example from an administrative department into a joint stock company, while full-scale public ownership is maintained (Ewers and Rodi, 1995: 13–15; Lane, 1994: 466–7).[10]

Basic rationales to privatization   The administrative departments or state-owned corporations which enjoyed monopoly positions in the major infrastructure sectors of many of the industrialized countries during the 1980s confronted each of their national governments with a similar set of problems. Politicians and trade unionists had 'captured' the management; the public enterprises were seriously overstaffed and instrumentalized for a wide range of non-profit, political objectives. The management was confronted with ambiguous and inconsistent goals set by the public authorities. Parliament, courts and the sponsoring minister had no effective control over the state-owned enterprises whose financial and operational performance as well as coordination with other (public) companies were deficient (Majone, 1994: 60). Most of these public enterprises operated in monopolistic conditions which were strongly protected by the regulation of potential competitors or the nature of the good produced.

Within the spectrum of possible economic and political reform motives Ikenberry (1990: 89–92) points to three basic rationales for privatization. The first is an answer to the fiscal crisis in most countries from the end of the 1970s onwards. In this sense, privatization became a way to finance governmental spending through the liquidation of assets. On the other hand, the operational deficits of public enterprises, infrastructures and administrative bodies can be lowered by enhancing the private involvement in those activities. The second and perhaps even more important rationale is through increasing the efficiency level. As the concept of efficiency, when applied in the social sciences, is sometimes overused while its meaning often remains blurred, it will be dealt with in more detail below. An important notion is that the efficiency rationale shows a close connection with the public budget rationale, since the only way to effect savings by privatization is via efficiency gains. The third rationale is a reworking of the instruments of economic and political management by the state, already referred to as a change of the governance regime. Under this banner come such objectives as the cutback of trade union power in the economic policy sphere and the establishment of a 'shareholder society' (population capitalism) together with a strengthening of national financial markets (see also Lane, 1994: 460; Suleiman and Waterbury, 1990: 3–4).

The term 'efficiency' covers a variety of rather different concepts – even if one limits its scope to a purely economic use. Table 3.2 illustrates the basic differentiations to be made, and the following may be noted:

Table 3.2   *Dimensions of economic efficiency*

Efficiency aspect	Dimensions
Static efficiency	Allocative efficiency (Pareto efficiency) Productive (operational, internal) efficiency
Dynamic efficiency	Rapid adaptation to changing circumstances through process or product innovations
Institutional efficiency	Transaction cost efficiency

Source: Bauer, 1988: 15; Ewers and Rodi, 1995: 16–18

Productive efficiency is enhanced by lowering the production costs (increasing the productivity). Common methods of increasing the productive efficiency are a reduction in the workforce, a rationalization of the production process or an out-sourcing of production steps.

Allocative efficiency is attained if the product or service price equals the marginal costs or – alternatively formulated – when the allocation is such that the utility of each individual is maximized given the utilities of the others (Pareto efficiency). In this form, allocative efficiency is the result of perfect markets described in neo-classical textbooks.

Dynamic efficiency involves an optimal or at least satisfying rate of innovations to keep up with the changing market environment. In contrast to the static concept of allocative and productive efficiency, a market process is introduced in which only those suppliers who show a high adaptation capacity can survive.

Transaction costs, a notion originally developed by Coase (1937) and further elaborated by Williamson (1975; 1985), refers to the overhead costs of transactions and their management. It is an important tool for the comparative assessment of different governance regimes (Williamson, 1991). The underlying assumption is that, in the long run, the governance structures with the lowest transaction costs are superior.

These efficiency considerations point to some important questions in relation to infrastructural privatization. What is its effect on the single dimensions of efficiency? Can certain approaches be differentiated according to their consequences for the different notions of efficiency? What is it that increases productive, allocative, dynamic efficiency in privatized enterprises and infrastructure sectors – if so? How about transaction costs? Is private supply of infrastructure superior to public provision in that sense?

Sectoral case studies on the privatization of infrastructures

The following empirical case studies will describe in detail the development towards privatization and the enhancement of private sector involvement in the major infrastructural sectors in Germany. The discussion is subdivided

into transport and communications sectors, thus covering the major infrastructures in contemporary German society.

Privatizing the transport sector

Transport infrastructures are material systems, often networks, facilitating
the physical transport of goods and passengers. Roads, railway tracks,
airports and air traffic control, inland waterways, harbours and pipelines
are the transport infrastructures to be distinguished. In Germany, the
complete transport sector is subject to exclusive federal legislation. The
administration is either a purely federal affair as in the case of sea and
inland waterway transport (Art. 87 Abs. 1 Grundgesetz) and air transport
(Art. 87d Grundgesetz), or under federal supervision assigned to the states
as in the case of the federal parts of the German road infrastructure. The
highways (Bundesautobahnen) and national roads (Bundesstraßen) belong
to the federal part while the rest of the road infrastructure either falls under
local government competence (local and city streets) or is a concern of the
states.

The German railways, however, provide a rather special case. Since their
structural reform in 1994, the economic responsibility for railway transport
now lies in the hands of the Deutsche Bahn AG (DB AG), a fully state-
owned joint stock company, whereas the Federal Railway Office (Eisenbahn-
Bundesamt) is responsible for technical and legal supervision. The planning
of railway infrastructure, as far as the DB AG is concerned, is still a matter
for the federal Ministry of Transport, whereas the administration of the more
than 100 'non-federal' railway companies in Germany and other local and
regional transport matters are controlled by the German state governments.[11]

The transport sector is thus a typical example of *Politikverflechtung*, a
type of cooperative federalism characteristic of the German political system
(Scharpf, 1988). The term refers to the decision and competence structure
being spread over all levels of government within the federal system and
resulting in high coordination requirements – horizontally as well as
vertically. As a result, most political decisions have to be taken and most
public responsibilities to be accomplished in cooperation with all levels of
German government instead of independent action by separate administrative bodies. This makes nation-wide infrastructural planning difficult and
costly (Denkhaus, 1995: 108–9).

Since 1973, the long-term planning of federal roads, railways, airlines
and inland waterways has been subject to the Bundesverkehrswegeplan
(BVWP). The objective of the BVWP is to coordinate the planning of the
entire federal transport network but it is not a financing instrument as its
actual investment sums are subject to the annual federal budgets. The
planning of the states, local road and public transport infrastructure has to
be coordinated by the respective bodies at state, regional or local level with

the federal infrastructure planning. In July 1992, the first federal transport infrastructure plan (BVWP) for the unified Germany was agreed upon. It constitutes the basis for investments in the federal transport infrastructure up to 2010. The planning decisions of the BVWP rest upon a traffic forecast up to the year 2010 predicting an increase in the transport of goods of 77% compared with 1988, and an increase in passenger transport of 39% (Engelkamp and Bison, 1994: 563).

The length and quality of transport infrastructures in Germany are comparable with those of other industrialized countries. The only specific pattern is the relatively high importance of inland waterway transport owing to a favourable natural inland waterway situation (especially the Rhine and Elbe) and early canal construction activities. A special situation arose from German unification, which united the deficient transport infrastructure of the former GDR with the rest of the network. The investment necessary for the maintenance of this existing infrastructure was estimated as amounting to roughly 130 billion DM alone, whereas the sum needed for its harmonization with West German standards amounted to a further 130 billion DM (Rothengatter, 1991: 19).

At the same time, investment in the transport infrastructure of Germany's western states began to show considerable shortcomings as well. The degree of modernity of an infrastructure describes such a condition, as the higher the degree of modernity (net fixed assets as a percentage of gross fixed assets) the 'younger' the infrastructure of an economy (Ostrowski, 1993: 50). Figure 3.3 illustrates that the degree of modernity of road and rail infrastructures in Germany is steadily falling. In the case of railways, the decline has stagnated since the mid 1980s. With respect to inland waterway infrastructures, the effect is less clear but also observable to some degree. Airport and air traffic control infrastructures are exceptions: their degree of modernity has constantly risen since the mid 1980s.

Together with the tightening of the German public budgets in the 1980s, and even more severely at the beginning of the 1990s, these conditions have laid down the structural framework in which the different sectoral privatization strategies have emerged. These are described in the following case studies.

Roads

Roads as travelled ways for wheeled vehicles, carriage animals and pedestrians have existed throughout recorded history. Between 1900 and 300 BC Etruscan and Greek traders developed the first European road system to transport amber from the north of Europe to the Mediterranean. Scientific road building reached its peak in the Roman empire with a network of more than 50,000 km of paved roads radiating from Rome to the frontiers of the far-flung territories. This sophisticated network fell into disrepair after the decline of the Romans, to be resurrected only by the advent of the automobile. The use of motor vehicles demanded high standards for roads

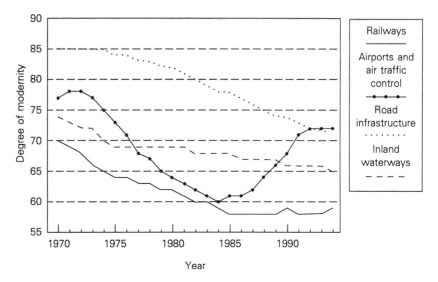

Figure 3.3 *Degree of modernity of transport infrastructure in Germany, 1970–94 (Net fixed assets as percent of the gross fixed assets). The figures of 1990–1994 refer to the territory of the old FRG only. 1971–74 railways and inland waterways: estimation. Source: Bundesministerium für Verkehr, annual statistics*

and led to an enhanced interest in road construction science *(Encyclopedia Britannica*, 1988, vol. 26: 360–3). In Germany those efforts have been state-led from the very beginning, especially since road construction provided job opportunities for the large number of unemployed between the world wars.

After the founding of the Federal Republic in 1949, all road infrastructures in West Germany as well as in the former GDR remained publicly owned and administered. However, in keeping with its federal political structure, its governance was strongly decentralized. After German unification, the property in East German road infrastructure was transferred to the 'new' FRG. Table 3.3. elucidates the complex distribution of administrative and financial responsibilities in the road sector.

As far as the construction of road infrastructure is concerned, competitive tendering is a procedure which is usually applied by the responsible bodies at all levels of government. But at this point, private participation in the transport infrastructure traditionally ends. The operation of transport infrastructure in Germany is subject to public responsibility and the usage of roads (highways) is basically free, with infrastructural investments being financed from the general tax revenue. The mineral oil and motor vehicle taxes are entitled to the federal budget, and may not be set aside for transport infrastructure investments exclusively (non-affectation principle).[12]

The so-called 'Eurovignette' is an exception to the German principle of cost-free road usage. According to the requirements of a European Community Directive (93/89/EEC), in 1995 a fixed highway usage fee for

Table 3.3 *Road infrastructure in Germany: property, financing and administration*

Road categories	Property and financing (construction and maintenance)		Administration	
	National parts	Local parts	National parts	Local parts
Bundesautobahnen (highways)	Federal government	– – –	States (Länder) Instructed by federal government (Art. 90 Grundgesetz)	– – –
Bundesfernstraßen (national roads)		< 80,000 inhabitants Federal government > 80,000 inhabitants Local authority < 30,000 inhabitants States (Länder)	States (Länder)	< 80,000 inhabitants States (Länder) > 80,000 inhabitants Local authority < 30,000 inhabitants States (Länder)
Landesstraßen (state roads)	States (Länder)	> 30,000 inhabitants Local authority < 30,000 inhabitants Regional admin. bodies	States (Länder)	> 30,000 inhabitants Local authority < 30,000 inhabitants Regional admin. bodies
Kreisstraßen (regional roads)	Regional administrative bodies (Kreise)	> 30,000 inhabitants Local authority	Regional administrative bodies (Kreise)	> 30,000 inhabitants Local authority
Gemeindestraßen (local roads)	– – –	Local authorities	– – –	Local authorities

Source: Bundesministerium für Verkehr, 1994: 15

heavy goods vehicles was introduced. This Eurovignette is valid in The Netherlands, Belgium, Denmark, Luxembourg and Germany. As far as road pricing is concerned, the EC has a strong hand in its member states' policy. The imposition of user fees for road infrastructure is legal according to European law only when connected to BOT models or the property transfer of the respective infrastructure from the public to the private sphere (as it is *de jure* in France and Italy) (Basedow, 1991: 75–6).

The German constitution (Grundgesetz) explicitly rules out the possibility of fully and permanently privatizing road, rail and inland waterway infrastructure (Klatt, 1990: 220). This legal requirement refers to the concept of 'material privatization', that is a full transfer of property rights from the public to the private sector. Therefore, the scope of possibilities for road infrastructure privatization in Germany is clearly limited, although amendments to the constitution are a viable possibility, as the case of the railways illustrates. Those amendments, however, require a two-thirds majority in both houses of Parliament (Bundestag and Bundesrat) which represents a high barrier. On the other hand, the law concerning the private construction and financing of national roads, enacted in 1994, has laid down the basis for the introduction of BOT models for selective infrastructures like bridges or tunnels. Such models include the imposition of user fees by private operating companies.

Altogether, increasing interest has been taken by governmental actors in modes and models of enhanced private involvement in the provision of infrastructure since the beginning of the 1990s. The tightening of public budgets, the special investment requirements in consequence of German unification, the investment delays in wide parts of western German transport infrastructure and the rising infrastructure capacity requirements due to increasing transport outputs have been mentioned above. Unique to the German situation was a particular impetus on the privatization of roads, especially highways, which is closely connected with the railways structural reform of 1993. The accumulated debts of both German public railways, the Deutsche Bundesbahn (DB) and the Deutsche Reichsbahn (DR), were transferred to a special federal body, the Bundeseisenbahnvermögen. In order to finance these debts (67 billion DM plus the additional financial burden arising from the preservation of the special status of the railways civil servants), the federal Minister of Transport had to offer new revenue sources to the Ministry of Finance. The original plan consisted of a combination of three elements: (1) an increased private involvement in building, financing and operating highway infrastructure; (2) a partial privatization of highways (Bundesautobahnen); (3) the imposition of road prices (Lehmkuhl and Herr, 1994: 639).

The plans encountered strong resistance from various sides. The automobile industry, major automobile associations and large proportions of the general public rejected especially the idea of road prices. The Greens (Green Party) and several environmental associations were against these road infrastructure privatization plans since they feared that individual motorized transport would be made even more attractive. The Social Democratic Party (SPD) opposed this policy mainly for social reasons (higher mobility costs would mainly affect the poorest). Since the governing liberal-conservative coalition was internally divided on this issue too, the required majority could not be attained. The railway reform finally was financed by an increase in mineral oil taxes, but the ideas of road and highway privatization still persisted. The benefits expected from a growing private involvement in the provision of transport infrastructures are centred around various concepts of efficiency: more demand orientation in infrastructure development, widened financial leeway for the public sector, cost savings, independence from economic trends, prevention of further public indebtedness and positive transport policy effects were connected with the privatization models proposed (Klatt, 1990: 217; Bergström, 1991: 187).

Initiatives, models and prospects In reaction to the lively discussion on privatization issues with regard to transport infrastructure, the federal Ministry of Transport in 1993 commissioned a consultancy, Roland Berger, to analyse the various privatization models proposed for the highways (Bundesautobahnen) as compared with the present organization. At about the same time, the Ministry also conducted a field test of various systems of electronic road pricing on highway 555 between Cologne and Bonn (Denkhaus, 1995: 81–5). Already in 1992–3 the federal Cabinet had taken the decision to implement the leasing model of private infrastructure finance for some federal road construction projects with a total investment sum of 4 billion DM. The realization of the BOT model is planned for three roads and three bridge projects which amount to a total investment of 11.25 billion DM.[13]

The Roland Berger consultancy assessed five concrete models of highway privatization:

Model A provided for the founding of a federally owned body for the financing of highway infrastructure. A public enterprise here would only gain from its financial autonomy through the general federal budget.

Model B consisted of a new federal highway company in a private legal form, but fully state-owned. All administrative functions would then be transferred to this federal highway company which would be comparable to the rail company at the final stage of German railway reform.

Model C intended the application of the BOT model to separate routes within the federal highway network. This meant the building and operation of distinct routes within the federal road network by private companies rediscounting road prices.

Model D consisted of the regional implementation of the BOT model, that is the founding of regional private highway network companies.

Model E provided for a private joint stock company as the owner of the whole federal highway network. The public responsibility for the highways would be largely given up (Gratza et al., 1996: 14).

Alongside the negative results of the practical tests of electronic road pricing systems,[14] the federal Ministry of Transport published the Roland Berger policy proposals. None of the models analysed was recommended for implementation without further qualifications. The policy proposals resulting from the study are:

1   alteration of the financing scheme for the federal highways from taxes to network-wide and appropriated usage fees (road prices)
2   introduction of distance-dependent, electronically measured highway charges at the moment only for heavy commercial motor vehicles
3   a gradual opening up of markets for planning, construction, operation and financing of highways for private firms through the implementation of the BOT model (Gratza et al., 1996: 18).

This scenario indicates one probable way in which the process of increasing the involvement of private actors in the financing of road infrastructures may be continued in Germany. Radical changes towards privatization of road infrastructure are highly unlikely owing to the resistance of important social groups against the plans.

Railways

The history of German railways began with the first line between Nürnberg and Fürth in 1835. Until the 1870s, private and public railway companies competed in the operation of rail transport in the German independent states. When Bismarck attempted to found a unified German railway company, the German states began to take over the private railway companies operating in their territory in order to oppose his plans.[15] At the beginning of the twentieth century, nearly all German railway companies, still decentrally organized, were state-owned. In the Republic of Weimar, the organization of German railways fundamentally changed. In 1920, a single Deutsche Reichsbahn was founded by uniting various regional railway companies. The Hitler regime then brought a further centralization of the railways (Fremdling, 1993: 422–33).

After the Second World War the centralized organization, despite the influence of the decentralization policy of the occupying powers, was taken over on behalf of the railways in both parts of Germany. Both railways were state-owned and formed a part of the general administration. The Deutsche Reichsbahn in East Germany was even more closely affiliated to the administration than was the case with the Deutsche Bundesbahn in the West. The Deutsche Reichsbahn also enjoyed the advantage of a more protective environment than its West German counterpart. Strict regulation – for all transport of goods over distances greater than 50 km, rail transport was compulsory – and slow automobilization helped to secure the market position of the Deutsche Reichsbahn; the Deutsche Bundesbahn's position, in contrast, deteriorated more and more. In freight transport the market shares of the Bundesbahn diminished from 60% in 1950 to 29% in 1990, and

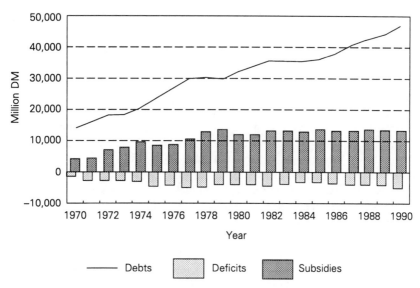

Figure 3.4 *Deficits, subsidies and indebtedness – Deutsche Bundesbahn 1970–90. Source: Deutsche Bahn 1994: 8*

in passenger transport from 36% in 1950 to only 6% in 1990 (Deutsche Bahn, 1994: 8). The consequences of this decline for the economic viability of the Deutsche Bundesbahn are highlighted in Figure 3.4.

The debts were constantly rising, the deficits were out of control, and federal subsidies were stagnating at a very high level. Since the 1970s, several attempts had been made to reform the public railways and road freight transport had been subjected to very strict price and quantity regulations. The Deutsche Bundesbahn staff had been reduced from about 510,000 in 1957 to around 320,000 in 1982. But its economic position continued to decline, and a further increase in debts was forecast. Further pressure originated from the EU level when the liberalization of road haulage – initiated by the EC Commission – intensified the competition in freight transport. This further endangered the market position of the state-owned railway company (Deutsche Bahn, 1994: 9; Link, 1994: 19–20).

The federal Cabinet in 1989 established an independent governmental commission for the future development of the Deutsche Bundesbahn. The initiative came from the federal Ministry of Transport and it was composed of representatives of sciences (2), business (3), politics (4) and labour (3). Only a few months after the commission had taken up its work, an unexpected event dramatically enlarged its area of responsibility. Within the context of German unification, the Deutsche Reichsbahn was united with the Deutsche Bundesbahn in 1991, thus multiplying the problems to be tackled by the commission's reform proposals. The Deutsche Reichsbahn was in a deplorable state, seriously overstaffed and rapidly losing market shares owing to the fall in the above mentioned regulation scheme of the former GDR as well as East German citizens catching up in motorization (Deutsche Bahn, 1994: 11–16).

A new wind from Brussels also influenced the governmental commission's work. After years of idleness and focus on road transport the EC Commission became more and more aware of the bad economic situation of its member states' railways. One of the reasons for this constant decline was the lack of international cooperation and technical harmonization of the European public railways in an age where international transport was the primary source of traffic growth. Therefore, the EC Commission took the initiative in rail policy and developed proposals for a restructuring of the national public railway companies which went hand in hand with the EC's liberalization policies and the completion of the internal market.

The Commission's proposals were discussed in the Council and with the national railway companies. In June 1991 the EC Regulation 1191/69 was amended (Regulation (EC) 1893/91) and in July 1991 the EC Directive 91/440 was adopted.[16] The Directive aimed at structural reforms of European public railway companies: it stipulates that the independence of the railway management has to be guaranteed and that a minimum separation in the accounting systems of 'infrastructure' and 'operation' should be implemented. In addition, third-party access to national railway infrastructure should be facilitated and a financial renovation of the railway companies should take place. Regulation (EC) 1893/91 contains some further rules with respect to the economic autonomy of transport companies, the application of commercial law to management, the limitation of cross-subsidies and the arrangement of contractual relations for the tendering of public services. This EC legislation set out a new framework for a structural reform of the German railway sector to which the legislators had to comply (Schmuck, 1992: 42–50; Kortschak, 1993: 103).

In December 1991, the governmental reform commission published its results. After intensive parliamentary discussion in 1992 and 1993, the legislation passed the Bundestag and the Bundesrat in December 1993 and the railway reform came into force on 1 January 1994 (Lehmkuhl, 1996: 73–8).

The railway reform programme   The main objectives of the railway reform were (1) relieving the public (federal) budget by profoundly improving the railway's economic and financial situation; and (2) enhancing the market share of rail compared with road transport by an increase in the efficiency, flexibility and customer orientation of the railway company.

The railway reform included the following measures:

Founding of a joint stock company, the DB AG In a first step, the former DB and DR were integrated into a separate budget 'federal railways' (Sonder-vermögen Bundeseisenbahnen). From this body, the railway infrastructure and transport operation departments were transferred to the newly founded Deutsche Bahn AG (DB AG) while the public regulation responsibilities were handed over to a new federal regulatory agency for the railways (Eisenbahnbundesamt), and the debts of both railways were assigned to the assets of this new economic entity (Bundeseisenbahnvermögen, BEV). The internal organization of the DB AG was effected in three separate areas: passenger transport, freight transport and infrastructure. Thereby an organizational separation of infrastructure and operation of rail transport was implemented. The share of the Deutsche Bahn AG are 100% owned by the state (Link, 1994: 20).

Regionalization A further change was the transfer of the responsibility for local passenger transport from the federal government to the state governments. Since the beginning of 1996, the German states have been responsible for the rail transport infrastructure of local passenger services as well as for the tendering of – mostly deficitary – passenger transport services at the local level. The concrete legal arrangement has to be made by the states themselves. In 1993, a special regionalization fund was decided upon by the federal and state governments from which the tendering of local transport services is financed. The regionalization transfer payments are financed through an increase in mineral oil taxes (Lehmkuhl, 1996: 81–2).

Regulation The federal regulatory agency for railways, the Federal Railway Office, (Eisenbahn-Bundesamt), is responsible for the assessment of infrastructural construction plans, the technical and structural supervision of rail transport, the issue and withdrawal of licences for operation and all other federal administrative tasks in relation to the DB AG. The Eisenbahn-Bundesamt is subordinated to the federal Ministry of Transport (Studenroth, 1996: 98) and the rail infrastructure planning is effected, as before, through the BVWP by the Federal Ministry of Transport.

Competition in rail transport According to a constitutional amendment, the infrastructural part of the German railway system has to remain in public control, that is at least 51% of the shares of the infrastructure company has to remain in the hands of the federal government. The federal government pays subsidies for infrastructural investments to the DB AG infrastructure department which manages the railway networks and levies user charges from the transport operators. In principle, all railway companies – whether national or from abroad – have the right of access to the federal railway infrastructure. The track area of DB AG is obliged to issue a price list and to guarantee non-discrimination of rail transport operators (Beuermann and Schneider, 1996).

Prospects for material privatization Within the scope of German railway reform, the provisions of EC Directive 91/440 and EC Regulation 1893/91 have been implemented to their full extent. But the final stage of the reform programme goes a step further: it provides for a conversion of the three DB AG areas into independent joint stock companies to be controlled by the

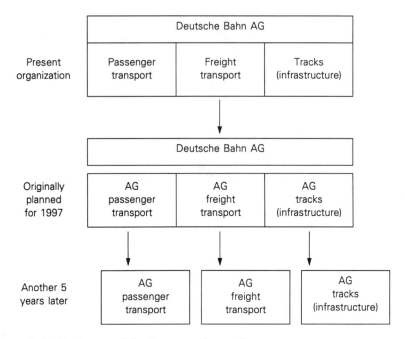

Figure 3.5   *Final steps of the German railway reform*

holding company Deutsche Bahn. This step was originally planned for 1997, but whether or not this date can be realized in time is still uncertain. As a second step, the holding company should be dissolved within five years, after which the three joint stock companies will act independently (Link, 1994: 22) (Figure 3.5).

Within this development process, 'material privatization' of the three separate joint stock companies is not compulsory but, in the case of the two transport operators, it is very likely. However, the infrastructure company will remain under public control. But through the divestiture of the Deutsche Bahn AG into three autonomous business areas, an institutional separation of infrastructure and operation of transport services will be implemented. Therefore, the German railway reform widely exceeds the requirements that are set by European regulations.

Air transport

Commercial air transport is an invention of the twentieth century. The First World War brought about further engineering progress and a considerable production expansion through the sudden demand for military aircraft. When the war ended, the pilots formed a recruiting pool for the further development of commercial air transport services – primarily air mail and passenger services. The first commercial flights occurred in Germany in 1909 with the founding of the Deutsche Luftschiffahrts Aktiengesellschaft for passenger and mail services. In February 1919 the Deutsche Luftreederei was founded, which established the first regular flight service in Germany and can be seen as a predecessor of Lufthansa. In those early days several air traffic corporations existed till the German Reichsministry decided to form a unified carrier in 1926, which was given the name Deutsche Luft Hansa AG. Of this 'old' Lufthansa, 26% was owned by the Reich, the federal government, 19% was owned by several different states, and the rest was in the hands of private owners. The flight services were maintained till 1945. From 1951 to 1965 the post-war Lufthansa organization was dissolved and in 1953–4 its West German successor organization was founded (Bittner, 1992: 139–41).

German air transport is subject to federal legislation and administration. The federal administrative body which is responsible for this area is a regulatory agency (Luftfahrtbundesamt) which is subordinated to the federal Ministry of Transport. The control of safety standards with regard to aircraft and airport infrastructure is one of the main responsibilities of the Luftfahrtbundesamt. Air traffic control is also subject to federal administration. The airports, while largely publicly owned, are organized as private firms (GmbH or AG) with the federal government owning shares in only a few of the more important international airports. The rest of the public airports belong to the state governments or local governments of larger cities.

Air traffic is the fastest growing transport sector in Germany, with passenger transport having more than doubled from 8.4 billion passenger km to 18.4 billion between 1975 and 1990. Amongst the transport sectors, air transport shows the clearest influence of EU policy-making on privatization strategies at the national level. The European air transport liberalization movement started in 1979 with the so-called First Memorandum of the EC Commission. This initiative was strongly motivated by the air transport deregulation in the US. The draft bills which had been proposed by the Commission during the early 1980s were watered down during decision-making at the Council level, to an extent that the original liberalization objective was no longer discernible.

In 1984, the Commission published its Second Memorandum on civil aviation. In spite of some positive experiences with US-style deregulation, the liberal tendencies have been weakened in the Second Memorandum compared with previous proposals. This can be explained by the strong influence of national, protectionist interests at that time. At about the same time the European Parliament sued the Council at the European court of Justice for passivity in the area of transport policy. In its opinion in 1985, the European Court of Justice obliged the Council to establish a common market in the transport sector within 12 years. Although it is unclear if the Court's decision directly applies to air transport, it caused a certain liberalization momentum, with direct effects on national civil aviation policies.

This momentum was enforced by another decision of the European Court of Justice, commonly called the *nouvelles frontières* decision. In its opinion the Court argued against several European airlines and a French travel agency that the price-setting system of the International Air Transport Association (IATA) would not comply with the competition provisions of EC law. In consequence, the Court charged the Council to liberalize the European air transport sector. In July 1987, the Commission formally accused 10 national airlines of EC member countries of violation of EC regulations in the competition area and this procedure was extended to the remaining three national airlines in the EC. In the end, all of the member states' airlines finally agreed to change their conduct according to the proposals of the EC Commission.

In 1988, the first European liberalization package came into force. It contained a series of regulations concerning competition rules, price-setting procedures, capacity questions, market access, multiple designation and the liberalization of international air transport. The second liberalization package was decided upon during the summer of 1990. It came into force in 1991 and provided for further liberalization steps, especially with respect to scheduled air traffic.

Immediately after the implementation of this second wave of European liberalization policy measures, a third and last package was launched. When the last of these provisions came into force in 1993, the 'open sky' policy of the EC Commission, providing for a fully liberalized air transport system within a common market, was completed and largely replaced the bilateral agreements between member states (Wassenbergh, 1992; Wheatcroft and Lipman, 1990; Niejahr and Abbamonte, 1996).

One of the main results of this European policy was that the national flag carriers lost a good part of their political importance.[17] The same trend has been amplified by the recent US 'open skies' policy towards Europe, supporting the gradual liberalization of transatlantic air traffic by bilateral 'open sky' agreements.[18] A major result has been increased competition, which the national airlines try to answer through the formation of strategic alliances (Wheatcroft and Lipman, 1990).

Privatization initiatives The German air transport sector has already experienced two major privatizations. In 1994 Deutsche Lufthansa AG, the German flag carrier, was materially privatized by a decrease of the federal share from 51.4% to 38%. Full privatization was originally intended for 1996 but had to be delayed because of constraints set by financial market developments as well as by EC regulations. Heavy fluctuations on the stock markets rendered the sale difficult. With respect to European law, the member states' airlines have to prove that the majority of their shares are owned by national or EU citizens. The monitoring of compliance with this regulation raises considerable problems and full privatization has recently been postponed until the end of 1997.

The 'new' Deutsche Lufthansa was founded in 1953, originally under the name of Aktiengesellschaft für Luftverkehrsbedarf (Luftag), while its predecessor organization was still in the process of liquidation. It was a joint stock company from the beginning, but major financial involvement by the federal government was needed for it to leave the deficit zone and to bargain for air traffic rights. After leaving the deficit zone in 1963 for the first time, the airline attained high profits for about 25 years before it ran into economic difficulties at the end of the 1980s. Since that time, the federal government has pursued profound economic and financial reforms, especially to reduce the high deficits (Bittner, 1992). The privatization plans formed an integral part of this restructuring and in 1994, the year of its 'material privatization', the Deutsche Lufthansa AG re-entered the profit zone with a surplus of 306 million DM prior to taxes (1993: deficit of 53 million DM).

The main reason for the Lufthansa privatization is the continued liberalization of the air transport market which has resulted in growing demands with regard to flexibility and competition orientation of the airlines combined with the desire – ubiquitous as far as privatizations are concerned – to attract extra revenues to (or to save costs in) the public budget. The first of these objectives was also prominent in the formal privatization of the German body for air traffic control, the former federal agency for air traffic control (Bundesanstalt für Flugsicherung). The capacity and safety of the air transport system depend to a large extent upon an efficient air traffic control system which provides for flexible adjustment to the continually growing aviation sector.

To this end, the German air traffic control system has been transformed into a private limited company (Deutsche Flugsicherung GmbH) in order to be released from legal constraints set by civil service regulations and the restrictive rules of the federal budget. The privatization became law in 1993 (Wissmann, 1994: 19). However, the federal government remains the full owner of the Deutsche Flugsicherung GmbH. Only recently, it confirmed the view that public interest in air traffic control is crucial and thus the public share in the air traffic control company will remain at 100%. Furthermore, Article 87d of the Grundgesetz provides for a federal administration. This was one of the main reasons why the President of the Federal Republic refused to sign a law which aimed at privatization of air traffic control in the form of a private limited company in which the federal government would only control the majority of the capital (Basedow, 1991: 77).

The main objective of the formal legal privatization of air traffic control in Germany was to escape from the tight constraints of German civil service regulations. Through these changes, flexible appointment rules could be applied, and the internal organization structure could be better oriented toward new technical requirements, thus enhancing the productivity and reliability of the control agency. Despite some complaints by the mergers control commission, a similar scheme has been proposed for the regulatory body in telecommunications (Soltwedel and Wolf, 1996: 10; *Frankfurter Allgemeine Zeitung*, 13 December 1995: 18).

German international airports   From 1951 onwards, the German airports were permitted to independently run their facilities although they were still under the control of the Allied forces. The basic structure of the decentralized airport system, which at present is typical for Germany, already existed at that time. The same is true for the importance of the Rhein-Main airport at Frankfurt as the main junction in international air transport owing to its troop supply function for the American army in Germany. The federal government acquired shares in several international airports, and during the 1960s, when air transport was rapidly expanding, federal financial aid was concentrated on the three airports with the largest international importance (Berlin, Cologne/Bonn, Frankfurt), whereas the federal shares in the other airports were sold. Later, federal shares in the new international airports of Hamburg and Munich were also acquired. The federal government refrained from formal influence on the airports' policy except through the introduction of a German coordination agency for flight plans in 1971 which improved air traffic flow considerably (Wolf, 1996: 79).

In a memorandum in 1994, the federal Minister of Transport announced a retreat from all federal shares in airports. The federal government also now supports the sale of the airport shares of the other public authorities (Wolf, 1996: 80–2; Wissmann, 1994). The main objectives of this retreat are again – in view of the high investment requirements due to fast growing air traffic – attempts to relieve the public budget (Wissmann, 1994: 25). Moreover the EC Commission is planning to liberalize the ground control services at airports too, which could increase the competition for the airport companies and therefore call for increases in efficiency of airport operation.[19]

In sum, privatization is widespread in the air transport sector. As the part of the transport infrastructure with the strongest international orientation, it displays the strongest influence of Europeanization and internationalization on national policy-making. In this context the relationship between liberalization (through deregulation) and privatization seems to be an especially interesting issue.

Privatizing the communications sector

Communications infrastructures differ from transport infrastructures in one basic respect: even when the movement of physical objects is involved in communication systems (such as letters in postal communication), their primary function is the transportation of *information content* over geographical distances, and the transport of objects only fulfils an intermediary function, namely, to carry the informational content.

Despite this clear functional difference, however, the boundaries between the two systems are not that indisputable. On the one hand, infrastructures like the postal system have always been second-order infrastructures based on first-order means of transport such as horses, ships, trains and aircraft.[20] On the other hand, the functioning of transport infrastructures in most cases – except the road system – presupposes the existence of communications systems. There are areas in which the two infrastructural systems overlap to a considerable extent.

In the case of transport infrastructure, the control of communications systems historically has been one of the core functions of the state. Since their very beginning, post and telegraphy have been subject to tight political control. In some cases, this was realized through governmental monopoly concessions such as (Thurn and Taxis) to a private operator, but in most cases through the direct operation of the system by a governmental department. The greatest influence in German postal communications has been in the previously mentioned form of the Prussian post which was established during the seventeenth century.

Optical telegraphy, the first modern telecommunications system, in contrast was exclusively restricted to political and military purposes, and the same was true for electrical telegraphy in its early stages of development. In the 1850s, when telegraphy was opened to the general public, the administration was separated from the military and was transformed into a specialized administrative unit, known as the Royal Telegraph Office of Prussia. After the foundation of the German Reich, branches of the post and telegraphy were integrated into the famous German Reichspost, which also later incorporated telephony (Thomas, 1994).

The public status of post and telecommunications in Germany was even established as part of the country's constitution, while the monopoly rights had been set up as part of specific pieces of legislation such as the Telegraph Act of 1892 and the Telecommunications Installations Act of 1928. The PTT had the exclusive right to install, operate and maintain the telegraphic and telephone systems which included transmission and exchange technology as well as the telephone terminals which were treated as a part of the technical network. Similar monopoly rights existed for postal communications and broadcasting. This traditional institutional regime remained stable during the Weimar Republic, the Nazi period, and also during the first three decades of the Federal Republic. When in 1952 a new postal administrative law was formulated, the exclusive public monopoly and the public character of administration were only adapted to the post-war period (Werle, 1990; Schneider and Werle, 1991: 104).

Despite some inherent development problems in state controlled communications, the old regime remained stable up to the 1980s. However, the first clouds over the old model had gathered during the 1960s, when the Bundespost ran into a large deficit. The financial crisis triggered two reform initiatives in the later part of that decade and the early 1970s which aimed at producing an organizational modernization and autonomization of the PTT administration. However, none of them survived their respective legislative processes (Grande, 1994; Werle, 1990). It needed another two decades to undermine the tradition and to open the road to liberalization and privatization. The main motives were no longer a more efficient public administration, but the opening of markets and the achievement of foreign trade and industrial policy objectives. In the broadcasting domain, the first changes occurred with the setting up of private TV channels in the early 1980s, and in telecommunications during the late 1980s with the opening up of terminal markets and the subsequent liberalization of telematic services. Since that time, privatization initiatives have broadened like a river in torrent. The different privatization initiatives in the three sectors will be outlined in more detail in the following sections.

Telecommunications

The old institutional model of German telecommunications, which lasted from the 1870s to the 1880s, can be characterized by the following facets. Most importantly, the telecommunications systems were completely controlled by a public administration which, since the 1920s, operated on a separate budget. Secondly, from an organizational aspect, the PTT administration was relatively autonomous from the general state administration, since it worked on a separate budget. And finally, the postal and telecommunications branches were integrated under one organizational roof, because they were considered to be 'holistic' entities: distinctions between infrastructures and services had not yet been applied.

From the late 1980s to the mid 1990s, however, this model was to be transformed in all these aspects. Markets were opened up, the post, telecommunications and banking branches were separated, and the former public administration was transformed into a private enterprise which has been partially sold on the stock exchange.

The starting point for the whole process was a *technological revolution in microelectronics in the late 1960s and 1970s* – often summarized under the key words of digitalization, satellites and mobile communication – which affected economic development in all major industrialized countries. As a consequence, computer firms and other electronic producers tried to enter these promising new business areas and exerted increasing pressure upon national governments to open up the formerly protected markets. Such liberalization efforts were targeted first towards telematic equipment, and later towards all kinds of telecommunications networks and services.

In Germany, computer manufacturers and other newcomers had started to ask for free entry into the telecommunications terminal market already at the end of the 1970s. In 1980, when the German merger control commission reviewed the market structures in this sector, it demanded far-reaching liberalization measures. However, such proposals were successfully rejected by the PTT, thus stopping the first assault on its protected areas (Schneider and Werle, 1991: 119).

The situation changed when a new federal government – a coalition of the Christian Democrats (CDU/CSU) and the Liberals – came to power in 1982 with the explicit goal of cutting back the scope of governmental intervention in society. In 1985, the government established an independent commission to review the situation in telecommunications and to elaborate reform proposals. It was composed of major social groupings, that is trade and industry, science and politics (Grande, 1994).

Parallel with the national process of policy-making, developments at the European Community level also supported such a national liberalization process. In 1987, the Commission of the European Communities issued a 'Green Paper on the Development of the Common Market for Telecommunications Services and Equipment' demanding a 'restructuring of national markets' to permit competition in the market for terminal equipment and for value-added services (Schneider et al., 1994). Only a few months later, the German government commission published its report on the possibilities of 'improving the fulfilment of tasks in telecommunications', proposing a restructuration of German telecommunications which was strikingly similar to the EC proposals (Schneider and Werle, 1991: 120–1).

The reform Act, drafted by the government a short time later, was largely based on the commission's report. The reform was declared a necessary adaptation to international and technological developments contributing to more efficiency and market orientation within the telecommunications infrastructure and to a strengthening of the German telecommunications industry in the world market. In 1989, the Postal Structure Law (Poststrukturgesetz) was enacted by the Bundestag (Werle, 1990).

The reform affected the political and economic organization of telecommunications in Germany at the following levels:

1   The new law split the Deutsche Bundespost (DBP) into three public corporations under the roof of a directorate with mainly coordinating competence. It separated the regulatory tasks from entrepreneurial functions by giving the Bundespost organizational autonomy *vis-à-vis* the Ministry of Posts and Telecommunications (BMPT). The BMPT's functions were now restricted to creating and guaranteeing the conditions of competition in telecommunications, although it was still the owner of the three DBP enterprises.
2   The separation of the telecommunications branch from the other branches ensured that each of them did business on the basis of their own revenues. Cross-subsidies between the branches are still possible, but now they are of known magnitude and direction, and thus subjected to a greater degree of public scrutiny.
3   While the new DBP Telekom still had monopoly powers with respect to transmission networks and the telephone service, the markets for mobile telephony and satellite transmission were partially opened. An almost complete liberalization of the markets was provided for enhanced services and customer premises equipment.

A problem which is still unresolved by the new law is that of the potential conflict between the regulatory and ownership function of the BMPT. As a regulator, the BMPT had to constrain and limit the actions of DB Telekom; in the role of the owner it certainly had an interest in increasing the value of the three DBP enterprises. This raised the issue of partiality in the regulations of the telecommunications sector, which several years later called for a new institutional solution. The fall of the Berlin Wall and the reunification of West and East Germany were also critical events in German telecommunications policy. Because of the massive capital requirements for the build-up of infrastructures in the new federal states, some observers expected that the push towards liberalization would lose momentum. This was most evident, however, when the government decided to collect from DBP Telekom an additional 2 billion DM annually over the next four years to finance the increasing deficit caused by German reunification (and originally also to finance Germany's contribution to the Gulf War).

However, the paradox of this complex conjuncture of events was that the reunification had rather the opposite effect. It broadened the scope of liberalization and helped to put the privatization issue onto the political agenda. First, after the reunification, DBP Telekom had great difficulties in responding to the accumulated telephone demand in the East (telephone density in the East was half that in the West). At the same time, business users were pushing for a speedy network build-up as a precondition for industrial investment. This forced the BMPT to liberalize satellite transmission for telephony in some restricted areas of the new federal states.

Secondly, when the Finance Minister started to collect an additional 2 billion DM from Telekom's revenues, even those factors of the opposition party SPD which tried to protect the institutional status quo in the 1989 reform became convinced of the necessity for Telekom to have more autonomy from political control – at least to hinder the Finance Minister in the use of Telekom as a cash cow. There were now a growing number of actors who considered DBP Telekom's privatization to be a policy option: that, in the late 1980s, was out of the question. The governing coalition needs the consent of the SPD since a change in the public status of the DBP requires a constitutional amendment which needs a two-thirds majority in the Bundestag.

Since 1991, the privatization issue has been on the political agenda, and was seen as the logical second step in the reform of German telecommunications (Jaeger, 1994; Schmidt, 1996). A strong proponent for this 'next step' was DBP Telekom itself.[21] The financial and human resources problems of DBP Telekom were exerting strong pressures for a quick move towards privatization. In 1991, it was expected that Telekom's equity capital would amount to less than 24% of its total capital in the coming years. This was far below the target minimum of 33% (of total capital and reserves) laid down in the Postverfassungsgesetz. An important supporter of the new reform step was the Finance Minister who tried to sell off further state-owned companies to finance Telekom's growing deficit. By transforming Telekom into a stock exchange corporation and by floating 49% of it he expected to raise about $20 billion. The BMPT was also strongly in favour of privatization.

The main privatization arguments were as follows. First, Telekom would gain more freedom to fulfil its capital needs. Secondly, more insulation from political pressure would ensure that Telekom's business policy was determined not by political timetables but by market requirements. Thirdly, with respect to the BMPT, privatization would separate the regulatory function much more clearly from the ownership function. Fourthly, changes in the civil service status would give Telekom more flexibility with respect to its human resources. For example, the civil service 'career principle' with its rigid qualification requirements and restrictive rules on pay restrict Telekom to offering its employees performance-related incentives. During these years Telekom had great difficulties in attracting highly qualified employees. Last but not least, through privatization Telekom would gain full freedom for international operations. In the current situation the definition of the Bundespost's institutional structure in Germany's constitution does not allow such ventures.

In order to find the necessary majority for a constitutional amendment, there were intensive talks between the coalition and the SPD during the whole of 1994. During the inter-party bargaining process, three models for a future Telekom ownership were discussed. One model provided that Germany's 16 federal states would hold a majority stake in the operator, and the remaining shares would be sold to private investors. An approach supported by the Social Democrats proposed to transform Telekom into a type of public service organization which raises capital by issuing non-voting, profit-sharing certificates. However, having abolished civil service status, such a company still would remain in public ownership. A further possibility was that DBP Telekom would spin off its competitive operations (digital cellular and data communications) into privately held companies. The latter was used as a 'last resort weapon' if the privatization project was blocked by the Social Democrats.

As part of the bargaining process between the coalition and the opposition parties, the first two options had been discussed, and by summer 1993 the stock exchange option was finally accepted by the SPD. In February the privatization bill was introduced into the Bundestag which passed it in July, and it came into force at the end of the year. By 1 January 1995 the three former branches of the Bundespost – Telekom, Postdienst and Postbank – were transformed into three private corporations which would later be sold on the stock exchange. A first portion of Deutsche Telekom shares was sold in November 1996.

Finally, a very recent reform initiative which led to a Telecommunications Act in the course of 1996 aims to eliminate the remaining monopoly barriers in the traditional telephone sector and to establish an independent regulatory agency, thus conforming with the major EU telecommunications policy goal to achieve complete liberalization in telecoms in 1998 (Schneider, forthcoming).

Broadcasting

A national broadcasting infrastructure has to be seen as a subsystem of a society's communications system. It differs from the two other subsystems (telecommunications and post) in the respect that its primary function is the facilitation not of *individual* communications but *mass* communications. However, in a 'genetic' sense, the first broadcasting technologies emerged from individual telecommunications (that is, radio telegraphy). The first radio broadcasting emissions appeared in the early 1920s, and at that time it was not yet clear by which organizational structure broadcasting would be governed. In its earliest phase it was a part of the telegraph monopoly,[22] and broadcasting was treated as a special service department of the German PTT. As soon as the media characteristics of broadcasting and its influence on public opinion became apparent, new institutional solutions had to be found. A solution whereby the responsibility for programming and programme scheduling[23] was shifted to separate private service organizations, which later re-entered the public sector, was based on a mixed private/ public legal form (Eckner, 1964).

At the political level, there have always been conflicts between central government and the different federal states with respect to responsibility for the programme domain. In 1926 a compromise between the empire and the Länder was arranged according to which the PTT only attained responsibility for the technical infrastructure, whereas programming was done by independent local or regional broadcasting societies (mostly controlled by the Länder), which were united by a private law broadcasting society (Reichsrundfunkgesellschaft mbH). Later the influence of the central state on programming increased again, when the Deutsche Reichspost took over 51% of the Reichsrundfunkgesellschaft. This arrangement did not last very long as in 1933, when Hitler and his Nazi Party came to power, the local broadcasting societies were dissolved and programming was entirely centralized. The shares of the Reichsrundfunkgesellschaft formerly held by the Länder were taken over by the German empire, and later, through the infamous decree on '*Volksaufklärung* and Propaganda' in June 1933, the German broadcasting system was turned into the most important ideological instrument of the Nazi government.

The *current* federal model of public broadcasting has developed since the early post-war years, 'largely imposed from outside' (Humphreys, 1994). The experience of the Nazi period led the Allied occupation forces to set the framework for a decentralized system in which the regulatory, operational and programming powers were given to the Länder – but organizationally insulated from direct governmental interference. Within this framework, during the late 1940s a number of independent broadcasting houses were created within the legal form of an 'institution of public law' (Anstalt des öffentlichen Rechts). Each of them exerted monopoly rights in the diffusion of radio – and later TV – programmes in its particular geographical area. These broadcasting organizations in turn were controlled by special broadcasting councils composed of socially significant groups (including trade unions and employers, religious, educational and cultural groups, etc.) rather than exclusively of the Länder governments and political parties. For matters of coordination and the collection of licensing fees a working group was founded, which later became the famous ARD (Humphreys, 1994).

In the early 1960s, the central government planned to introduce a second TV channel based on a new broadcasting society named Deutschland Fernsehen GmbH. This objective, however, was challenged by the federal states in the Constitutional Court which declared the plan to be unconstitutional, and decided that broadcasting should be organized as a public monopoly as long as there was a shortage of broadcasting frequencies. In addition the Court also confirmed the Länder competencies in matters of broadcasting law (Holtz-Bacha, 1991: 221). As a consequence, the 11 states founded a second TV channel with a similar legal form as the ARD (the ZDF, the 'Second German Television').

Interestingly, it is in this judgement of the federal Constitutional Court that the first indications for private opportunities in broadcasting were made. The Court declared that its decision would not mean that private companies *per se* could not be involved in broadcasting, but rather the government (in any form) could not. This ruling therefore is generally considered to be a cornerstone in German broadcasting policy, in principle opening the door to private broadcasting (Williams, 1985: 99).

The traditional institutional arrangements remained stable until the early 1980s. As in telecommunications real changes in the traditional order of broadcasting have only happened since then. In the same way as in individual communications, these changes were largely triggered by technological innovations, that is cable and satellite TV, undermining the scarcity rationale for the public broadcasting system. The setting up of broadband cable infrastructures in Germany began at the end of the 1970s. After a short politically motivated break by the Social Liberal government, this expansion strategy was taken up again and even broadened when the Kohl government[24] came into power, seeing this as an opportunity not only to support political allies[25] but also to react toward business requests seeking investment opportunities in this emerging sector. In June 1981, the federal Constitutional Court provided a legal basis for cable pilot projects in four German states. Although the Court recognized that technological advances had weakened the scarcity rationale, it resisted giving up the public broadcasting system entirely. In the following years a number of Bundesländer with CDU governments legislated new broadcasting laws enabling commercial broadcasting that is mainly financed by advertising. In 1987 a treaty among the 11 Länder was ratified, setting the ground rules for a 'dual broadcasting system' where private and public broadcasters coexisted and where public broadcasting was given the responsibility of providing 'basic services' mainly financed by a quasi-compulsory broadcasting fee.

During the early 1980s also the age of satellite broadcasting began in Europe. In June 1983 the telecommunications satellite ECS 1 was launched, providing two German TV channels. Two years later INTELSAT V was launched with six additional TV channels for Germany. Parallel to – and partly triggered by – the emergence of these new technological opportunities, the EU started some initiatives to abolish traditional institutional barriers for the use of these new communications technologies. Although

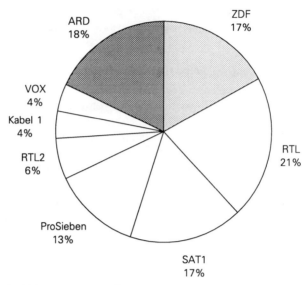

Figure 3.6 *Television viewing figures in Germany (October 1996) Source: GfK Fernsehforschung/mediaResearch*

the birth of the EC's broadcasting policy can be traced back to 1982 (see European Parliament document 1-1013/81, asking for a unified European television channel), the most visible sign of EC engagement was the 'Green Paper on Television without Frontiers' in 1984 on the establishment of the common market for broadcasting, where the emphasis was especially put on satellite and cable technology. Since then, several Directives have followed which called for the market access of private broadcasting companies, and the abolition of monopoly barriers (Collins, 1994).

To summarize, the greatest changes in German broadcasting have happened over the past 10 years. Until the early 1980s, all television services were provided by the public broadcasting houses, and there was no private commercial TV or radio terrestrial broadcasting. Since then, a number of new private programme services have emerged, often delivered by cable and satellite, and in some areas also by terrestrial transmitters. For some time, the public channels were even beaten by the private channels in the viewing figures, where, at the moment, RTL is the top ranking station. The current 'dual' TV market structures are depicted in the pie chart of Figure 3.6, where the patterned slices represent the two public broadcasting channels, which only cover one-third of the market share. In the coming years, it is expected that the public share will decline even further.

Postal Services

The institutional evolution of the postal sector has been partially described in the telecommunications sections. In as much as the two infrastructural subsectors were integrated under one organizational roof over the last 100 years, public status and monopoly rights in both have been very similar. A major particularity in the postal domain was that in the late 1960s the traditional monopoly rights in these sectors had been confirmed by a 'law on the postal system' of 28 July 1969 (Gesetz über das Postwesen, PostG).

Only since the first postal reform in 1989 has the development of the two branches diverged. While the organizational reform in the three branches of the Bundespost was more or less the same, the monopoly rights in the postal system remained untouched by the changes transforming the telecommunications sector. However, it is important to note that an exclusive monopoly only exists in the letter services where the Deutsche Post AG fulfils an infrastructural mandate imposed by federal government. The transmission of letters is considered to be a universal service which has to be provided nation-wide to the public. In other areas like the delivery of parcels, the new DBP Postdienst competes with other public (the German railway) and private firms (private carriers and delivery firms).

In 1984, international couriers services claimed market entry and after a tenacious bargaining process the DBP and the German Federal Association of International Courier Services reached an agreement that the DBP would tolerate delivery by international courier services under certain conditions.

Further exemptions from postal monopoly rights are books, non-addressed advertising pamphlets, and also letters that cost more than 10 DM. According to a recent press release, the Deutsche Post AG pretends to provide 50% of its services in a competitive environment. It is estimated that there are about 40,000 firms competing with the German Post in the parcel and courier market segments, and that the 10 largest providers employ more than 40,000 people (Berger and Knauth, 1996: 17).

There are some policy actors who wish to move even further down the path of liberalization. The EU proposed to open the national postal markets for all letters exceeding certain price or weight limits, and it plans to do the same with printed papers and direct mail. European liberalization initiatives in the postal sector have been especially strong since the early 1990s when the EC Commission issued its 'Green paper on postal Services' (Saramago, 1991). In December 1995 the European Commission published a draft Directive representing a compromise between the supporters of far-reaching liberalization measures and those who still support important aspects of the traditional institutional arrangements. Its main policy strategy is to identify a set of reserved or mandatory services which are necessary for the provision of a universal postal service, whereas the services which are not considered as reserved should be supplied on the basis of free competition. To maintain a universal postal service it is believed that this requires the postal administration to retain a monopoly over the basic letter service (that is, collection, sorting and delivery of items up to 350 g). According to the Commission's proposal the post offices would also be able to retain control of the distribution of incoming cross-border mail and direct mail until the end of the year 2000 if this will be necessary for their financial viability. To ensure that the post offices are not subsidizing services such as parcels and express mail, which do not fall into these reserved categories, they will be required to maintain separate accounts for the reserved and non-reserved sectors (*Financial Times*, 14 February 1996).

Also in the postal sector EU policy-making is closely coordinated with policy processes in the national arena. Within the German ministerial administration currently a legislative draft is being prepared by which the EU Directive will be transposed into national law. According to the current reform bill the Deutsche Post AG will have a protected monopoly in the basic letter services[26] up to the end of the year 2002. After this period a licensing system will be introduced similar to the provisions in the telecommunications reform Act. According to the current compromise formula, the transport and distribution of letters up to 2000 g then has to be licensed. Licences are principally open to all commercial actors having the necessary capacities and resources.

With respect to the property status, there have been changes during the last few years, too. Parallel to the legal privatization of DBP Telekom, DBP Postdienst has also been transformed into the legal form of a joint stock corporation (Post AG). The conversion became effective at the beginning of 1995. It is planned that the Post AG will float an initial tranche of its shares on the stock market in 1998.

Comparing and explaining German infrastructure privatization processes

The above case studies show that the institutional structures of major German infrastructure systems are in radical transformation. After the period of stability in the late 1980s and early 1990s, all of the six sectors outlined above began to move towards privatization and liberalization, or at least towards the greater involvement of private actors. In this section, we first summarize these developments from a comparative perspective, and secondly try to contribute to an understanding of why these institutional transformations occurred at all, and why they have evolved differently in the various sectors.

Sketching the basic directions of transformation

The major institutional transformations in each of the six sectors are depicted in Table 3.4, which outlines the following dimensions in each sector: (1) the traditional governance structures before the 1980s; (2) the current institutional model after the transformations; and (3) the presumed future changes. For the sake of simplicity, as mentioned above, the transformations are outlined as changes in market structures (degree of liberalization) and changes in property forms (shifts from public to private). This perspective shows that the traditional model was a public monopoly, which differed only with respect to the degree of administrative and political

Table 3.4 *Old and new models in the governance of infrastructures*

	Old model before 1980s	New model after realized transformations	Additional changes planned
Roads	Public monopoly; decentralized federalist governance through public administrations	Public monopoly; partial implementation of franchising and BOT models	Introduction of road usage fees; network-wide application of BOT model
Railways	Public monopoly; centralized governance through public administration at the federal level	Partial liberalization by access rights to infrastructure; private corporation fully owned by federal government	Divestiture into three separate corporations (freight, passenger, tracks); complete sale of operational units; partial sale of infrastructure units
Air transport	Public monopoly; decentralized federalist governance through public enterprises	Nearly complete liberalization; former flag carrier is private corporation; air traffic control run by private company fully controlled by federal government	Complete privatization (except air traffic control)
Telecommunications	Public monopoly; centralized governance through public administration at federal level	Far-reaching liberalization of markets; dominant network provider and operator is private corporation fully controlled by government	Complete liberalization, partial sale (up to 49%)
Broadcasting	Public monopoly; decentralized federalist governance through autonomous public institutions	Far-reaching liberalization through increasing access of private firms; public area still governed by public institutions	Further expansion of the commercial area in the dual broadcasting system
Posts	Public monopoly; centralized governance through public administration at federal level	Partial liberalization of markets; dominant network provider and operator is private corporation fully controlled by government	Partial liberalization, partial sale (up to 49%)

centralization. Political centralization was particularly high in the roads, air transport and broadcasting sectors, while being low in the other infrastructure systems.

With respect to the present model, after the recent transformations and the planned changes, the general features are the break-up of monopolies and the transformation of public administrations or state enterprises into private companies which are still under partial or full public control. Only in the air transport market are liberalization and the sale of capital almost complete. Air transport and telecommunications are the infrastructure sectors in which the most radical transformation have taken place; these are also the sectors which are most strongly exposed to international competition.

In the following sections, we will discuss the different factors and conditions which may explain these institutional transformations as well as their cross-sectoral variation. According to our analytical framework outlined earlier, we will point to technical and economical structural properties as well as to specific political conditions under which these changes came about.

Structural properties of infrastructures

Privatization efforts are influenced by structural properties of the goods or services produced in the relevant sectors. This argument can easily be illustrated by the example of telecommunications, where technological innovations of various kinds led to an international trend towards liberalization and privatization. Technological developments in telecommunications changed the basic properties of the goods and services produced and therefore had an effect on the property rights structure, as well as opening the door to a greater degree of competition within the sector. Applying the conceptual considerations basic to this chapter, the major changes of structural features of the infrastructures are now analysed in detail.

Shrinking the core of a natural monopoly through the separation of infrastructure and operation   A prominent pattern in all our cases of infrastructure privatization was the fact that the physical infrastructure was somehow separated from the operation of a given transport or communication system or the provision of services. Such processes were of some importance in each of the depicted cases of infrastructure privatization. This pattern is the least conspicuous in road transport, since here the infrastructure – roads – had always been separated from the actual transport services owing to the nature of the technical system. The argument becomes clearer, however, if one looks at the German telecommunications and railways privatization. Here the separation of network provision and service operation was crucial to the privatization process. Air transport is an exception in this respect, since it does not require a physical infrastructure network but needs only geographically dispersed points for infrastructure bases (airports, air traffic control facilities).

As a general reform pattern, the separation of infrastructure and service operation[27] points to a highly significant strategy for infrastructure privatization. By the separation of the physical network from the operation of services, the natural monopoly characteristics are eliminated for the service operations, that is the natural monopoly is shrunk to the infrastructure. Therefore, the area of political regulation can be restricted to the infrastructure domain, whereas the operation of transport and communication services can be governed by market relations. In some sectors, however, separating the infrastructure from the operation of services was made possible only recently through technological innovations. Railways are a fitting example: they require highly advanced information systems to coordinate the train operations of different companies on a common rail network. Telecommunications are another example, since modern, computer-based clearing systems were a prerequisite to the separation of the infrastructure from the services part.

Furthermore, limiting a natural monopoly implies the introduction of competition, as the former monopoly is replaced by a system of market governance. Usually this strategy is accompanied by the imposition of utilization fees, which have the side-effect of making the infrastructure costs more transparent. Moreover, this strategy is an adequate means of ending the traditional practice of cross-subsidization in the public sector.

Changes in the goods character of infrastructures Infrastructures are 'lumpy goods' and thus tend to natural monopolies. As depicted above, 'lumpiness' or 'indivisibilities' influence the nature of a good as soon as capacity problems occur. Capacity bottlenecks were a frequent phenomenon for most of the cases analysed, most notably in road and air transport. Decreasing free capacity on an infrastructure increases the rivalry of consumption and therefore causes an upward movement towards private good characteristics (see Figure 3.1).

But the dimension of 'control over exclusion from consumption' is also subject to changes which usually occur with technological innovations. Road transport is a good illustration since it was the development of electronic road pricing systems that initiated the debate on the privatization of German highways. In broadcasting, technologies like cable TV reduce the cost of controlling 'free riding'. When new technologies lead to decreasing marginal costs of exclusion, the result is a leftward movement of a formerly public good toward mixed good characteristics.

Through these two mechanisms, the character of the good 'infrastructure' can change radically over time and have considerable impacts on privatization strategies. The decrease in exclusion costs has been strongest with road infrastructure owing to the development of electronic road pricing systems,[28] whereas the changes in the structural properties of airports occurred largely at the level of increasing rivalry for access among consumers as a result of growing capacity bottlenecks. Telecommunications and railway infrastructures[29] show little movement in this respect. Whereas the change in the characteristics of airports and broadcasting has been a strong influence on privatization and liberalization (shifting the good from the zone of mixed or public goods into the zone of private production), the changes in roads, telecommunications and postal services are less influential. Both sectors still remain in the zone of mixed goods.

Political factors and new regulatory demands

Infrastructures exhibit various kinds of political characteristics which render them specific as far as state interventions are concerned. Obvious cases are externalities, particularly if they are negative ones, natural monopoly situations and beneficial economic or social effects.

Regulation of negative externalities   Negative externalities connected with infrastructures can occur either directly, such as destruction of natural landscape or sealing of the soil, or indirectly via the operation of services on the respective infrastructure, such as noise, pollution, accidents, lacking protection of personal data etc. The direct negative externalities are usually dealt with by planning rules in the construction process. This also holds for the indirect negative effects of those infrastructures which can be subject to additional public policy instruments such as specialized rules by sectoral regulatory agencies, tax incentives or market access requirements. Direct negative externalities occur in the sectors encompassing physical networks (railways, roads, telecommunications and, to a smaller extent, postal services). Indirect negative externalities and therefore public regulation requirements are prominent in road and air transport.

Positive network externalities and natural monopolies   The term 'positive network externalities' refers to various benefits which infrastructures bring about apart from the direct operation of services on them. As was mentioned above, infrastructures are 'support systems' for a wide variety of social activities and therefore subject to a multitude of political or public policy considerations. The regulation and intervention requirements arising from the external benefits of infrastructures are dealt with by public planning rules, but often also by further public involvement in the sector. Air traffic control is such a case owing to its high security relevance and therefore unaltered public ownership.

The 'sub-additivity of the cost function' condition continues to exist after the privatization although it can be limited to certain parts of the physical network and sometimes moderated by regional division. Further regulation requirements arise from this fact, for example the federal government has to make sure that the infrastructure part of the DB AG refrains from using its monopoly power to keep other railway operators off the network and thereby informally eliminating the formally guaranteed rights of network access. In the postal sector, monopoly prices for customers from remote areas are to be prevented by public regulations. The creation of new, considerably independent regulatory bodies (such as the Eisenbahn-Bundesamt) is one strategy by which government may deal with these new regulatory demands common to our cases.

Public or universal service requirements Another common phenomenon concerning infrastructure sectors is the fact that the services related to those sectors are often subject to political goals such as obligations to nation-wide uniform rates, conveyance obligations or social fares. These are often referred to as merit goods for which an undersupply situation will occur when they are purely governed by market forces and consumer sovereignty. Local passenger transport by railways and the provision of telecommunications and postal facilities in remote areas are examples of this merit character ascribed to some parts of the infrastructure. Most local rail passenger services create deficits but are politically desirable in order to promote the mobility of the lower social classes as well as to bring some relief to urban traffic congestion. Under the old governance regime, those transport services were secured by general subsidization of the public railways by the federal government. When privatizing an infrastructure sector, a new way to ensure these politically preferred services and service conditions must be found. Concerning local rail services for passenger transport, the solution was the introduction of a tendering process for these services at the state or local government level. Another possibility is reintroducing government regulation, although compliance is often difficult to control.

The role of budget constraints and liberalization

As shown above, technical innovations and capacity bottlenecks played an important part in the trend towards privatization. But nevertheless these structural properties were only conditions enabling privatization strategies where they were formerly impossible or at least problematic. Therefore, the above section dealt with the necessary conditions for the infrastructure privatization observable in Germany, but not with the sufficient conditions. Technical and economic changes are setting the stage for privatization, but politics accounts for the players, their differential resources and strategies, and the rules of the game. Therefore, the political context of German infrastructure privatization will now be scrutinized.

The empirical cases we dealt with involve two major types of objectives for privatization: (1) the concern about growing public budget deficits and the rising indebtedness of the public sector; (2) internationalization (or Europeanization) in the form of an international liberalization movement creating strong pressure on national institutional structures to adapt in order to maintain their competitiveness. These two objectives, however, were not equally important for all the privatizations analysed. The importance of each of these goals varied widely according to the specific properties of the infrastructure sectors concerned. Sectors with a high budgetary importance naturally were those with the greatest amount of government funding, subsidies and deficits, such as the railways and the road infrastructure, or those with the highest probable revenues from privatization, such as telecommunications. Internationalization or Europeanization especially influenced privatization in air transport, telecommunications and broadcasting, but to a smaller degree, and predominantly as a result of the European Union, also the railways and postal services. The influence of international trends is weakest in the road transport sector.

The first objective – unburdening the state budget by privatization – is closely connected with the notion of efficiency, as introduced earlier. The dimensions of efficiency addressed by the public budget objective are primarily the allocative and productive efficiencies, since those are the areas in which direct decreases of the financial burden can be achieved, that is through rationalization, reducing the workforce, and leaner administrative structures. The notion of dynamic efficiency points more to the question of international competitiveness since the rapidity of adaptation to new technical economic circumstances determines the international market position of national industries. Public budget, allocative and productive efficiency questions were very prominent in the railway reform and road infrastructure privatization initiatives, and in the reforms of the postal services. In telecommunications, air transport and broadcasting, improvement in dynamic efficiency and catching up with international liberalization and new market opportunities were more prominent as rationales for privatization. In both cases, moreover, the high influence (sometimes even 'hegemonic coercion') of the USA seeking access to the European markets for its industries was an important factor.

Institutional efficiency in terms of transaction costs reduction is another objective in the context of lowering the state's financial burden, albeit on a more abstract level. Here, the question of the most appropriate governance structure for infrastructure sectors is addressed. In a comparative static perspective, transactional risks and coordination costs of market systems may be compared with the monitoring and policing costs of hierarchical, bureaucratic systems. Privatized large technical telecommunications, air transport and railway systems which are primarily coordinated through market systems imply a different level of risk and reliability than systems that are hierarchically monitored and controlled.

Political actor systems and institutional arenas

As the preceding sections have shown, the various cases display differences with respect to changing structural conditions as well as basic motives for privatization. However, this level of explanation is still incomplete. From an actor-centred and institutionalist perspective (Mayntz and Scharpf, 1995), several additional explanatory elements are relevant: political actors, typical conflict lines and interest structures, and the 'institutional landscapes' constraining the action and interaction among these units.

At this level of analysis, the major differences between the sectors concern: (1) possible power differentials between the coalition of privatizers on the one hand, and the opponents (aiming to preserve the status quo) on the other; (2) the degree to which the status quo is institutionally entrenched in the constitution or in law (thus implying veto position); and (3) the degree of political centralization in the related sectors.

In general, institutional transformations towards privatization and liberalization are more likely in sectors with strong and broad privatization coalitions, low institutional entrenchment, and high sectoral centralization – and vice versa. In telecommunications, air transport and broadcasting, a broad transitional privatizing coalition is at work, ranging across industry (expecting access to new business areas), international or transnational actors (supporting an international harmonization of privatization policies), and domestic governmental actors (expecting large proceeds from these sales). In such sectors, veto coalitions will have more difficulty in defending the status quo. By contrast, in the postal, railway and road sectors, the actor set was not only restricted to domestic actors, but also characterized by the less important role of business actors, as the new industrial opportunities seemed to be less obvious than in other sectors.

The sectors displayed some similar institutional characteristics such as the political centralization or decentralization (that is, decentralized, federalist political decision-making structures versus concentration of competencies at the federal level, and centralized versus fragmented unions) of the various sectors, as well as the related 'veto positions' of certain governmental actors and organized interests. Such positions are largely based on a strong institutional entrenchment within the old model – mostly in the constitution.

Synopsis: factors influencing the privatization policies

Table 3.5 summarizes the properties and factors influential for infrastructure privatizations in Germany. The causal implications of these structural and situation features are illuminated below.

Looking at the technical and economic properties influencing the privatization approach, whether or not the relevant infrastructure sector is a natural monopoly is important regarding whether the sector is split up into several regional entities or into the two levels of physical 'network' and 'operation'. Furthermore, the existence of a natural monopoly results in public control requirements which necessitate some form of regulation and sometimes even some degree of remaining direct public control. Therefore, given a natural monopoly situation, privatization and full deregulation are unlikely to occur together. As far as the character of goods is concerned, additional regulation requirements can arise from mixed goods which raise problems of non-rivalry (jointness in supply) or non-control of exclusion

Table 3.5 *Factors contributing to infrastructure privatizations in Germany*

Factor	Telecommunication	Air transport	Railways	Posts	Broadcasting	Roads
Technical-economic properties						
Natural monopoly	Partial, cable network	No, partly with airports	Yes, physical infrastructure network	Partial, post offices	No	Yes, regional restrictions
Goods character	Private	Private	Mixed	Private	Mixed	Mixed
Socio-political aspects and requirements						
Public or universal service obligations	Relevant, solved by regulation	Irrelevant	Relevant, solved by local tendering	Relevant, solved by regulation	Solved by Rundfunkräte	Relevant, unsolved
Public budget objectives;						
Burden on public budget	None	Low	High	None	None	High
Expected revenues from sale	High	High	Low	Medium	None	None
Internationalization; Europeanization	Highly influential; strong influence of EC liberalization	Highly influential	Some influence of EC liberalization	Some influence of EC liberalization	Some influence of EC liberalization	Not important
Veto positions based on institutional entrenchment of status quo	Potentially unions with SPD, solved by safeguarding civil servants' preferential status	None	Potentially unions with SPD, solved by safeguarding civil servants' preferential status	Potentially unions with SPD, solved by safeguarding civil servants' preferential status	Yes, SPD and states' governments defending their position and competencies	Yes, SPD, Greens, PDS; majority of the citizens
Corporatist integration	Strong, high degree of unionization, strong interest groups	Weak	Strong, high degree of unionization, strong interest groups	Strong, high degree of unionization, strong interest groups	Medium, medium position of unions, but strong interest groups	Medium, weak position of unions, but strong interest groups

and therefore can be subject to free riding as well as sub-optimal production levels.

Public or universal service conditions can be imposed either by regulation or by competitive tendering. Tendering solutions are generally superior to regulation, since they introduce cost awareness and therefore enhance efficiency at the level of production and allocation. In situations where tendering is unfeasible, however, it has to be substituted by regulation to ensure a socially desired level of public or universal service conditions. Public budget objectives determine the likelihood of a full sale of the respective infrastructure corporations as well as the general climate for privatizations. The prominence of internationalization and Europeanization in the relevant sector determines the degree of national liberalization and again the commitment to materially privatize, that is to sell the public infrastructure corporation to the private sector.

In the German political system with its general trend towards joint decision-making (cooperative federalism and high degree of corporatist integration), socio-political veto positions play an important role since they can preserve the status quo. This is especially true of infrastructure sectors showing a high constitutional and legal entrenchment: an amendment to the German constitution requires a two-thirds majority in both houses of Parliament and a high percentage of laws – and their amendments – needs to be approved by both houses. These incentives for joint decisions are further strengthened if the degree of corporatist integration of the relevant infrastructure is high, as unions and other societal interest groups can potentially build up additional veto positions – or at least exert strong influence on the privatization approach and the new governance structure to be implemented. Thus the preservation of the preferential condition of the civil servants and the employees in the public sector as well as the non-disruptive and gradual course of the privatization process was a pattern common to all the cases analysed.

Conclusions

Similar to many other advanced industrial countries, Germany has significant parts of its public sector currently in transformation. The empirical cases analysed in this chapter show that the privatization of infrastructures in Germany in the late 1980s and early 1990s depicts a state-led reform of the sectoral governance regimes as a response to changing environmental conditions. As Campbell and Lindberg (1990) have shown, one prominent way of shaping governance structures in a societal sector is the manipulation of property rights through the state. In several of our cases such shifts have occurred, and mostly in the direction of greater market control and more private involvement in public production. As we have pointed out in our comparative interpretation, most of these transformations can be conceptualized as structural adaptations towards more appropriate institutional arrangements in the governance of economic sectors, reducing transaction costs and therefore enhancing sectoral efficiency. According to Olsen (1992: 280–1), such institutional transformations generally occur in the context of severe external crisis, and they are more likely to happen when existing institutional arrangements are unable to adapt. The major adaptive pressures in the infrastructure sectors dealt with in this chapter were caused by changes in the goods characteristics which mostly were related to technological innovation and capacity bottlenecks as well as an enhanced ability to deal with natural monopoly structures. These 'necessary' conditions again were supported by other factors of which the occurrence of severe public budget constraints and the internationalization or Europeanization of the respective sectors were the most prominent. The result is a fundamental transformation of public infrastructural sectors, leading to an increased involvement of private actors in the provision of formerly public or para-public goods.

Notes

We want to thank Carles Boix, John Halligan, Joachim J. Hesse, Jan-Erik Lane, Edward C. Page and Thomas Plümper for useful comments on this chapter as well as Gregory Jackson, Scott Rogers and Martin C. Lodge for improving our English.

1 Smith (1976) points out in Book V of his *opus magnum*: 'The third and last duty of the sovereign . . . is that of erecting and maintaining those publick institutions and those publick works, which, though they may be in the highest degree advantageous to a great society, are, however, of such a nature, that the profit could never repay the expence to any individual or small number of individuals, and which it, therefore, cannot be expected that any individual or small number of individuals should erect or maintain.'

2 For instance, in 1988 the German government sold off its remaining holdings of VW, oil concern VEBA and the conglomerate Viag AG.

3 A recent overview of this conceptual landscape is given by Schneider and Kenis (1996). The most prominent authors in the area of 'economic governance' are North (1990) and Williamson (1985). Recent approaches with a socio-political orientation are represented by Campbell and Lindberg (1990), Hollingsworth et al. (1994), Scharpf (1993) and Mayntz and Scharpf (1995).

4 In French the term *infrastructure* depicted the material facilities enabling the operation of services in distinct sectors such as railways, air transport and military devices from an early stage onwards, whereas in German the term gained acceptance only in the late 1950s. In English the expression 'social overhead capital' (SOC) as introduced by Albert O. Hirschman is somewhat more common, but carries a slightly different meaning (Schatz, 1996: 124–6).

5 For an overview of such network effects see Blankart and Knieps (1992).

6 Since non-exclusiveness implies rivalry the respective dimension is more appropriately depicted as control over exclusion (Snidal, 1979: 539).

7 Thereby Snidal comes quite close to the theory of club goods (Buchanan, 1965; Sandler and Tschirhart, 1980).

8 This refers most notably to road and air transport (air pollution, noise, accidents, etc.) but can be a matter of citizens' protest concerning noise from or new tracks for railways or canal construction plans as well.

9 Merit goods are goods whose political importance is so high that their supply by public subsidies is greater than if the provision was subject to market forces and consumer sovereignty (Böhme, 1994: 28).

10 The German legal system differentiates clearly between public and private law. The area of public law is destined for the public administration and contains specialized civil service obligations and rights. Therefore, the autonomy of public law organizations and bodies is restricted as compared with the requirements for organizations according to private law.

11 Which again have the possibility to transfer this control or part of it to the Federal Railway Office or to regional administrative bodies.

12 After the railway reform, however, a part of the mineral oil taxes revenue is distributed to the states to pay for local passenger rail transport.

13 The road infrastructure projects cover two national road connections (B10 near Karlsruhe and B178 Weißenburg–Zittau) and one highway (A94 Ampfing–Winhöring). The bridge projects are the Elbe crossing near Glückstadt, the Fehmarn Belt crossing and the Strelasund crossing towards the island of Rügen. All these projects will be financed via user charges (*Frankfurter Allgemeine Zeitung*, no. 91, 18 April 1996: 17).

14 The project failed more or less. The plan to implement electronic road pricing for private cars had to be given up owing to data protection shortcomings, so the system will in the near future at best be used to levy charges from heavy commercial vehicles where the data protection requirements are less severe.

15 Bismarck's objectives were gaining a military advantage and introducing a unifying element to Germany's states (Fremdling, 1993: 426).

16 Council Directive 91/440/EEC of 29 July 1991 on the development of the Community's railways (*Official Journal* L 237, 24 August 1991). Council Regulation (EEC) 1893/91 of 20 June 1991 amending Regulation (EEC) 1191/69 on action by member states concerning the obligations inherent in the concept of a public service in transport by rail, road and inland waterway (*Official Journal* L 169, 29 June 1991). EC Directive 91/440 has been amended and specified several times since then.

17 The term *national flag carrier* refers to those national airlines which were entitled to observe the traffic rights distributed in the framework of the restrictive bilateral air traffic agreements. Usually those flag carriers were at least partly state-owned. This was justified with the argument that the granting and withdrawal of international traffic rights are often subject to foreign policy objectives (Soltwedel and Wolf, 1996: 5).

18 Although the new head of the Commission of Transport, Neil Kinnock, has made a big effort to ensure that the EC Commission retains responsibility for bargaining and completion of 'open skies' agreements.

19 In general, the competitive pressure on airport companies is lower than that on airlines. With the hinterland and the high sunk costs involved in airport investments, this area is in practice a 'non-contestable market' which requires political regulation (Soltwedel and Wolf, 1996: 13). On airport privatization in general see Truitt and Esler (1996).

20 For the distinction between first- and second-order infrastructures see Braun and Joerges (1994), which contains an analysis of second-order large technical systems.

21 Its 1991 business report explains this necessity as follows: 'It must . . . be said that Telekom has already come up against the limits of its entrepreneurial freedom. This triggered the discussion of a second structural reform. Sure, the first critical review of the Deutsche Bundespost reforms of 1989 had initially been planned for the mid 1990s, but unpredictable developments such as German unification and changing international circumstances have brought forward the need for such review.'

22 Referring to legislation in 1908 ('Gesetz betreffend die Abänderung des Gesetzes über das Telegraphenwesen des Deutschen Reichs vom 6 April 1892' from 7 March 1908) in which radio communications was defined as a variant of telegraphy.

23 The vertical chain of the broadcasting production process usually is divided into producing programming, packaging programming into schedules by programme services or networks, and delivering programming to the consumers via telecommunications technologies.

24 Since 1982, the Bundespost has invested about 1 billion DM p.a. in the extension of the broadband cable network.

25 The Christian Democrats were particularly keen on supporting private TV because they

expected that commercial broadcasters and private TV channels would be more sympathetic to the conservative political parties.

26 This is related to letters having a weight not more than 350 g, and of fees lower than 5 or 6 DM.

27 The term 'operation' refers here to the actual services produced with the aid of the infrastructure and not to the maintenance and running of the network itself.

28 This phenomenon, however, should not be interpreted as an automatic or inevitable change: every technological innovation encompasses push as well as pull elements and therefore the development of such automatic toll systems can be effected by political demands as well.

29 Those small changes result from innovations in the field of telematics and capacity scarcities on main routes of the railway network.

References

Alessi, Louis de (1987) 'Property rights and privatization', *Proceedings of the American Academy of Political Science*, 36: 24–35.

Basedow, Jürgen (1991) 'Rechtsfragen der Privatisierung im Verkehr – Verfassungsgrenzen und europäische Dynamik', in Deutsche Verkehrswissenschaftliche Gesellschaft (DVWG) (ed.), *Privatisierung im Verkehr*. Schriftenreihe der DVWG, Heft B 145. Bergisch Gladbach: DVWG. pp. 74–90.

Bauer, Johannes, M. (1988) *Alternative Governance Structures for Infrastructure Sectors. Notes on an Insitutional Design Problem*. EUI Colloquium Papers DOC IUE 256/88. Florence: European University Institute.

Baumol, William J. (1985) 'Industry structure analysis and public policy', in Georg R. Feiwel (ed.), *Issues in Contemporary Microeconomics and Welfare*. London: Macmillan. pp. 311–27.

Berger, Heinz and Knauth, Peter (1996) 'Zur Notwendigkeit einer Änderung des Ordnungsrahmens im Postsektor', in Heinz Berger and Peter Knauth (eds), *Liberalisierung und Regulierung der Postmärkte*. München: Oldenbourg. pp. 11–46.

Bergström, Siegfried (1991) 'Vorzüge und Grenzen einer Privatfinanzierung', *Internationales Verkehrswesen*, 43: 183–8.

Beuermann, Günter and Schneider, Jürgen (1996) 'Das Infrastrukturunternehmen der DBAG: Monopolistischer Gigant oder Partner für alle Schienenverkehrsbetreiber?', *Zeitschrift für Verkehrswissenschaft*, 67: 34–48.

Bittner, Werner (1992) 'Die Geschichte der Lufthansa als Grundlage von Unternehmenskultur und Öffentlichkeitsarbeit', in Deutsche Verkehrswissenschaftliche Gesellschaft (DVWG) (ed.), *Verkehrshistorischer Workshop*. Schriftenreihe der DVWG, Heft B 148. Bergisch Gladbach: DVWG. pp. 139–53.

Blankart, Charles B. and Knieps, Günter (1992) 'Netzökonomik', in *Jahrbuch für Neue Politische Ökonomie 11*. Tübingen: Mohr. pp. 73–87.

Böhme, Hans (1994) *Eine Strategie für den öffentlichen Personennahverkehr*. Kiel: Institut für Weltwirtschaft.

Braun, Ingo and Joerges, Bernward (1994) 'How to recombine large technical systems: the case of the European organ transplantation', in Jane Summerton (ed.), *Changing Large Technical Systems*. Boulder, CO: Westview Press. pp. 25–52.

Buchanan, James M. (1965) 'An economic theory of clubs', *Economica*, 32: 1–14.

Bundesministerium für Verkehr (ed.) (1994) *Strassen in Deutschland*. Bonn: Bundesministerium für Verkehr.

Bundesministerium für Verkehr (ed.) (annual) *Verkehr in Zahlen*. Berlin: Deutsches Institut für Wirtschaftsforschung.

Campbell, John L. and Lindberg, Leon N. (1990) 'Property rights and the organization of economic activity by the state', *American Sociological Review*, 55: 634–47.

Coase, Ronald H. (1937) 'The nature of the firm', *Economica*, 4: 306–405.

Collins, Richard (1994) 'Unity in diversity? The European single market in broadcasting and the audiovisual, 1982–1992', *Journal of Common Market Studies*, 32(1): 89–102.

Denkhaus, Ira (1995) *Verkehrsinformationssysteme. Durchsetzbarkeit und Akzeptanz in der Bundesrepublik Deutschland*. Wiesbaden: Deutscher Universitäts-Verlag.

Deutsche Bahn AG (ed.) (1994) *Die Bahnreform*. Frankfurt a.m.: Deutsche Bahn AG.

Domberger, Simon (1986) 'Economic regulation through franchise contracts', in John Kay et al. (eds), *Privatisation and Regulation – the UK Experience*. Oxford: Clarendon. pp. 269–83.

Eckner, Herbert (1964) 'Der Rundfunk als bundesstaatliches Problem', in *Jahrbuch des Postwesens 4*. pp. 9–81.

Engelkamp, Paul and Bison, Gunhild (1994) 'Die Verkehrsentwicklung bis zum Jahr 2010', *Internationales Verkehrswesen*, 46: 563–8.

Ewers, Hans-Jürgen (1994) 'Privatisierung und Deregulierung bei den Eisenbahnen. Das Beispiel der Deutschen Bundesbahn und der Deutschen Reichsbahn', in *Jahrbuch für Neue Politische Ökonomie 13*. Tübingen: Mohr. pp. 178–208.

Ewers, Hans-Jürgen and Rodi, Hansjörg (1995) *Privatisierung der Bundesautobahnen*. Beiträge aus dem Institut für Verkehrswissenschaft der Universität Münster, Heft 134. Göttingen: Vandenhoeck & Ruprecht.

Fremdling,Rainer (1993) 'Eisenbahnen', in Ulrich Wengenroth (ed.), *Technik und Wirtschaft*. Düsselforf: VDI. pp. 418–37.

Grande, Edgar (1994) 'The new role of the state in telecommunications', in Wolfgang C. Mueller and Vincent Wright (eds), *The State in Western Europe: Retreat or Redefinition?* Essex: Cass. pp. 138–57.

Gratza, Hugo, Hahn, Wolfgang and Steenken, Nicolaus (1996) 'Möglichkeiten einer Privatisierung von Bundesautobahnen', *Internationales Verkehrswesen*, 48(6): 13–19.

Hesse, Joachim Jens and Benz, Arthur (1988) 'Staatliche Institutionspolitik im internationalen Vergleich', in Thomas Ellwein et al. (eds), *Jahrbuch zur Staats- und Verwaltungswissenschaft Band 2*. Baden-Baden: Nomos. 69–112.

Hollingsworth, Joseph R., Schmitter, Philippe C. and Streeck, Wolfgang (eds) (1994) *Governing Capitalist Economies: Performance and Control of Economic Sectors*. New York: Oxford University Press.

Holtz-Bacha, Christina (1991) 'From public monopoly to a dual broadcasting system in Germany', *European Journal of Communication*, 6: 223–33.

Horn, Mechthild (1994) 'Betreibermodelle – Herausforderung und Chance für die Regionalbahnen', *Österreichische Zeitschrift für Verkehrswissenschaft*, 49(3/4): 19–36.

Humphreys, Peter J. (1994) *Media and Media Policy in Germany: the Press and Broadcasting since 1945*, 2nd edn. Oxford and Providence, RI: Berg.

Ikenberry, G. John (1990) 'The international spread of privatisation policies: inducements, learning, and "Policy Bandwagoning"', in Ezra N. Suleiman and John Waterbury (eds), *The Political Economy of Public Sector Reform and Privatisation*. Boulder, CO: Westview Press. pp. 88–110.

Jaeger, Bernd (1994) *Postreform I und II: Die Gradualistische Telekommunikationspolitik in Deutschland im Lichte der Positiven Theorie Staatlicher Regulierung und Deregulierung*. Koeln: Inst. F. Wirtschaftspolitik.

Klatt, Sigurd (1990) 'Die Finanzierung der Verkehrsinfrastruktur', in *Hamburger Jahrbuch für Wirtschafts- und Gesellschaftspolitik 35*. Tübingen: Mohr. pp. 207–23.

Kortschak, Bernd Helmut (1993) 'Richtlinie 440/91 (EWG): Quersubventionierung ade? Auswirkungen auf das Produktionsprogramm im Bahngütervekehr', *Internationales Verkehrswesen*, 45: 103–110.

Lane, Jan-Erik (1985) 'Introduction: public policy or markets? The demarcation problem', in Jan-Erik Lane (ed.), *State and Market: the Politics of the Public and the Private*. London: Sage. pp. 3–52.

Lane, Jan-Erik (1994) 'Ends and means of public sector reform', *Staatswissenschaften und Staatspraxis*, 5: 459–73.

Lehmkuhl, Dirk (1996) 'Privatizing to keep it public? The reorganization of the German Railways', in Arthur Benz and Klaus H. Goetz (eds), *A New German Public Sector?* Aldershot: Dartmouth. pp. 71–92.

Lehmkuhl, Dirk and Herr, Christoph (1994) 'Reform in Spannungsfeld von Dezentralisierung und Entstaatlichung: Die Neurordnung des Eisenbahnwesens in Deutschland', *Politische Vierteljahfresschrift*, 35: 631–57.

Link, Heike (1994) 'German railway reform – chances and risks', *Japan Railway & Transport Review*, June: 19–22.

Majone, Giandomenico (1994) 'Paradoxes of privatisation and deregulation', *Journal of European Public Policy*, 1(1): 53–69.

Mayntz, Renate (1995) 'Progrès technique, changement dans la société et développement des grands systèmes techniques', *Flux*, no. 22: 11–16.

Mayntz, Renate and Scharpf, Fritz W. (eds) (1995) *Gesellschaftliche Selbstregelung und politische Steuerung*. Frankfurt a. M.: Campus.

McKay, Charles (1989) *Möglichkeiten der privatwirtschaftlichen Finanzierung von Verkehrsinfrastruktur-Investitionen in der EG*. Göttingen: Vandenhoeck & Ruprecht.

Musgrave, Richard A. and Musgrave, Peggy B. (1976) *Public Finance in Theory and Practice*, 2nd edn. New York: McGraw-Hill.

Niejahr, Michael and Abbamonte, Giuseppe (1996) 'Liberalization policy and state aid in the air transport sector', *EC Competition Policy Newsletter*, 2(2).

Nijkamp, Peter and Rienstra, Sytze, A. (1995) 'Private sector involvement in financing and operating transport infrastructure', *Annals of Regional Science*, 29: 221–35.

North, Douglass C. (1990) *Institutions, Institutional Change and Economic Performance*. Cambridge: Cambridge University Press.

Olsen, Johan P. (1992) 'Rethinking and reforming the public sector', in Beate Kohler-Koch (ed.), *Staat und Demokratie in Europa. 18. Wissenschaftlicher Kongreß der Deutschen Vereinigung für Politische Wissenschaft*. Opladen: Leske Budrich. pp. 275–93.

Olson, Mancur (1965) *The Logic of Collective Action: Public Goods and the Theory of Groups*. Cambridge, MA: Harvard University Press.

Ostrowski, Rüdiger (1993) 'Neue Wege der Infrastrukturfinanzierung', *Zeitschrift für Verkehrswissenschaft*, 64: 49–66.

Rothengatter, Werner (1990) 'Germany', in European Conference of Ministers of Transport (ECMT) (ed.), *Private and Public Investment in Transport*. Report of the Eighty-First Round Table on Transport Economics. Paris: ECMT. pp. 49–92.

Rothengatter, Werner (1991) 'Möglichheiten privater Finanzierung im Verkehrswesen Infrastruktur', in Deutsche Verkehrswissenschaftliche Gesellschaft (DVWG) (ed.) *Privatisierung im Verkehr*. Schriftenreihe der DVWG, B145. Bergisch Gladbach: DVWG. pp. 18–38.

Sandler, Todd and Tschirhart, John T. (1980) 'The economic theory of clubs: an evaluative survey', *Journal of Economic Literature*, 18: 1481–521.

Saramago, José Luis (1991) 'Perspectives of a European postal policy – the view of the CEC', in *Die Zukunft der Postdienste in Europa. Proceedings der internationalen Konferenz Die Zukunft der Postdienste in Europa*, Bonn, 25–26 October 1990. Berlin: Springer.

Scharpf, Fritz, W. (1988) 'The joint-decision trap: lessons from German federalism and European integration', *Public Administration*, 66: 239–78.

Scharpf, Fritz, W. (1993) *Games in Hierarchies and Networks*. Frankfurt a. M.: Campus Verlag.

Schatz, Klaus-Werner (1996) 'Zur Entwicklung des Begriffs Infrastruktur', in Heinz Berger (ed.), *Wettbewerb und Infrastruktur in Post- und Telekommunikationsmärkten*. Zeitschrift für öffentliche und gemeinwirtschaftliche Unternehmen, Beiheft 19. Baden-Baden: Nomos. pp. 122–36.

Schmidt, Susanne K. (1996) 'Privatizing the federal postal and telecommunications services', in Arthur Benz and Klaus H. Goetz (eds), *A New German Public Sector? Reform, Adaptation and Stability*. Aldershot: Dartmouth.

Schmuck, Herbert (1992) 'Die Eisenbahnen in der Gemeinsamen Verkehrspolitik der EG', *Transportrecht*, no. 2: 41–53.

Schneider, Volker (forthcoming) 'Staat und technische Kommunikation. Zur politischen Entwicklung der Telekommunikation in den USA, Japan, Deutschland, Großbritannien, Frankreich und Italien'.

Schneider, Volker, Dang Nguyen, Godefroy and Werle, Raymund (1994) 'Corporate actor networks in European policy making: harmonizing telecommunications policy', *Journal of Common Market Studies*, 32: 473–98.

Schneider, Volker and Kenis, Patrick (1996) 'Verteilte Kontrolle: Institutionelle Steuerung in modernen Gesellschaften', in Patrick Kenis and Volker Schneider (eds), *Organisation und Netzwerk. Institutionelle Steuerung in Wirtschaft und Politik*. Frankfurt a. M.: Campus. pp. 9–43.

Schneider, Volker and Werle, Raymund (1991) 'Policy networks in the German telecommunications domain', in Bernd Marin and Renate Mayntz (eds), *Policy Networks. Empirical Evidence and Theoretical Considerations*. Schriften des Max-Planck-Instituts für Gesellschaftsforschung Köln, Bd. 9. Frankfurt a. M.: Campus.

Smith, Adam (1976) *An Inquiry into the Nature and Causes of the Wealth of Nations*, vol. 2. Oxford: Clarendon Press.

Snidal, Duncan (1979) 'Public goods, property rights, and political organizations', *International Studies Quarterly*, 23(4): 532–66.

Soltwedel, Rüdiger and Wolf, Hartmut (1996) 'Privatisierung öffentlicher Unternehmeneine ordnungspolitische Reflexion', in Deutsche Verkehrswissenschafliche Gesellschaft (DVWG) (ed.) *Privatislerung Deutscher Flughäfen*. Schriftenreihe der DVWG, B185 Bergisch Gladbach: DVWG. pp. 4–20.

Starr, Paul (1990) 'The new life of the liberal state: privatisation and the restructuring of state–society relations', in Ezra N. Suleiman and John Waterbury (ed.), *The Political Economy of Public Sector Reform and Privatisation*. Boulder, CO: Westview. pp. 22–54.

Studenroth, Stefan (1996) 'Aufgaben und Befugnisse des Eisenbahn-Bundesamtes', *Verwaltungsarchiv*, 87(1): 97–114.

Suleiman, Ezra N. and Waterbury, John (1990) 'Introduction: analyzing privatization in industrial and developing countries', in Ezra N. Suleiman and John Waterbury (eds), *The Political Economy of Public Sector Reform and Privatisation*. Boulder, CO: Westview. pp. 1–21.

Thomas, Frank (1994) *Telefonieren in Deutschland. Organisatorische, technische und räumliche Entwicklung eines großtechnischen Systems*. Frankfurt a. M.: Campus.

Truitt, Lawrence J. and Esler, Michael (1996) 'Airport privatization: full divestiture and its alternatives', *Policy Studies Journal*, 24(1): 100–10.

Wassenbergh, Henri (1992) 'The globalization of international air transport', in Chia-Jui Cheng and Pablo Mendes de Leon (eds), *The Highways of Air and Outer Space over Asia*. Dordrecht: Martinus Nijhoff. pp. 337–49.

Werle, Raymund (1990) *Telekommunikation in der Bundesrepublik: Expansion, Differenzierung, Transformation*. Frankfurt a. M.: Campus.

Wheatcroft, Stephen and Lipman, Geoffrey (1990) *European Liberalisation and World Air Transport: towards a Transnational Industry*. The Economist Intelligence Unit, Special Report 2015. London: Economist Intelligence Unit.

Williams, Arthur (1985) 'West Germany: the search for the way forward', in Raymond Kuhn (ed.), *The Politics of Broadcasting*. New York: St Martin's Press. pp. 83–118.

Williamson, Oliver E. (1975) *Markets and Hierarchies: Analysis and Antitrust Implications. A Study in the Economics of Internal Organization*. New York: Free Press.

Williamson, Oliver E. (1985) *The Economic Institutions of Capitalism*. New York: Free Press.

Williamson, Oliver E. (1991) 'Comparative economic organization: the analysis of discrete structural alternatives', *Administrative Science Quarterly*, 36: 269–96.

Wissmann, Matthias (1994) *Luftfahrtkonzept 2000*. Bonn: Bundesministerium für Verkehr.

Wolf, Peter (1996) 'Die Rolle des Bundes in der Flughafenpolitik', in Deutsche Verkehrswissenschaftliche Gesellschaft (ed.), *Privatisierung Deutscher Flughäfen*. Schriftenreihe der DVWG B185. Bergisch Gladbach: DVWG. pp. 76–82.

Yarrow, George (1986) 'Privatisation in theory and practice', *Economic Policy*, 2: 324–64.

4

Rebuilding the State: Public Sector Reform in Central and Eastern Europe

Joachim Jens Hesse

The Central and Eastern European public sector: 'odd man out' or 'member of the European family'?

The countries of Central and Eastern Europe are still undergoing fundamental, if not revolutionary, changes affecting the very foundations of their political, social and economic life. Although both the extent of the transformation processes that have thus far taken place and the pace differ considerably from country to country, it is no doubt possible to detect a number of shared characteristics which suggest a common pattern of political and social change. The distinguishing features include: the transition of what were effectively, if not in name, systems of one-party rule, in which the leading role of the Communist Party in all sectors of society was firmly entrenched, to pluralist, multi-party parliamentary systems with democratically elected and accountable governments; the abandoning of the principle of 'democratic centralism' in favour of a far-reaching deconcentration and decentralization of political power to be exercised under the rule of law; the rejection of the principle of unity between politics and the economy which involves the emergence of distinct spheres of political and economic life; and far-reaching economic reforms whose principal aims are the strengthening of private enterprise, the denationalization (or rather privatization) of a large share of the previously state-controlled productive capital and a substantial deregulation and liberalization of the national economy.

The underlying ideas spurring the ambitious reform attempts at replacing a nationalized, centralized and planned economic system with a market economy are, in principle, also being applied to the task of reorganizing or, rather, refounding the public sector. Thus, there are moves to strengthen democratic controls over state administration to increase its accountability to democratically elected bodies; efforts are under way which aim at the deconcentration and decentralization of the bureaucratic apparatus; the need to bring public institutions strictly under the rule of law and to guarantee the legality of public acts is stressed; and it is universally accepted that public efficiency, effectiveness and flexibility must be increased. All this implies that the organization of governance is subject to the same pressures for change which have already led to radical political reforms, which transformed the economy profoundly and, partly by extension, revolutionized the fabric of society.

The events unfolding since the late 1980s have led not only to processes conventionally described as transforming former command-like political systems into democratically accountable statehoods, but also to a growing recognition that the conventional and convenient perception of 'Europe' as 'Western Europe' is no longer applicable to the realities of the continent. Whereas the political process has reacted with various assistance programmes and a drive at enlarging the European Union to incorporate the fledgling democracies of Central and Eastern Europe, academic reactions have been characteristically slow. Comparative research on public sector reform is still dominated by Western European 'cases'; journals continue to focus on 'Western Europe', failing to notice the profound changes experienced since 1989; and the analytical and empirical approaches employed are often more striking in their benign neglect of the Central and Eastern European environment than they are convincing in trying to catch up with the developments of the last decade. This is not to deny that there have been attempts at improving the situation by adding a Central and Eastern European dimension to the agenda of comparative research, but there are very few publications indeed that indicate more of a challenge than just adding two or three countries to the number of empirical units under observation anyhow. This way, Central and Eastern Europe threatens to remain the 'odd man out' instead of being perceived as a 'member of the European family' – contrary to the historical experiences and the numerous political declarations during the early stages of the transformation process.

As regards the present state of public sector reform in Central and Eastern Europe, two observations stand out: the scarcity of reliable information on the various attempts at reform within the Central and Eastern European context; and the paucity of appropriate analytical approaches that are capable of catching at least the most crucial characteristics of the still ongoing processes of democratization and marketization. Although various attempts have been brought forward both within the practical world of government and administration and within the main academic disciplines covering the public sector, it is the absence of informed analyses and the dominance of those concentrating on the transfer of 'Western' know-how that increase the danger of losing touch with the realities of public sector reform. It is, furthermore, not only sheer prudence which suggests greater analytical and empirical efforts in this field, but also the opportunity that this might mean for an almost stagnant Western debate itself. The more the public sectors in the industrialized countries of the 'West' are under critical observation themselves, the more it dawns that the experiences observed in Central and Eastern Europe could potentially form a framework of analysis that might serve as a source of inspiration. Given the often circular debates today, this might be a very welcome innovation.

This chapter tries to pave the way towards such an analysis of public sector reform in comparative perspective. It will try to compare reform attempts in the OECD world with what is to be observed in Central and Eastern Europe; it puts emphasis on the striking mismatch of 'soft theory' and 'hard cases'; and it aims at the identification of crucial issues that might be different to those identified within 'mainstream analysis'. As externally induced change has to be complemented with policies of internal adjustment, there might be different options for reform in Eastern Europe than observed in the countries of the West. It is hoped that the categories put forward and the empirical evidence provided will contribute to a broader understanding of public sector reform, thus benefiting a debate that so far seems to feed its participants but threatens to lose touch with basic normative and functional demands.

A disclaimer is, however, appropriate. If the chapter refers to the countries of Central and Eastern Europe, it tries to generalize but is mostly based on the experiences observed in the Visegrad countries (Poland, the Czech Republic, Slovakia and Hungary), and in some cases the so-called SIGMA-countries as well. It furthermore refrains from the temptation to provide more than a few sector-specific data. Although the statistical bases for sector-specific analyses have improved dramatically over the last two years, the material provided so far is still no more than just basically 'comparable', thus short of evidence that would allow for a truly comparative analysis.

Models to emulate in public sector reform in the OECD world: pressures towards global convergence?

Following the unheavals of 1989, the necessity to reform their public sectors led the countries of Central and Eastern Europe quite naturally to look to the West for inspiration. However, one would be mistaken in assuming that Western advice was valued only for the democratic accountability and economic success of Western systems. To be seen to adhere to the recommendations of Western experts quickly became politically expedient in as much as it promised to open up new sources of financial assistance and co-operation, or access to other tangible benefits. Today, the legal, institutional and administrative approximation, which is thought a necessary precondition for EU membership, serves as a further argument to adopt Western practices. The question remains, however, what exactly it is that needs to be copied, given that the public sector is under critical review world-wide. Is it wise to assume that we witness pressures towards global convergence?

It may in this context be helpful to summarize the developments in Western environments by looking at the most recent synopsis provided, for example, by the Organization for Economic Cooperation and Development (OECD). In one of its latest reports (*Governance in Transition*, 1995), one clearly detects a preoccupation with issues of public management. It is said that the role of government is evolving in OECD countries in response to fundamental changes in economies and societies. In adjusting to these new demands and conditions, governments of OECD member countries are reviewing and reforming their systems of management. They are reconsidering how governing relates to citizens and enterprises, how best to ensure the provision of public services and how to define the inherent functions that governments must perform. In short, they are deeply concerned with maintaining the capacity to govern in the face of great change.

Although the report acknowledges that pressures for reform, national cultures and stages of development differ widely, it concludes that OECD countries have increasingly come to pursue a common reform agenda driven by the need for fiscal consolidation, by the globalization of the economy and by the impossibility of meeting an apparently infinite set of demands on public resources. The dynamic changes in strategies of governance are, therefore, to be looked at, not least to offer countries an opportunity to compare their own ideas and progress with those of others.

Examining this approach further, one quickly realizes that it follows a kind of overarching 'ideology', according to which unchanged governance structures and classical responses of 'more of the same' are inappropriate for today's policy environment. The challenge is, therefore, one of institutional renewal. Setting an appropriate framework for both public and private sector activity under conditions of increasing global interdependence, uncertainty and accelerating change seems to be the major challenge. That requires a reappraisal of the rationale for government intervention and a re-examination of the cost-effectiveness of public sector institutions, their programmes and regulatory activities. Governance must, the report stresses, strive to do things better, with fewer resources, and above all differently.

> Outdated institutions and practices need to be redesigned or replaced with ones that better match the realities and demands of dynamic market economies with the objectives and responsibilities of democratic systems. If the public sector is to remain responsive to the needs of those it serves, governance must foster the development of organisations that perpetually adapt and reshape themselves to reach changing client needs, and that develop new ways to cope with a changing world. (OECD, 1995: 7)

The programmes outlined in such proposals concentrate on various policies to reform management and to set priorities for further action, culminating in different functions of government such as policy-making, securing performance, enhancing strategic capacity, enabling output and reforming the internal and external environment.

In this process, it becomes quite clear that the favoured approach is dominated by an Anglo-Saxon perception of what the public sector is all about. Under headings such as 'Administrative reform revisited', 'The new public management', 'Towards a new civil service' or just 'Renewing the public sector', we seem to observe the emergence of a new global paradigm, at least an almost ubiquitous attempt at reforming public administration. But what precisely is meant by claims of a 'global paradigm' often remains dark. Do we indeed witness a 'radical departure' from previous routines? Does a close analysis of both the concepts and the empirical evidence of 'New Public Management' sustain the perception of historical inevitability and global convergence? To avoid riding just another issue cycle, a careful look at what is happening might be appropriate instead, shedding light on the variety of reforms pursued, their different components, national characteristics and preconditions. Whether there are, in comparative perspective, leaders and laggards very much depends on the definition of the perceived ills and the proposed remedies, varying across state traditions, administrative cultures and bureaucratic routines.

In doing so, it is certainly true that in most of the 'developed' nation states the number of convergent pressures on the public sector seem to lead to a rethinking of its place, role and ultimate objectives, as governments nearly everywhere seek to adjust the balance between state, market and society. The broad, often interconnected pressures that are to be discerned entail a number of rather different developments and issues (Hesse et al., 1996): the ideological prejudices against the state, against budgetary expansionism, big government and universalistic solutions; the economic and financial pressures caused by stagnant revenues and fiscal resistance, leading to policies of resource squeeze and cutback management; the internationalization of the economy and especially of industrial and financial markets, which is creating immense problems of international or better transnational cross-border cooperation and regulation; the growing impact of regional integration processes on domestic policies, administrative arrangements and the routines of national policy-making and implementation; the technological challenges resulting especially from the increasingly intimate marriage of telecommunications and electronics; the rapidly changing political environment, where a questioning of the established routines of representative government is taking place and traditional administrative structures disintegrate under the impact of territorial, ethnic-cultural and social challenges; the changing policy agendas in many countries with, for instance, the increasing political salience of new issues and problems, which often cut across traditional administrative boundaries; and, last but not least, the democratic pressures with their many and often conflicting demands for more and better services, for smaller, more personalized and more open and transparent administrations, for greater accountability and for a more representative bureaucracy.

The various reactions to these pressures led to first attempts at empirical generalization and interpretation from the late 1980s onwards. Whereas some stressed that reform policies predominantly aimed at overhauling administrative systems and rejuvenating public organizations, being prompted largely by a world-wide decline in public finances and the need to get more for less (Caiden, 1988) – which meant cutting back, reducing expenditure, staff, investment and services, and demanding higher productivity and better performance from the sluggish public sectors – others went much further. Looking predominantly at Britain, Australia and New

Zealand, they, too, referred to the need to respond to the fiscal stress brought about by changes in the international economic system and by the unrelenting demands for government services and regulations in national political systems, but added a kind of context analysis (Aucoin, 1990). Public choice theories (that appeared to offer an explanation for the crisis in representative government in the context of the modern administrative state) were here contrasted with 'managerialism', emanating from sources external to public management *per se*, especially the literature on private sector and business administration. The assumptions underlying this paradigm stress that the capacities of modern complex organizations to realize their objectives can be enhanced by management structures and practices which debureaucratize organizational systems. In doing so, bloated bureaucracies can be trimmed of fat and become economical in their use of organizational resources; productivity can be improved by doing things more creatively and thus more efficiently; and effectiveness can be achieved by paying closer attention to the organization's mission, its personnel and its customers/clients. These approaches and similar attempts paying tribute to the challenges facing public administration, not least popularized by Osborne and Gaebler (1992), have attracted significant interest over the last years, representing a critique of 'bureaucracy' as a mode of organizational design and management. It was (and is) based on the belief that public sector management is superior to public sector activity, denoting a concern for the use of resources to achieve results in contrast to the presumed focus on 'administration' as the adherence to formalized processes and procedures.

But even the proponents of these approaches soon realized that the available empirical evidence calls for more systematic and disaggregated analysis of public sector reform. They stress that the principles of governance and management that are linked to the reassertion of the political dimension of representative government and the simultaneous ascendancy of the managerialistic school of thought (centralization, coordination and control, on the one hand, and decentralization, deregulation and delegation on the other) lead to a number of obvious paradoxes which, in turn, refer to obvious cross-pressures in public management. The pendulum may, therefore, be swinging in different directions between centralization–decentralization, coordination–deregulation and control–delegation. The corresponding policies very much depend upon national characteristics and pressures, but can be located somewhere between these poles.

Mainstream analysis: soft theory and hard cases

Given that the complexity of public sector reform experience defies simple categorizations, it does not come as a surprise that some of the more recent literature has begun to suggest a further differentiation of patterns of change. Whereas some have stressed the impact of state traditions on policies such as privatization and deregulation, personnel management, customer orientation, empowerment and deconcentration, others have discussed the influence of economic performance records, government size or party political incumbency, or aimed at advancing the analysis by distinguishing between stages of development and the political, legal and economic legacies (and opportunities) going along with that. Such attempts at refinement need further work and are to be complemented by other basic distinctions that call the claim of global paradigm shift into question.

In evaluating the attempts at analysis so far, we witness a number of detailed descriptions of reforms under way, whereas much less effort has been expanded on the systematic (rather than impressionistic) explanation of the similarities and differences that are found among those examples. There are usually a number of implicit generalizations about the rules of change, but these ideas have rarely been elaborated and examined. Relatively few governments have actually engaged in the systematic evaluation of their own reforms. It might, therefore, be necessary to look beneath the occurrences of events to examine the political dynamics that undergird them. To do so might help to overcome the weaknesses of mainstream analyses that have been summarized as 'soft theory and hard cases' (Hesse et al., 1996).

At the most general level of explanation, four 'i's' are used almost as a litany when attempting to explain social and political phenomena: ideas, interests, institutions and processes of internationalization. These categories are somewhat vague and general and, while probably collectively exhaustive, they are rarely mutually exclusive. In case of explaining public sector reforms, for example, ideas are being spread through international organizations, and many institutions within the public sector also have a collective interest in producing certain types of change. Further so-called explanations can merely be truisms or clichés, with no real variation in their independent variables that could explain change. It might, therefore, be necessary to ensure that there is some real variance in the independent and dependent variables. A careful selection of critical cases might be a useful strategy to secure that.

Another possible way of looking at the causes of reform activity and of examining the relative success of reforms is to distinguish between exogenous and endogenous sources of change. That is, some attempts at change appear to arise outside government and outside the administrative structure, while others come from within the public sector itself. One working hypothesis could be that those arising within the public sector, and therefore being 'owned' by the occupants of the organizations in question, are more likely to be successful than those imposed from the outside.

The prevalence of public sector reform efforts in the 1980s and into the 1990s has led to the argument that there is a *Zeitgeist* that contributes to the diffusion of reform ideas. Again, to investigate such an assumption one would want to find the most difficult case for investigation to determine the extent to which diffusion is occurring. One would, therefore, want to look at cases that are most culturally distinctive and/or cases which have a stronger commitment to governmental solutions as regards social problems, this way being less likely to accept the anti-governmental bias motivating some of the contemporary reforms elsewhere.

If one goes beyond general explanations for administrative change and public sector reform, one could identify at least six more specific explanations warranting greater elaboration and 'testing'. Most of these concepts would need to be elaborated within different national contexts and a careful selection made of those to provide the most suitable challenges to the given theoretical assumptions. The concepts are: the *stages of development* a country is in; *cultural perspectives and traditions; institutional variables*; the given *resource base*; the degree of *reform professionalization*; and *policy entrepreneurship and political will* (see Hesse et al., 1996: 13ff). Such a systematic examination of the roots of public sector reform seems indeed to be needed, as the multi-causal world of government asks for complex theoretical and analytical considerations. Without these, the literature on public sector reform will stay to be biased towards descriptive analyses of 'hard cases'.

There are, therefore, a number of obvious paradoxes encountered in pursuing public sector reforms within the OECD world and beyond, which ask for sustained and broadened, yet at the same time more focused, research. Why is it, we ought to ask, that some countries engage in far-reaching if not radical reforms of their public sectors whilst others do not react at all or adopt policies of incremental change in an attempt to continuously adapt towards an ever changing environment? What could explain that even within comparable groups of countries or 'families of states' we are able to detect patterns of both convergence and divergence; and why do countries with much less similar system characteristics engage in often comparable policies? Do 'regional regimes' play a role in this respect; do we witness an internationalization of reform attempts and an 'export' of expertise going along with that; does 'conventional wisdom' play a role by now, as innovations seem to travel fast? But given that they do, why are there such significant differences in the reactions of, for example, the Anglo-Saxon countries and the member states of the European Union, or between the major liberal democracies of the West, the reborn nation states of Central and Eastern Europe, and the economically driven innovators of South East Asia? To try to answer these questions, our research agenda has to be extended quite considerably. It needs not only a close look at the possible roots of reform in various environments, but also a solid analysis of different reform approaches and outcomes, their intended and unintended effects. Contemporary research does not offer much in this respect so far. It either refers to broad 'issue cycles' that oscillate between a 'permanent revolution' and policies of continuous adaptation, or presents specific case studies that have their merits in making us aware of the policies pursued but do not help in answering the questions raised above. Comparative research asks for more.

A tale told differently: the Central and Eastern European experience

If it is indeed accepted that there is no global paradigm shift to be identified even amongst Western countries, the individuality of reform needs and the possible responses to be observed in the countries of Central and Eastern Europe require further analysis. To merely recommend the introduction of management practices will hardly do justice to the extraordinary historical opportunity, the variety of pressing needs and the diversity of country-specific preconditions.

The limited value of a blanket transfer of 'Western' models to Central and Eastern European countries is particularly obvious if one considers that reforms initially had to overcome understandable but still damaging anti-state attitudes by stressing the positive contribution of a modernized public sector to a functioning market economy. In such a context, the need for an inclusive approach at reform is acknowledged. This means that tasks, organizational structures, administrative procedures and issues of personnel are not to be considered in isolation. It also implies that horizontal and, in particular, vertical linkages and interdependencies between different levels of government are taken into account. In doing so, it becomes obvious that the contextual conditions under which the Central and Eastern European public sector operates are subject to a degree of change which has made larger-scale adjustments inevitable. Public administration systems have on occasion proven capable of absorbing – or at least of cushioning the impact of – 'external shocks'. Yet, transformation processes in Central and Eastern Europe are as unprecedented as they are comprehensive in nature, and can therefore not be answered by adaptive modifications alone. Here, the public sector is simultaneously the target and agent of reform, thus more fundamental approaches are required. As reform efforts aim at introducing stability, dependability and continuity into the administrative system, they must, at the same time, not hamper later revisions and modifications, which are bound to be required as the environment continues to be transformed. Thus, stability needs to be combined with flexibility, dependability with openness, continuity with adaptability. Under such conditions, one needs to be careful in prescribing specific institutional, procedural or personnel arrangements, let alone an elaborate public management approach.

Despite the apparent complexity of public sector reform needs, it might nonetheless be possible (and indeed helpful in structuring the debate) to identify some common trends or stages of development that are to be distinguished in the Central and Eastern European reform process. Four phases may be discerned.

During the initial phase of *transformation* the old legal, political, social and economic orders irrevocably broke down and new structures began to be formed. Characteristics of this transformation phase include: the emergence of multi-party systems; regular elections at the national, regional and local levels; the overhaul of public sector institutions, in some cases amounting to an attempt at recreating the entire governmental machinery;

the formulation and partial implementation of what often were radical economic reform programmes; as well as thorough and in some cases heated constitutional debates. As all-encompassing as the developments appeared, the results were varied and often fragmentary. Volatile voting patterns, unstable coalitions and unresolved power struggles between different governmental institutions were as common as constitutional debates were inconclusive, privatization programmes incomplete and institutional arrangements and rearrangements short-lived.

The initial transformation phase was followed slowly by what one could call a process of *consolidation*, during which increased political stability allowed for a more systematic approach to de-étatization, privatization and marketization. Whilst the demarcation between the executive and the legislative as well as that between the political and administrative spheres remained somewhat fuzzy, and whilst constitutional issues remained unresolved, the programmes of economic transformation began to show first encouraging results. Less erratic voting behaviour supported the expectation of continuity, which proves to be necessary to stimulate and sustain private sector investment, and that also turns out to be conducive to a more rational approach at evaluating and reforming the public sector. As 'big bang' approaches lost their appeal, designing and implementing crucial and more specific policies became the staple rule of the game.

The said stability in turn allowed for at least a medium-term approach, instead of *ad hoc* measures, which – combined with enhanced problem awareness – led to the third phase of *modernization*. The need to overhaul institutional arrangements and to look out for 'best practice', not least triggered by the need to secure various policies, characterized this stage. Unresolved problems and newly emerging deficiencies suggested, finally, a redefinition of the public sector, its extent, role and institutional make-up. It became increasingly clear that marketization and privatization would in the long run only produce the hoped-for results if based on a comprehensive and binding legal framework accompanied by the necessary safety provisions, checks and balances, and if supported, regulated and controlled by an efficient and reliable public sector. Yet, the reorganization of the machinery of central government as well as both the functional and the territorial demarcation of competencies proved notoriously difficult undertakings. Added to this was a widespread problem of discontinuity in personnel, resulting on the one hand from the increased attractiveness of private sector employment, and on the other from the practice of incoming governments of replacing large fractions of the administrative leadership. In some cases, the mentioned unresolved constitutional issues continued to hamper the modernization process.

A fourth and partly overlapping phase to be distinguished in the process of reforming the public sector is that of *adaptation* towards the state of the art of public sector performance, as observed in Western environments, as well as towards the pressures brought about by the preparation for European Union membership. Ten Eastern European countries have deposited their applications for membership at the Commission and have already ratified association agreements. The remainder are also working towards membership. The administrative capacities as well as the regulatory instruments (legal approximation) needed in order to fulfil the *acquis communautaire* will require enormous legislative, institutional and procedural adjustments to be made by the applicant countries. Given that the extent to which these preparations have been completed will be one of the determining factors in the European Union's decision on the opening of formal negotiations – expected after the conclusion of the Intergovernmental Conference – this adaptation process has been given high priority in the countries concerned.

In distinguishing these phases or stages of transformation, consolidation, modernization and adaptation, one has, of course, to be aware of their contingency when applied to such widely different countries. The succession of these phases should, furthermore, not be taken to suggest a 'logic', a time continuum, let alone a uniform experience. Neither should different stages be distinguished merely depending on the respective developmental process. In each case they represent the outcome of different settings such as specific legacies, state traditions or indeed different administrative cultures. Instead, they may serve as broad categories wherein all countries of Central and Eastern Europe can be located. If the most advanced have gone through this typical development process, the four phases might help to identify a kind of state of the art as far as the reform and its constituent parts are concerned. This should not, however, be confused with convergence of the administrative systems of Central and Eastern Europe, let alone with global convergence. Nonetheless, there are a number of important similarities in the external and internal challenges facing public administration in Central and Eastern Europe which warrant a closer examination of the contextual conditions of public sector reform.

Rebuilding the boat in the open sea: framework conditions revisited

Using Jon Elster's (1993) eye-opening metaphor for describing the difficulties faced by legislators in Central and Eastern Europe sheds light not only on the crucial importance of contextual difficulties when engaging in an analysis of public sector reform, but also on the empirical and analytical challenges brought about by developing a public sector within an environment that itself is in flux. It is therefore, rather obvious that the dynamics of public sector reform in the post-communist countries of Central and Eastern Europe cannot be fully understood in terms of adaptation and/or adjustment to a changing environment. Concentrating on contextual developments and their impact on the public sector, it should first be remembered that the initial period of political and economic transition was, unsurprisingly, characterized by a great deal of instability, volatility and changeability in contextual conditions. Key elements of the framework in which public administration had to operate were subject to abrupt change, whose direction was frequently unpredictable. As a result, the formulation and implementation of realistic adaptation strategies proved extraordinarily difficult, if not impossible. Public sector reform was, accordingly, guided less by an assessment of the new requirements associated with political and economic change than by the intention to overcome the legacy of socialism. Put differently, transformation provided the prevailing reform pattern because the turbulence of political and economic developments impeded a performance-oriented analysis of tasks, structures, procedures and personnel.

There are, however, signs of increasing consolidation in contextual conditions. In the political sphere, the process of institutionalizing a framework of democratic governance has been more or less concluded, and the main outlines of the future political order have become increasingly apparent. The unpredictability and uncertainty of political life which characterized the transition years are gradually declining, as more settled patterns of political behaviour evolve. As regards economic reconstruction, it is, of course, still far from being completed; the transition from socialist planning to market-based economies through privatization, liberalization and marketization has proved a much more complex and drawn-out process than many had originally predicted. Moreover, the disruptive effects of this process, in terms of falling production, rising inflation, mushrooming unemployment or declining living standards, were much more severe than the proponents of reform were initially ready to admit. However, whilst economic policy faces still significant problems, the basic structural foundations of the different national economies have begun to emerge quite clearly. Generic declarations in favour of creating market-based economies are, therefore, increasingly replaced by more differentiated policies. This concerns, for example, the role of publicly owned enterprises; the mix between small, medium and large firms; or the sectoral composition of the economy.

For the development of the public sector at large, the stabilization of important variables of political and economic reform implies an increased degree of dependability and predictability. As the context of and for the public sector begins to settle, political expectations and functional demands in the medium and long term become more apparent. Consequently, there is a more realistic chance for a positive, purposive reform, which goes much beyond the rejection of the inheritance of 'democratic centralism'.

Looking at the different environments of the public sector in some detail, the break with the communist past has been most obvious and most far-reaching in the *political-institutional* framework. Since autumn 1989, a largely competitive multi-party system has evolved, and a number of elections have been held for the presidency, the chambers of national parliaments, and regional and local governments. As a result, there has been a far-reaching change of personnel in the major positions of executive leadership. However, whilst the old order has been broken, the new political framework is, despite the positive signs mentioned, still evolving in some

some cases. The party system, for example, often remains fragmented. The formation of a government enjoying a workable parliamentary majority or at least tacit support has sometimes proved difficult. Perhaps even more importantly, the popularly elected presidents on the one hand, and the national assemblies on the other, appear occasionally in fundamental disagreement about their respective roles, resulting in a situation of political deadlock and potential paralysis of the policy-making system. The according instability in government and executive leadership has for some time been accompanied by a lack of clear policy orientation. Even where clear-cut government policies had time to develop, support in parliament was often difficult to obtain. In the event of a ruling coalition not commanding a reliable majority, for example, the withholding of parliamentary approval for key government proposals is almost commonplace.

The picture that emerges, then, is still one of transition and volatility: the old political framework has irrevocably broken down, but the new framework has yet to be consolidated. In particular, key aspects of the triangular relationship between president, government and parliament remain contentious. It is unlikely that this will change until their respective powers and privileges are authoritatively redefined in new constitutional agreements. However, a decisive breakthrough in the constitutional debate has not yet been achieved. Contrary to the high hopes in 1989 when many expected a swift new constitutional settlement, the preparation and adoption of completely new constitutions have not yet progressed significantly. As time has passed, the process of constitutionalization has, perhaps inevitably, become more and more subject to the same political pressures affecting other areas of reform. No longer is there a common spirit of opposition against a hostile regime which could hold the contending forces together.

It cannot be denied that the failure to resolve fundamental constitutional questions introduced a critical element of fluidity into the reform process at large. However, it should also be recognized that 'for countries undergoing rapid social and economic change, commitment to standing rules may not be desirable. The future of many Eastern European countries may prove to be a succession of emergencies, in which constitutional self-finding might be disastrous' (Elster, 1993). It would, therefore, make more sense to talk of an open rather than an unstable constitutional situation at the present time. Yet, as Elster also notes, the potentially tragic element is that the future without a constitution to regulate expectations and behaviour might be equally bleak.

Moving on to *economic transformation*, it is worth noting that even under communist rule, the economies were peppered with some elements of a market-based system. Yet, this does not imply that for the introduction of a market economy an evolutionary approach could have been sufficient. Rejecting gradualism and a piecemeal approach, most governments embarked, often under the guidance of the IMF, on a radical economic reform programme, whose key elements included stabilization, liberalization, the creation of market institutions and privatization. With some distinct modifications, these programmes still provide the basis for ongoing reform policies.

In the early 1990s, Poland and what was at that stage still Czechoslovakia opted for macroeconomic stabilization based on restrictive monetary and fiscal policies, whilst Hungary sought to maintain purchasing power by following a liberal wage policy in order to avoid a dramatic decline in total demand. Concerning prices as well as the opening of the economy to imports, Poland and Czechoslovakia took swift liberalization measures: nearly 90% of all prices were liberalized by early 1990 in the former, and by January 1991 in the latter. Although the Hungarian government also aimed to free 90% of its prices, the implementation of a respective 1991 decision was to be spread over a longer period. Import liberalization – as a crucial step towards currency convertibility – was beginning to be introduced in Hungary even before the political turnover of 1989. Within three years, the liberalization of 80% of imports was achieved. That meant that not all industrial sectors were exposed to world market conditions at once, as was the case in Czechoslovakia and Poland. Here, convertibility and the lifting of import restrictions had to be accomplished almost overnight.

Since 1989, privatization has been regarded as a key element in the reform process in Central and Eastern Europe. High expectations were associated with privatization over and above the aim of converting a planned into a market economy: there were hopes for an increase of state revenues from privatization proceeds (and later through tax receipts), for a reduction of the inflationary effect of assistance programmes and for a positive impact on the efficiency of enterprises, to name but a few (Engerer, 1996: 15). Given that privatization often involved fictitious values placed on company assets, the success of privatization programmes is difficult to measure. The most commonly used indicator is the proportion of state enterprises privatized since the start of the reform process. Measured as such, nearly 90% of Czech state enterprises have been privatized already. The Hungarian government is still planning to have nearly 80% of formerly state-owned enterprises privatized before the end of 1997.

The countries discussed here vary not only in their progress towards privatization, but also in the method chosen to convert state enterprises into private property. The main objective of the Czechoslovakian privatization policy was to speed up the process whilst at the same time keeping tight control over the actual transfer of ownership (Hoen, 1996: 12). To this end, a Ministry of Privatization was put in charge of reviewing every single application of prospective investors. In a second step, private capital was to be raised by involving citizens in large-scale 'voucher schemes'. Vouchers entitle the public to buy equity in state-owned companies ranging from heavy industry to breweries. Investment funds invest the capital thus raised on behalf of ordinary people, with the vouchers ultimately being converted into tradable shares on the stock markets. The great number of investment funds set up and administered by private banks has, however, made the process difficult to control.

Although Poland followed the voucher policy of Czechoslovakia, a number of other privatization methods are being used simultaneously. Whereas 'small privatization' of small and medium enterprises was reasonably successful and could gain broad public support, 'big privatization' is still subject to political conflicts. Here, a distinction has to be drawn between the privatization of whole branches of industry and the so-called *Mass Privatization Programme* (MPP). Both modes are directed towards privatization of unprofitable industrial giants. Given the great variety of privatization methods, Poland can still be regarded as lacking a consistent implementation policy in this area of reform.

Not least owing to decentralization efforts in the 1980s, privatization in Hungary started as 'spontaneous privatization' at the local level, where enterprises themselves tried to bring in investors. The Antall government, which was in favour of 'gentle' privatization, sought to regain control by centralization and the establishment of a privatization agency. The Horn government then increased transparency in privatization by defining three categories of enterprises. The first group includes strategic companies such as energy, transport, telecommunications and selected banks. The second group is composed of small and medium enterprises with less than 500 employees, whilst the third category comprises the remainder. Privatization of the first group is still problematic, although foreign investment in these sectors was particularly marked in 1995. Foreign investors now control nearly 50% of enterprises in energy and gas, for example. Yet these two sectors form the exception, with almost 70% of the group as a whole remaining in public ownership. Attracting private investors is made more difficult by the fact that the government has to give its consent to each privatization project and may decide to retain a certain proportion of the company's equity.

Some caution should be applied to over-optimistic assessments of privatization efforts in the countries under consideration here. A large part of the companies sold are said to be technically bankrupt while others are on the brink of bankruptcy. The Czech and Polish governments have not enforced tough bankruptcy laws yet. Many companies are still inefficient and will probably need to undertake serious restructuring. Often strategic investors have to be encouraged to take on managerial responsibility and to inject desperately needed capital for modernization. Another crucial issue is, therefore, the establishment of market institutions such as an effective banking sector and proper institutional guidelines; the recent collapse of Czech banks serves as a powerful reminder. It can also be said that in all former socialist countries privatization appears to have slowed and public sentiment has grown sceptical towards further privatization: either privatization becomes subject to political conflicts within governmental coalitions, as was recently the case in Poland, or privatization agencies face growing public distrust following allegations of corruption, as has beset the Hungarian privatization programme. Whether political instability will negatively influence further efforts remains an open question.

In macroeconomic terms, privatization, marketization and deregulation policies had some impact on the main economic performance indicators, although the available statistical data should still be treated with caution. In many cases the figures not only tentatively suggest that economic collapse has been halted, but also reveal growth rates which have led economic activity to recover to its 1989 levels. Poland and the Czech Republic are undoubtedly leading the group of former socialist countries in this respect, with 1995 GDP growth rates of 7% and 5% respectively. This represents a breakthrough particularly for Poland, which had suffered a near collapse of industrial activity.

Since 1992, the rate of unemployment in the Visegrad countries had been declining steadily (with the exception of Poland which had to transform the most labour-intensive public sector), though it cannot be ruled out that it will rise again in the wake of necessary structural adjustment policies. As regards the employment situation, the Czech Republic is usually referred to as the most successful, with an official unemployment rate of a mere 2.9% of the active population in 1995. By contrast, unemployment stands at 10% in Hungary and around 15% in Poland. It has to be added that regional variations in economic performance have produced unemployment rates much higher in rural than in urban areas.

Perhaps the most significant progress has so far been made with regard to inflation. Though most of the annual rates are still in double figures, they seem to be falling steadily. This is the case even in Poland, where the 1995 inflation rate of 27.8%, though high by any standards, represented a marked improvement on the 1994 rate of 43%. There are several countries with similar experiences, where inflation has been more than halved over the last five years. However, as the figures indicate, inflation continues to present one of the most serious problems to the countries concerned. Further measures to reduce inflation have, therefore, to be taken in order to reach the ambitious economic targets set by each government for the upcoming years.

A different picture emerges with regard to foreign direct investment (FDI). Here, Central and Eastern European countries appear tremendously successful. 'Group 1' countries – a World Bank classification which includes primarily but not only the Visegrad countries – were able to attract $22 billion in FDI since 1989. More specifically, the World Bank points out that they were those countries pursuing the most transparent reform strategies that were able to bring in the largest share of foreign investment. This applies in particular to Hungary, absorbing almost 50% of all foreign investment into Central Europe since the beginning of the reform process, with $10.5 billion invested in 1995 alone. To attract still further foreign investment will be problematic. In the Czech Republic and Hungary, FDI may actually fall in the short run, given that the inflows into those two countries (1995: $2.6 billion and $4.6 billion, respectively) were artificially expanded by unique sell-offs to foreigners (telecommunications in the Czech Republic, utilities in Hungary). These were one-off transactions that will not be repeated, since neither country has further 'crown jewels' left for privatization.

Budget deficits are still modest in all countries discussed here, though only some were able to close with budget surpluses of between 1% and 3% in 1995. In Poland, by contrast, budget deficits have been necessary ever since 1989 in order to finance privatization programmes as well as cushioning the social impact of economic transformation. However, spending on social security in the countries of Central and Eastern Europe has led to levels of government expenditure (on average 50% or more of GDP) that are higher even than in many OECD countries. To finance these outlays, high taxation is required which in turn could hamper investment in the longer run.

Foreign debt has been reduced, but Central and Eastern European countries remain significant borrowers on the international money markets; this still justifies the stringent conditions imposed by the International Monetary Fund (IMF). Hungary has improved its position significantly in this respect, having serviced a large proportion of its liabilities. This has been made possible not least by the country's successes in terms of privatization and foreign direct investment as described above. Yet, if compared with the Czech Republic, the absolute level of Hungarian foreign debt remains considerable, standing at $17 billion in 1995 as against the $4.5 billion accrued by the Czech Republic, though the latter has risen since.

The positive overall outlook suggested by macroeconomic indicators should not lead to an underestimation of the tasks ahead. In this context, short-term success has to be distinguished from long-term prospects. The new market economies show impressive growth rates, significant improvements concerning inflation, and increases in direct investments after only a short period of reform. Yet, the low base level of all these indicators after 1989 may lead to an overestimation of the success since then; the sustainability of recovery may thus be in doubt. Above all, the challenge of structural change cannot be ignored given the still large and labour-intensive agricultural sectors; and the obstacles to EU membership are exemplified by the fact that none of the countries under consideration can equal the GDP per capita of the poorest member state of the European Union.

The last contextual category to be mentioned here refers to processes of *societal* disclosure. Whilst economic change is on its way, some of its negative repercussions have become increasingly obvious and visible. These include not only unemployment, a temporary fall in living standards and increasing absolute poverty, but also the emergence of new types of broader-scale and longer-lasting social disparities. At the same time, the quite comprehensive social safety and benefit provisions, which used to take care of basic life necessities, are under threat. The squeeze on public resources has led to attempts at cutting back social expenditure; social benefits in the public sector are disappearing as many enterprises are transferred to private ownership; other provisions are considered incompatible with the market economy. In short, there is the danger that the safety network will disintegrate at the moment when it is most needed. As a consequence, individuals are faced with the task of adjusting to an environment which is changing rapidly and fundamentally. Moreover, the profound qualitative changes in the triangular relationship between the state, society and the individual are certainly not yet concluded. What we may witness in future is a re-emergence of a civil society, associated with processes of de-étatization, the depoliticization of social and private life, and the redefinition and expansion of the private against the social and political.

In sum, it is obvious that the contextual conditions under which the public sector operates are subject to a degree of change which has made large-scale adjustments inevitable. Although bureaucratic organizations are, of course, capable of absorbing considerable external shocks without having to resort to fundamental institutional reforms, the unprecedented character of the Central and Eastern European transformation processes calls into question some of the most basic principles of statehood. The public sector is, therefore, under tremendous pressure to adapt. Secondly, however, adjustment is still made difficult by the lasting volatility of the contextual conditions. The elements of the framework in which the public sector operates turn out to be rather unpredictable. Dependable information is scarce, and effective implementation strategies are, therefore, hardly to be formulated. Under these conditions, political priorities and preferences can alter very quickly. Moreover, reform attempts require an increasingly high degree of horizontal and vertical coordination. However, firm decisions on the future allocation of powers, responsibilities and finances between the different levels of government have only been partially attained. In short, public sector reform is urgent and under way, but it can often be no more than tentative and provisional as long as crucial external parameters remain undetermined.

Crucial issues of institutional stability, economic performance and social guarantees: a vicious or a virtuous circle?

Putting it this way, the transition from socialist one-party rule to democratic pluralism has a number of immediate consequences for the structures and procedures of the public sector. As regards organizational questions, the implications of a break with the principle of 'democratic centralism' deserve particular attention. 'Democratic centralism' had at least two dimensions: vertically, much emphasis was placed on a hierarchical administrative structure in which lower-tier units enjoyed limited discretion and were subject to comprehensive control by central institutions, whereas the horizontal organization of state power was characterized by a lack of an effective separation of powers. There were, of course, separate legislative, executive and judicial institutions. The rule-making powers of the executive were, however, extremely extensive, so that, in effect, legislative and executive functions were merged. The institutional consequences of the renunciation of the principle of 'democratic centralism' are, therefore, far-reaching. They include the obvious need not only to separate party bureaucracy from public administration, but also to establish clear institutional boundaries between legislative and executive institutions and to combine this with new forms of democratic accountability; to lessen control of sub-central administrative units and to create a sphere of local government; and to provide effective legal controls over administrative activities.

Therefore, if the implications of democratization point to the need for structural and procedural reforms, the processes of privatization and marketization focus attention on adjustments in public tasks and the modes of public action. Public administration is losing some of its former tasks as the state is partly withdrawing from the economy by means of liberalization, deregulation and privatization. At the same time, however, there is an urgent need to create or stabilize administrative capacities which can support economic transformation and development. Consequently, different tasks call for different instruments of intervention. Regulations and restrictions, as well as requirements to seek administrative permission for private actions, will remain important instruments of public activity. In addition, however, executive policy will need to rely increasingly on the provision of incentives and services, persuasion and public–private cooperation.

In the longer term, the perception of the public sector and its role in and towards society will, perhaps, be most decisively reshaped by the processes of de-étatization. The partial withdrawal of the state from civil society, and the acceptance of the domain of private life protected and, to a certain extent, immune from political interference, imply that public administration will have to assume a much less extended and far-reaching role than under the previous regimes. This means that non-public forms of service delivery will play an increasingly central role. In this context, one should not just think in terms of the replacement of the state by the market, although privatization and marketization at present dominate the political agendas. What might emerge in the longer term is a rigorous 'third sector' between state and market, comprising a wide variety of institutions of societal self-organization and self-administration. The redrawing of the boundaries between the state, the social and the private sector promises to be accompanied by a positive recognition of the potential contribution of associational self-government.

In sum, institutional stability, economic performance and socially conscious policy-making form, therefore, an inevitable circle. It aims, given the logic of democratic government, at a virtuous circle but could turn vicious if the balance is impaired. Sensible economic policies and further moves at strengthening the market forces may, for example, fail owing to the lack of legal certainty and institutional-administrative underpinning; institutional rigidity, in turn, might hamper economic performance and harm the chances of the less privileged in society. Putting social issues to the fore, without regarding the necessities of securing economic performance and allowing for institutional stability, virtually leads nowhere. Given the direction of public sector reform in Central and Eastern Europe, all three 'points of entry' into the vicious circle seem unlikely dangers, though.

However, given the dominant emphasis on economic policies, it seems very important indeed to realize that without institutional stability and guarantees for social safety, marketization and privatization might lead to an excessive and, in part, ruthless form of free market behaviour. The divisive social consequences of the latter may well undermine the still precarious political stability on which the reform process as a whole rests. It is, therefore, the virtuous circle at which the countries of Central and Eastern Europe have to aim. There is hardly an alternative. One-sided reform processes threaten to be counterproductive.

Externally induced change: learning from experience?

If the pitfalls of a mere transposition of 'Western' reform designs are to be avoided, it is only after consideration has been given to the contextual conditions, and the need to avoid one-sided reform policies has been recognized, that the analysis can turn to reform options. Given the historically oriented analysis of the reform stages that most of the Central and Eastern European countries have been through since 1989, it might now make sense to look at the different approaches pursued. Here, a distinction between externally induced change and internal adjustment seems appropriate.

Looking at externally induced change first, it is to recall that, given the sudden and unexpected change, the degree to which not only élites but also the organizational and procedural characteristics of the old systems had been discredited, and the numerous economic challenges as well as normative demands placed on a democratic future, the search for proven models should not have come as a surprise. A new and often inexperienced political leadership had hardly any other options at hand. Hence, *'big bang'* *approaches*, shock treatment and other potential options characterized the early debate. As understandable as these may appear in retrospect, given the magnitude and simultaneity of the economic, social and political challenges of systemic transformation, they proved counterproductive owing to their almost exclusive focus on economic rationality. What had gravely been ignored was the fact that economically successful Western societies do not exclusively rely on the rules of the market, but also provide stabilizing elements in the form of institutional permanence, legal dependability and social guarantees. German reunification, which some critics have depicted as a 'colonization' of the former GDR, should have provided an early warning of the consequences of too hasty an adoption of Western principles.

'Big bang' approaches, therefore, made headlines for a very brief period before being replaced by an approach perhaps most suitably described as *experimenting with public sector reform*. This characterization applied in particular to initiatives designed to adapt constitutional provisions, to democratize public institutions and to secure privatization and market reforms. Again, Central and Eastern European reformers tended to look towards Western Europe for different examples and 'models', but were at that stage not really equipped to choose the most appropriate ones concerning their own institutional and political environment. Themselves short-lived, governments often selected individual reform steps because of a certain political initiative or on the advice of foreign experts present at the right moment. A lack of coordination led to a situation characterized by a multitude of reform attempts frequently contradicting or duplicating one another. This approach is, therefore, best labelled as 'learning by doing'.

The experimenting approach – in any case limited in both time and depth – was swiftly followed, and in many cases replaced, by *supply-led approaches* at reform, induced mainly by international organizations such as the International Monetary Fund. Much less as a matter of choice than as victims of circumstance, Central and Eastern European countries were subjected to detailed programmes of economic and budgetary reforms. These certainly helped in so far as they provided the basic principles for a successful process of marketization. They were also credited with focusing formerly dispersed technical as well as financial assistance. However, as we know by now, there was and still is an enormous number of overlapping programmes as regards World Bank, IMF, EBRD, EU and other initiatives. More fundamentally, supply-led and other externally induced programmes were yet again unduly biased towards the economic rationale of the reform process and overlooked basic legal and institutional adaptations.

It then took some time for the governments of the reform countries to regain the initiative. Before moving on to a more *demand-led approach*, necessary conditions for internal adjustment had to be met. That included policies of capacity-building and institutional stabilization, which themselves were the result either of planned change from the outside or of growing awareness on the part of incoming or reformed élites that reform attempts would have to rely on the specific needs of the country. Outsiders may, of course, be able to offer advice, but will never be equipped enough to judge the full complexity of the domestic situation.

Towards internal adjustment: recognizing their own potential

Increased political stability, improved economic performance and prospects as well as the growing expertise of public sector personnel are only now beginning to combine to allow for a drive at demand-led public sector reforms. So far, such reform attempts have only been aimed at crucial bottlenecks to the reform process at large. Partly home-made, they often failed but put emphasis on a number of crucial issues that could have been identified only by domestic experts rather than being glossed over by foreign consultants. This process of 'recognizing their own potential' has gained pace. In the meantime, it is hoped that the assistance offered by international organizations and the demand raised within the recipient countries will meet in a coordinated effort to build up domestic capacities for reform.

Such an emphasis on domestic expertise does not, of course, rule out close collaboration with the partners within the EU or the World Bank. Seeking their advice and financial assistance certainly does no harm to the development of the countries under observation here; in some cases they still form the basis of the transition.

Looking at legal and institutional prerequisites, modes of public activity and human resources as examples, a number of interesting developments are to be distinguished. As regards the legal and institutional setting, functional considerations have gained ground, as issues of implementing crucial reform policies have been receiving growing attention. As mentioned before, grand reform designs were viewed with increasing suspicion; instead, policy-makers were beginning to underline the need to secure what had already been achieved, to complete the reform process, and to pursue selective corrections where initial transformation processes resulted in dysfunctional arrangements. As the idea of a complete and immediate change on virtually all levels of government was discarded, there were more and more calls for a phased approach to public sector reform. The understanding of the reform process as a one-off act was, therefore, beginning to be superseded by a conception which stressed the continuous character of institutional adjustment.

As regards *legal prerequisites*, the importance of variable implementation strategies for creating a responsive and accountable public sector and an effective system of rule of law had been dangerously underestimated during the early stages of the transformation process. In reforming constitutional law and secondary legislation, for example, the emphasis has firmly been on substantive issues; the normative content of legislative acts has been at the centre of the political and legal debates. By contrast, procedural aspects have tended to be neglected. In particular, the decisive questions of how constitutional and secondary law can be made effective, what difficulties may arise in the implementation process and how they could be minimized, have not been addressed in a systematic manner. West–East knowledge transfer was of marginal help in this respect, as the efforts focused almost exclusively on assisting legislative activity (in particular the legal adaptation to a market economy). In fact, one may well argue that law-making was for a rather long period largely dissociated from its own implementation; new legislation was often adopted although it was recognized that the pre-conditions for giving effect to these new laws were lacking and could not be created within a short period. Legislation, therefore, degenerated (and partly still degenerates) into symbolic politics. The resulting dangers should be obvious: the adoption of laws which cannot be enforced (or which legislators do not intend to see enforced) discredits not only the legislative process but also, in the longer term, the very idea of a polity based on the rule of law.

In the rare cases where implementation issues have been given explicit consideration in the reform process, it would appear that the potential for the direct application of Western experience was viewed here too optimistically as well. Western implementation research over the last two decades has undoubtedly helped to highlight the complex preconditions for giving effect to legal regulations and political decisions; to a certain extent it has also improved the capacity for designing more efficient implementation processes by identifying key actors and resources. However, the lessons drawn from Western experience seem of little immediate use in trying to improve implementation in Central and Eastern Europe. Western analyses have mostly focused on implementation in comparatively stable environments, whereas the normative frameworks in Central and Eastern Europe are, of course, still undergoing a process of dynamic change. More generally, the often still turbulent context in which implementation does (or does not) take place means that few of the basic assumptions and units of analysis with which Western researchers are used to operating can directly be applied to the Central and Eastern European situation. That is why reformers now rightly stress building up the domestic potential to implement crucial policies; it is, once again, the process of recognizing their own potential that is important in this respect.

As regards the *institutional setting*, two things stand out. There is first of all the uncertainty about the future shape of the intermediate/regional level and of intergovernmental arrangements at large. Whilst the previous district offices were abolished almost everywhere, since they served as organs of state governments, the future of the regional level is wide open. In none of the countries under closer examination was it possible to provide a satisfactory solution. Whereas the old intermediate authorities have been discredited and, accordingly, decisively weakened, the new ways promoted have led to a proliferation of specialized deconcentrated units of state administration (Hesse, 1996b). What emerges is an attempt to disentangle governmental levels, although there is a growing awareness that problems of coordination and control might be at the forefront of reform processes for the years to come. Owing to the multitude of institutions with partly overlapping competencies, it should not come as a surprise that tangible performance deficits tend to worry reformers. Unusual models, such as the Commissioners of the Republic in Hungary, failed, and it remains to be seen whether the new approaches both in this country and in the Czech Republic, following the election results of spring 1996, will provide workable solutions. Here again, it has been the domestic debate, focusing on both normative and functional deficiencies, that has triggered crucial discussions; foreign expertise has played a rather modest role.

Another telling example for the growing recognition of their own potential – and according policies of internal adjustment – is the attempt to rebuild local government in Central and Eastern Europe. Contrary to most of the literature, it is important to distinguish here between changes in the normative framework on the one hand, and the actual practice of local government on the other. Although the reform legislation mostly adopted in 1990 was not free of internal contradictions and ambiguities and is, in part, still in need of clarification and specification, it did provide solid legal bases for a separation of state administration from local government and constituted an independent sphere for the localities. In view of the relative recentness of the reforms and the still unstable constitutional, political, economic and social environments in which they have been implemented, it should not come as a surprise, however, that the reality of local government partly lags behind the normative ideal. Looking at the legal framework alone, as provided by foreign experts, would give an incomplete and, in fact, distorted view of the state of local government. Whilst reform legislation has, undoubtedly, strengthened the role of the local level and succeeded in establishing a sphere of genuinely autonomous government, it has to be argued that the reforms have shown too little appreciation of the need for effective implementation and intergovernmental coordination and cooperation. The resulting problems of sectoralization are compounded by the fragmented nature of the local government map. Weak intermediate institutions mean that central bodies are increasingly expected to build direct links with local government, a task made more difficult by the great number of local units and, especially where there are too many small localities, the lack of professional capacity. In sum, it seems that reformers may have placed too high hopes in local government reform. The understandable emphasis on what one could call a 'bottom-up' approach at reform led to significant shortcomings; the capacities of local governments were partly overestimated; conversely, there has been a significant under-estimation of the need for central steering, guidance and control. As a result, there are growing domestic calls for a partial 'reform of the reform', seeking to adopt a more pragmatic approach towards local government, to reconcile normative demands and functional requirements.

As regards *procedural questions*, reference has already been made to the elusiveness of 'global convergence', let alone that of a new 'paradigm'. This has not, however, prevented 'management gurus' or 'academic tourists' from advocating their 'products'. Only now is it being recognized that within the environments of Central and Eastern Europe it needs 'rowing' as well as 'steering' to keep the boat afloat, as even the most attentive steering is conditional upon the day-to-day success of those implementing public policy. To go even further, the introduction of business approaches in public administration, as advocated by New Public Management concepts, may well prove disastrous in systems based on a continental European tradition in which either the preconditions may not be in place or they may be rejected due to their inherent logic. Particularly problematic in the trans-formation context will be the all too limited ability of New Public Management systems to cushion the impact of unrestrained free market behaviour. At best, a drive towards improved management methods may be appropriate, while it appears impossible to simply adopt Anglo-Saxon administrative cultures. A note of caution is therefore appropriate: with regard to procedural issues, 'recognizing own potential' has to be read as a recommendation rather than an identification of an already prevailing trend.

A fourth example is to be found in the realm of *personnel policies*, which can be said to have undergone a significant shift in emphasis since 1989.

The only policy 'successfully' implemented in the immediate transformation phase was that of removing those officials who had been compromised in discharging their responsibilities under the previous regimes. Given the historical experience of an ideologically controlled public administration, the focus on these so-called 'lustration' policies was as understandable as the near absence of more positive measures in the area of personnel policy seems counter productive. It was only after this 'external shock' had been dealt with that personnel policies were starting to become demand-led in so far as pressing needs began to draw a more concentrated and sustained response. The legal, organizational and procedural changes enacted during the transformation and consolidation phases of public sector reform gave rise to a need for suitably qualified public servants. However, while there was certainly more continuity, the decisions taken with regard to recruitment, retention and training lacked structured aims and objectives and represented *ad hoc* reactions. By the early 1990s, this shortcoming led to a significant drainage of the most skilled public servants to infinitely more attractive private sector employment. Given that there was little intra-administrative expertise, the countervailing initiatives which focused on the training of remaining and new employees opened up countless opportunities for foreign consultants as well as domestic entrepreneurs to exploit a niche 'market'. Frantic institution-building, widespread duplication and even contradictory initiatives were among the unintended consequences.

It is only now that the need for institutional stabilization (in the form of civil service legislation) and domestic expertise (often in the form of coaching domestic trainers and institutionalizing public sector training schools) is beginning to receive the recognition it deserves. Yet, political agreements concerning the adaptation of Civil Service Acts are still difficult to reach within the countries of Central and Eastern Europe. Hungary is one of the few exceptions; it passed a Civil Service Act in 1992 as the result of preparatory activities which had already started in 1988. After a two-year parliamentary debate as well as several amendments, the original concept was adopted. The Act regulates the most important principles of the status of civil servants, such as recruitment, promotion and salary levels. Other countries have been slow in putting forward similar legislation. In Poland, for example, a Civil Service Law ranked high among the reform objectives. Since 1990, several commissions, committees and task forces have been appointed to prepare the law. Between 1993 and 1995, several drafts were put forward (not least owing to frequent changes of government), but none of them got to be voted on in Parliament. The recruitment and training of administrative staff lack comprehensive approaches, particularly in countries where basic legislation is still being discussed. At the same time, the obvious lack of basic administrative skills often hampers the implementation of reform itself, while newly defined tasks frequently require specialist economic training. The development of 'human capital' and a personnel policy deserving the name is, therefore, increasingly being recognized as a crucial category and a long-underestimated bottleneck of reform.

Looking at the empirical evidence, public administration in the post-communist countries of Central and Eastern Europe is conventionally perceived as being vastly over-extended and over-staffed. However, to measure the exact number of public employees is still a difficult undertaking. Privatization policies obviously had a significant influence on the size of the public service. While such measures helped to reduce public sector employment, new tasks necessitated the recruitment of further officials. The number of public servants is, therefore, constantly in flux. The figures provided reveal the total number of public servants to vary considerably between the countries discussed here, though it should be kept in mind that great differences in the size of government employment also exist between Western industrialized countries. For example, Albania and Lithuania – countries similar in size and population – show an impressive variance: whereas the former supports a rather large public service of 160,000 employees including 3,900 ministerial staff, the latter claims to employ only around 16,700 civil servants working in ministries and municipalities. Public servants in the Czech Republic numbered 140,000 in 1995. This figure includes 66,000 civil servants working in central, district or local governments, with a further 74,000 employees in finance, labour and school offices. Yet the statistics exclude public sector employees who do not exercise state administration in a narrow sense, such as teachers, hospital staff and others. In Poland, there are around 133,400 public servants (1994) of which approximately 100,000 work in central government, with the remainder exercising their duties in territorial administration.

These few figures indicate that a cross-national comparison of the size of the public service is extremely difficult. Among the factors reducing the comparative value of the statistics provided is the fact that proper employment records are often non-existent, particularly with regard to those working in lower levels of government or in non-administrative capacities. A further statistical complexity is found in the various meanings of the terms 'civil servant' and 'public servant'. At times, the former term is extended to cover as diverse positions as doctors and roadsweepers, while elsewhere 'civil servant' is used in its most narrow sense, referring to central government officials only. The figures provided are, therefore, to be treated with extreme caution and do not seem to provide a secure basis for comparative assessments of the quantity of state employees in the countries under consideration.

What can tentatively be examined, however, is the development of the overall number of civil servants of particular countries over time. In Hungary, for example, the number of civil servants increased from 65,000 to nearly 100,000 between 1989 and 1995, whereas the respective figures for Bulgaria were 49,000 in 1990 and 60,000 in 1994. While estimates concerning the overall size of public sector employment in Central and Eastern Europe are notoriously difficult, a steady increase can be detected with regard to the number of civil servants employed to perform core administrative duties. Multiplication of tasks and duplication of organizational structures have been held responsible for this trend, yet the lack of a coherent human resource policy can be expected to contribute to the problem. As each country seeks to speed up reforms, personnel policy, which follows the current legal, organizational and procedural changes, is evidently a crucial issue.

The great benefit of utilizing domestic expertise in training and personnel policy has at last been realized. Yet, 'recognizing their own potential' is not to be confused with severing the valuable links to international organizations and foreign donors in general. Instead, the latter may in future play an important role in providing independent needs assessment and quality control. Personnel policies as such, however, will have to be formulated and executed within a given environment.

Options for reform: analytical and empirical perspectives

In trying to summarize externally induced changes and policies of internal adjustment, a number of analytical and empirical observations stand out. In analytical perspective, to begin with, we seem to witness the disappearance of large-scale, macro-oriented global approaches and paradigms. They anyhow served at best the purpose of provoking and never reached the level of being accepted as a sensible approach to cope with the challenges at hand. What might be called for in place is to react to the growing awareness that public sector reform in the still fledgling democracies in Central and Eastern Europe is complicated by the fact that the task of modernizing the public sector at large goes much beyond subjecting it to the basic legal norms of conduct which govern the execution of public responsibilities in the majority of the industrialized countries of the Western hemisphere, and to engage in a process of marketization that allows previously regulated environments to free themselves from the grip of a command-like system. The challenge with which public institutions are faced in Central and Eastern Europe is to redefine even their role in society, or, more concretely, their relationships with politics, the economy and the civil community. One is well advised, therefore, to recall that the dynamics of institutional transformation are intimately linked to changes in the political, legal, economic and social environments in which public institutions operate and on whose material and immaterial inputs they crucially depend. Although the public sector is both an object of reform and, almost invariably, its chief agent, the reform process is an interactive one.

This means that there are hardly any analytical certainties to build upon; that it is often almost impossible to distinguish between dependent and independent variables in analysing ongoing reform processes; and that it seems necessary to replace broadish and one-sided analytical approaches (from public choice theories to 'managerialism') or at least to complement them with attempts to take into account both normative and functional demands.

Here, we realize that the predominant paradigm of change *via negationis*, that is the negation of the legacy of democratic centralism, has lost in importance. There are growing signs that functional considerations, focusing on performance issues and the implementation of the various policies adopted, are gaining ground. The emphasis is here on complementing structural reforms at the central government level with processes of internal differentiation; defining the intermediate tiers of government and taking into account the demand for horizontal and vertical cooperation and coordination; and pragmatically reorienting reform efforts at the local level, adapting over-ambitious reforms to the given needs and capacities. So the task is to give effect to a framework partly in place, whilst adopting corrective strategies where necessary. What seems, furthermore, to be significant is a need to differentiate reform policies segmentally and sequentially, to recognize their interdependence whilst focusing on particular tiers, branches and institutions of government at the same time. Given the still enormous task of implementing the mostly ambitious reform agendas, a certain prioritization and consequent phasing of policies is turning out to be inevitable. Different perceptions of policy-makers and implementors need not be judged negatively in this respect. They may rather induce 'creative tension' or indeed a 'climate of reform' that reinforces the need for an effective collaboration between different actors and institutions. Questions of policy design remain of importance in this respect as well, complemented by a recognition of growing institutional self-interests, and an acute awareness of the time and resources needed.

Employing a somewhat simplified supply and demand model, it is time to realize that at least in the most advanced of the reform countries of Central and Eastern Europe, the prerequisites for successful public sector reforms are mostly in place. Basic decisions on the form and function of the new statehood have been taken (though quite a number of them have not reached the stage of implementation yet); attempts at securing most basic services and regulatory provisions are supported by an established institutional framework; policy-making and the resulting decision-making processes are being routinized. Although crucial bottlenecks, such as the lack of intergovernmental arrangements or of qualified personnel, threaten to hamper successful reform attempts, this is not to deny that the legal, political and institutional preconditions for public sector activities have been met, and in a few cases have even reached 'Western standards'.

As regards the demand side for public sector reform, it is encouraging to see that the anti-state attitude which long prevailed in most of the countries of Central and Eastern Europe is beginning to be superseded by the growing awareness of complementary approaches at private sector development and public sector reform. Though one can still detect a number of prejudices against bureaucratic organizations, most observers agree that there cannot be a successful completion of the marketization and privatization programmes without securing basic standards. This applies to such diverse issues as securing property rights, institutional responsiveness and increased social awareness. Even the representatives of the private sector and, not least, of international organizations have developed an interest in public sector reform by now, acknowledging that economically driven reforms will not succeed without a stable legal, institutional and administrative under-pinning. It appears as if not only the demanding public but the ruling élites as well have realized that institutional issues are not at all peripheral but are at the heart of the still ongoing processes of change, that to stabilize the political and social situation, to create markets, to secure investment and to reach target groups, a solid and acceptable public sector is needed. This should be interpreted as an encouraging sign in the midst of a reform process that is moving slowly from basic transformation to consolidation, modernization and adaptation.

Conclusion: an attempt at comparison

In comparative terms, it should be argued that by taking the Central and Eastern European experience into account, the often circular world-wide debate on public sector reform could be given a new and somewhat unexpected direction. As suggested in this chapter, the Central and Eastern European case is unusual in so far as reformers first embarked on the direct application of Western models in an attempt to cope with an extremely turbulent environment. It was only after dysfunctional 'reform' outcomes led to significant disillusionment that the need to involve, and even to rely predominantly on domestic expertise became an acceptable and broadly followed policy. Now, and partly as a result thereof, it is no longer only international organizations that develop an interest in the Central and Eastern European reforms. The countries of Western Europe start to take note of the experiences encountered in the Central and Eastern European context as well. Given that their own public sectors are currently under-going critical reviews that call into question even their most basic principles, they are in frantic search for examples of successful renewal.

Having had the opportunity to 'start nearly from scratch', the fledgling democracies of Central and Eastern Europe are now the subject of increas-ing international attention, as they have had the historically unprecedented chance to redefine the size, form and function of the public sector. To determine 'core public tasks' was and is a normative and functional necessity here as opposed to being the latest 'fashion' within the Western European debate. Their undeniable need for interventionist and regulatory policies is to be contrasted with the all too numerous calls for more flexible, moderative, communicative and cooperative policy-making and implemen-tation within Western environments. The role of a reformed public sector in society and a reborn civil service in securing necessary public tasks and in safeguarding the *bonum commune* could also serve as a reminder of restraint to 'Western' reformers. Here, the heated debates about undeniable reform needs are more often than not dominated by those advocating more radical 'blanket solutions', the realization of which would undoubtedly endanger basic principles of public activity (at least in democratic polities). In many respects it might make sense, therefore, for Western experts and reformers alike to replace their one-sided top-down attitude of informing and influencing Central and Eastern European processes of change by an attitude that includes at least 'listening' if not 'learning'. That is why it might be of mutual benefit to examine closely the Central and Eastern European experiences since 1989. At the very least, there is a chance to detect certain patterns of change and perhaps even an outline of a future public sector that would be of interest to the debates within Western environments as well.

Apart from that, it should have become obvious by looking at public sector reforms in comparative perspective that 'global convergence' is indeed not a characteristic to be detected within the environments of Western and Eastern Europe. What has become more than clear over the last decade is that state traditions, administrative cultures and specific historic legacies (that embrace in the case of Central and Eastern Europe much more than the communist period) have to be taken into account, and that the fashionable way of introducing public management formulae into the routines of handling public affairs carries only limited and much too timely weight. It might make sense, therefore, to recall some of the categories put forward in this chapter.

Stages of development, for example, are of importance in so far as they seem to rule out *ad hoc* approaches, one-off policies or indeed the adoption of 'grand designs'. What the Central and Eastern European experience has highlighted instead is that stages of development strongly suggest a phased approach at public sector reform. Only an ongoing, step-by-step reform strategy aiming at broadly defined long-term objectives allows for the necessary corrections to be made due to changed circumstances, or new and upcoming functional demands.

The Central and Eastern European experience also suggests that *cultural perspectives and traditions* are to be taken much more seriously than originally expected. They not only stand in the way of transplanting models onto different environments, but remind us also that in the case of Central and Eastern Europe there is more than just one legacy. The different ways to recall even structural characteristics of the Austrian-Habsburg empire or French influences in redeveloping the unitary state systems clearly indicate the pros and cons of specific reform paths in a given environment.

Institutional variables are of extreme importance not only in restructuring central government, the intermediate tier or local administration, but also in deciding on basic state structures. Though most of the countries of Central and Eastern Europe have adopted unitary state systems, there are, of course, significant processes of differentiation to be observed. The experiences made within federal systems are, therefore, of interest, especially with regard to the workings of multi-tiered governmental units. The accommodation of social and territorial disparities and the cleavages going along with that are further elements to be considered.

Last, but not least, *reform professionalism* and *political will* are of crucial importance. This applies not only to the limited help foreign assistance can provide, so that the building up of domestic expertise has come to the fore of today's orientation. It also has to be noted that, owing to the dominance of economically driven reforms, politicians were reluctant to engage in a process of rebuilding a democratic statehood. It is only now that they have begun to learn that marketization, democratization and institutional stabilization form a complementary relationship that is essential in establishing a workable and accepted body politic and a functioning market economy. Under the current fiscal squeeze and the problems of legitimacy and acceptance going along with that, Western politicians would be ill-advised to disregard this interrelationship.

Given those observations, one seems to be well equipped to conclude that modern statehood in both Central and Eastern as well as Western Europe is certainly not in the process of being 'hollowed out'. What we witness instead is a modernization process that seems to be inevitable in a period of growing uncertainty and systemic change, in which not only the private sector but the public sector as well have to undergo policies of significant adjustment. This should not be confused with a 'withering away' of the democratic state and its principal elements; what we might be faced with instead is the need to redefine the balance between the private and the public sectors, and with it, the *raison d'être* of modern democratic statehood.

Bibliography

Author's work

This chapter is based on a number of the author's previous writings on public sector reform in Central and Eastern Europe:

Hesse, J.J. (1991) 'Administrative modernisation in Central and Eastern European countries', *Staatswissenschaften und Staatspraxis*, 197–217.

Hesse, J.J. (1992–3) *Public Sector Reform in Central and Eastern Europe: the Case of Poland, Czechoslovakia and Hungary*. Reports for the International Labour Office (ILO), Oxford/ Geneva.

Hesse, J.J. (1993a) 'From transformation to modernisation: administrative change in Central and Eastern Europe', in J.J. Hesse (ed.), *Administrative Transformation in Central and Eastern Europe: Towards Public Sector Reform in Post-Communist Societies*. Special issue of *Public Administration*. Oxford: Blackwell. pp. 219–57.

Hesse, J.J. (ed.) (1993b) *Administrative Transformation in Central and Eastern Europe: Towards Public Sector Reform in Post-Communist Societies*. Oxford: Blackwell.

Hesse, J.J. (1995) 'Administrative reform in the Czech Republic: report for the Czech government', *Staatswissenschaften und Staatspraxis*, 477–506.

Hesse, J.J. (1996a) *Rebuilding the State: Public Sector Reform in Central and Eastern Europe*. Baden-Baden: Nomos.

Hesse, J.J. (1996b) *Deconcentrated Administrative Units: the Case of Hungary*. Report for the World Bank, Oxford/Washington.

Hesse, J.J. (1996c) 'Training and public sector reform', in OECD, *Training Profiles*. Oxford and Berlin: OECD.

Hesse, J.J. and Goetz, K.H. (1993–4a) 'Public sector reform in Central and Eastern Europe. I:

The case of Poland', in T. Ellwein, D. Grimm, J.J. Hesse and G.F. Schuppert (eds), *Jahrbuch zur Staats- und Verwaltungswissenschaft*, Bd. 6/1992–3. Baden-Baden: Nomos. pp. 237–82.

Hesse, J.J. and Goetz, K.H. (1993–4b) 'Public sector reform in Central and Eastern Europe. II: The case of the Czech and Slovak Federal Republic', in T. Ellwein, D. Grimm, J.J. Hesse and G.F. Schuppert (eds), *Jahrbuch zur Staats- und Verwaltungswissenschaft*, Bd. 6/1992–3. Baden-Baden: Nomos. pp. 283–323.

Hesse, J.J. and Goetz, K.H. (1993–4c) 'Public sector reform in Central and Eastern Europe. III: The case of Hungary', in T. Ellwein, D. Grimm, J.J. Hesse and G.F. Schuppert (eds), *Jahrbuch zur Staats- und Verwaltungswissenschaft*, Bd. 6/1992–3. Baden-Baden: Nomos. pp. 237–82.

Other works

Ágh, A. (ed.) (1994) *The Emergence of East Central European Parliaments: the First Steps*. Budapest: Hungarian Centre for Democracy Studies.

Aucoin, P. (1990) 'Administrative reform in public management: programmes, principles, paradoxes and pendulums', *Governance*, 3: 115–37.

Batt, J. (1991) 'The end of communist rule in East Central Europe: a four-country comparison', *Government and Opposition*.

Baylis, T.A. (1994) 'Plus ça change? Transformation and continuity among East European elites', *Communist and Post Communist Studies*, 315–28.

Bolton, P. and Poland, G. (1992) 'Privatization policies in Central and Eastern Europe', *Economic Policy*.

Brzezinski, M. (1993) 'The emergence of judicial review in Eastern Europe; the case of Poland', *American Journal of Comparative Law*, 153–200.

Caiden, G.E. (1988) 'The vitality of administrative reform', *International Review of Administrative Sciences*, 54(3): 331–58.

Comisso, E. (1995) 'Legacies of the past or new institutions? The struggle over restitutions in Hungary', *Comparative Political Studies*, 200–38.

Crawford, B. and Lijphart, A. (1995) 'Change in post-communist Eastern Europe: old legacies, new institutions and international pressures', *Comparative Political Studies*, 171–99.

Dallago, B., Brezinski, H. and Andreff, W. (1991) *Convergence and System Change: the Convergence Hypothesis and Transition in Eastern Europe*. Aldershot: Gower.

Derlien, H.-U. and Szablowski, G.J. (eds) (1993) 'Regime transition, elites and bureaucracies in Eastern Europe', special issue of *Governance*, 304–453.

East European Constitutional Review (1994–5) Country-by-country constitutional updates. Chicago. 1994–1995.

Elster, J. (1993) 'Constitution-making in Eastern Europe: rebuilding the boat in the open sea', in J.J. Hesse (ed.) *Administrative Transformation in Central and Eastern Europe: towards Public Sector Reform in Post-Communist Societies*. Oxford: Blackwell.

Engerer, H. (1996) 'Privateigentum, Privatisierung und Transformation', *Vierteljahreshefte zur Wirtschaftsforschung*. Deutsches Institut für Wirtschaftsforschung. pp. 14–30.

Filatotchev, I., Grosfeld, I., Karsai, J., Wright, M. and Buck, T. (1996) 'Buy-outs in Hungary, Poland and Russia: governance and finance issues', *The Economics of Transition*, 67–88.

Gärtner, W. (1995) 'Eigentumsgarantien in den Verfassungen Polens, Ungarns, der Tschechischen und der Slowakischen Republic – Verfassungsrechtliche Grundlagen und Verfassungspraxis', *Recht in Ost und West*, 75–9.

Giersch, H. (ed.) (1991) *Toward a Market Economy in Central and Eastern Europe*. Springer Verlag.

Gomulka, S. and Polonsky, A. (eds) (1990) *Polish Paradoxes*. London: Routledge.

Hesse, J.J., Hood, C. and Peters, B.G. (1996) 'Paradoxes in public sector reform: soft theory and hard cases'. Unpublished manuscript.

Hoen, H.W. (1996) 'Shock versus gradualism in Central Europe reconsidered', *Comparative Economic Studies*, 1–20.

Illner, M., Baldersheim, H., Patocka, J. and Surazska, W. (eds) (1993) *Regional Organisation and Administrative Performance in Eastern Europe*. The Institute of Sociology, Academy of Sciences of the Czech Republic.

König, K. (1992) 'The transformation of a "real socialist" administrative system into a conventional western European system', *International Review of Administration Sciences*.

Lane, J.-E. (1995) *The Public Sector. Concepts, Models and Approaches*, 2nd edn. London.

Lijphart, A. (1992) 'Democratization and constitutional choices in Czechoslovakia, Hungary and Poland 1989–91', *Journal of Theoretical Politics*, 4(2).

McGregor, J.P. (1996) 'Constitutional factors in politics in post-communist Central and Eastern Europe', *Communist and Post-Communist Studies*, 2: 147–66.

Müller, K. (1992) 'Modernising Eastern Europe: theoretical problems and political dilemmas', *Archives Européennes de Sociologie*.

OECD (1991) *Transformation of Planned Economies: Property Rights Reform and Macroeconomic Stability*. Paris: OECD.

OECD (1993) *Public Management Profiles: Sigma Countries*. Paris: OECD.

OECD (1995) *Governance in Transition: Public Management Reforms in OECD Countries*. Paris: OECD.

Offe, C. (1991) 'Capitalism by democratic design? Democratic theory facing the triple transition in East Central Europe', *Social Research*.

Offe, C. (1994) *Der Tunnel am Ende des Lichts: Erkundungen der politischen Transformation im Neuen Osten*. Frankfurt: Campus Verlag.

Olsen, J.P. (1992) 'Rethinking and reforming the public sector', in B. Kohler-Koch (ed.), *Staat und Demokratie in Europa*. Opladen: Westdeutscher Verlag.

Osborne, D. and Gaebler, T. (1992) *Reinventing Government: How the Entrepreneurial Spirit is Transforming the Public Sector*. Reading: Addison-Wesley.

Pridham, G. (1994) *Building Democracy? The International Dimension of Democratisation in Eastern Europe*. London: Pinter.

Rose, R. and Makkai, T. (1995) 'Consensus or dissensus about welfare in post-communist societies?', *European Journal of Political Research*, pp. 203–24.

Schade, W. (1995) 'Zur Verfassungsdiskussion in Polen', *Osteuropa*, pp. 638–50.

Schwartz, H. (1992) 'In defense of aiming high: why economic and social rights belong in the new post-communist constitutions of Europe', *East European Constitutional Review*, 1(2).

Squires Meaney, C. (1995) 'Foreign experts, capitalists and competing agenda: privatization in Poland, the Czech Republic, and Hungary', *Comparative Political Studies*, 275–305.

United Nations (1994) *A Comparative View on Economic Reform in Poland, Hungary and Czechoslovakia*. Economic Commission for Europe Discussion Paper, vol. 3 no. 2, 1993. Geneva: United Nations.

Van Zon, H. (1994) *Alternative Scenarios for Central Europe: Poland, Czech Republic, Slovakia and Hungary*. London: Ashgate.

Welfens, P.J.J. (1995) *Die Europäische Union und die mittelosteuropäischen Länder: Entwicklungen, Probleme, politische Optionen*. Berichte des Bundesinstituts für ostwissenschaftliche und internationale Studien.

World Bank (1991) *The Reform of Public Sector Management: Lessons from Experience*. Washington, DC: World Bank.

5

Farewell to the British State?

Michael J. Goldsmith and Edward C. Page

The scale of reform

If we look at public sector reform attempts in the post-war period in Britain there is a general tendency among contemporary observers of whatever era to believe that what they are witnessing marks a fundamental change in state organization as we know it. The Fulton Committee of 1968 seemed to open the doors for change in an archaic civil service that had last been examined early in Queen Victoria's reign (Fry, 1983: 249). The merging of ministries in super-departments as well as the merging of small local government units into larger entities were part of the 'planning mood' that also involved the creation of strategic policy planning units and similar organizations within both central and local government in the 1960s and 1970s (Hogwood and Gunn, 1984). In the 1970s the development of 'corporatist tendencies' which produced consultative mechanisms was ended by the introduction of techniques which were supposed to bring private sector techniques, disciplines and management to the public sector (Rhodes, 1988: 378–81).

What distinguished the Conservative government's approach to reform after 1979 from earlier episodes in reform was its apparent breadth, its tenacity and its impact. The transfer to the private sector of organizations and functions previously belonging to the state, or the application of techniques and principles which emulate those from the private sector, have affected the whole public sector – from coal mines, the army, schools, hospitals, dental surgeries and universities to the provision of policy advice and inspection. Moreover it is possible to find continuity over the whole 18 years of the Conservative government – from the earliest forays into this territory to the promises in 1997 that even more was to come. While it was possible to argue that reform attempts before 1979 were in many cases largely superficial – Whitehall 'defeated Fulton' (Kellner and Crowther-Hunt, 1980) or the Central Policy Review Staff became 'routine punctuated by orgies' (Hennessy, 1985), others simply 'evaporated' (Gray and Jenkins, 1985; Rose, 1977) or were otherwise forgotten – it is only at an absurdly high level of abstraction that anyone could claim the British state in 1996 resembled that of 1979. The Conservatives appeared to have proved wrong Sidney Webb's dictum that 'In Britain it is easy for good reason to change the form of an institution without changing the substance, or the substance without changing the form, but one should never try to change both the substance and the form of anything at one and the same time' (quoted in Beveridge, 1953: 72).

Moreover, internationally Britain seems to be at the forefront of a new public management revolution (Hood, 1991). If we look at comparative evaluations of new public management, and associated reform measures, commentators point out 'British distinctiveness'. Vincent Wright's (1994: 117) comparison shows similarities among West European countries, but talks of a distinctive 'imposed radicalism' in Britain, which also displayed a 'frenzy' of reform. Moran (1995) points out that while many other countries have reformed their health care systems, the only other European countries which experienced change on the scale of that found in Britain were those political systems in which change was forced by the extreme upheaval following the collapse of communism.

Yet there may be some danger of talking up the 'revolution' that has taken place in Britain's public sector. In few 18-year periods this century has the whole of the public sector stood still; if we think in 18-year periods – going backwards through 1979, 1961, 1943, 1925 and 1907, for example – we might argue that to expect anything less than fundamental change in the public sector is fanciful. War, decolonization, booms and depressions may help account for some of the major changes in the contours of the state. Yet in few such periods can one talk about a *set of guiding principles* with which the character of changes across such a wide area may be described, as is conventional when looking at the period since 1979. How might we offer an assessment that avoids the tendency to exaggerate impacts that comes from proximity to reform? In this chapter we seek to examine the overall effect of these changes on the public sector. In the next section we set out what it is that is commonly associated with the 'revolution' in the public sector. After a brief discussion about the difficulties of evaluating the effects of this revolution we go on to look at the effects on the *size, hierarchy, reach* and *culture* of the public sector in Britain.

Outlining the intended revolution

The reforms of the public sector in the United Kingdom since 1979 have been diverse. While the precise character of the reforms in different sectors cannot be easily encapsulated in such terms, one can give a broad indication of what was intended in the major reforms of the public sector over the past 18 years by the terms *privatization, the removal of subsidies, marketization, consumerism* and *management decentralization*. These terms are related, and some of them have given rise to an extensive literature all of their own. Their use in this chapter is intended not to settle long-standing debates about their meaning, but to give a flavour of the diverse strategies that go to make up the 'revolution' in the British public sector. Table 5.1 outlines the

Table 5.1 *Contours of government reforms, 1979–97*

Privatization

Sale of major public enterprises to the private sector including British Petroleum (after 1979), Cable and Wireless (1981), Britoil (1982), British Telecom (1984), British Gas (1986), Rolls-Royce (1987), British Steel (1988), water companies (1989), electricity companies (1990) and British Coal (1994)

Sale of parts of the civil service including the Product Services Division of the Property Services Agency (1992), the Chessington Computer Centre (1995), Her Majesty's Stationery Office (1996)

Compulsory competitive tendering (services such as refuse collection, cleaning and catering) have to be put out to tender by local authorities. Introduced in the 1980 Local Government (Planning and Land) Act 1980, and extended in the 1988 Local Government Act

'Market testing' introduced in the civil service 1992

NHS hospitals contract out cleaning and ancillary services after 1983

1991 Criminal Justice Act establishes principle of private prisons (four in operation in 1996) and the use of private security firms for prisoner escort functions

Removal of subsidies

Local government subsidies for public housing curbed in Housing and Planning Act 1989; transport subsidies reduced

Creation of 'social fund': repayable loans for social security benefit recipients to buy capital goods such as cookers and furniture

Setting up of Child Support Agency with powers to trace and require family maintenance payments from absent fathers

Student maintenance grants progressively reduced: shortfall to be made up through student loans

Charges for health services increased: prescription medicines, eye tests and dental charges

Marketization

Creation of 'internal market' in National Health Service through 'purchasers' (district health authorities and fundholding family doctors) and 'providers' (self-governing hospital trusts) and similar purchaser–provider split in social services

Consumerism

Tenant's Charter 1980 for public sector housing tenants

Use of performance indicators in education including the publication of national tests and nation-wide exam results (school league tables); publication of OFSTED school inspections and university teaching and research quality assessments

Publication of hospital league tables after 1994 based on performance in matters such as speed of processing accident and emergency cases

Citizen's Charter established 1991 with over 40 separate charters for specific services including a Patient's Charter and a Taxpayer's Charter as well as charters for social security benefits recipients, road users and court users

Management decentralization

Financial Management Initiative of 1982, aimed at devolving financial management within the civil service; setting up of Next Step agencies after 1988 major reforms by the institutions of government which are most closely affected.

Privatization refers to the selling off of formerly publicly owned bodies to the private sector. This includes the mandatory sale of local council houses on demand, the sale of major nationalized industries and utilities including telephones, electricity, gas and water as well as the sale of parts of the civil service such as Her Majesty's Stationery Office in 1996. Compulsory competitive tendering, according to which local authority as well as health services have to be offered out to tender, thus allowing private sector organizations a role in public sector service provision, can be viewed as a form of privatization of service delivery (Kane, 1996). In local government this initiative originally applied to tasks carried out by manual workers, but has since been extended to white-collar employees. In 1996 targets were set for tendering out local government legal, financial and technical services. Even in one of the core 'defining' services of government (Rose, 1976), prisons, private sector security firms have developed a modest and still growing role. The 'market testing' initiative in the national civil service may be considered as an alternative to privatization since it sought to introduce the rigours of the private sector without necessarily privatizing by making civil service departments tender for jobs that they already do (Oughton, 1994; Richards and Newman, 1996).

The removal of subsidies refers to the increasing substitution of public by private funding to provide services. Subsidies have been reduced in a variety of different areas. The scope for local authorities subsidizing public housing and transport has been substantially limited since 1979, above all after the 1980 Housing Act and the 1985 Transport Act (Malpass and Warburton, 1993). A general squeeze on local government finance has led many local authorities to levy charges for services such as museums. In education, students in higher education rely increasingly on repayable loans from the Student Loans Company. There has been an increase in fees and user charges in the National Health Service for prescriptions, eye tests and dental surgery (see Slater, 1996). After 1988 the government embarked on a process of encouraging employees to take up personal pensions and opt out of the State Earnings-Related Pension Scheme (Gough and Shackleton, 1996). The Private Finance Initiative introduced in 1992 was designed to attract private sector finance for capital projects, mainly in transport, such as the renovation of the Northern Line of the London Underground or the Channel Tunnel Rail Link.

Marketization refers to the creation of market mechanisms of resource allocation to replace bureaucratic ones. Here the main example is in the health service reforms, following the 1990 National Health Service and Community Care Act, which have transformed health service organizations into sets of purchasers and providers of services, where purchasers are encouraged to shop around for cheaper forms of treatment for their patients, and providers must compete for their custom (Ellwood, 1996; Lewis, 1996). The 1990 Act also introduced a similar distinction between purchasers and providers in local authority social services (Charlesworth et al., 1996). More widely in local government, service departments have tended to develop new relationships with those departments they serve through charging for services and negotiating 'service level agreements' with them (Blackman and Stephens, 1993).

Consumerism refers to the increase in information about levels and standards of service available to recipients and the ability to make choices on the basis of this information. This includes the development of means of judging the performance of public bodies: university departments are assessed on the basis of their teaching and research; primary and secondary schools are judged on the basis of ostensibly standard indicators of performance in national examinations published in league tables in national newspapers, and they also have to be evaluated by teams of OFSTED (Office for Standards in Education) inspectors, the reports of which are similarly widely published, especially in the case of 'failing' schools. As well as information, consumerism also generates sets of expectations of performance of public bodies set out in the Citizen's Charter movement according to which standards of service are explicitly set out – how late a train may run before a passenger has the right to claim a rebate or how long a client may be kept waiting for an appointment at a Job Centre – and good performance is rewarded with Charter Marks (Goldsworthy, 1994; Pollitt, 1994).

Management decentralization has been pursued at a variety of different levels. At the most obvious level it has meant the setting up of Next Steps agencies; here (currently) 109 agencies, in which a claimed 72% of national civil servants are employed, are responsible for the operational tasks that used in many cases to be carried out by officials formally employed by a ministry. Hogwood (1995) correctly warns us to be sceptical both about the percentage employment in agencies and the notion that there is anything approaching a clear division of labour between ministries and agencies with respect to 'policy' and 'operational' tasks. Management decentralization also includes a variety of measures at the local government level, reducing the role of the local authority and increasing the autonomy of those running institutions that provide services. In education this has entailed the local management of schools initiative, according to which local authority-run schools must devolve budgetary authority to headteachers and governing bodies; and the ability of some schools to 'opt out' of local authority control and have greater control over things such as school admissions. Housing Action Trusts allowed local authority tenants to opt out of local authority management of housing. A related trend has been the setting up at the local level of special-purpose organizations outside the control of elected local government aimed at promoting local economies: the early 1980s experiment with Enterprise Zones, the Urban Development Corporations of the 1980s and the Training and Enterprise Councils of the 1990s (Deakin and Edwards, 1993).

Of course, one should not over-emphasize the degree to which all of these initiatives were part of a conscious plan to transform the public sector.

While some of the reforms, such as the sale of council houses, were part of the Conservative manifesto in 1979, others appeared to be almost stumbled across. For example, managerial reform in the British civil service was a consistent theme of Conservative policy since 1979, yet there were many experiments as well as false starts before the Next Steps were developed. These included the 'Rayner scrutinies', which looked at the efficiency of management and recommended the restructuring of tasks; experiments with information systems, such as MINIS which sought to identify activities of ministries and the costs associated with them; and the Financial Management Initiative (FMI) of 1982, which sought to decentralize financial administration in the civil service. The Next Steps initiative was in large part a reaction to the failure of the FMI (Zifcak, 1994).

The whole issue of local government reform shows a variety of distinct approaches of which we can set out only the high points (Stoker, 1996). Conservative policy in the early 1980s took the form of a squeeze on local finances exercised by several separate, and sometimes contradictory, spending penalty regimes. Then came the abolition of the Greater London Council and the metropolitan counties, local tax capping, and the disastrous 'Poll Tax' episode which sought to make each citizen pay the same flat-rate 'charge' for local services. After the Poll Tax the government was forced into another major reform of local finances, shifting much of the burden of local finance to national taxation and introducing a new property tax to replace the Poll Tax. It also announced a major review of the structure of local government, although when its work was nearly finished its chairman, Sir John Banham, resigned in protest against the government's initial refusal to follow the Commission's recommendations (Waddington, 1995).

While reforms such as the restructuring of the NHS do fit in with the logic of a Conservative admiration for the market, this admiration might have manifested itself in many other forms. Most obviously it may have led to the development of an insurance-based system, mooted in 1981 in a leaked Central Policy Review Staff report but countered by Mrs Thatcher who crushed any further discussion of this plan and made the promise that the NHS is 'safe in Conservative hands'. Thus while many reforms reflected some general overall principles, the precise contours of the reforms reflected more ephemeral interpretations about how such principles might be applied as well as the political conditions for their acceptance.

Evaluating the revolution

If Rip van Winkle had fallen asleep in May 1979, he would have found much that is different about the public sector when he woke in 1997. He might have had an inkling that retrenchment was on the cards – as it had been since the oil crisis of the early 1970s – but would have been hard pressed to have predicted the precise effect this would have on public sector organization, even if he went through the 1979 Conservative election manifesto with a fine-tooth comb. How much difference these changes have made depends entirely on the criteria and perspective one uses to evaluate change. The perspective of a consultant paediatrician will differ from that of a local councillor or an official in a social security office. We would get a different impression of the scale of the effect of the changes according to whether we look at, for example, the effect on public spending, house prices, business confidence or the ideology of the Labour Party. Moreover an evaluation might look at the unintended as well as the intended effects of reform. If we consider that the attribution of causation is very difficult in the social sciences anyway, and that even attempting to attribute causation would entail very detailed examination of each of the components of reform over the past 18 years individually, it is important to specify what any evaluation of the charter of the changes in a chapter such as this can achieve.

In what ways would we expect the public sector to have changed? There are four main ways that the transformation of the British state which emphasizes market virtues and practices might be expected to change. First, we would expect the public sector *to shrink in size*. One of the main purposes of reforms in the civil service, the National Health Service and local government has been to decrease the role of the public sector and increase the role of the private. Consequently, the most obvious sign of the effect of these measures would be in the reduction in the resources, mainly labour and financial resources, taken up by the state.

Secondly, in so far as the government has sought to model its organization and practices upon the private sector, we would expect the public sector to be far *less hierarchically organized* than the public sector before 1979. It would be mistaken to view the British state pre-1979 as reflecting the classic principles associated with continental bureaucracies of the nineteenth century – a more or less integrated hierarchy with an unbroken chain of superior and subordinate relationships running from the apex to the base. Nevertheless, one of the purposes of the introduction of reforms was to bring about greater efficiency through greater flexibility in organization, and to that end the effect can be assessed by movement away from hierarchical models of organization. While hierarchy is a difficult feature of organizations to assess with precision, we can look at the degree to which old hierarchical relationships within central government, as well as between central government and other public organizations, have been replaced by newer coordinate authority relations (for a discussion of coordinate and hierarchical models see Damaška, 1986).

Thirdly, we may expect the *reach* of the public sector to have diminished following the reforms of the Conservative years. Not only should there be a lighter touch of authority within the governmental structure, but the logic of valuing the market as a mechanism of distributing goods, benefits and sanctions means that the state should become less involved in the regulation of non-state actors, whether individuals, firms or groups.

Finally, and perhaps most difficult to formalize, we would expect the Conservative reforms to have affected the *culture of the public sector*.

Culture is capable of a diverse array of different interpretations. In the British context it may be associated with the culture of the civil service characterized by Fulton as one of 'amateurism'; for Heclo and Wildavsky (1981) it was a close community of 'chaps' who got to know each other over years. However, here we understand culture to refer to the pattern of thought which Mrs Thatcher among others believed characterized public officials – an unwillingness to innovate, take risks and treat citizens as consumers rather than captive clients (Hennessy, 1989: Chapter 15). As we will see, one of the important objectives of several of the reforms set out in Table 5.1 was to 'change the culture' of the organization or organizations which they were supposed to transform.

The size of the public sector

Since one of the prime objectives of the revolution was to 'roll back the state' (for a discussion of Thatcherism see Kavanagh, 1990), we might expect the revolution to have had an impact on the size of the public sector itself. This, of course, takes us back to the definition that we use for size. The most common measures of the size of government are the number of people working for the public sector, the amount of money government spends and the amount of legislation and regulation. On the basis of the level of expenditure, the British state has not been rolled back. Figure 5.1 sets out levels of expenditure at constant prices, excluding the receipts of privatization (for a discussion of the effects of this see Hogwood, 1992) and confirms that the most significant cuts in expenditure in real terms came under the Labour government of 1974–9. Some areas of public expenditure, notably housing (with a reduction of 64% in real terms since 1979, continuing a sharp decline that began under Labour in 1974) and defence (reduction of 6%), have faced substantial cuts while other big spending areas have increased, including education (increase of 32%), social security (84%), law and order (110%) and health (70%). As Hogwood (1992) shows, in the longer term such variations in programmes do not fit any consistent patterns that might be derived from our expectations of the effect of party ideology (such as, for example, less spending on social programmes under the Conservatives than Labour). Thus it would be hard to fit either the overall trend in public spending or the patterns of spending in broad programme areas into a picture of radical change in the British state since 1979.

A rather different picture emerges if one looks at the levels of employment in the state sector (Table 5.2). Government figures published in *Economic Trends* tend to overestimate the diminishing size of public sector employment (see below). Nevertheless, even taking account of these apparent rather than real reductions in the size of the public sector, the number of public employees has dropped by 1,995,000. This is in large part due to the privatization of public enterprises (the reduction from 1.9 million employees in 1981 to 0.4 million in 1995 shows the scale of privatization) and the

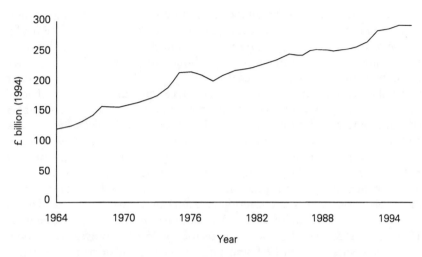

Figure 5.1 *Public expenditure 1964–1994. Source: Public Expenditure. Statistical Analyses 1996–7, March 1996, Cm 3201, pp. 8, 10 and 11 (adding privatization proceeds)*

Table 5.2 *Public employment, 1961–95*

	1961	1971	1981	1995	Change 1961–81	Change 1981–95
Total employed workforce	24,457	24,533	24,498	25,743	41	1,245
Private sector	18,598	17,906	17,313	20,278	-1,285	2,965
Training	0	0	0	237	0	237
Public corporations	2,200	2,009	1,867	442	-333	-1,425
General government of which:	3,659	4,618	5,318	4,788	1,659	-530
Central government:	1,790	1,966	2,419	2,144	629	-275
armed forces	474	368	334	230	-140	-104
NHS	575	785	1,207	1,183	632	-24
other	741	813	878	731	137	-147
Local government:	1,869	2,652	2,899	2,644	1,030	-255
education	785	1,297	1,454	1,188	669	-266
social services	170	276	350	412	180	62
police	108	152	186	208	78	22
construction	103	124	143	83	40	-60
other	703	803	766	753	63	-13
Total public sector*	5,859	6,627	7,185	5,467	1,326	-1,718

* *Economic Trends* definition excludes several categories of employees more conventionally classed as public sector such as general practitioners in the health service, university employees, employees of sixth form colleges and further education colleges and many employees of the civil service whose organizations were reclassified. Next Steps agencies are included in the public sector.

Source: HMSO, *Economic Trends*, February 1996.

continued declining numbers in the armed forces (104,000). Outside of these areas, some of the decline in Table 5.2 can be accounted for by the reallocation to other public organizations not included in the table. In education, for example, the 23,000 teachers in opted-out schools are no longer counted along with the 1.2 million in local authority schools even though they are still public employees, and the 180,000 education staff taken out of local government employment owing to the reorganization of further and higher education are also removed from the figures in Table 5.2 even though they still remain in the public sector. Many employed in the education sector as ancillary workers are employed by private cleaning or catering companies but work for the public sector. Much of the decline in NHS and local government employment is accounted for by ancillary and manual workers, many of whom now work for organizations that have had to tender for contracts. According to Table 5.2, the health sector declined by 2% between 1981 and 1995, and the education sector by 18%. However, the labour market statistics between 1979 and 1995 tell a different story: the education sector has *increased* over the period by 12% and the health sector by 33%, suggesting that there has actually been a net increase in the numbers directly or indirectly employed by the state in these areas (Annual Abstract of Statistics, 1982; 1996).

The demise of the hierarchical state?

While Terry Heiser (1994: 14), a former Permanent Secretary, talks of a traditional 'sense of hierarchy' in the post-war British civil service, it is nevertheless doubtful that Britain ever came close to being a hierarchical state in the Weberian ideal-typical sense of government being an integrated and unbroken chain of superior and subordinate relationships. Whether one is talking about relationships between government and the National Health Service organizations or local government, or the relationship between ministerial headquarters and the people actually on the ground delivering services, there is a danger in assuming that just because recent changes have restructured these to a greater or lesser degree, in the old days they were rather simple. Take, for example, the Next Steps agencification of government. While it is assumed that such an innovation marks a fundamental change in the nature of the civil service, it is possible to overestimate precisely how fundamental by assuming that ministries were integrated hierarchies before 1989. As a senior civil servant wrote in 1956, the British civil service is a 'single unified service, but its members serve under some scores of separate and partially independent employing authorities, and the duties which they perform are of almost limitless variety' (Padmore, 1956; see also Hogwood, 1995).

In fact, if we look at *intra* governmental relations more closely we get a very mixed picture. In terms of the relationship between local and national government it is commonly argued that government has become more of an integrated hierarchy since 1979. We can list the sorts of things that lead to this conclusion: local governments have been mandated to do things many of them probably would not otherwise have done, such as sell off their housing stock or tender out services; and have been forbidden to do other things, such as subsidize housing and transport or give money to homosexual groups. The government tells local authorities what they should spend, penalizes them if they spend too much and sets upper limits on the amount they can raise locally. Levels and standards of service in education are becoming increasingly the subject of central direction. In education, the government introduced in 1988 a 'national curriculum' – an arrangement that was hitherto commonly associated with Napoleon's France – and transformed school inspections from an institution which had been in the 1960s and 1970s geared towards spreading good professional advice to a form of supervision which is widely disliked by teachers and regarded as a significant cause of absenteeism within the profession (Bright, 1996).

In the National Health Service the picture is likewise mixed. Although the creation of NHS trusts and fundholding GPs has, on *a priori* grounds, appeared to reduce further the direct hierarchical control over medical practitioners, a couple of developments suggest stronger central control. The 1996 abolition of the regional health authorities (which had some independent status) and their replacement by regional offices – direct outposts of the Department of Health which may be staffed by ministerial civil servants rather than NHS managers – could involve an enhanced hierarchical role for the Ministry. Moreover, the requirement that fundholding GPs submit an annual report to district health authorities might also bring stronger administrative control over the activities of medical professionals (Hunter, 1996).

In the civil service, the creation of Next Steps agencies was widely expected to diminish the direct ministerial control over the agencies since ministries concentrate on 'policy' while 'operations' are delegated to the 109 agencies which, despite government claims, employ just under one-half of central government civilian employees. While the creation of agencies might have had a profound effect on government (see the later section on culture), it appears to have had a minimal effect upon its hierarchy. As Hogwood (1995) points out, commentators on the Next Steps programme are apt to assume that ministries before Next Steps were far more hierarchical than they in fact were. Moreover, as the sacked head of the Prison Service, Derek Lewis, found out in 1996, Next Steps status did not prevent the minister from intervening directly in specific details of the operation of the agency.

In a variety of other areas national government has taken a more direct hierarchical responsibility than in the past. In education, polytechnics (now 'new universities') and further education colleges have been taken out of local authority control and are now funded by national bodies directly responsible to the Department for Education and Employment. Universities, old and new, have experienced a shift towards a more intrusive funding regime which has entailed submission by universities to research and teaching assessments as well as firm guidance on the structure of undergraduate and postgraduate courses and on the way in which the teaching year should be organized (for performance measurement in higher education see Cave et al., 1995).

Hoggett (1996: 23) sees the variety of new types of formal devices as constituting 'new modes of control' just as hierarchical as the ones they replaced. The

> detailed performance specification, routine monitoring and proceduralization, can all be thought of as elements of a rational-systems control. Together they spin a myriad of little threads around different parts of the public sector. Contrary, therefore, to what is sometimes thought to be the current trend, there is no obvious sign of a reduction in this formalization of organization within the UK public service; if anything, quite the reverse appears to be true.

It is, of course, impossible to make any direct equation of the net increase or decrease in hierarchical control produced by so many changes across such a broad range of activities in the public sector. However, Hoggett's analysis does highlight the fact that changes in the public sector have produced new hierarchical relationships as well as dismantling or transforming older ones.

The reach of government

Has the British state shrunk in terms of the range of aspects of the lives of its citizens which it regulates? We may have two apparently contradictory expectations here, both of which are consistent with the overall trend of less state and more private sector. The first is simply that of deregulation. The Conservative government came to power in 1979 promising a bonfire of petty legislation that prohibited businesses from making money. The second is one of increasing reliance on regulation to achieve the objectives of state influence that used to be achieved through other means. Thus while the state might sell off public enterprises, it passes regulations controlling prices and service standards which give the state the same sort of control it had when it owned the enterprises. Giandomenico Majone argues along these lines that we are witnessing 'the rise of the regulatory state to replace the dirigiste state of the past' (1994: 97).

As with our understanding of the impact of Next Steps we must be cautious not to exaggerate the strength of ministerial control in the good or bad old days in the nationalized industries. Kelf-Cohen (1961) argued, for instance, that 'For a government to exercise anything resembling supervision over a nationalised industry will be tantamount to a constitutional revolution and it is difficult to see how it will be brought about and what kind of Government Department can be devised to undertake the responsibility' (see also Fry, 1994). Nevertheless, nationalized industries have been privatized, and government regulatory organizations – OFWAT, OFFER, OFTEL, OFGAS – have been given powers to control prices and charging

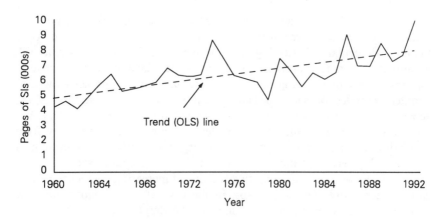

Figure 5.2 *Statutory instruments, 1960–92*

structures, to shape decisions affecting the provision of services and to require that, among other things, public utilities meet environmental objectives. This suggests two features of the reform of the British public sector. First, the reach of the state – the influence it can exert over those parts that it has lost to the private sector – has been diminished far less than might at first appear to be the case. Secondly, while the government may have substituted regulation for the powers it lost through transferring ownership to the private sector, to argue that privatization followed by regulatory supervision agencies is a new form of state 'to replace the dirigiste state of the past' exaggerates the role of government in the status quo ante.

Moreover, the suggestion that a broad trend in the way in which government intervenes in society or a general tendency to use different tools of government – 'authority' instead of 'treasure' or 'organization', to use Hood's (1983) terms – cannot be based on the treatment of the formerly nationalized industries alone. If we look at the development of regulation more generally (Figure 5.2), we see that the volume of regulation as measured by Statutory Instruments – decree laws that do not go through the same process of parliamentary approval as Acts of Parliament (see Miers and Page, 1982) – though fluctuating annually, shows no substantial discontinuity. Critics of the Conservatives, in fact, alleged that the government was responsible for an *increase* in the level of regulation (McSmith, 1995), yet the evidence points to a longer-term upward trend. Certainly one must be cautious when interpreting Figure 5.2 since the volume of regulation is not necessarily the same as the degree to which any society is regulated. However, the coming of the Conservative government in 1979 neither marked the beginning of an increasing use of regulation nor demonstrated a significant decline in regulation: there is a continuing upward trend in the amount of regulation passed each year.

This is not to suggest that the Conservatives made no difference in the reach of government. The government, for example, abolished the National

Dock Labour Scheme according to which port employers could only employ workers registered with the National Docks Labour Board. Here the term 'deregulation' affecting, for example, air and road transport as well as shipping refers to a process not of wide-scale relaxation of rules governing, say, safety or planning (although there have been examples as well as counter-examples of such measures), but of opening up sectors of the economy to more private firms by removing statutory barriers to entry. Yet it is doubtful whether such forms of deregulation are a move away from regulation as an instrument of government, or a significant diminution of the role of government more generally in the economy and society, rather than a more specific programmatic objective of increasing competition. This can be seen more clearly, perhaps, in the case of wage negotiation. The Conservative government repealed some of the Employment Protection Act (notably Schedule 11) which provided for employees to take employers to arbitration where wages were significantly below industry norms, yet it also passed trade union legislation limiting the freedom of unions in their handling of industrial disputes.

Changing the culture

When commentators examine assessments of the intended as well as the observed impact of Conservative reforms of the public sector, many emphasize the role of 'changing cultures' (see, for example, Colville and Packman, 1996; Greenaway, 1995; Wilson and Doig, 1996). There is, however, a variety of dimensions of culture that may be changed by the reforms of the Conservative period. Perhaps the most prominent of the 'cultural' objectives of the reforms has been to create a 'stronger customer focus' in the provision of public services. This sort of objective is seen in the creation of Citizen's Charter initiatives – setting out standards of service in a charter for the length of time one should wait for a hip operation or a train, and the award of honours in the form of Charter Marks for organizations which afford conspicuously good public service. The same sort of cultural objective is also to be found in the development of school and hospital league tables. The creation of greater discretion for 'operational' levels of service provision (including Next Steps, the setting up of NHS trusts, the local management of schools as well as direct grant schools) is also aimed at providing a 'stronger customer focus'. David Curtis, Chief Executive of the Driver and Vehicle Licensing Agency in 1994, expressed a common view among chief executives appearing before parliamentary scrutiny committees when he argued that 'the agency ethos is very consistent with focusing on customers . . . It has helped us focus on our customers better and has provided a stimulus to finding efficiency gains within the organization' (quoted in Public Accounts Committee, 1994: 16).

It is extraordinarily difficult to assess the significance of a 'culture'. Culture is hard to measure: the extent to which it spreads throughout an organization requires the sort of cross-time survey evidence that does not exist, and the lack of correspondence between expressed attitudes and actual behaviour makes questionable the impact of 'culture' beyond paying lip-service to norms (for the political relevance of the attitudes–behaviour debate see Marsh, 1971). Moreover, the significance and scale of any change that might be found in any such study is exceptionally difficult to evaluate. The evidence that does exist, however, offers a mixed picture and does not unambiguously suggest a radical shift in the culture of public sector officials generally.

A recent survey of local government chief executives, undertaken as part of the wider UDITE study (Goldsmith, 1996), strongly suggests that most now see their role in management terms not dissimilar from private sector managers, stressing such key tasks as promoting innovation and vision, and believing that they had a key role to play in influencing decision-making processes. Secondary to such objectives are such tasks as using resources efficiently and promoting inter-departmental cooperation. Such views were held generally, regardless of difference in size, type and political control of the local government concerned. In interviews, a number of chief executives stressed the importance of the networking and brokering role which they increasingly play with other local agencies, and of the way in which they had undertaken delayering exercises, increasingly delegating responsibility to subordinates so that they would be free to deal with the strategic issues. Others stressed the impact on their role of the marketization of local government, remarking on the costs and benefits of contracting out and compulsory competitive tendering. Others expressed concern that the traditional legal background of a chief executive was no longer so relevant to modern local government, where a willingness to take risks and to assess them, as well as thinking strategically, were all new values to be stressed.

Poole et al. (1995) set out evidence from a British Institute of Managers survey which reported on managers' attitudes in 1980 and 1990. Managers were asked which interests management should promote within the organization (Table 5.3). While the survey relates to a period before changes such as Next Steps had started to take off, there is little evidence of a strong cultural change among managers in the public sector. Consumers become more important for public sector managers over the 10-year period, but they were slightly more important to public sector managers even in 1980, and the increase over the decade is of the same order as that experienced in the private sector in this respect. Poole et al. conclude

it is clear . . . that emphasis at the macro-level on the enterprise culture and on market values has impacted on managerial attitudes in Britain. This is particularly evident in the importance attached to the consumer and customer interests among public sector managers. On the other hand, a long-standing public sector ethos has probably encompassed these interests in any case. (1995: 284)

The importance of the 'public at large' has also increased (Table 5.3), suggesting that a customer-based ethos has not developed at the expense of a broader ethos of public service.

Table 5.3 *Attitudes of public and private sector managers: percentage agreeing which groups management should promote within the organization*

	Public sector		Private sector	
	1980	1990	1980	1990
Owners/shareholders	71	78	70	83
Managers	49	56	59	59
Other employee groups	46	62	54	60
Consumers	78	91	72	83
Suppliers	28	23	23	31
Public at large	62	73	41	51

Source: derived from Poole et al., 1995

Pratchett and Wingfield, looking at local government, argued that one of the main concerns about the public sector reforms of the Conservative years is that the 'distinctive character and attitudes of public servants, which provided the essential cohesive force for traditional public administration, are being lost' (1996: 106–7). They go on to define distinctive elements of a 'public service ethos': accountability, impartiality, sense of serving a collective good, non-profit motivation and loyalty. Using the results of a 1994 postal survey, Pratchett and Wingfield show that a public sector ethos was still widespread: 77% of local government employees believed they still worked according to one. Pratchett and Wingfield concluded that the main source of the public sector ethos was 'professionalism' rather than the fact of belonging to a traditional public sector organization. This suggests that despite the changes to local authority service provision, the 'public service' ethos among officials remains strong, and that changes such as contracting out might not be expected to undermine it.

In the National Health Service, an analysis of the early managerial reforms of the 1980s (Pollitt et al., 1991) suggested that one of the most important cultural changes was that doctors had become more cost-conscious, but that this might have been a result of the general financial climate as much as a fundamental change in culture brought about through managerial change.

A customer orientation is not the only type of cultural change that reforms of the public sector might have been expected to produce. However, a customer focus is a particularly important cultural dimension which we might have expected to show change. The evidence does point to some form of cultural change in this respect, but one somewhat more modest than a cultural revolution, not least because clients appear to have been important in a public sector ethos before the reforms of the 1980s and 1990s and because any increase in the consideration of the client does not appear to have occurred at the expense of a broader concern with 'the public'. Moreover, Young (1996: 365) questions, in the context of local government, the degree to which any new public sector doctrines have produced a culture which produces or sustains a new type of public sector rather than a set of ideas which accommodate the new reality. The fact that 'cultural' change is driven by imposed reforms 'suggests not that the "reinvention" of local government is driven by an entrepreneurial spirit, but [that] its transformation, [is] driven by central government's own purposes and its readiness to use the bluntest of weapons to enforce its will'. Such changes in culture are not 'forces with their own transformational power' (1996: 365–6).

There are other dimensions of culture within public bureaucracies that might have been expected to have changed, such as the attitudes towards initiative, risk and colleagues (see Hofstede, 1980), although there is little current survey evidence on changes in such dimensions of culture. It is quite possible that changes in culture in the public sector have been most marked at more senior levels in the administrative hierarchy and thus less amenable to broad survey instruments. Senior officials in Next Steps agencies, for example, tend to emphasize the impact of agency status on increasing the entrepreneurial culture of management within the organization when asked to comment on the impact of the Next Steps initiative in their organizations. More widely in the public sector, professional jobs have changed in such a way that entrepreneurial skills are now a requirement for headteachers, university teachers and doctors among others (see Evetts, 1994 for a discussion of the changed job of headteacher; and Fisher and Best, 1995 for a discussion of medical professionals).

Conclusions

In 1979, when Labour left office, it seemed difficult to imagine that the Conservatives really would be able to 'roll back the state'. The early failure of Mrs Thatcher to secure substantial reductions in public spending seemed to confirm the apparent resilience of the public sector to change, and to confirm the description of the mass of commitments to public service provision inherited over decades if not centuries as the 'juggernaut of incrementalism' (Rose and Peters, 1978). Moreover, the era of cutbacks had begun in earnest under Labour in 1976, and an observer of the public sector in the early 1980s might well have drawn the conclusion that not much was going to change. Certainly times were going to be hard for the public sector, but Mrs Thatcher did not seem in the early years to have the capacity or even the authority within government to make the sorts of changes that the market rhetoric of her mentor, Sir Keith Joseph, suggested (Kavanagh, 1990).

The Conservative years appear especially revolutionary because they introduced changes on a scale that had previously been considered very difficult – certainly without extensive consultations with the major interests concerned. But the Thatcher and Major administrations introduced reforms against the expressed interests of the type of group – doctors, local authority associations, teachers and civil servants – that had been considered by many observers to be on the inside track in policy-making. Thus the contentious nature of the changes in the public sector, and the absence, in most cases, of any consultation about the *principle* of reform, add to the revolutionary image of the transformation of the public sector.

So how revolutionary actually was the 18 years of Conservative government? The most dramatic of the changes remains the reduction in size through the privatization of publicly owned enterprises. Yet no significant areas of government remained immune from the wave of reforms: civil service, armed forces, National Health Service, local government services and institutions of higher and further education all experienced massive changes on a scale that few would have thought possible in 1979 (for a discussion of the scepticism of even the Conservative establishment about the scope for radical change see Kavanagh, 1990: 207). Any answer to the question of how such changes were possible would include the weakness of the Labour opposition, the immediate benefits many such policies brought (such as the cut-price shares of the first British Telecom flotation), the ascendancy of Margaret Thatcher within the Conservative Party after the Falklands War and the progressive weakening of trade unions. In this sense, such changes reflected a degree of opportunism and cannot be viewed entirely as the systematic unfolding of a clear 'reinvention' strategy.

Yet the character of the changes should not be exaggerated. The size of the public sector has been dramatically reduced by the sale of the public corporations. In many other cases the 'privatizations' took the form of using private sector companies to carry out tasks which remain the responsibility of the public sector. Moves towards management 'decentralization' have not necessarily diminished the hierarchical control of the state over those it employs; in some cases, such as Next Steps, the changes in hierarchical control are generally quite small, and in others, such as the local management of schools, they are replaced by new forms of control. The reach of the state – the range of activities it seeks to regulate – has altered; some things are no longer the subject of regulation. Yet in the 1990s the government continued to regulate at the same rate as it did in the 1970s. It is by no means clear that if we were able to compare the volume of human activity that remains regulated and that which remains unregulated, the ratio between the two would have changed substantially over the 1980s and 1990s.

There is evidence of 'cultural' change in the public sector, but the change is somewhat more subtle than a cultural revolution. Managers and professionals in the public sector have had their jobs redefined to include tasks such as budget and personnel management, and in an era of retrenchment they are bound to become cost-conscious. A customer orientation among officials at all levels was, as far as one can tell, present among public employees before 1979, and there is evidence that this might also be a feature of changing management attitudes outside the public sector. The available evidence does not show that the growing lip-service that is paid to 'private sector' ideas about management and service has transformed the thinking of public sector employees in a radical way. Moreover, it is difficult to establish whether such cultural change constitutes a motor for further reform or is a form of cognitive dissonance – a psychological mechanism for making sense of many of the undesired and imposed changes in the public sector.

Note

This chapter was written before the Labour election victory in May 1997.

References

Beveridge, L. (1953) *Power and Influence: an Autobiography*. London: Hodder and Stoughton.

Blackman, T. and Stephens, C. (1993) 'The internal market in local government. An evaluation of the impact of customer care', *Public Money and Management*, 13(4): 37–44.

Bright, M. (1996) 'Teachers go sick as inspectors pile on pressure', *The Guardian*, 5.

Cave, M., Hanney, S. and Henkel, M. (1995) 'Performance measurement in higher education – revisited', *Public Money and Management*, 15(4): 17–23.

Charlesworth, J., Clarke, J. and Cochrane, A. (1996) 'Tangled webs? Managing local mixed economies of care', *Public Administration*, 7(1): 67–88.

Colville, I. and Packman, C. (1996) 'Auditing cultural change', *Public Money and Management*, 16(3): 53–61.

Damaška, M.R. (1986) *The Faces of Justice and State Authority: a Comparative Analysis of the Legal Process*. New Haven, CT: Yale University Press.

Deakin, N. and Edwards, J. (1993) *The Enterprise Culture and the Inner City*. London: Routledge.

Ellwood, S. (1996) 'Pricing services in the United Kingdom National Health Service', *Financial Accountability and Management*, 12(4): 281–301.

Evetts, J. (1994) 'The new headteacher: the changing work culture of secondary headship', *School Organization*,14(1): 37–47.

Fisher, C. and Best, W.A.A. (1995) 'Management or medics: how professionals adapt to management', *Public Money and Management*, 15(2): 48–54.

Fry, G.K. (1983) *Reforming the Civil Service. The Fulton Committee on the British Home Civil Service 1966–68*. Edinburgh: Edinburgh University Press.

Fry, G.K. (1994) 'The path to the privatization of public enterprises in Britain: a public policy analysis', *Public Policy and Administration*, 9(3): 19–32.

Goldsmith, M.J. (1996) 'The British local government chief executives', in *3rd UDITE Conference*, Odense, Denmark, September.

Goldsworthy, D. (1994) 'The Citizen's Charter', *Public Policy and Administration*, 9(1): 59–64.

Gough, O. and Shackleton, J.R. (1996) 'The Pensions Act 1995: unfinished business?', *Public Money and Management*, 11(3): 41–8.

Gray, A. and Jenkins, W. (1985) *Administrative Politics in British Government*. Brighton: Wheatsheaf.

Greenaway, J. (1995) 'Having the bun and the halfpenny: can old public service ethics survive in the new Whitehall?', *Public Administration*, 73(3): 357–74.

Heclo, H. and Wildavsky, A. (1981) *Private Government of Public Money*. London: Macmillan.

Heiser, T. (1994) 'The civil service at a crossroads', *Public Policy and Administration*, 9(1): 14–26.

Hennessy, P. (1985) *Routine Punctuated by Orgies: the Central Policy Review Staff 1970–1983*. Paper 31, University of Strathclyde, Glasgow.

Hennessy, P. (1989) *Whitehall*. London: Fontana.

Hofstede, G. (1980) *Culture's Consequences*. London and Beverly Hills, CA: Sage.

Hoggett, P. (1996) 'New modes of control in the public service', *Public Administration*, 74(1): 9–32.

Hogwood, B.W. (1992) *Trends in British Public Policy: Do Governments Make any Difference?* Buckingham: Open University Press.

Hogwood, B.W. (1995) 'Whitehall families: core departments and agency forms in Britain', *International Review of Administrative Sciences*, 62(4): 511–30.

Hogwood, B.W. and Gunn, L.A. (1984) *Policy Analysis for the Real World*. Oxford: Oxford University Press.

Hood, C. (1983) *The Tools of Government*. London: Macmillan.

Hood, C. (1991) 'A public management for all seasons?', *Public Administration*, 69(1): 3–19.

Hunter, D. (1996) 'Health', in P.M. Jackson and M. Lavender (eds), *Public Services Yearbook 1995/6*. London: Chapman and Hall.

Kane, M. (1996) 'The nature of competition in British local government', *Public Policy and Administration*, 11(3): 51–66.

Kavanagh, D. (1990) *Thatcherism and British Politics: the End of Consensus?* Oxford: Oxford University Press.

Kelf-Cohen, R. (1961) *Nationalisation in Britain: the End of a Dogma*. London: Macmillan.

Kellner, P. and Crowther-Hunt, L. (1980) *The Civil Servants*. London: Futura.

Lewis, J. (1996) 'The purchaser–provider split in social care: is it working?', *Social Policy and Administration*, 30(1): 1–19.

Majone, G. (1994) 'The rise of the regulatory state in Europe', *West European Politics*, 17(3): 77–101.

Malpass, P. and Warburton, M. (1993) 'The new financial regime for local authority housing', in P. Malpass and R. Means (eds), *Implementing Housing Policy*. Milton Keynes: Open University Press.

Marsh, D. (1971) 'Political socialization: the implicit assumptions', *British Journal of Political Science*.

McSmith, A. (1995) 'Tories stack up back-door legislation', *The Guardian*, 6.

Miers D. and Page, A.C. (1982) *Legislation*. London: Sweet & Maxwell.

Moran, M. (1995) 'Explaining change in the National Health Service: corporatism, closure and democratic capitalism', *Public Policy and Administration*, 10(2): 21–33.

Oughton, J. (1994) 'Market testing: the future of the civil service', *Public Policy and Administration*, 9(2): 11–20.

Padmore, T. (1956) 'Civil service establishments and the Treasury', in W.A. Robson (ed.), *The Civil Service in Britain and France*. London: Hogarth.

Pollitt, C. (1994) 'The Citizen's Charter: a preliminary analysis', *Public Money and Management*, 14(2): 9–14.

Pollitt, C., Harrison, S., Hunter, D.J. and Marnoch, G. (1991) 'General management in the NHS: the initial impact 1983–1988', *Public Administration*, 69: 61–85.

Poole, M., Mansfield, R., Matinez-Lucio, M. and Turner, B. (1995) 'Change and continuity within the public sector: contrasts between public and private sector managers in Britain and the effects of the Thatcher years', *Public Administration*, 73(2): 271–86.

Pratchett, L. and Wingfield, M. (1996) 'The demise of the public service ethos', in L. Pratchett and D.Wilson (eds), *Local Democracy and Local Government*. London: Macmillan.

Public Accounts Committee (1994) *The Driver and Vehicle Licensing Agency: Quality of Services to Customers*. PAC Report 34. Session 1993–4, HC 279, House of Commons.

Rhodes, R. (1988) *Beyond Westminster and Whitehall: the Sub-Central Governments of Britain*. London: Allen and Unwin.

Richards, S. and Newman, J. (1996) 'Shaping and reshaping market testing policy', *Public Policy and Administration*, 11(2): 19–34.

Rose, R. (1976) 'On the priorities of government: a developmental analysis of public policies', *European Journal of Political Research*, 4(2): 247–89.

Rose, R. (1977) 'Implementation and evaporation: the record of MBO', *Public Administration Review*, 37(1): 64–71.

Rose, R. and Peters, B.G. (1978) *Can Government Go Bankrupt?* London: Macmillan.

Slater, A.E. (1996) 'Privatizing medicines in the National Health Service', *Public Money and Management*, 16(1): 39–44.

Stoker, G. (1996) 'The struggle to reform local government 1970–95', *Public Money and Management*, 16(1): 17–22.

Waddington, P. (1995) 'The Local Government Review: a packet of allsorts', *Public Money and Management*, 15(2): 4–6.

Wilson, E. and Doig, A. (1996) 'The shape of ideology: structure, culture and policy delivery in the new public sector', *Public Money and Management*, 16(2): 53–61.

Wright, V. (1994) 'Reshaping the state: the implications for public administration', *West European Politics*, 17(3): 102–37.

Young, K. (1996) 'Reinventing local government: some evidence assessed', *Public Administration*, 74(3): 347–67.

Zifcak, S. (1994) *New Manageralism: Administrative Reform in Whitehall and Canada.* Milton Keynes: Open University Press.

6

Anglo-Saxon Public Management and European Governance: the Case of Dutch Administrative Reforms

Walter J.M. Kickert

As in most Western countries, the administrative reforms that have taken place in the Dutch administration have been primarily a response to the economic recession and the resulting public sector deficits. The larger the necessary budget cutbacks, the more inevitable the need for structural changes in government and administration. As the main rationale of the reforms was to increase the effectiveness and efficiency of the organization and functioning of government, the reforms understandably tended to be managerial. As a consequence, the Dutch administrative reforms also seemed to reflect the common 'managerial' trend in most administrations throughout the Western world to adopt more business-type management techniques.

The adoption by many Western administrations of a seemingly similar kind of 'new public management' is quite surprising. Various states differ in economic, socio-political, cultural, constitutional and institutional senses, and so do the ways in which these public administrations are managed. The differences in states, politics, governments and administrations between the United States and Europe, and between the various European countries, make the common adoption of the same kind of public sector management rather surprising. For, unlike the natural sciences, it is not possible to derive a universally valid theory of public administration which holds true anywhere and anytime. Neither is a universal theory of public management conceivable.

In this chapter, first, a brief account of the Dutch reforms in central administration will show that, in practice, the reform process has passed the stage of managerialism. Although clearly started as a managerial reform process, the constrained frame of reference of business-type management no longer suffices to validly describe the factual reforms at the moment. The frame of reference of the actual reforms has shifted from a strict managerial one towards the broader concept of 'public governance'. Elsewhere (Kickert, 1993; 1997) the concept of 'public governance' has been introduced and presented as an alternative to Anglo-American managerialism. Therefore, the conceptual explanation of 'public governance' in this chapter will remain brief.

In this chapter we will try to further explore the concept of public governance in an international institutional sense. If we broaden our scope from a constrained business-type interpretation of management towards a wider concept of governance – including the socio-political context of complex public policy sectors, including the complexity of such public sector networks, implying that classical top-down 'steering' by government is unfeasible, leading to multicentric, pluriform, multirational forms of 'steering' – then the institutional context of a state and an administration becomes the more important. A first exploration of a number of institutional aspects that might influence the form of governance in a country will be carried out.

Reforms in national administration: beyond management

Centre-right Cabinets, 1982–9

The 1980s were dominated politically by the two centre-right Lubbers coalition Cabinets (1982–9) between the Christian democrats and the conservative liberals. Their 'no-nonsense' policy was based on three main objectives: first of all the public budget deficit had to be drastically reduced; secondly the oversized and unaffordable public welfare sector had to be reduced; and thirdly the languishing private market economy had to be stimulated and revitalized. The welfare state gave way through a major retreat by the state from many social welfare arrangements. The 1980s were tough times of massive cutbacks throughout the public sector.

The first Lubbers Cabinet in 1982 launched a number of government reform activities which became known as the 'great operations' (van Nispen and Noordhoek, 1986; de Kam and de Haan, 1991). The first of the 'great operations' was decentralization. The constitutional Dutch 'decentralized unitary state' had increasingly centralized during the post-war expansion of the welfare state. Many promises for decentralization had also been made by previous governments.

The second of the 'great operations' was deregulation. The initial objective was to stimulate the market economy. Gradually that objective gave way to the aim of improving the quality of legislation. The legal system had to be purged of unnecessary and counterproductive regulations.

Privatization was considered an important instrument to reduce the budgetary and personnel size of government and to strengthen the private sector by transferring formerly public tasks to the market economy. Initially the objectives were of a rather ideological market-belief nature: a transfer of tasks would stimulate the market, and a market production of these tasks would be more efficient. Moreover the state could make budgetary gains by selling off state property. These financial-economic objectives were gradually replaced by managerial ones, as we will see later.

The fourth of the 'great operations' was the so-called 'reconsideration', more or less the Dutch equivalent of the British so-called 'Rayner scrutinies'.

Policy areas were scrutinized to find out whether all existing activities were absolutely necessary, and if so, whether and how the effectiveness and efficiency of the particular activities could be improved. Such 'reconsiderations' had to result in a number of budgetary cutback proposals.

The next was the reorganization of the civil service. Shortly before the start of the Lubbers Cabinet a major advisory committee – the so-called Vonhoff Committee – had produced a substantial and influential report on the issue, which led to the instalment of a government commissioner for the reorganization of the civil service.

Last but not least, the reduction of the number of civil servants was a major policy issue of the Lubbers Cabinets. During the first Lubbers Cabinet (1982–6) this was called the 'minus 2%' operation and resulted in a decrease of some 6,000 of the total number of about 160,000 civil servants. During the second Lubbers Cabinet (1986–9) about 20,000 people were additionally removed from the civil service. About half of that figure was realized by 'privatizing' government organizations.

Centre-left Cabinet, 1989–94

In the third Lubbers Cabinet the conservative liberals had to cede their place to the social democrats in the coalition with the Christian democrats. The new political figurehead of that Cabinet became the so-called social renewal (in Dutch *sociale vernieuwing*). Social activities should be initiated and realized by local citizens and neighbourhoods themselves, and local government should stimulate and assist those grass-roots activities in neighbourhoods.

Social renewal was to be a bottom-up activity at local level. The main task of national government was to decentralize tasks, authorities and funds to the local level to enable them to actively stimulate and support the grass-roots activities. The second main characteristic of the concept of 'social renewal' was its integrative comprehensive meaning: the hitherto separate policies on inner city renovation and poor area housing, on social welfare for excluded groups, on education and health for the poor and immigrants etc. ought to be viewed integratedly.

Decentralization was one of the main policies of the third Lubbers Cabinet as well. The Cabinet reached an agreement with the Association of Dutch Municipalities (VNG) about a so-called decentralization initiative, which was a compromise between on the one hand the decentralization of certain tasks and budgets and on the other hand a certain cut in the budgets, thus decentralizing not only tasks but also deficits.

In 1990 the Cabinet launched a so-called great efficiency operation. The objective was not only to realize budget cutbacks but also to qualitatively improve the organization and functioning of the civil service. At many ministerial departments this operation resulted in proposals to autonomize executive parts of the ministry, an administrative reform trend which will be discussed later on in this chapter.

Constitutional and administrative renewal

Another important political context of the national administrative reforms was the instalment, soon after the elections in 1989, of a parliamentary committee on constitutional and administrative renewal, headed by the President of the Second Chamber of Parliament, Deetman, and consisting of the parliamentary leaders of all major political parties. Administrative reform therefore figured not only on the agenda of the civil service and of the Cabinet, but also on the political agenda of Parliament. The 1991 report of the parliamentary Deetman Committee contained proposals which were compromises between the political parties and therefore far from revolutionary, but a movement had been set in place. A number of follow-up committees were installed to elaborate certain issues. One of these – the Wiegel Committee on the reshuffling of ministerial departments – played a marked role in the administrative reform of the civil service, presumably because its subject (mergers and abolishment of departments) constituted an existential threat for the existing ministries. This might well be a major reason why the College of Secretary-Generals of all departments produced a report on a drastic reorganization of the civil service in the spring of 1993, shortly before the publication in the summer of 1993 of the report of the Wiegel Committee. Both reports more or less had the same contents: the autonomizing of executive agencies and the creation of policy-making core departments. Departmental shifts and mergers were explicitly rejected in the Wiegel Report. Neither did the coalition formation after the 1994 elections lead to the abolishment of certain ministries.

Reforms within departments: strategic policy, integral management and quality of execution

The downsizing of the public sector, the 'retreat' of the welfare state, the withdrawal of government from policy fields, have resulted in fundamental shifts in policies and governance relations. Without the explicit development of long-term strategic policies, such fundamental ruptures – if governable at all – tend to become beach balls on the waves created by incidental social and political winds. At several departments, units for long-term strategic policy-making have been established.

Developing coherent, integral policy is the principal 'core business' of a ministerial department. The notorious sectoralization of Dutch departmental policies implies the necessity of coordination and integration. The urgent need to bridge the cleavages between the separate worlds of the policy sectors has for decades been the major message of almost all reports and advice on the organization of the Dutch civil service.

One attempt to overcome the boundaries of sectoral policies has been the instalment at various ministries of so-called 'governing boards' (in Dutch *bestuursraad*), consisting of the secretary-general and his or her deputy, and the director-generals. Some ministries have even abolished directorate-generals. The members of the governing board, who maintain the title 'director-general', are no longer in charge of a sectoral directorate, but have certain directions in their 'portfolio'. A further step is that the members of the governing board do not have directions in their portfolio but have strategic policy projects. Moreover the portfolios of the members of the governing board can be reshuffled every few years.

Another attempt to increase coordination and integration was the introduction of 'integral management'. At the Ministry of Transport and Waterworks a business-type concern-division model was adopted at the three levels of department, directorate-general and direction, the so-called D/D/D model. The first D-level is the governing board of secretary-general and director-generals; the second D-level is the directorates; and the third D-level is the directions at regional or district level. The relations between the three levels should be governed by management contracts, output financing and result-oriented planning. Integral management implies that all staff functions are fully subordinated to the line management.

Autonomization of executive tasks

Government not only has the task to 'serve' politics by preparing policy documents, but above all to 'serve' the citizens by executing policies and delivering services. From that point of view executive tasks and service delivery seem to be the actual 'core tasks' of government.

A clear common reform trend which took place in the early 1990s at ministerial departments during the so-called 'great efficiency operation' is the distinction between policy-making and policy execution, the organizational separation of executive task units from the policy-making department and the increase in the managerial autonomy of executive units, the so-called autonomization (in Dutch *verzelfstandiging*) of executive tasks (Kickert et al., 1993; Kickert and Verhaak, 1995). The idea behind this reform was that central departments should concentrate on their 'core tasks', that is, policy preparation, and that executive tasks should be performed at a distance of politics and policies so that management could concentrate on its own 'core task', that is, the production and delivery of goods and services, without interference from The Hague, thus resulting in better quality and higher efficiency. Managerial autonomy would lead to better quality and efficiency in public service delivery. Apparently this type of reform had a clear managerial rationale (Kickert and Jorgensen, 1995).

The 'great efficiency operation' which was launched in the Dutch national administration in the autumn of 1990 resulted in many departmental proposals of autonomization. The autonomization trend initially began as mere budget cutbacks. In many instances however the initial budgetary reforms gradually evolved into qualitative organizational reforms. The considerations for the reforms gradually changed into a managerial frame of reference. The advantages of autonomous executive agencies were increasingly viewed in terms of managerial and organizational improvements in the functioning of the affected task units.

Special regime 'agency'

The development of internal autonomous agencies was actively supported by the Ministries of Finance and Home Affairs in a report in 1991 which contained several proposals to substantially increase flexibility and autonomy in financial and personnel regulations for the new autonomous agencies, which would remain within the organizational boundaries of a ministry and under ministerial responsibility. The distinction between personnel and material expenditure was terminated, integral top formations were proposed, and more annual budget reservation possibilities were created. A separate administrative regime was proposed in the form of an *agentschap*, with a striking resemblance to the British Next Steps agencies. Although the proposals for relaxing the administrative regulations for government agencies were reticent in two major respects – a further differentiation in labour conditions and payments was rejected, and the authority to loan on the capital market was denied – the positive support of further developments of internal autonomizing of executive agencies was however undeniable.

Sint Committee and National Audit Office

More recently some critical and sceptical noises have been made about the widespread growth of various forms of autonomization, particularly from the viewpoint of the 'primacy of politics' and democratic control of such organizations.

In 1993 the College of Secretary-Generals installed a committee to further investigate the pros and cons of the various forms of autonomizing and to derive some form of systematic reasoning. The content and tone of the report of this so-called Sint Committee were widely perceived as a 'step back' in the autonomizing trend, as a warning against too easy and too much autonomizing, particularly against too easy external autonomizing. The 1994 report of the Dutch National Audit Office contained a highly critical investigation into independent administrative bodies and ministerial responsibility. The Audit Office concluded that a substantial clarification of that type of organization was necessary, particularly in view of the large multitude of such bodies and the huge public expenditures concerned. The Audit Office observed that the minimally necessary forms of supervision and inspection were lacking in more than half the cases. The lack of financial information from and control of such bodies was considered unacceptable. After the restrictive remarks on external autonomizing in the Sint Report, this report of the National Audit Office seems to form a next step in the counter-movement against the autonomizing trend. Both Cabinet and Parliament have seized the opportunity presented by this report to publicly restate their firm support for the 'primacy of politics' and 'democratic control'.

Core departments and steering at a distance

After the domination of the reform agenda at the beginning of the 1990s by the issue of 'autonomization', in 1993 another issue was added to that agenda, that is, the issue of a 'core department'. The College of Secretary-Generals published a report on the organization and functioning of the civil service, introducing the issue of 'core department'. In the same year the advisory committee on the reshuffling of departments, the so-called Wiegel Committee, issued its report 'towards high-quality and flexible core departments'. The Wiegel Committee argued that core departments should not be the leftovers of autonomizing executive tasks. The autonomization of an agency in order that it can more or less independently execute its public tasks does have consequences for the policy behind those tasks. Autonomizing is not merely an organizational restructuring but also a matter of a substantive reconsideration of tasks and policies. The separation of policy execution from policy preparation implies reconsideration not only of the executive tasks but also of the policy tasks at the department.

The separation of policy execution from policy preparation signifies three issues:

1   reconsideration of policies and core tasks of the ministerial department in the political and official context of The Hague
2   reflection on executive tasks, services and products in the context of clients, customers and target groups, as well as that of 'competing' products and services
3   reflection on the administrative relations between department and agency, about mutual 'steering' or better 'governance'.

In summary the Dutch reforms in the 1990s started with an emphasis on the autonomization of executive task units, then shifted to the issue of 'core departments', and now entail most departments searching for operationalization of the 'steering at a distance' of their autonomized executive units.

In the UK the Next Steps operation has also reached the phase where the issues of central core departments, and particularly the relationships between departments and agencies, have been added to the reform agenda. The Fraser (1991) report explicitly raised this problem. An evaluation report (Trosa, 1994) indicates that the British experiences with so-called 'Fraser figures' and 'ministerial advisory boards' as possible communication, monitoring and advisory instruments have not yet produced an adequate resolution of this problem.

In The Netherlands the picture is more diverse. Some departments have established central communication and coordination units for their relationships with executive organizations, but most have not. Contrary to the British civil service, where administrative reform is centrally guided by the Cabinet Office, in The Netherlands there is no central director of the stage. Each ministry is free to choose its own way of reform, resulting in more variety.

Public governance: conceptual exploration

Public managerialism

The shift in Dutch administrative reform from autonomization, via core departments, towards steering at a distance also implies a shift in the kind of reasoning and the frame of reference. The original reasoning behind autonomizing was primarily managerial. The argument was that if executive tasks units were distanced from politics and policies, away from the disturbance and interference of The Hague, they would be able to concentrate better on their actual executive tasks. Granting the management of such task units more autonomy would lead to an improvement in the quality, effectiveness and efficiency of the production and delivery of goods and services.

This line of reasoning runs remarkably parallel to the Anglo-American trend of 'new public managerialism' (Hood, 1991; Pollitt, 1990). According to this new managerialism the public sector should adopt more business-type management techniques, should become more customer-oriented and should introduce more market-like competitive methods. The urge towards 'entrepreneurial' government, following Osborne and Gaebler's *Reinventing Government* and Al Gore's *National Performance Review*, is an example of this managerialist trend in the United States. The trend is even more apparent in the United Kingdom where the government policy papers on Next Steps, on the Citizen's Charter and on Competing for Quality form a perfect illustration of, respectively, business-type management, client-orientedness, and market competition.

Managerial reforms are the dominant trend throughout the Western world, according to the reviews of the OECD (1990; 1993) on public management developments. From these reviews, it appears that more or less the same kind of developments have occurred in all of the OECD member countries. In a recent analysis of public management reforms (OECD, 1995), it is concluded that notwithstanding differences in the nature of, size of, and approach to reforms, a common agenda has developed, 'a new paradigm for public management has emerged, aiming at fostering a performance-oriented culture in a less centralised public sector'.

Public governance

The empirical evidence of the process of Dutch administrative reforms illustrates the restricted nature of the business-type interpretation of 'managerialism'. After an initial stage of predominantly managerial reforms, the frame of reference of the reforms has nowadays moved on to the more general question of mutual 'steering' relationships between core departments and agencies. The Dutch ministerial departments are now busy searching for new forms of 'governance'. The stage of mere intra-organizational management has been superseded in The Netherlands. Public management, government steering, or better 'public governance', requires more than the effective and efficient running of the 'government business'.

In our opinion, public governance has a broader meaning than the usual restricted businesslike market-oriented interpretation of the concept of 'management'. Public management is more than business management, client orientation and market competition. Public management is not merely a matter of effectiveness and efficiency, but also a matter of legality and legitimacy and of value patterns other than strictly business patterns. Public management is not only internal but also and primarily external management in a complex socio-political context.

Rechtsstaat, *Democracy and Public Values*

In the public sector, the management of organizations occurs within the context of *Rechtsstaat* and political democracy. The 'environment' of public management consists of the societal, political, juridical and economic context of state and administration. The principles of democracy and legality should be the starting points of any consideration of public organizations. The criteria which a democratic nation should meet, such as democracy, efficiency and professionalism, can well be mutually conflicting. For a large degree of democracy, a sacrifice in the degree of rationality and efficiency must be made. A public organization is not a commercial business. Without denying whatsoever the great importance of effectiveness and efficiency in the public sector, other norms and values play a role as well – values such as liberty, legality, legitimacy, equity and social justice.

Context, complexity and governance

In the governance of complex public sector networks three aspects are of major importance (Kickert, 1993; 1997): the context, defined as the environment; the complexity, defined as the number and variety of the system's elements and the relations between the elements; and governance, defined as 'directed influencing'. The specific context of the public sector implies a high degree of complexity – a network of many different actors – and this complexity implicates a different form of governance, neither central nor top-down. Context, complexity and governance are interrelated in a certain line of argument.

Context Public governance cannot be isolated from the societal and political context, neither generally the context of political democracy and the legal state, nor specifically the context of the specific policy sectors with their diversity of political, social, public and private actors. Management and organization within the public sector cannot be isolated from this context. An outside-in approach is to be followed.

Complexity The specific context of administration, the specific policy sectors, leads to the second aspect, the complexity. Public governance is 'steering' in complex networks in a specific societal sector. The participants in such a network are, besides manifold government (which even at the national level is no monolith but often consists of many divisions, directorates and departments apart from the various regional and local governments), the multitude of advisory and consultative bodies in typically consociational democracies and the typically neo-corporatist intermediate layer between state and society. Besides the formal official political actors such as parliamentary committees and party representatives, a great number of other participants can be involved. In addition to this impressive list of various actors in the public domain, actors from the private sector also play a part in many policy processes such as firms, project developers, building contractors, and so on. A large number of actors with large differences and a multitude of differing relationships means high complexity. A theory on public governance will have to deal with this kind of complexity.

Governance   In a network of many different actors, with different and often conflicting goals and interests and with diverging power positions, no single dominant actor exists. Such complexity means negotiating, pushing and pulling, giving and taking, and implies a different form of governance than monocentric, monorational, hierarchical top-down control by an omnipotent government (Hanf and Scharpf, 1978). On the other hand, public governance in complexity is not identical to the extreme opposite of hierarchy, that is, total autonomy of actors. Networks are characterized by the many dependencies and relationships which exist among the actors. The economic model of the market with free competition, in which buyers and sellers are autonomous and only the 'invisible hand' of the price mechanism functions, or the mathematical model of game theory in which all participants are making decisions in a completely independent way, are not applicable in public policy networks.

Governance between hierarchy and autonomy

The distinction between a complex multi-actor network and completely autonomous actors is not without meaning. It means that actors in a network are not entirely independent. It also means that, although actors are not hierarchically sub- or superordinate, they are not completely equivalent. Government will always maintain a different position from other societal public and private actors. Government cannot dominate and unilaterally dictate in a hierarchical manner, but at the same time it is not a complete horizontal equivalent to all other actors. This is not a normative view, but an empirical observation. The question here is not whether government should play a stronger steering role. Such a normative model of 'harder' government steering, for instance in the complex environmental policy area, is not inconceivable. It would however imply a return to some form of hierarchical top-down steering by government; yet the denial of the possibility of such a role was the very starting point of the network approach. It is not a normative statement but an empirical observation that the role of government in complex networks is special and unlike the roles of the many other actors. This does not imply a return to top-down control. It does imply that full horizontality and total autonomy of actors require an unrealistic model of a public sector network.

The concept of governance lies somewhere in the grey area between the two extremes of hierarchy and market (Thompson et al., 1991; Koppenjan et al., 1993; Kickert et al., 1997).

Public governance: institutional context of state and administration

Uniqueness of American public management

The Anglo-American trend of 'public managerialism' seems to spread over the entire Western world. The introduction of business-type management, customer-orientedness and market competition into Western public sectors does however raise serious questions. One should be cautious in the trans-position of American public management methods onto other parts of the world, especially onto continental Western Europe.

Contrary to the natural sciences, where the researcher's nationality does not matter, the administrative sciences do depend upon a nation's charac-teristics, for the state, government and public administration are the very object of study and this object differs considerably between countries. The administrative sciences are logically dependent upon their object. In a number of respects which are highly relevant from an administrative science point of view, the United States of America is exceptionally unique, to put it mildly. The concept of nation state does not exist there; the government, particularly central government, is viewed with the greatest suspicion, even in the American constitution which created checks and balances in order to prevent government from usurping too much power. In public opinion polls, Washington politicians score about as high as the mafia. Bureaucrat bashing is a most popular sport in the States. In view of the dominant culture of utilitarian individualism, American citizens primarily behave like individually calculating consumers of goods and services, no matter whether these are provided by private commercial firms or by public agencies.

One should therefore be extremely careful and cautious in the imitation of American public administration and public management elsewhere in the world. States, governments and administrations differ too much between the United States and Europe, and within Europe itself, to be able to simply imitate and transpose American theories of public management onto the various European public sectors.

Institutional context and historical awareness

When public management is more broadly interpreted as public governance, the institutional context of a country's administration evidently becomes even more important. Public governance cannot be separated from its institutional context, the organization and functioning of a nation's administration, and the latter cannot be viewed detached from its historical development and traditions. Maybe the internal organization and management of some public service in a particular short episode might be examined separately from the national historical context, but the way an administration 'governs' its societal public sectors can surely not be regarded without that socio-political historical context.

The usual lack of historical consciousness in today's policy and organizational analyses becomes untenable if one proceeds from organizational to institutional analysis. Whereas organizational analysis emphasizes structure, the sociological meaning of the concept of institution emphasizes its culture, that is, the patterns of norms and values, the behavioural patterns, the development of relatively stable, orderly patterns of social relationships. In particular the dynamics of institutionalization require attention to the historical context.

Institutional and historical traditions become more relevant when making international comparisons. Particular administrative reforms in the British or French government, for example, cannot be fully and rightly understood without some historical insight into the particular traditions of the British civil service or the French *haute fonction publique*. The same holds true for a study of the German, Dutch or Danish administrations, even when the particular interest is in the latest reform trends (Kickert and Jorgensen, 1995). This is especially so when the reform trends tend to resemble the managerialism which is typical of the highly unique United States. Some insight into the institutional and historical differences between the administrations of various countries might be useful to understand the contemporary trends in administrative reform, especially when these apparently form a departure from traditional administrative practice, which undoubtedly is the case when public management is introduced in the traditional continental European 'Weberian' bureaucracy.

Legal systems compared

It is common knowledge that lawyers dominate the German and French administrations, whereas within the British civil service and the North American administration that profession is markedly absent. Also widely known is the difference between the Anglo-Saxon common law system and the continental European public law system.

To begin with, one should realize the private law difference between the continental Roman law tradition and the Anglo-Saxon common law tradition. The first consists of a deductive, rational, comprehensive system of generally applicable, detailed rules. Jurisdiction is the rational deduction from the general regulations which are applied to the particular juridical case at hand. The latter is, on the contrary, based on inductive casuistic empiricism. Starting from the particular empirical case at hand, the judge inductively looks for precedent in similar cases from which parallels and conclusions might be drawn. The basic philosophies behind continental and

Anglo-Saxon legal thinking fundamentally differ. That holds true in private law and in public law as well.

The second important watershed between the continent and the Anglo-Saxon world is that the same common law also applies to the British and American public sector, whereas in continental Europe a separate administrative law system is in force. So on the continent government and administration are subject to judicial review in a Roman law type deductive, rational, comprehensive system of general rules of administrative law. Of course Great Britain is also a legal state where administration has to ensure the legality of its actions, but the fundamental difference in legal philosophy, thinking and system, equally in the private and public sector, has major consequences for the style of public governance. British administration is definitely not so dominated by legal thinking as, for example, the German and French administrations. It is not a coincidence that in the German and French language no separate word exists for 'policy' besides 'politics'. Policy-making in a German ministerial department solely consists of the preparation of legislation. White Papers or other policy documents, sent to Parliament preceding legislative proposals, are non-existent or at least highly unusual. Administrative activities are predominantly juridical in the German and French administrations. Although legalism dominated also in the Dutch and Danish administrations till after the Second World War, that monopoly has been broken in the post-war welfare state.

Notice that although the main legal characteristic of the Anglo-Saxon administrations is the non-existence of a separate administrative law, that does not hold true for constitutional law. Britain has no written constitution but the United States certainly has. The American constitution is considered there to be the 'holy pillar' supporting their democracy. Judicial review by the constitution is well known in the United States. Constitutional review in America differs from that in continental Europe in that US courts and the Supreme Court feel politically much more free to judge on constitutional incompatibilities than their European counterparts. This of course has to do with the difference between rational-deductive and empirical-inductive legal thinking.

The all-pervasive dominance of administrative law, combined with the rational, deductive, comprehensive, systematic way of legal thinking, must have serious implications for the form of 'public governance' that is adopted. The typical German legalistic way of thinking and acting does seem at odds with a managerial attitude, to put it mildly. From this point of view, one is bound to expect that 'new public management' is more likely to be introduced in the continental European states that have already diverged from the *Juristenmonopol*.

Political system

There is no such single thing as 'a' democracy. Administrative scholars are well aware of the variety of types of democracies, such as the distinction between a presidential and a parliamentary one, and the distinction between a two-party and a multi-party one. Many Anglo-American observers of the European type of coalition Cabinet governments, in their eternal pursuit of compromise and consensus, often wonder how decisions are ever taken at all. The political science theory on consensus democracy, which enjoyed much popularity in the 1960s and 1970s (Lijphart, 1968; 1969; Lehmbruch, 1967; Huyse, 1970; Daalder, 1971), ought, however, to be rescued from obscurity. The relative oblivion of that theory was probably related to the revolutionary democratic movement of the 1970s, when politicization and polarization seemed to put an end to the compromise and consensus culture. The revolutionary *élan* has, however, evaporated, and the typical multi-party coalition forming and consensus reaching has reappeared on the political scene. Deliberation, consultation, compromise and consensus have become once more the fundamental traits of the political culture in many small continental European states.

The resurrection of compromise and consensus politics does not imply the resurrection of the underlying political fragmentation that originally induced political scientists to study that form of democracy. The 'pillarization' in The Netherlands has almost disappeared; the ethno-linguistic fragmentation in Belgium has been solved by transforming the unitary state into a federal one; and the Austrian *Lager* seem to have buried the hatchet. This seems to support the thesis that consociationalism and consensus have much deeper historical roots than modern politics.

It goes without saying that such dominant traits of political culture must have consequences for the style of public governance, let alone management. Top-down hierarchical steering and control are concepts that are hardly adequate in such a political context. Although the author is well aware that modern management science consists of more than only the classical hierarchical control archetype, a slight warning does not seem redundant. In the political context of a multitude of political participants, which ought at least to be consulted, with which compromises have to be reached, and which should consent to the proposed agreement, decision-making and governance rather take shape in terms of 'management of complex political networks'.

Corporatist interest intermediation

The previous remarks about the resurrection of a political culture of consultation, compromise and consensus applied to the internal functioning of the political system. The neo-corporatist model of interest intermediation (Schmitter, 1974; Lehmbruch, 1976; Williamson, 1989) applies to the 'external' relationship of government with societal interest organizations. The consensus model of democracy explains the stability of the political system of government; neo-corporatism explains the stability of the social economy of a state, that is, the system of relationships between government, employer associations and labour unions.

On the surface the phenomena are equal: deliberation, consultation, compromise and consensus. Here, however, the interrelations take place not amongst political parties only, but also with societal organizations. Neo-corporatism is a model of a particular type of state–society interrelations. In a certain sense it is also a model of public governance, the way in which government 'deals' with societal actors.

Neo-corporatism can be extended from the macro-level of socio-economics to the meso-level of sectoral policy-making (Cawson, 1986). The management of complex political networks is now extended to the governance of complex networks of many social actors in public policy sectors. All these actors have different objectives, interests and strategies. There is no single dominating actor 'in command' of the network, not even government; all actors have some influence on the policy-making. Public governance in such a complex situation requires more than legislative authority, democratic legitimacy and financial means alone.

The issue is closely related to the questions that were raised in the 1980s about the shaping and controlling of society by the state. The economic crisis and the subsequent public budget deficits had forced Western states to withdraw from many welfare arrangements. The heyday of the integral government planning of the welfare state was over. Government proved unable even to control the ever growing unemployment. Belief in the governability and controllability of society waned (Mayntz, 1987). The limitations of a more modest state were realized (Crozier, 1987). Insight into the complexity of social policy networks led to the recognition that government could indeed not unilaterally and hierarchically 'steer' such processes. Another form of public governance was needed – a form of governance in public sector complexity.

Other aspects of public governance

In the foregoing overview only three aspects of public governance have been considered. Of course many more dimensions can be distinguished in the broad concept of public governance. In the definition of public governance as government 'steering' in a complex network of social actors, a simple systems theoretical model would already consist of the various types, numbers and forms of actors, their different relationships, their various environments, etc. The distinction between pluralism and corporatism specifies one such dimension of social actors, that is the number of actors (many or a limited number), and specifies a certain sort of relationship with government, that is recognition and delegation.

Besides the aspects of legal and political systems, of course, the financial-economic dimension ought also to be included in a comparative review of public governance. The importance of the financial-economic aspect of public governance is self-evident. It does make an enormous difference whether government is trying to 'govern' a policy sector such as primary education, which in economic terms is an example of a 'collective good'; or whether government is trying to interfere in the policy sectors of fishery or agriculture, which in economic terms are examples of 'private good' producing sectors of the 'free market'; or whether government is trying to develop health policy, a sector of 'quasi-collective goods'. In the first case it is legally compulsory for every youngster to follow primary education, which as a consequence is financed by the state. The legislation and financing system enables government to pursue educational policies. In the second case, in principle the free market economy should regulate the agricultural and fishery sector, and government should refrain from interference in that sector of the market economy. For political reasons, however, many governments pursue an active agricultural policy of subsidizing grain and dairy products, supporting farmers, or, on the other hand, of prohibiting fishing by imposing maximum quotas. Government interference in the agricultural 'market' sector substantially differs from educational policy in a legally and financially 'public' sector. Health policy is an intermediate case, in the sense that on the one hand public health is considered throughout the Western world to be so important that the state feels obliged to interfere, whereas on the other hand the financing of that sector usually is not part of the public budget, and hence is not in the government's control but in the hands of legally independent sickness funds or private health insurance companies. The Dutch government has to its distress experienced the difficulties and limitations that dual position implies for public governance of the health sector.

An international review of the financial-economic aspect of public governance seems therefore to tend in the direction of an international comparison per sector.

Discussion: public governance in Europe

From public management to governance

'New public management' 'managerialism', 'entrepreneurial government' or any synonymous fashionable terms are undeniable trends in the Western public sectors, calling for more business-type, more market-like and more client-oriented management in the public sector. It is, however, doubtful whether these private sector management concepts can easily be transposed onto, let alone simply be imitated by, the public sector.

The recognition that the usual interpretation of management is too constrained a concept to be adequate for public administration has led to the introduction of the broader concept of 'public governance', that is, the governance in complexity, in the socio-political context of complex public policy networks. This concept implies a different form of 'steering' than monocentric, monorational, hierarchical top-down control by government. The awareness of the limitations and constraints of central government control led to scientific theory formation on policy networks and on the management of networks. The central concept in the Rotterdam research programme on 'governance in complex networks' is that 'network governance' is located between the one extreme of hierarchical, central, top-down control and the other extreme of horizontal, fully autonomous actors in a free market. The first results of the exploration and elaboration of the meaning of network management have been published (Koppenjan et al., 1993; Kickert et al., 1997).

Elsewhere (Kickert, 1997) the author has presented a conceptual outline of public governance as a possible alternative to Anglo-American 'public managerialism'. Let me explicitly repeat that it is by no means my objective to create unnecessary fissures between scientific communities studying administration and management anywhere in the world. The rising scholarly interest in public management has undoubtedly yielded most interesting and relevant results in the United States. Neither should one create an unnecessary split between business and public administration. Both scientific areas can learn a lot from each other and are actually doing so. The only statement here is that the adequate form of 'governance' does depend on its context. It does make a difference whether governance is taking place in the private business sector or in the public sector. Likewise it does make a difference whether public governance takes place in the United States, the United Kingdom or continental European states. Or to put it more generally, public governance depends on its institutional context. In this chapter the concept of public governance has been developed one step further by paying explicit attention to this aspect of institutional context of different national states and administrations.

It is clear that we have only been able to offer a preliminary conceptual exploration of some of the institutional aspects – legal systems, political systems and systems of interest representation – that might influence the particular form of public governance which is adopted in a country. An elaborate, well-developed, systematical theory of public governance is still far beyond the horizon.

Although the road is apparently still very long, some steps have already been taken. The first step was the recognition of the difference between private and public sector management. Since the end of the 1970s and the early 1980s, that hurdle has definitely been passed in our field of science, to the extent that the private–public discussion has almost become obsolete and sometimes even counterproductive. Business administration, generic management and organization sciences are by no means to be accused of irrelevance. On the contrary, we can still learn a lot from them. Other steps in the theory development of governance have also been taken (Rhodes, 1997). The recognition that public governance is not top-down hierarchical control by government is widespread. Complexity, pluriformity, pluricentrism, self-steering are widely accepted as concepts underlying governance.

Public governance in Europe

The ultimate aim is to develop a conceptual framework of public governance which is contingent on international institutional characteristics. It is hard to believe that European public administrations, with their century-long tradition of running government business, should or could adopt the new 'managerialism'. The deeply rooted institutional tradition of the French *haute fonction publique* or the German *Beambtentum* seems to make a simple adoption of managerialism quite impossible. On the other hand the equally deeply-rooted institutional traditions of the British civil service apparently did not prevent them from becoming 'public managers' (Hennessy, 1989). My aim is to develop a framework of governance which is not only particularly adjusted to the public sector, but also particularly suited for the European states and administrations. Allow me therefore to conclude this chapter with some perhaps provocative remarks about the typical characteristics of European states.

Usually, the European states and administrations are distinguished according to a typology which consists of three main categories. The first is the Napoleonic type of state, with post-revolutionary France as the main example. Spain and Italy are typically considered to belong to this type, and so is Belgium. The second is the Germanic type with its Prussian and Habsburg roots, in which post-war Germany and Austria can be placed. The third is the Anglo-Saxon type, with England as the main example. The smaller Northern European states, such as The Netherlands and the Scandinavian countries, are usually considered to be a mixed form of the Anglo-Saxon and Germanic types of state.

One might, however, follow a different line of argument in categorizing European states. The large European states like France, Britain and Germany are all highly unique and highly dissimilar. There are many more small states in Europe than the few large ones, and most of the smaller continental European nations are highly similar in three respects which seem highly relevant for the form of public governance, as follows.

State and politics They all have a consociationalist type of consensus democracy (Lijphart, 1984). Contrary to the majoritarian Anglo-American two-party system of democracy, they have a multi-party system with proportional elections where governments consist of coalitions between more parties. The search for compromises and consensus is a main ingredient of their political culture. This search is seen in the post-war *Grosse Koalition* in Austria, in the *Proporz* system of division of seats in government in Switzerland, in the coalition governments between the Flemish Christian democrats and Wallonian socialists in Belgium, in the varying coalitions between the social democrats, Christian democrats and conservative liberals in The Netherlands, in the multi-party coalition Cabinets in Denmark and Norway which sometimes do not even have a parliamentary majority; these forms of consociationalism explain the political stability in these societies.

State–society relations They all have a neo-corporatist type of democracy. Contrary to the American pluralist type of democracy, in a neo-corporatist democracy interest representation takes place through a few well-organized groups which are recognized by the state and to which many public tasks and state authority have been delegated. Sweden has a social democratic type of corporatism, The Netherlands a typically confessional type, Belgium a linguistic, regional and confessional type, Austria again another type, but all are variations of the same basic type of neo-corporatism.

Society They all have socio-political cleavages and fragmented political and social subcultures. Austria has its Christian and socialist *Lager*. Switzerland has its regional and linguistic fragmentation into various *Kantons*. Belgium has the linguistic cleavage between Flanders and Wallonia and the political cleavage between socialists and Christians. The Netherlands has a 'pillarization' as a consequence of its history of confessional division into Protestant, Catholic, socialist and liberal-neutral pillars. The theory of consociationalism, later renamed consensus democracy, originated from the question of how these countries with their fragmented societies, and hence potentially unstable political democracies, could nevertheless end up being politically highly stable.

The whole range of countries from the far north to the middle of continental Europe – Finland, Sweden, Norway, Denmark, The Netherlands, Belgium, Switzerland, Austria – all have these three characteristics in common, albeit in greater or lesser degrees and in different variations. The Netherlands – in population and economy the largest of the small Western European countries – is an extremely clear and highly institutionalized example of the three characteristics.

So if one is interested in Europe, perhaps one had better pay somewhat less than the usual attention to the big states of Germany, France and Britain, pay somewhat more attention to the many small continental ones, and take The Netherlands as a *pars pro toto*. The study of public governance in the tiny royal kingdom of the Lowlands is not merely an amusing token of the author's nationality. It is an interesting and relevant prototypical case in the European landscape.

References

Cawson, A. (1986) *Corporatism and Political Theory*. Oxford: Basil Blackwell.

Crozier, M. (1987) *État moderne, état modeste*. Paris: Editions Seuil.

Daalder, H. (1971) 'On building consociational nations: the cases of The Netherlands and Switzerland', *International Social Science Journal*, 23(3): 355–71.

De Kam, C.A. and de Haan, J. (eds) (1991) *Retreating Government: an Evaluation of the Great Operations* (in Dutch). Schoonhoven: Academic Service.

Fraser, A. (1991) *Making the Most of Next Steps*. London.

Hanf, K. and Scharpf, F. (1978) *Interorganisational Policy Making*. London: Sage.

Hennessy, P. (1989) *Whitehall*. London: HarperCollins.

Hood, C. (1991) 'A public management for all seasons', *Public Administration*, 69(1): 3–19.

Huyse, L. (1970) *Passiviteit, pacificatie en verzuiling in de Belgische politiek.* Antwerpen: Standaard Wetenschappelijke Uitgeverij.

Kickert, W.J.M. (ed.) (1993) *Changes in Management and Organisation at Central Government* (in Dutch). Alphen: Samsom.

Kickert, W.J.M. (1997) 'Public governance in The Netherlands: an alternative to Anglo-American managerialism', *Public Administration.*

Kickert, W.J.M. and Jorgensen, T.B. (eds) (1995) *Management Reform: Executive Agencies and Core Departments.* Mini-symposium in *International Review of Administrative Sciences,* 61(4): 499–587.

Kickert, W.J.M. and Verhaak, F. (1995) 'Autonomising executive tasks in Dutch central government', in W.J.M. Kickert and T.B. Jorgensen (eds), *Management Reform: Executive Agencies and Core Departments.* Mini-symposium in *International Review of Administrative Sciences,* 61(4): 499–587.

Kickert, W.J.M., Mol, N.P. and Sorber, A. (eds) (1993) *Autonomisation of Government Services* (in Dutch). Den Haag: VUGA.

Kickert, W.J.M., Klijn, E.H. and Koppenjan, J.F.M. (eds) (1997) *Managing Complex Networks: Strategies for the Public Sector.* London: Sage.

Koppenjan, J.F.M., de Bruyn, J.A. and Kickert, W.J.M. (eds) (1993) *Network Management in Public Administration.* The Hague: VUGA.

Lehmbruch, G. (1967) *Proporz Demokratie, Politischa Systeme und Politische Kultur in der Schweiz und in Oesterreich.* Tübingen: Mohr.

Lehmbruch, G. (1976) 'Liberal corporatism and party government', *Comparative Political Studies,* 10: 91–126.

Lijphart, A. (1968) *The Politics of Accommodation: Pluralism and Democracy in The Netherlands.* Berkeley, CA: University of California Press.

Lijphart, A. (1969) 'Consociational democracy', *World Politics,* 21(2): 207–25.

Lijphart, A. (1984) *Democracies: Patterns of Majoritarian and Consensus Government in Twenty-One Countries.* Yale: Yale University Press.

Mayntz, R. (1987) 'Political control and societal problems', in Th. Ellwein et al. (eds), *Yearbook of Government and Public Administration.* Baden: Nomos. pp. 81–98.

OECD (1990) *Public Management Developments Survey.* Paris: OECD.

OECD (1993) *Public Management Developments Survey.* Paris: OECD.

OECD (1995) *Governance in Transition: Public Management Reforms in OECD Countries.* Paris: OECD.

Pollitt, C. (1990) *Managerialism and the Public Services.* Oxford: Blackwell.

Rhodes, R.A.W. (1997) *Understanding Governance.* Buckingham: Open University Press.

Schmitter, P.C. (1974) 'Still the century of corporatism', *Review of Politics,* 36: 85–131.

Thompson, G.J., Frances, R., Levacic, R. and Mitchell, J. (eds) (1991) *Markets, Hierarchies and Networks.* London: Sage.

Trosa, S. (1994) *Next Steps: Moving On.* London.

Van Nispen, F.K.M. and Noordhoek, D.P. (eds) (1986) *The Great Operations* (in Dutch). Deventer: Kluwer.

Williamson, P.J. (1989) *Corporatism in Perspective.* London: Sage.

7

Public Sector Reform in the Nordic Countries

Jan-Erik Lane

Public sector reform attempts have been numerous in the Scandinavian countries as well as in Finland. Perhaps Sweden has been the most aggressive in engaging in these activities, not only in the scope of reforms but also in the depth of changes sought. Why is this so? Does the search for public sector reform in the Nordic countries simply reflect general tendencies in all the advanced countries with a democratic regime? Or are there special circumstances in Norden which make public sector reform urgent, such as the sheer size of public expenditure as a percentage of GDP, or the heavy reliance upon one institution for the delivery of public services, the local government?

The public sectors of the Nordic countries have a few distinctive features. In a comparative perspective, characteristic of the Nordic countries is on the one hand the strong public commitment to both allocative and redistributive expenditures and on the other hand the special division of labour between the national and local governments, the former concentrating upon public goods and redistribution and the latter being responsible mainly for welfare state services. The local government sector is very large in Scandinavia and Finland with a larger allocative responsibility than the state itself.

When local governments play a major role in the public sector as in the Nordic model, efficiency in local government operations becomes a critical concern. But how is efficiency in these authorities to be investigated when at the same time the local governments claim autonomy from the state? This is the crux of the matter in the Scandinavian countries and Finland, where most welfare state services and much infrastructure are allocated by local governments simultaneously as they claim and have been recognized as having an autonomous position in relation to the national government. What are the efficiency enhancing mechanisms in the Nordic type of local government?

The existence of these huge local governments raises not only problems of economic efficiency but also a fundamental question about political participation. When local governments become the largest organizations in society, outcompeting private sector firms and challenging the state, then there are good reasons to be concerned not only with efficiency but also with accountability. In the Nordic context, countries have tried to increase political accountability by means of participatory reforms. The problems of productivity and effectiveness in the Nordic model were realized in the mid 1980s, as public sector reforms have been attempted since then. In Sweden the reforms have been extensive, whereas the other countries have been more cautious. However, in all countries we find examples of reforms which we may classify as oriented towards efficiency.

Efficiency and accountability

Countries with a huge public sector face two chief problems. They must frame their decision-making and implementation processes in such a manner that the taxpayers feel that politicians are accountable for their huge budgets. Why should citizens put up so much money for a public sector if they feel that decisions are taken that do not reflect their preferences? The question of accountability concerns how the huge resources of modern government are handled in a legal fashion. The political accountability of the public household involves concerns of democracy and administrative legality.

At the same time, public expenditures must make economic sense. The huge tax state is hurt if inefficiencies occur, because the occurrence of waste could undermine the legitimacy of the entire public household. The critical question is to design institutional mechanisms that promote efficiency in public expenditures. Economic efficiency in the public household may refer to either allocative expenditures or redistributive expenditures. And it may be tackled by means of different reform efforts, as efficiency in terms of productivity of effectiveness may be promoted by institutional mechanisms or changes in these. Governments may search for rules or changes in rules which enhance economic efficiency, because a government as an agent faces pressure from its principal, the population, to deliver – given the quid pro quo assumption which is at the heart of democratic politics in a market economy.

Economic efficiency and political accountability may not go together, meaning that there may occur goal conflicts, the former calling for less public expenditure whereas the latter could demand more resources. Clearly, both objectives – efficiency and accountability – have played a major role in the efforts at public sector reform in the huge Nordic welfare state. Yet, distinctive of the public household in the Nordic countries is the major role played by the local government, the so-called *kommuner* (communes) and *landsting* (county councils).

Both objectives – economic efficiency and political accountability – are to be accomplished by the Scandinavian local government system, which operates under broad discretion from the national government, including taxation powers as well as budgetary autonomy. Much of the welfare state

Table 7.1   *Public sector reform types in the Nordic countries*

| | Efficiency | | Accountability |
	Allocation	Redistribution	
Central government	1	2	7
State enterprises or public joint stock companies	3	4	8
Local governments	5	6	9

is concentrated in the local governments. Whereas public sector reform of the state has focused almost exclusively upon economic efficiency, local government reform has attempted to achieve both objectives, accountability and efficiency. This double objective function has no doubt strained the local governments. At the same time, the measuring rods of efficiency and accountability may be applied to the national government or the entire public sector as well. Below we will examine reform efforts in the national governments also.

Besides the quid pro quo demand, there are in Western Europe strong requests for more accountability of public officials, when numerous voices are raised for the protection of minority rights by means of public sector programmes. Legality is emphasized by groups who seek to protect collective rights by means of public policy. In a few countries, corruption and the fight against it are given much attention. The notion of human rights has been given an increasingly prominent place in both policy and the legal order in several West European countries, partly as a response to demands for minority protection. And the concept of judicial review in one form or another has been given much more attention at both the national and international levels – the judicialization of politics.

The search for efficiency may refer to either allocative or redistributive expenditures. This is the basic functional division. And it may be raised in relation to the central government and its bureaux, in relation to the state enterprises and public joint stock companies at both the national and the local government level, as well as in relation to the local government system: this is the basic institutional separation. Using these distinctions, we arrive at Table 7.1.

What follows is an examination of these nine types of public sector reform with special reference to a few examples from Scandinavia and Finland. One should mention that Sweden and Finland have been forced to bring down their public sectors simply because deficit spending at the national government level took on drastic proportions, threatening overall financial stability. What, more specifically, is the place of the local governments in the public sector in these countries?

Only the Swedish government has attempted a comprehensive public sector reform policy, initiated in 1989 (Hæggroth, 1991: 30–2). Each year the central government presents to the Riksdag its efforts at a renewal of the public sector, but one must remember that the central government has few tools for steering one large part of the public sector, namely the local governments. A comprehensive public sector reform policy may be a rational means for the accomplishments of clearly stated goals, if the central government can identify transparent objectives and suggest reliable means. But it can do little if the sublevel governments do not cooperate.

The so-called renewal of the Swedish public sector aimed at the following goals: (a) changes made by reorientation of given resources within existing programmes; (b) new means of financing in demand; (c) increased competition in supply; (d) reduction in administration; (e) increased scope for citizen choice (1991: 30–2). However, the government also made it very clear that the core function of the public sector – law and order, care, education and income protection – cannot be changed in any substantial manner. Thus, it stated:

> The general welfare policy ambitions remain intact. Health care, education and child care must be available to all on equal terms. Everyone has the right to security at old age and when sick. The public sector must be financed in a solidaristic manner. (1991: 30)

What, then, is the scope for policy change? There is a real risk that public sector reform attempts result in so-called garbage-can processes.

Structure of the public sector

The Nordic public sector is so large in terms of outlays as a proportion of GDP that one needs to unpack it into various parts. First, the distinction between allocative and redistributive reforms appears to be highly relevant, although it is sometimes difficult to decide whether a programme belongs to the allocative side or the redistributive part of the budget. Since the Scandinavian model recommends a public sector that harbours deep commitments in both service provision – public resource allocation – and income redistribution, one may examine the reform attempts by relating to the allocative or the redistributive part of government.

The distinction between the allocative and the redistributive programmes is the first basic characteristic of the Scandinavian model. The huge involvement of the local governments in the allocative side is the second fundamental feature. Table 7.2 has a few figures relating to the first dimension.

Given such a huge public sector, with about 50% of the population deriving their main income from government (public employees, unemployed and pensioners), how are reforms to be identified which enhance economic efficiency?

The sharp public sector expansion in the Nordic countries, involving more than a doubling of the share of public expenditures of the GDP at the same time as the GDP has more than doubled, has been evenly divided between allocative and redistributive types of expenditures. During the last decade, the redistributive part of the public household has outpaced the

Table 7.2　*The Nordic public sector as a percentage of GDP*

	Total outlays		Final government consumption		Transfer payments	
	1960	1990	1960	1990	1960	1990
Denmark	21.7	58.8	12.7	25.7	11.1	19.7
Finland	21.9	56.9	12.6	24.8	31.2	23.7
Norway	28.0	57.7	14.0	21.5	9.4	20.5
Sweden	28.7	64.3	17.1	27.9	10.9	23.4

Source: Political Data Handbook: OECD countries, 1996.

allocative part in yearly growth. The cost explosion in the redistributive programmes has called for reforms, which however are not easily accomplished. The Scandinavian model implies that a number of services are provided gratis, or almost free of charge, to the citizens or the population – education, health care and social care – in the allocative budget, and that income maintenance programmes or transfer payments are immense on the redistributive side. Table 7.2 does not include the costs for public infrastructure, which is paid for by means of user fees and which has also been targeted in the search for more efficiency through massive deregulation.

In relation to the allocative side of the public sector there is a search for efficiency as well as accountability, whereas the debate about the redistributive part has focused mainly upon efficiency. Allocative efficiency refers to micro efficiency, or the search for productivity and effectiveness in each public sector programme. Efficiency in redistribution deals with the effects on the economy of extensive transfer payments, as what is at stake is incentive compatibility, that is whether income maintenance programmes hurt or benefit the economy, i.e. macro efficiency.

The second major characteristic of the Scandinavian model is the size and importance of the local government system. The local governments are either communes or county councils, which are both representative bodies elected by direct proportional elections – democracy *von unten*. The local governments have achieved a highly independent position in relation to the national government, as they have legal recognition as well as taxation powers. The growth in the number of employees has been immense, turning these participatory bodies into formal organizations which are the largest employers at the local level (communes) or the regional level, the county councils being responsible mainly for health care. Table 7.3 indicates the size of the local governments, where the sharp increase reported for Finland and Sweden concerning the relative size of local government employment as a percentage of all public sector employment reflects ongoing institutional changes, transferring employees lost from the state enterprises to public joint stock companies.

Given such a heavy concentration of the workforce in local government employment, how can these organizations frame their activities so that they become efficient, or more so? What are the institutional alternatives between which local governments can choose?

Table 7.3 *Local government employees*

	Total number (000s)			% of all employed			% of public sector employment		
	1975	1985	1995*	1975	1985	1995*	1975	1985	1995*
Denmark	–	605	607	–	23	24	–	64	65
Finland	233	427	400	12	21	23	55	67	72
Norway	200	285	382	15	15	21	61	68	75
Sweden	847	1,212	1,146	23	31	33	68	74	82

* The numbers for Denmark and Sweden refer to 1994.

Source: *Statistical Yearbooks*, national accounts

Allocative reforms

Both the national and the local governments in the Nordic countries have searched for reforms in the allocative branch of government that would improve economic efficiency, meaning either productivity or effectiveness. One is well aware of the risk of inefficiency in a large public sector, as several studies in a few countries have pointed to productivity difficulties as well as problems in targeting goal achievement in the public sector. Since the local government sector possesses a substantial degree of autonomy in Scandinavia and Finland, one must look at the reform efforts at the national and the local level separately. The national governments cannot order the regional or local governments to engage in public sector reform. Besides, the national government or the state has problems of its own in handling productivity and effectiveness.

The national governments

The national governments in the Nordic setting focus upon protective tasks like defence and law and order, transfer payments and higher education and some infrastructure. They have focused upon evaluation as the chief tool for improving public sector programmes on the allocative side besides deregulation.

Evaluation is employed in almost all programmes with varying degrees of assertiveness. Thus, for instance, the Swedish national government budgetary process has been extensively changed in order to make room for evaluation within a three-year period, as each bureau has to display its productivity numbers in order to receive new appropriations. The emphasis upon evaluation is part of the general drive away from planning towards an understanding of actual accomplishments. Within most ministries there are today operating systems of performance indicators, but the use of these in the budgetary process is not always transparent.

The Nordic governments have been very interested in deregulation in general as well as in changing their own state enterprises in particular,

Table 7.4 *The protective state: costs and output or outcome measures, 1994*

	Cost per capita* (SK)	Numbers of persons found guilty per 100,000	Prisoners per 100,000	Number of offences†
Denmark	1,880	1,337	97	550,000
Finland	1,800	1,992	97	370,000
Norway	1,880	542	90	245,000
Sweden	2,230	1,208	97	1,080,000

* Costs are standardized and calculated in Swedish crowns (SK).
† The crimes reported are crimes against the penal code in each country.

Source: State budgets and the *Nordic Statistical Yearbook 1995*

although they have been hesitant to move to full-scale privatization. The state enterprise sector has by tradition been fairly large in the Nordic countries, being concentrated in the infrastructure sector. This is also the sector where most efforts at large-scale deregulation have taken place. State enterprises have been transformed into public joint stock companies in order to make them more efficient.

Evaluation The search for improved productivity and effectiveness through the more and more refined use of evaluation is common to all four governments. One works with both evaluation surveys done by the bureau internally and with bureau-wide evaluation studies conducted by separate information bureaux such as an audit office or a parliamentary board for financial review. The studies of efficiency have used both simple measures of physical productivity and more refined tools for the measurement of cost effectiveness, including cost–benefit analysis.

What the Nordic governments have done far too little of is to compare public sector efficiency between the countries. A major study in the early 1980s revealed that costs per unit of production were substantially higher in Sweden than in the other Nordic countries, which could at least partly be explained by the higher ambitions concerning service coverage and service quality in that country (Statskontoret, 1985). Yet, the question is whether Sweden also has a general problem of inefficiency in several of its public programmes, reflecting too rapid a process of public sector expansion since the Second World War. Take the case of the allocation of pure public goods such as in the protective state, the costs of the Ministry of Justice and Internal Affairs for police, prisons and the courts. Table 7.4 has the comparative data.

It appears from the data in Table 7.4 that the Swedish *Rechtsstaat* is about 15% more costly than the *Rechtsstaat* in the other Nordic countries, when one holds population and currencies constant. At the same time the Swedish *Rechtsstaat* does not seem to produce more output or achieve better outcomes than the *Rechtsstaat* of the other comparable countries. On the contrary, both output and outcome measures indicate that productivity and effectiveness are problems in the Swedish state public administration. We will examine the evidence from local governments later.

Deregulation All four Nordic governments have conducted deregulation policies within the infrastructural area, opening up for competition by abolishing legal monopolies. The most spectacular changes have been made within the energy sector and the communications sector with regard to both telecommunications and transportation. Extensive deregulation has been made in the airline sector, the taxi-cab sector and the energy sector.

The Nordic governments have instructed their price and competition agencies to monitor the occurrence of cartels and tacit collusion more effectively, if indeed that is possible. The Swedish government has changed its competition laws in order to strengthen the legal framework for competition, increasing the powers of the market court to inflict penalties on parties who break the rules. No doubt, Scandinavian competition policy and anti-trust laws have been influenced by the European Union framework, as Sweden and Finland entered the Union in 1995, more than 20 years after Denmark became a member.

There can be no doubt that most of the outcomes have been beneficial for consumers, as prices have come down and output has expanded. In some sectors it seems as if the deregulation came much too quickly, resulting in a lack of adequate controls in, for example, the banking sector and the taxi-cab sector. However, within airlines, telecommunications and energy, deregulation has worked according to intentions.

In the Nordic countries the governments have not only regulated infrastructure but also operated state enterprises in order to make sure that governments could exercise as much control as possible. In all four countries these state enterprises have had a huge number of employees, as postal services, energy production and distribution, and telecommunications, not to mention the railways, require many employees. What is to be done with state enterprises in a deregulated market situation? The general solution to the problem of adapting the state enterprises to a world of competition has been their transformation into joint stock companies owned by the state, although some of the state enterprises have been kept as a special type of institution between the bureau and the joint stock company. What are the experiences with incorporation of public firms on the Nordic scene?

Incorporation The Finnish government has pursued a most consistent policy of incorporation. In order to downsize the budget responsibilities a number of state agencies were transformed after 1989 first into public enterprises and then into public joint stock companies. Almost half of all state employees were concerned, as the organizations included postal services and telecommunications as well as the state railways in addition to some 10 smaller enterprises. This has meant a sharp reduction in the number of personnel employed on the state budget – about 40%.

The pros included flexibility and efficiency. Table 7.5 shows that in all these new companies the number of staff has been reduced considerably. A market orientation has been introduced into these restructured agencies in combination with a requirement that the activities be paid for by means of charges to the consumer directly. The increased discretion of the organizations provides the politicians with less responsibility for painful decisions, including the sacking of redundant people or the taking of decisions not to rehire people who go on pensions. The cons refer mainly to a lack of transparency about the place of these new public joint stock companies in the market economy. What is it that they maximize? And how does one level the playing field when huge public joint stock companies operate with large discretion in a market environment with private sector competitors?

In Denmark, public sector reform has focused upon the emergence of what is called the 'grey zone'. It involves new organizational structures for the delivery of public services, mixing public and private institutional principles (Greve, 1996). First, there is incorporation at the state and local government levels: the transformation of public organizations into joint stock companies, owned by public principals or handled by means of private–public mixtures. Secondly, there is the hiving off of public tasks to voluntary organizations of various kinds, and – from the other side – the acceptance by private organizations of public responsibilities, for instance the job recruitment activities of trade unions.

The incorporation reforms have attracted much attention, as a number of public organizations have been transformed into public joint stock companies: Copenhagen Airport, TeleDenmark, Statens Konfektion, Eksport-kreditrådet and Det Danske Klasselotteri. Privatization has not been resorted to except with regard to Danica (a public insurance bureau) and Giråbank (privatized up to 51% of the shares). The structure of the grey zone is contested, as it raises questions about how accountability is to be safeguarded when market institutions are employed. In Denmark there was a long debate about the choice of a governance form for the postal services, after which PostDenmark was identified as a hybrid organization or an 'independent public activity'.

The grey zone not only comprises the new joint stock companies with a public principal, but also harbours the new public–private mixtures under which private organizations accept responsibility for welfare state services. Thus, various social organizations have been drawn into the administration and implementation of welfare services, for instance Dansk Flygtingehjælp. Or private profit-making companies take over the delivery of services like health care and waste disposal, such as ScanCare and WasteManagement. Similarly, sports organizations have entered into partnerships with public authorities.

The Finnish government has conducted a strong policy including institutional changes among its state enterprises. Actually, the policy involved an interesting two-step procedure, first moving a number of former government agencies or other budget financed bodies into the institutional status of

Table 7.5   *State sector employees in Finland,* 1987–96*

Year	Public administration	State enterprises	Total
1987	214,268	–	214,268
1988	215,326	–	215,326
1989	211,633	3,415	215,048
1990	146,948	66,516	213,464
1991	145,877	64,958	210,835
1992	145,100	60,299	205,399
1993	139,886	53,214	193,100
1994	132,918	23,268	156,186
1995	124,670	6,453	131,123
1996	122,300	5,314	127,614

* Personnel transferred to the new public joint stock companies are not included.

Source: Ministry of Finance, Helsinki

public enterprises, and then later transforming some of these into public joint stock companies. By 1995, about 24 formerly budget financed bodies at the central government level had been turned into enterprises or companies. The outcome was a drastic reduction in the number of state employees, close to 40%, from about 213,000 in 1989 to 130,000 in 1995 (a similar trend is to be found in the number of employees in the Swedish state sector). The critical question is, though, whether productivity and effectiveness have changed for the better. Table 7.5 has some details.

All state enterprises on the Nordic scene, whether operating in the special form of an enterprise having both properties of bureaux and firms or in the new shape of a public joint stock company, have been under increasing pressure to improve their performance record in the deregulation era. Governments have usually had to accept losses in these enterprises as they filled the functions of utilities and secured considerable employment. However, the marketization drive has had the result that government have been able to free themselves from these enterprises, confronting them with the demand that they not only cover their costs but also return a small profit to their owners, the state. Faced with the threat of privatization, these enterprises could do nothing else than adapt by raising productivity or output per employee. Thus, we find in all Nordic countries that state enterprises have cut back on employment. In the Finnish case the change from budget status to independent status meant not only that employees became private instead of public, but also that the workforce could be cut back by some 8%, consisting in shedding some 11,000 jobs.

The national telecommunications enterprises as well as the railways have raised their productivity, the former owing to international competition and the latter owing to pressure from its owner. These enterprises, having lost their monopoly position, have adapted by stressing their market orientation, claiming at the same time from the state a more independent position where the objectives to be accomplished should be more strictly market goals. Sometimes these enterprises have been incorporated, sometimes not, but whatever the institutional form they have started to act as private firms. The reduction in employees has in some cases been considerable, from about 20,000 in 1990 to 15,000 in 1995 for the Finnish railways and from almost 11,000 in 1990 to 7,000 in 1995 in Finnish telecommunications.

The Swedish policy in relation to its sector of enterprises and joint stock companies has similarly targeted efficiency, managerial discretion and market objectives. In 1992 all these firms had about 250,000 employees, compared with about 250,000 civil servants. The number of employees in the firm sector has been reduced mainly through job reductions and less so through privatization. At the same time there has been incorporation, for example of the energy enterprise Vattenfall and the telecommunications Telia AB. States Järnvägar within the railways sector has managed a substantial decrease in employees and at the same time turned a loss-making activity into a profitable one. Thus, SJ has been shrunk by 46,300 employees to 29,300 within a six-year period, and a profit of 709 million SK in 1994 replaced a loss of 416 million SK in 1988 at the same time as turnover increased from 17.7 billion SK to 23.7 billion. Yet, one cannot conclude that all these effects constitute efficiency gains. First, about 6,000 employees have simply been moved to another enterprise (Banverket), responsible for the tracks and paid for by the state budget, including substantial new investments. Secondly, the management team of SJ has been allowed to restructure activities, meaning that loss-making routes have been cutback in favour of a concentration on the profitable routes, which mainly connect the large urban areas.

The Norwegian policy towards its enterprise sector has followed much the same lines. Thus, there has been incorporation of the telecommunications firm Telenor as well as the energy firm StatKraft in combination with extensive deregulation of these sectors. The Norwegian government has been eager to distinguish between business activity and regulatory tasks in relation to the former state enterprises, placing the former in new joint stock companies and the latter with a bureau. At the same it must be pointed out that the Norwegian policy has been much more cautious, finding a legal form for the old public enterprises which is slightly different from a full-scale joint stock company. The Norwegian government has maintained its stake in the economy through its extensive ownership of equity in both the oil-producing sector and the banking and insurance sector, while government regulation of oil production remains tight.

Privatization There has hardly been a major movement towards real privatization in Scandinavia or Finland. A few public enterprises have been hived off to the private sector, but there has been much hesitance to use privatization on a large scale, mainly among the social democratic parties which are strong in all of Norden.

Thus, there remain large state enterprises within all four countries, especially in Norway where the government is more involved in the economy than in the other three countries, mainly through its huge oil company Statoil and its 51% share in Norsk Hydro, but also by means of its large ownership in the banking and insurance sector. If changes have been made, then they have mainly concerned the legal status of the state enterprises, as some have been transformed from bureaux to joint stock companies with state ownership of the shares. Here we find the trans-formation of the various state telecommunications companies, the postal services and the energy companies. Yet, there have been a few spectacular privatizations in Sweden such as Celsius Industries, ASSI/DOMÄN/Ncb and Pharmacia.

The local governments: internal markets

The local governments have in a similar fashion been hesitant about full-scale privatization, although some have hived off their companies in the infrastructural sector. The communes and the county councils have pre-ferred to transform their public enterprises into joint stock companies where they own all or the bulk of the shares, especially within energy. The market drive has affected the local government in a different fashion, especially in Sweden. We are referring to the attempts to change the entire organiza-tional framework of the local governments by means of the creation of so-called internal markets.

The internal market efforts have a heavy supply side orientation, as they focus upon cutting costs in service production by the use of bidding and short-term contracting. However, these reforms have done little on the demand side, as it is still the case that politicians represent the consumers/citizens communicating to the managers the quantity and quality of service that they wish to see. Few attempts have been made to place the demand for public sector services directly with the consumers/citizens, as for instance user fees are not used very often outside the infrastructural sector. In Sweden some local governments have introduced voucher-like schemes, for example in the primary and secondary school sector.

When local governments are given such a prominent role in allocation, then efficiency will be a major consideration. It is certainly not the only one, as consumer choice could also be taken into account. When local govern-ments provide much or almost all of the services in the fields of health care, social care, education, infrastructure, housing, culture and sports, library, fire protection and environment and physical planning, then there will be no markets for such services, reducing consumer sovereignty.

Probably the best way of understanding how immense the Nordic local governments are is to look at the metropolitan governments which handle both primary and secondary local government tasks, that is they are both *kommun* and *landsting*. Table 7.6 presents data about the size of some of these units.

The average costs per capita for these metropolitan governments go as high as 70,000 SK which should be related to a total GDP per capita of roughly 180,000 SK. This explains not only the high taxes in the Scandinavian welfare

Table 7.6	*Metropolitan governments in Norden, 1995: costs and staff*

	Population	Total costs* (billion SK)	Cost per capita* (SK)	Number of employees	Employees per capita
Copenhagen	471,000	37	79,000	56,000	0.120
Göteborg	449,000	31	68,000	60,000	0.134
Oslo	488,000	28	58,000	53,000	0.109
Helsinki	525,000	26	51,000	37,000	0.071
Stockholm†	711,000	49	69,000	86,000	0.122

* Costs recalculated in Swedish crowns (SK) (including infrastructure).
† Stockholm is only a primary local government; in order to achieve comparability the costs for health care and other services of the Stockholm County Council have been added to the costs of Stockholm, which procedure also applies to the number of employees.

state but also the focus upon one supplier. Often the term 'monopoly' is used in reference to the position of the local government as the sole provider of many vital services. One may dispute the use of such a term in relation to the local governments, which are basically democratically elected governments, but it remains the case that there is a danger of concentration here, this time not at the central government level but at the local government level.

It has been argued that the local government contains a system error when it tries to combine the role of a large producer with the role of being the representative of the citizens, that is having a demand role. In Sweden in particular, one has been eager to move away from the traditional conception of local government as Weberian bureaucracies, to be governed by politicians but run according to public law principles. The new model of internal markets has attracted lots of attention mainly in Sweden, but also in Norway, as a new institutional mechanism for raising productivity and effectiveness in the local governments. Thus, entire local governments have broken up their Weberian bureaux and installed a demand board, which is instructed to negotiate with any supplier about the delivery of services, on the condition that the local government picks up the final costs. The outcomes of the new internal market model are mixed in Sweden, there being a few cases of failure as well as a few cases of success.

Local governments: service and efficiency

One may note an interesting difference between the Swedish local governments and the local governments in the other countries. Excluding Copenhagen, which has high costs owing to its transfer of state money to unemployment and pension programmes, the Swedish local governments of Stockholm and Göteborg have a considerably higher cost per capita than Oslo in Norway and Helsinki in Finland. Looking at the number of personnel we observe that the Swedish local governments far outnumber the others. These differences in costs and staffing would cause little concern if indeed the output of services was higher in the Swedish local governments.

Table 7.7   *Metropolitan governments in Norden, 1995: service production per capita**

| | School | | Day | Elderly | | Library | Health care | |
	Primary	Secondary	Care	Home assistance	Care	visitors	Beds	Visits
Copenhagen	68	10	69	51	19	7.4	7.1	1.2
Göteborg	81	32	56	26	16	9.5	6.8	5.1
Oslo	71	51	53	35	18	4.7	4.5	1.0
Helsinki	85	62	42	39	16	11.0	8.9	5.1
Stockholm	81	27	47	24	23	6.0	3.8	2.4

*   In each category the output of services has been divided by the population and standardized.

But is this the case? Table 7.7 presents information about the production of services by the local governments.

One may note somewhat surprisingly that Stockholm and Göteborg only produce marginally more services than Oslo, Copenhagen and Helsinki. Whereas Göteborg and Stockholm have been eager to change their organizations institutionally, the other Nordic capitals have retained the Weberian administrative model, although Copenhagen and Oslo have recently decentralized their overall administration into numerous areas or townships.

Symbolic policy responses

The enormous size of the Scandinavian local government involves a clear risk for the economy: allocative inefficiency. When about 30% of GDP is entrusted to the local governments, how can one devise mechanisms that ensure social efficiency and productivity? The Nordic governments typically engage in large-scale evaluation projects in relation to their local governments at the same time as the central governments have few control instruments in relation to the communes and county councils, except in Norway where the Stortinget possesses great financial control on taxation. The outcome is a search for efficiency that sometimes results in garbage-can processes. We will give two examples here, the internal market reform in Sweden (Montin, 1996) and the Nordic project concerning special autonomous local governments (Albaek et al., 1996).

One should perhaps underline that lots of real results have been accomplished by the drive for evaluation, both at the central government level and at the local government level. The techniques for conducting evaluation studies have been greatly improved and evaluation has become integrated into decision-making affecting appropriations and requests in the budgetary process. We focus here upon two policy pathologies, because they indicate the basic problem with a public sector founded upon local governments with huge allocative responsibilities and substantial taxation powers, but where it is problematic to arrive at a quid pro quo judgement for ordinary citizens as well as politicians.

The internal market drive in Sweden is large-scale organizational reform, as it involves an almost complete remake of the local government. Instead of bureaux, the local government is divided into a few purchaser units and a number of production units, which may amount to over 200. In order to maintain control the parliamentary committees of the local government body also have to be changed. Sometimes there is one so-called production board, or all the production or result units are placed under the command of the administrative head of the local government. Although the idea is to maintain a sharp institutional separation between the purchaser units and the production units, it is still the case that the main political board of the local government has the overall responsibility for both organizations.

The aims of the internal market reform include an improvement in the demand side of the local government household by means of a strengthening of the purchaser role, increasing the purchasers' access to information as well as forcing them to clarify objectives and arrive at priorities. If demand is organizationally separated from supply, then resource allocation at the local government level will improve in terms of social efficiency, meaning that politicians know what they want and what they are prepared to pay. Also productivity on the supply side is to be increased, it is hoped. By changing the interaction pattern between demand and supply towards tendering/bidding, one aims at removing X-inefficiencies. In principle, all production is based upon short-term contracts between the purchaser board(s) and the set of production units, which theoretically includes also private organizations. Since the demand side is no longer bound up with the supply side in the form of long-term contracted hierarchies, value on the demand side will be clearly separated from cost at the supply side. However, in order to handle the mounting transaction costs involved in the move towards short-term bidding/tendering, many purchaser boards have concluded long-term cooperation deals with productions units, stating intentions which limit competition. The gain is to get rid of potential switching costs and reduce opportunistic behaviour on the part of the suppliers in relation to possible contractual conflicts. The outcome has been a bewildering set of contracts between the purchasers and the providers, some of which are short-term supply arrangements whereas others are letters of intent, which raises the entire question of what is a contract in the local government household (Häggroth, 1993).

The outcomes of the internal market reform in the local governments which have tried it include a number of deviations from the model and its principal aims. First, the use of short-term contracting has been diluted as a result of the tendency to replace strict competitive tendering with coordination of developmental agreements and promises. Secondly, the demand side has not become as strong as envisaged. Thirdly, there is a general increase in the power of managers, who collaborate across the purchaser–provider separation, and at the same time lots of worries among the employees, who generally speaking are tired of the many local government reforms since 1980. At the end of the day, the purchaser–provider model does not bite, meaning reduce costs considerably, because the new production units tend to contain the very same people that the local government used to have authority over. Thus, one is now negotiating instead of commanding, which by itself does not improve efficiency or reduce costs. Outside competition has been limited, except within certain sectors.

The project concerning certain so-called free local governments is an interesting one, because it was tried in all four Nordic countries on an experimental basis, where a few local governments asked for permission to function without central government directives (Ståhlberg, 1990). The free commune scheme may be seen as the last step in a long process of decentralization, increasing the power of the local governments at the expense of the central government. It has not been possible to show that service efficiency increased or that costs were reduced. The outcomes of the free commune experiment were more marginal than comprehensive. It paved the way for changes in the regulation of the local governments, increasing autonomy, but the status as a free commune was not entrenched in law. At the same time other local governments made other efforts at adaptation, increasing democracy within the local governments by means of the introduction of town councils.

Redistributive reforms

That the public sector in the Scandinavian welfare state is so large is due to the heavy commitment to income maintainance for all kinds of groups. The redistributional programmes include not only pension schemes, unemployment benefits and sickness payments, but also a range of other programmes such as child allowances, housing support and poverty relief payments. The critical questions are as follows. First, how are the various redistributional programmes to be coordinated in order to avoid inefficiencies, for instance people drawing upon several support programmes or people choosing one support programme instead of another simply because the levels of income maintenance differ? Secondly, what level of income maintenance is the proper one, either from a justice point of view or when efficiency considerations are being taken into account?

The Swedish reforms are interesting from this angle, as Sweden has made the most extensive changes of all the four Nordic countries in their redistributional programmes. Not only has the general level of compensation been reduced from 90–100% to 75%, but Sweden has also implemented the same level of income maintenance in all programmes.

The redistributional reforms have two targets, one fiscal and the other efficiency oriented. The protection of the public purse looms large when the Nordic governments have attempted to reform the transfer payments. There is simply not enough money to pay for all the redistributional programmes, especially since the governments employ the pay-as-you-go framework. Sweden provides an example of how drastic changes may become necessary,

Table 7.8   *Transfer programmes in the Nordic countries, 1995*

	Sweden	Finland	Norway	Denmark
Unemployment	75% for 300 days	45–77% for 500 days	62% for 173 weeks	90% for 7 years
Sickness insurance	75% and one day without	100%	100% for 52 weeks	90%
Maternity leave (either parent)	300 days 75% + 60 days 85%	263 days 100%	42 weeks 100%	140 days 90%
Child allowances (SK monthly)*	1 child 640 4 children 3,360	1 child 828 4 children 4,444	1 child 922 4 children 4,140	Between 953 and 655 according to child age

* Allowances in Swedish crowns (SK).

as it used to have the most generous transfer payment programmes but was forced to cut back severely in the early 1990s. Table 7.8 shows that the other Nordic countries now have better protection for their citizens than Sweden.

The major single transfer programme is the pensions, which in the Nordic countries are basically public on the model of one fixed portion and one supplementary portion which varies in relation to working life experience. All the governments have tried or wish to change the finance system in order to introduce individual payment. Thus, Sweden has increased the individually targeted payments sharply and at the same time lowered the level of compensation. Similar reforms are being contemplated in the other countries.

The transfer payment programmes were built up over a very short period when the economy displayed impressive growth figures. When the rate of economic growth decreased and the age distribution shifted, the Nordic governments faced profound difficulties. Table 7.9 testifies to the trend towards a larger and larger share of the population that lives off public income distribution programmes in some form or other, with Denmark as the case.

At the same time as the age structure has changed, the level of unemployment has risen as well as the number of people that suffer from working life accidents, meaning that the share of the population that is occupationally active has to support a large section of the population that is not occupationally active. The increase in income burden of those active in employment is several hundred per cent in relation to both the elderly (14% to 27%) and those that are outside occupational life (7% to 36%), at the same time as the number of youngsters who will enter occupational life is down both relatively and absolutely (41% to 34%).

The redistributive state in the Nordic context faces the problem of paying for huge commitments made in the past as well as the problem of controlling cost developments. The basic feature of all the transfer programmes has

Table 7.9   *Welfare recipients in Denmark, 1960–94 (thousands)*

	1960	1970	1980	1990	1994
Number of people of occupational age	3,000	3,251	3,407	3,553	3,599
Number of welfare recipients	189	309	626	760	946
Number of people 0–14	1,163	1,150	1,081	881	889
Number of people over 67	403	506	633	701	709

Source: Petersen, 1996: 72

been that they are based upon the principle of pay-as-you-go systems, that is they are basically financed by taxation and without any individual insurance component, although the social security charges may not be called 'taxes'. The efficiency problem in such a system concerns the incentive structure in the economy, which becomes aggravated the more generous the rules guiding the transfer programmes are. By rejecting the insurance principle, these systems break the connection between individual payments and benefits, making them heavily redistributive. And when the criteria of the programmes become connected with parameters which governments cannot control or even predict the development of – unemployed, inflation, age structure, migration, birth cohorts, etc. – then the financial difficulties may soon become extremely burdensome for the budget. Often taxes or charges have to be raised in order to meet the cost explosion. However, then governments face the problems of excess burden in taxation on tax wedges, meaning that efficiency in the economy is hurt, causing further costs in the transfer programmes, and so on.

The Nordic governments have taken steps to change their redistributive programmes, reducing the incentive problems as well the costs. Thus, the Swedish government in 1995 decided to insert some insurance principles into the pension programmes while at the same time lowering the level of pension payments as a percentage of the salary received. The direction of change is clearly to link more of the pension to payments made during the active years of the employees, although retaining pensions as fundamentally a public concern.

In the Norwegian debate there has been an awareness of the problem of excess burden in taxation when public programmes are undertaken. Thus, Brendemoen and Vennemo (1993) estimated the real cost to the economy of one unit of public expenditures to be roughly 1.5 units. They state:

> The marginal cost of a general public project financed by means of a proportional increase in all taxes is about 1.5 when one takes external effects into account. Disregarding externalities the marginal cost is about 10–15% higher.

The argument is based upon the well-known leisure–work trade-off where a rise in taxation hurts incentives:

> Higher taxes mean less real wages. This is conducive to a reduction in work effort by the consumers, who get more spare time but can afford less consumption of goods which causes negative external effects. (1993: 27)

One may add that the excess burden will be multiplied when higher taxes are used to finance the consumption of people who are not active in the economy, as some of these persons would otherwise have taken up a job in the official economy. Adding the costs for excess burden in taxation to the excess burden in subsidizing persons outside the economy entails that redistributive programmes can become extremely expensive.

Accountability

Efficiency has been far from the only relevant consideration in the making and implementation of public sector reforms. There has been a constant worry that democratic legitimacy would be hurt if accountability was not improved. Again, the quest for accountability must be related to the immense public sector size. When for example local government units command almost one-third of the GDP, how are citizen preferences to be channelled in such a manner that they become reflected in the decisions of politicians and administrative personnel? Of if about 60% of GDP is channelled through the public sector programmes, then can the rules governing all the public programmes become transparent and fair enough to warrant such a heavy reliance upon public organizations?

Speaking of accountability, one can distinguish between political and administrative accountability, the former being promoted through mainly participatory reforms and the latter chiefly by legal institutions. Attempts at increasing citizen influence by various participatory mechanisms have been launched, from voluntary presence when programmes are to be implemented to the introduction of district councils in the major metropolitan areas.

Now, the public sector in the Nordic countries has changed as a response to the call for more equity in politics. The seminal process of public sector expansion since the Second World War has left politicians with a huge set of tasks and promises to be fulfilled by means of various programmes. There is increasingly a realization that a big public sector does not simply offer a set of tools for solving social problems. It also has efficiency problems of its own. Can politicians deliver on their promises? If so, how are the resources of government to be organized? Can parliamentarians really control the civil service? And there is a search for new institutions in the public sector which result in improved state performance. This is one side of state reform in Europe and it takes several expressions. The other side concerns the call for more accountability and rule of law in the public sector. Here there is a focus upon justice and the ethos of governments.

There is a tension between these two values: performance or effectiveness of government operations and justice as the rule of law in the state. Efficiency may run into conflict with the requirements of due process and legality. Efficiency and the rule of law are extremely valid values for the state. As objectives they are entirely different, one being on the economic or technological side and the other on the legal side. Managerialism, with its emphasis upon efficiency in performance, is not the sole concern of parliamentarians and executives in Scandinavia and Finland. They also face an increasingly strong demand for more accountability and ethos in state operations.

The public sector encompasses all the various programmes that governments at different levels run by means of taxation in a broad sense, including social security schemes. The public sector deals mainly with three functions: public resource allocation, income redistribution and public regulation. In all these branches of government there are equity concerns and considerations about legality. The degree of comprehensiveness of state reform varies from one country to another. Much attention in state reform has focused upon privatization. However, this is too simplistic a picture, because at the same time there is a renewed emphasis on citizens' rights in relation to government. People have sought to enhance accountability by focusing upon both participatory reforms and legal mechanisms, including: more political accountability by devolving power and influence; the bolstering of the role of parliamentarians in checking government; the establishment of citizen tribunals as well as more scope for judicial review; new codifications of comprehensive human rights; an increased recognition of the European Court of Justice; a strengthening of the control of administrative processes; and more power for ombudsmen/women. What the call for more legality and the rule of law in the public sector may lead to is an increased judicialization of politics, although only in Norway is there a tradition of strong legal review.

Conclusion

Public sector reform in Scandinavia and Finland has almost become an industry. It is debated all the time, with new solutions searching for old problems, institutional changes being initiated from time to time, numerous investigations making long enquiries, as well as lots of consultants making lots of money with their contributions to public sector reform.

The key words in the debate about the public sector in the Nordic countries are 'restructuring', 'reorientation' and 'rejuvenation'. What is to be found behind these phrases is a strong ambition to reform the public sector, functionally or institutionally, as well as a feeling of uncertainty about where things stand and where one should go.

The motive for public sector reform is expressed in new ideas about how to change the public sector so that it operates more efficiently. The uncertainty in the push towards public sector reform reflects an awareness that efficiency is difficult to enhance. Perhaps there is a realization that the basic problem of public sector reform in the Nordic context is the size of the entire sector as well as some of its major programmes or its many small programmes. And you do not solve the *size problem* by mere institutional reforms.

References

Albaek, E., Rose, L., Strömberg, L. and Ståhlberg, K. (1996) *Nordic Local Government*. Helsinki: The Association of Finnish Local Authorities, *Acta* 71.

Brendemoen, A. and Vennemo, H. (1993) *Hva koster det å øke skattene?* Økonomiske Analyser 8, Statistisk sentralbyrå, Oslo.

Greve, C. (1996) 'Den grå zone'. Unpublished paper, Institute of Political Science, Copenhagen.

Häggroth, S. (1991) *Offentlig sektor mot nya mål*. Stockholm: Publica.

Häggroth, S. (1993) *From Corporation to Political Enterprise*. Ministry of Public Administration Ds 1993: 6, Stockholm.

Montin, S. (1996) 'Erfarenheter från beställar-utförarkonceptet'. Mimeo.

Petersen, J.H. (1996) *Vandringer i velfaerdsstaten*. Odense: Odense Universitetsforlag.

Ståhlberg, K. (ed.) (1990) *Frikommunförsöket i Norden*. Åbo: Åbo Akademi.

Statskontoret (1985) *Kostnader för offentliga tjänster i Norden*. Stockholm: Kron-projektet.

8

Public Sector Reform in France

Thierry Postif

In France the state is a very old institution, which tradition anchors particularly in the characteristics that the French Revolution and the empire granted it. Three can be named here. The first is the pre-eminence, strongly established in political practice if not in the constitution, of the executive institutions and particularly of individual authorities (emperor, king, president of the Republic, prime minister) in relation to Parliament and even more to the judiciary. The second characteristic is the corresponding concentration of administrative powers in the hands of individual authorities at the national level, and of the prefects who closely depend on them at the departmental level. As Sieyès put it, 'to deliberate is the fact of several people, to execute is the fact of one person only.' And finally, there is the authority of the state over the public companies, meaning that the public service, in the modern sense of the expression, has for many decades had only one centre of decision-making. We must add that the public sector has been expanding for a long time, especially since World War I; in this respect this period renewed the tendency of the *ancien régime* where the king's principal ministers behaved like managers and interventionists.

The constant development of the public sector transcends, by its permanency, the many political changes. One can note that the ideology of the right, namely national independence, as well as that of the left, namely social progress, have contributed to public sector expansion. The important recent periods are still the Popular Front years, the liberation and the beginning of François Mitterrand's first seven-year term. This movement of state expansion has never been reversed. A few figures may be employed to give the current size of the public sector: in 1994 public expenditures represented 55.5% of GNP and non-commercial public employment accounted for 26% of all salaried employment.

Yet, these traditional and therefore more or less permanent characteristics of the French state and consequently its public sector have not prevented a constant succession of reforms since the end of World War I. Here we will not go back to the end of the nineteenth century when the Conseil d'Etat laid down instructions concerning public service change, theorized half a century later by Louis Rolland and expressed in this way: 'the public service must always be adapted to the necessary changes in the general interest'. Is it accidental that a Third Republic minister should say 'Administrative reform is the order of the day and will remain so'? In 1922 a decree instructed the so-called Martin Commission to search for the deep reforms which could be introduced into the public services operation. We will stick to the reforms implemented after the events of May 1968, and several successive waves can be highlighted following their inspiration. First of all the participation of the personnel and to some extent the consumers in public services management has been aimed at. Then the transparency of the activities and the decisions of the public powers and of the public enterprises became the target. More recently, priority has been given to decentralization by transferring important competencies from the state to the local collectivities: 36,763 communes, 100 departments and 25 regions. France now happens to be one of the members of the EU where public powers are the most decentralized, where decision-making organs have been democratized as well as where the autonomy of the public utilities has been reaffirmed.

Thus, the state and the entire public sector were in 1986 deeply renewed in their structures and in their operation modalities. But they remain important in a secular perspective of increased public ascendancy in national life and the economy. It is from this perspective that one must look at the policy implemented by the government of Jacques Chirac between 1986 and 1988, which involved the privatization of several important state-owned companies.

From this period dates the initiation of the present public sector reform, of which we present here a general outline limited to the state, the local collectivities and the public companies without extension into social security. After having recalled the reasons for, the objectives of and the means to public sector reform, we will give illustrations concerning the central functions of the state as well as the local public powers and the state-owned companies.

Reasons and objectives

One may claim that the reasons for reforming the central functions of the state, the local public powers and the state-owned companies are to a large extent similar. Regarding the reform of the state the reasons have been explained by J.-L. Silicani. As the commissioner for the state reform, he asked: why should a state that has remained for a long time a model of a republican state, having achieved its phases of maturity in the 1950s and 1960s, be reformed? And he formulated the following four circumstances which lead to this imperative.

Until the end of the 1950s the state was almost the only public actor in the life of the nation. At the beginning of the 1960s the number of public actors increased greatly: first appeared the European Union, which has seen its power extend considerably; and then with the development of social protection systems, other public structures were created. Even if the status of the regional funds adheres to private law, these organizations are in charge of public interest missions and their budget today exceeds the budget of the state. With the important movement towards decentralization in the 1980s, the local collectivities now play a major role. Finally, there has emerged a series of parapublic structures or third-sector organizations which serve missions of general or public interest.

Thirty years ago the public power identified itself as a strong and powerful state. Today the public landscape is extremely diversified, indeed reflecting, as in most developed nations, a more complex society. But this diversification is a great innovation in France with its unitary state tradition, and this situation creates for the citizens a large complexity of structures and procedures. A few examples underline this.

For the past three or four years, more than half of the new rules of legislative or statutory level applied in France are of European origin. The sources of law and therefore the juridical restrictions have exploded in number, becoming also more complicated. For example, in the social domain an elderly person in a position of dependence can call on as many as nine different services to which he/she is entitled according to position and need. The public system has become extremely complex both at the top, where the rules are made, and at the bottom, in the interface with the citizens. Over the past 30 years, the expectations of the citizens and the civil servants have changed considerably. Forty years ago, the citizen who went to the post office had an average level of education slightly superior to the primary certificate; now this consumer often holds a university degree. The same applies to the producers of public services, as many more than half of the civil servants now have a level equivalent or superior to the baccalaureate. These users or these civil servants do not accept the same kind of relations with the administration and with the state employer that existed a generation ago. Their expectations change as new service supply techniques appear.

The fourth fact to focus upon is the financial crisis, which has become particularly severe as the public deficit has for several years gone beyond the record level reached at the end of the Fourth Republic. The stakes in the reform are to build a state which on the one hand is a central actor and promotes French competitiveness in the world, and on the other hand guarantees national solidarity. The political choice made by President Chirac was to opt for a better state, able to adapt to a rapidly changing environment without the values of the republican state disappearing. The reasons for the reform of local collectivities are the same as those for state reform, to which one should add the concern, especially worrying in the recent period, to prevent corruption. The reasons for the reform of the public companies consist especially in the concern given to their customers as well as to their staff and not least to the financial situation they are going through.

Having considered this, the figures are informative, as the government indicates that in 1994 the whole set of public companies – about 30 divided into seven sectors – lost FF19 billion on a total turnover of 1,487 billion.

Only three sectors display profits: the energy sector (FF6.7 billion), information and electronics (5.5 billion) and intermediate goods and equipment
(258 million). All the others are in deficit. The public sector banks have
FF13 billion in losses, the transportation sector 10 billion, the weapons
sector 5.5 billion and the insurance sector 2.5 billion. The debts of those
companies amount to FF620 billion, compared with their funds which
amount to 535 billion. The commentators note in addition that between
1991 and 1994 the number of employees in public companies (except the
financial sector) has changed only marginally, while over the same period
industrial employment in France has been reduced by nearly one million.

The objectives of the public sector reform, successively expressed by
various prime ministers for about 10 years, strengthen each other. As of
1986 the Chirac government gave the first impulse to the yet ongoing public
sector reform, which essentially aims at improving public service efficiency.
The most important task of this policy is the privatization of several of the
largest public companies. Drawing upon the lesson that the private company is more qualified to respond to market tendencies, and relating France
to world-wide international moves towards state disengagement from the
economy, the government has reacted to a policy of nationalization that
had reached extreme dimensions.

It is telling to note that even before the change that brought Chirac to
office, the government with a Socialist Prime Minister carried out 72
privatization operations in public companies. This demonstrates the tacit
agreement of the right and the left concerning the need to break the secular
perspective of growing expectations on the state with regard to national life
and the economy.

More generally, the idea that 'too much state kills the state' is gaining
ground, as we may note about the successive responsibilities of Camille
Cabana. He had in fact been named minister in charge of privatization just
after the elections which made Jacques Chirac Premier, but five months
later under cover of a ministerial reshuffle he became minister in charge of
administrative reform. In this post he declared that: 'While the extension of
the role of the state, since the last war, was held by a majority of our
citizens to be synonymous with the improvement of welfare, public opinion
has for ten years perceptively observed and remained conscious that state
interventions have reached a critical level.' He went on to say: 'It is
necessary, consequently, to stop this evolution; it is essential in fact, in a
context of slowing growth and of international competition, to reduce
unproductive expenditure and to ease the nation's budget.' Thus, he
concluded that: 'Administrative reform, essentially consisting in action to
reduce the state lifeline, appears as an irreversible necessity.'

In the same way, but eight years later, the Picq Report on the organization and responsibilities of the state, sent to Prime Minister Edouard
Balladur, emphasized that the state must not do what others can do better.

In 1988 the expansion of the public sector was frozen, President François
Mitterrand having established a 'neither/nor' principle (meaning neither

privatization nor nationalization) in his letter to the French people which outlined his platform for his second seven-year period. This temporarily served the objective of containing the public sector by focusing upon efficiency. In these circumstances, the Prime Minister in 1989 stated the second objective of the public sector reform, the improvement of the state by public management reforms called 'public service revival'. Having established that the necessary adaptation to accompany or to precede the deep transformations of society would take time, Premier Michel Rocard strongly underlined that the state and the public services must be able to ensure under the best equity and efficiency conditions the indispensable missions of the republican values, as guaranteeing the general interest and as originators of economic and social progress. Yet, recognizing that the conditions under which those public service missions are accomplished are not entirely satisfactory, either for the public service agents or for the citizens or the enterprises, Rocard affirmed his determination to conduct this revival fully and strongly, proposing policies articulated around the following four ideas. The first two were to be implemented with more determination, although not more systematically then the other two.

1 a policy of renewal of workplace relations, a more dynamic management of staff, and the development of social dialogue in administrations
2 a policy for development of responsibilities, allowing for experimentation with the centres of responsibilities (see below)
3 an evaluation duty for all public policies
4 a policy for the treatment of the customer, that is a service policy in considering the users.

In addition, we cannot ignore the development of corruption, as several scandals were disclosed as early as the beginning of the second seven-year period of François Mitterrand. Numerous observers connect it with the decentralization movement. The call for transparency in the decisions and the activities of the local collectivities was increased, and the publicness of their services/delegations became the objective of a special series of reforms.

In 1995, as soon as he was elected to the presidency, Jacques Chirac put the state and public services reform at the first level of government consideration in line with the statements made during his electoral campaign. The new Prime Minister assigned to the government policy in this field five priority objectives, of which some were inspired by the Picq Report referred to above. The first is to clarify what the state is doing and what the public service field is like; this is a repeat of 1986 although with a renewed content, particularly following EC pressures. The second objective, and the main innovation, is an emphasis on the needs and wants of the citizens, because state reform, as Premier Alain Juppé hammered out, has no purpose other than to serve better our fellow citizens. The third target, to be seen in the context of a long-term deconcentration process, is also an important innovation in French administration: it is to decentralize the state, because the operation of public services need not be centralized. The fourth and fifth objectives concern the delegation of responsibilities and the renewal of public management.

We must for the sake of truth point out that the two main innovations in this communication by Alain Juppé formed for several years the very ambitions of some public companies, aiming on the one hand at putting the customer at the centre of their preoccupations and on the other hand at reforming their central functions. Asking the government to mobilize itself to undertake with determination the reconstruction of the state and the public services by the year 2000 through a permanent effort of innovation and adaptation, the Prime Minister indicated that he would appoint not only a particular government minister but also and for the first time a permanent administration which would handle state reform.

Means

We will examine successively the legal means and then the human means of the French state reform, or more generally of the public services reform. One may ascertain that the legal means were developed especially for this reform. The instruments emanate from Parliament as laws and from the Prime Minister in the form of circular letters. One can note that the former have the character of compulsory and uniform requirements, more particularly to change the structures and to prescribe or to modify the proceedings, whereas the latter are more flexible, as a means to initiate and to permit, particularly in the fields of human resources management and of public management. In any case they all express a political impulse giving them a voluntarist dimension and in this regard they do not deviate from the French classical top-down approach, even if one finds agreements with trade unions and the support of the staff.

If it is the case that the decrees or unilateral decisions emanating most of the time from the Prime Minister result in a number of measures of reform, it is all the more certain that the contract to implement them holds only when the law requires recourse to it – especially between the state and the public companies, a subject developed later in this chapter. We must still note that the juridical means of the public sector reform do not constitute the bulk of the experimentation, as the circular letters only invite organizations to try reform in 1989 in the matter of the centres of responsibilities and in 1995 in service contracts. It is true though that these concepts of new modes are central for public management.

Following the 1995 circular the government presented in June 1996 the triennial plan of the public services and state reform. Its goal is to commit the government to the new responsibilities where the main ideas of the effective realization of several reforms precisely identified had been laid down during a government seminar held in September 1995. The Prime Minister insisted on the concerns which inspire this plan to make the administration altogether simpler, closer to the citizens, and more responsible, announcing a new procedure for the individual evaluation of civil servants. A number of new laws will essentially implement these orientations.

The human means of the reform are – and this is nothing new – governmental in nature. An interministerial committee for state reform created for three years in September 1996 is charged with setting the direction of governmental policy, aiming at reaching the above mentioned priority objectives. Chaired in principle by the Prime Minister, this committee brings together the ministers in charge of the civil service, the budget, the interior, the territorial development, the plan and if necessary other members of the government. The minister in charge of state reform, in 1995 Dominique Perben, titled Minister of the Public Service, State Reform and Decentralization, can be called on to chair this committee by delegation from the Prime Minister. He is generally entrusted with carrying out state reform to bring public administration closer to the citizens. Within the interministerial committee for state reform a permanent committee is instituted to prepare the work under the leadership of the minister in charge of state reform or by delegation by the commissioner for state reform. The latter is an innovation without real precedent in French administration. He directs a commissionership for state reform instituted like the above committee for three years and at the disposal of the minister. The commissionership must make all the proposals aimed at achieving the objectives, coordinate the preparation of governmental decisions in this domain, watch over their implementation and more generally stimulate the political reform of the administration. The commissioner for state reform, Jean-Ludovic Silicani, notes that if the commissionership intervenes in these three successive areas, its mission concerning the first is rather classical, as it was the normal work of commissions which in previous years have deliberated and made reform proposals. On the other hand, he goes on, accompanying and preparing public decisions constitutes an important innovation, but the quality of a permanent body to follow the implementation of decisions constitutes undoubtedly the major innovation which presupposes the largest important investment from the methodological point of view. Jacques Chevallier, whose work has enriched this report, indicates that the creation of those specialized structures in charge of orienting the reform obviously creates problems of the allocation of responsibilities in relation to the classical structures, and especially with the national headquarters of public administration.

National state level

We noted above that the third of Prime Minister Alain Juppé objectives, assigned to governmental action in public services reform, involves important innovations changing the central government. As mentioned above, there was already a long-standing perspective on deconcentration of which a decree of 1992 expressed the intention. In terms of the latter, deconcentration is the general rule of division of tasks and means between the different levels of the state civil administration. One can regard this 1992 charter as the reflection, at the national level, of the subsidiarity principle established in the European Community by the European Union Treaty signed in Maastricht a few months earlier. Certainly, this deconcentration objective derives from the disposition itself of the same decree, according to which the central administrations take on at the national level a role of conception, animation, orientation, evaluation and control. But it is no use pretending to outline here a picture of ongoing deconcentration in France, as we must agree with Jean-Ludovic Silicani's analysis that before 1995 administrative reform avoided making a real issue of the question of the central state, its major stake in power.

In fact, it was up to Alain Juppé to give instructions that management tasks still handled by the central administration were to be resolutely transferred to the deconcentrated services, which process needed to be accompanied by a significant reduction in real manpower in the central administration as well as in an improvement of their information and decision capacities. One may interpret the ambitions of the key power holder as follows. The objectives were now to shrink the central state in terms of staff and the number of division headquarters. The 215 central administrative headquarters existing today are conducive to a compartmentalization and an excessive separation in the handling of public policies, which make public decision-making very difficult. It was therefore considered necessary to free human resources in order to strengthen the deconcentrated services and the conduct of certain strategic functions which at central level are badly executed, namely the functions of evaluation and forecast. Perhaps this 'strategic state', according to the formula of the National Plan Commission, to which power-holders often refer, is not a modest state in Michel Crozier's (1991) conception; according to the President of the Republic, the state must be strong.

The government decided, at the time of the above-mentioned seminar held in September 1995, that the codification of legislative and statutory texts, started a long time ago, should be achieved in a five-year period, under the umbrella of a High Commission for Codification under the Prime Minister's chairmanship. It is aimed at stopping the proliferation of rules as well as the confusions about rules which are characteristic of the French juridical system. In other words, it is to facilitate the implementation of the principle according to which 'no one is entitled to ignore the law'. In fact in 1991, the Conseil d'Etat counted about 7,500 applicable laws; evaluated at some 82,000 the statutory decrees in effect; and indicated that according to the records of the Economic Community data bank Celex, more than 21,000 regulations are applicable in the Community.

The strategy here is one of codification of existing law, meaning that the codes are applied while retaining the presentation of the texts as at the time of the codification with no attempt to change the basic sense of the law. Yet it seeks a regrouping and clarifying of the texts which improves law and its application. It is to be continued by an effort to simplify the texts which it prepares and facilitates. Since the new codification effort began in 1989 several codes have been published, among these one concerning the financial jurisdictions and one concerning local collectivities, and 15 others have been prepared. The general codification plans for 1996–2000, constituting the last step of this effort to organize French law, comprise 42 codes of which more than half are entirely new.

The fifth – and last – of the objectives that Prime Minister Alain Juppé assigned as an action for the government in the field of public services reform targets the innovation of public management. It is, more specifically, a question of carrying out a modernization of the French civil service, that is involving more than five million people employed.

Jacques Chevallier notes that civil servants have for a long time considered themselves subjugated and have felt the impact of reforms decided without their consideration; since the 1980s it has been clear that the administrative changes must be conducted with and perhaps by the agents themselves. The public authorities assert, however, that it is not a question of modifying the status of the civil service which, according to J.L. Silicani, does not appear to block the process of renovation; on the contrary.

The three-year plan for state and public services reform presented in June 1996, already mentioned above, calls for an updating of the civil service involving four orientations:

1   their day-to-day management, which is accompanied by corresponding training as well as a renewed procedure for grading and individual assessment
2   professional mobility as well as multifunctionality, which should be achieved through a reduction in the number of professional corps, some 1,200 only for the state public functions
3   review of salaries, with priority to be given to compensation and bonuses for sectors which are subject to mergers and regroupings
4   the implementation of tools enabling high-level civil servants to better manage their team by the generalization of contracted objectives.

Observing that these human resources management clauses have a direct continuity with reforms previously started, Jacques Chevallier remains sceptical of their import. Nevertheless, it is the idea of promoting professional mobility and multifunctionality among the professional corps that in his eyes is most likely to shift the structure. The example of the PTT – nowadays La Poste and France Telecom – shows that the opposition to such measures may be overcome but at the cost of social dialogue, and also if such measures are seen as favourable by those concerned, that is leading to a reform of qualifications and an increase in salaries. It is not inappropriate to make a comparison between what has been discussed here, and the claims which arose at the announcement of a 0.3% decrease in the number of active state civil servants in 1997.

Local level

At the level of the local public powers we witness the 1992 decree which lays down the principle whereby the department district is to be the territorial division of implementation of national and community policies. Therefore, it is to the 100 departments of the Republic that the role of operator belongs, which consists in managing, in applying rules, or in giving services, following the expression used in 1995 by the Prime Minister. Much activity has to a large extent already been decentralized.

No one will be surprised by the fact that the decentralized services represent a large majority of the centres of responsibilities, that is the functional units of public management by those responsible, to whom enlarged possibilities are given to adapt to the targets aimed at by means of the human materials and financial possibilities which they can dispose of. Every centre of responsibilities commits itself to implement a service project of which the objective is to improve the service given. A commission chaired by Hervé Sérieyx has provided an assessment, made public, of all the service projects existing in 1994, that is 594. Each of the 207 centres of responsibilities outlined as of 1 January 1994 had concluded with its minister a three-year contract specifying the fixed quantified objectives and attributing the means to reach them. The Ministries of Equipment, Industry and Youth and Sports were those where the centres of responsibilities were relatively the most numerous. Even if those responsible for the centres judge positively the measures of modernization and flexibility in management with which they are concerned, they have regretted that the 'contractualization' of the links with the ministers to which they are attached remained superficial.

In 1995, the Prime Minister asked each minister to take necessary measures in order that the decentralized services overall would function following the managing rules for the centres of responsibilities by the end of 1996, adding that service contracts would be experimented with from 1 January 1996 in several ministries. Alain Juppé further indicated that the operating services, especially those which are not decentralized, face a call to be relocated outside the Paris conurbation. No doubt the relocation announced raised more than reservations on the part of the staff concerned. It can be pointed out that on all joint decisions the interministerial committees for territorial planning held on 3 October and 7 November 1991, 29 January and 23 July 1992, and 10 February 1993 announced the transfer into 80 towns of 88 services representing 15,500 jobs, but up to now only 2,000 jobs have actually been transferred.

We have already underlined that since the beginning of the second seven-year period of President F. Mitterrand, several scandals have revealed an expansion of corruption which has restricted more and more the decisions and activities of the local communities within juridical constraints aimed at satisfying an increased demand for transparency. A series of reforms have paid particular attention to the publicness of local services delegations: water supply, sanitary improvement, transports, etc. to which the local communities previously used to have less recourse than they have today. For instance the number of municipalities delegating their public service of water supply has multiplied by 10 (from 2,000 to 20,000, comprising 55% of the French municipalities) between 1970 and 1990. However the regulations, already weak in 1970, were even less binding in 1990 under the effect of the decentralization impulse, whereas it appeared that the delegation of public services involved objectionable payments of large sums.

A law of 1993 known as 'loi Sapin' henceforth codified in the general code of territorial communities, has bound them to a publicity procedure, allowing the submission of several tenders. These proceedings are similar to the procedure used in public contracts but without binding the local collectivities' choice, and they include not only the announcement of the projects of the delegation of the public service in several publications, but above all the intervention of the municipal council. Thus, the delegation of public services and the choice of the provider are openly examined, especially by the local opposition on the presentation of substantial documents. This reform, and others – but of lesser importance – also concerning the local public services delegations, have without doubt renewed their practice which is now perhaps a little in decline but is being conducted more rigorously.

After a country-wide debate for one year, a 1995 law has substantiated the French government decision to rehabilitate an ambitious territorial planning policy. This text establishes various frameworks: a national scheme, sectoral schemes, urban and country planning, a regional scheme etc. into which the state will implement the planning of the French territory. In addition it refers to the extent of the country, which without being a new administrative district is targeted to become a reference for the geographical coherence of public policies. To tell the truth this appears as one of the major innovations of the law, as it is in this framework that the local collectivities and their groups are called upon to define common projects of development, the state taking into consideration its presence in the organization of services.

Public enterprises

It is only as a reminder that we raise here the privatization of public companies concluded between 1986 and 1988 and since 1993. This was not an insignificant change: the proportion of the public companies in salaried employment should have been reduced by almost half – from 10.6% to 5.5% – between 1985 and 1993, if all the companies named in the 1993 law to be privatized had been. Since this was not the case this proportion went down only to 9% but, considering the transformation of the position of La Poste and France Telecom in 1991 with an increase of about 470,000 in the staff of public companies, this was an achievement. The amount of privatization reached FF 22 billion in 1996 – whereas the objective was 40

– but the Minister of Economy, Finance and Planning counts on an amount of FF 27 billion in 1997 which happens to be the year of the sale of a portion, although minor, of France Telecom.

But this movement deserves more than the brief analysis to which it is necessarily subjected here; one needs to consult the thorough published works which specialists have devoted to it. Especially in the last 10 years several public companies have changed their juridical status, owing to various pressures more or less combined in each case. One can in particular cite the policies of the European Union, the adaptation to the industrial structures induced by technological evolution, and the economic necessity to make capitalistic links with other companies, possibly foreign ones. The most recent notable example of this change concerns France Telecom, which first operated in the French telecommunications network as a general agency of central administration and therefore part of a state ministry until 1990; then operated as a public operator, meaning almost a commercial and industrial public company (EPIC), from 1991 till 1996; and will become a national company in 1997. It will be essentially submitted to the legislative dispositions applicable to public companies, and the state will directly control more than half of its capital.

In the context of the transition within telecommunications from monopoly to competition each of these steps demonstrates, as compared with the previous one, progress in economic and juridical autonomy and in the search for entrepreneurial behaviour on the part of France Telecom. Therefore, the public authorities are presenting the latest step as the best way to guarantee the long-term viability of the mission of public service of which France Telecom is in charge, as it gives the company the overall competitive advantages of a less administrative structure. This is certainly relevant as France Telecom, the fourth largest world operator of telecommunications, is today the only one, out of the 20 main world operators, not to be structured as a commercial company, on the basis of the argument that its current status of public operator makes difficult the conclusion of durable alliances, and deprives it of the flexibility which its competitors have.

The EC Council has set down two successive Directives concerning not only the public powers, but also the national and even private companies, which operate in the water, energy, transport and telecommunications domains. They aim at obliging them to abide by the competition rules at the European level in relation to their major work, supply and service contracts. These rules, certainly, force the public companies involved into a fundamental restraint which is, however, less than the one which usually applies to public agencies for the management of their tasks. In particular, the negotiated proceedings constitute normal proceedings and not exceptional ones. Anyhow, they bind these companies to special formalized proceedings aiming at informing their contractors, suppliers and service providers via the European Community of the contracts they intend to allot. The implementation of these proceedings enables them in return to improve their awareness of the European supply likely to meet their demands, whereas experience shows that they used to have almost exclusive access to their national markets. Hence, it is a matter of reform of European origin, presently registered in French law only in relation to the work and supply contracts, which concretely leads a large number of French public companies altogether to adjust their purchasing practices.

As mentioned, the contract constitutes a means of reform only when the law enforces one to employ it; this in particular is the case of the so-called planning contracts decided between the state and various public companies of which the origin is found in a law of 1982, related to planning. It is interesting to devote a few lines to the Electricité de France (EDF) planning contract for the 1993–6 period as an illustration. The public utility company endorses in this plan very significant commitments concerning its management targets to get out of debt and lower rates, to improve the quality of the product and service supplied to its customers, and to increase the effort in favour of the environment. Further, one can note with interest that the planning contract gives EDF's social policy the three following directions: to permit, while guaranteeing employment to everyone, the accomplishment of the necessary changes of competencies and geographical locations meeting company needs and the ambitions of employees; to seek with its social partners the signing of a national social agreement aiming essentially at an understanding of the needs linked to the modernizations of public service and to open the way for local collective negotiations on subjects such as professionalism, the evolution of capacities, adjustment of working time, etc.; and to strengthen the remuneration components related to work effort and the professionalism of the agent and to acknowledge the collective and individual contribution to the results.

The counterpart of these commitments is the respect by the government of the autonomy of the firm and the allocation of agreed means. Within EDF which is a very large company with a staff close to 120,000, and where the annual turnover is almost FF 200 billion, it is also by contracts that the central management decides together with the divisions their objectives and means. The same procedure applies to the divisions themselves in relation to their units and services. These objectives and these means are part of the scheme of the planning contract but also of the middle-term strategic plans which the public company itself, and its divisions, units and services, elaborate. Therefore, these objectives are formalized and contractualized as well as made public, and are endorsed by a certain necessary vigour, and these means constitute in the managers' hands a powerful tool, their operation being subject to a relatively close supervision.

Conclusion

One must conclude that public sector reform, and especially reform of the state, is in process in France. However, one must also admit that far from being uniform the movement displays clear differences in its extent and in its rhythm, depending on the services and the aspects concerned in the reform.

In September 1996 the public authorities focused on the objective of bringing the public state administration closer to its users. Consequently a draft bill, increasing the amount of cases where silence kept by the administration upon a request provokes an implicit decision of acceptance, will eliminate some 120 regulations of administrative authorizations – out of, it is true, roughly 4,500. It will also reinforce the mediators' powers and establish public services houses, created by agreements between the concerned administrations in view of ensuring a public service of proximity, especially in districts in difficulty.

The aspects of public sector reform which appear particularly difficult to implement are related to the public policy assessment. If nobody can fail to recognize particularly the Court of Accounts and various inspection procedures, it remains the case that the initiatives taken in this regard over almost 10 years by public authorities, like the creation in 1989 of an interministerial committee and of a scientific evaluation council, do not seem to have met with the expected success.

Nevertheless a renewed approach is noted with the experimentations during 1996 of an impact study, accompanying the draft bills and the decrees in the Conseil d'Etat. This study takes into account the effects of law and decrees on employment, on public finances, on administrative formalities and on the complexity of juridical organization.

Finally let us point out that Parliament, by a law of June 1996, has given itself a parliamentary office for public policy assessment composed of two delegations, one constituted at the Assemblée Nationale and the other at the Senate, of which the prerogatives are important, and which has access to all the information that facilitates its mission.

Bibliography

Balladur, E. (1994) 'L'Etat de droit au quotidien', *La Revue administrative*.

Barbier, C. (1995) 'L'usager est-il devenu le client du service public?', *La Semaine juridique (J.C.P.)*, édition G, Doctr. 3816.

Barreau, J. (1995) *La Réforme des P.T.T.: quel avenir pour le service public?* Paris: La Découverte.

Bernard, P. (1994) 'La déconcentration de l'Etat: un nouveau regard sur l'administration du territoire', *La Revue administrative*.

Bodiguel, J.-L. (1996) 'Les fonctionnaires en proie au changement', in *Le Service public en recherche: quelle modernisation?* Paris: La Documentation française.

Brillaud, F. (1996) 'L'Administration et ses usagers', *Le Courrier juridique des finances*, no. 67.

Cabana, C. (1986) 'Coût et rendement: la réforme administrative', *La Revue administrative*.

Caillosse, J. (1991) 'La modernisation de l'Etat', *L'Actualité juridique, Droit administratif*.

Cascales, M. (1995) 'Territoires et développement, l'Etat aux commandes', *La Revue administrative*.

Chevallier, J. (1993) 'Les fonctionnaires et la modernisation administrative', *La Revue administrative*.

Chevallier, J. (1996) 'La politique française de modernisation administrative', in *l'Etat de droit: mélanges en l'honneur de Guy Braibant*. Paris: Dalloz.

Chevallier, J. (1996) 'La réforme de l'Etat et la conception française du service public', *Revue française d'administration publique*.

Chevallier, J. and Lochak, D. (1982) 'Rationalité juridique et rationalité managériale dans l'Administration française', *Revue française d'administration publique*.

Choussat, J. (1996) 'La modernisation, est-ce l'efficacité?', in *Le Service public en recherche: quelle modernisation?* Paris: La Documentation française.

Crozier, M. (1991) *Etat modeste, Etat moderne: strategies pour au autre changement*. Paris: Le Seuil.

Dugueperoux, G. (1994) 'Le contrat de plan 1995–1997 de La Poste', *Juris P.T.T.*, no. 38.

Forges, J.-M. de (1995) 'L'Administration, les mots et les choses', *La Revue administrative*.

Fraisse, R. (1996) 'Le service public saisi par la modernisation', in *Le Service public en recherche: quelle modernisation?* Paris: La Documentation française.

Groshens, J.-C. (1994) 'Moderniser l'Etat?', *La Revue administrative*.

Guillaume, E. (1991) 'La réforme des Postes et Télécommunications comme le passage du statut d'usager d'un service administratif à celui de client d'un service public industriel et commercial', *Revue française de droit administratif*.

Joudon, L. (1993) 'Le contrat de plan entre l'Etat et Electricité de France 1993–1996', *Cahiers juridiques de l'électricité et du gaz*.

Koubi, G. (1995) 'Responsabilisation des fonctionnaires et modernisation de l'Administration', *La Revue administrative*.

Lasserre, B. (1994) 'L'entreprise publique du monopole à la concurrence', *Cahiers juridiques de l'électricité et du gaz*.

Loosdregt, H.-B. (1990) 'Services publics locaux: l'exemple de l'eau', *L'Actualité juridique, Droit administratif*.

Perego, B. (1994) 'Une nouvelle organisation de l'Administration centrale pour favoriser des synergies', *Juris P.T.T.*, no. 35.

Perrin, B. (1995) 'Déconcentration, décentralisation: la réforme administrative reste à faire', *La Revue administrative*.

Picq, J. (1995) *L'Etat en France: servir une nation ouverte sur le monde*. Paris: La Documentation française.

Pontier, J.-M. (1993) 'L'état de la décentralisation', *La Revue administrative*.

Pontier, J.-M. (1994) 'Une décennie de décentralisation vue par le Conseil d'Etat', *La Revue administrative*.

Rossinot, A. (1994) 'La réforme administrative: nouveaux enjeux – nouvelles étapes', *La Revue administrative*.

Rouban, L. (1991) 'Le client, l'usager et le fonctionnaire: quelle politique de modernisation pour l'Administration française', *Revue française d'administration publique*.

Rouban, L. (1996) 'Les cadres supérieurs de la fonction publique face à la modernisation', in *Le Service public en recherche: quelle modernisation?* Paris: La Documentation française.

Salon, S. (1991) 'Le statut des personnels', *Juris P.T.T.*, no. 24.

Serieyx, H. (1994) *L'Etat dans tous ses projets: un bilan des projets de service dans l'Administration*. Paris: La Documentation française.

Silicani, J.-L. (1996) 'Actualité de la réforme de l'Etat en France', *Revue française d'administration publique*.

Stirn, B. (1993) 'La conception française du service public', *Cahiers juridiques de l'électricité et du gaz*.

Thoenig, J.C. (1996) 'Réforme de l'administration et réforme de l'Etat', *Revue politique et parlementaire*.

Tholon-Pommerol, V. (1994) 'Le secteur public d'entreprises de 1980 à 1992', *Cahiers juridiques de l'électricité et du gaz*.

Vié, J.-E. (1995) 'Décentralisation et corruption: les ratés de la démocratic locale', *La Revue administrative*.

Woerhling, J.-M. (1992) 'Réflexions sur le renouveau du service public', *La Revue administrative*.

Circulaire du 23 février 1989 relative au renouveau du service public. JORF, 24 February 1989.

Circulaire du 26 juillet 1995 relative à la préparation et à la mise en oeuvre de la réforme de l'Etat et des services publics. JORF, 28 July 1995.

Circulaire du 21 novembre 1995 relative à l'expérimentation d'une étude d'impact accompagnant les projets de loi et de décret en Conseil d'Etat. JORF, 1 December 1995.

Circulaire du 15 mai 1996 relative à la mise en oeuvre du plan de réforme de l'Etat: réduction du nombre des autorisations et déclarations administratives préalables. JORF, 27, 28, 29 May 1996.

Circulaire de 30 mai 1996 relative à la codification des textes législatifs et réglementaires. JORF, 5 June 1996.

9

Local Government in Britain after Thatcher

Gerry Stoker

The reform drive in Britain aimed at local government has been one of the more extensive and active in Western democracies. The early years of the Conservative government elected in 1979 saw a concentration on attempts to hold back local government spending. In the mid 1980s this theme was joined by a commitment to changing the way public services were managed and run in order to ensure greater efficiency in the use of resources and a greater responsiveness to the users of services. A raft of legislation was introduced in Thatcher's administration which came into office after a general election in 1987. The Audit Commission, a government appointed spending 'watch-dog', wrote at the time: 'Local authorities are in the throes of a revolution' (1988: 1). When auditors write of a revolution in local government clearly something unusual and significant is happening. When Thatcher resigned in 1990, in part because of the political difficulties raised by the new system of local finance (the Poll Tax) which was part of her revolutionary package, the new administration – led by John Major – retained and indeed added to the reform measures aimed at local government. However the new administration did abolish the Poll Tax.

One new element introduced by the Major administration was to launch a structural review and reform of local government. This chapter does not dwell on this issue since the focus of the book is more on other dimensions of public sector reform (see Leach and Stoker, 1997 for an analysis). In broad terms a single tier of local government has been established throughout Scotland and Wales. The major urban areas in England have also obtained 'unitary' local government. A single-tier system of local government was established in London and the main metropolitan areas in 1986.

The structural reorganization pales in impact compared with the extensive and profound revolution in local government's ways of working, rationale and purpose launched by the Conservatives in the mid 1980s. The impact of the reform package launched by Thatcher and continued under Major has been substantial. It has left a system of local government in 1997 characterized by:

1 financial constraint and fiscal stress
2 a focus on performance and best value

3 a flagging commitment to the 'customer revolution'
4 an embryonic vision of a wider role as community governance.

Each of these characteristics will be examined in more detail in the remainder of the chapter. In a concluding section an overall assessment of the impact of the public sector reform process on British local government is made.

Financial constraint and fiscal stress

In the mid 1980s local authorities were responsible for raising over half their own revenue through two locally determined taxes: domestic and business rates. These taxes on property were subject to certain controls and limits from central government. Legislation in 1988 removed business rates entirely from local authority control and gave central government responsibility for setting its level and redistributing the money raised. Domestic rates were abolished and replaced by the Community Charge or Poll Tax, a local tax to be paid at a flat rate by most adults. The poorest members of each community were expected to pay at least a part of the standard Poll Tax. The taxation change proved to be enormously unpopular. The arrival of Major in Downing street signalled a retreat. The Poll Tax was abolished and replaced by the Council Tax, a graduated property-based fiscal measure. The burden of money to be raised locally was reduced still further by a 2½% increase in VAT to enable national taxation to fund local services to a greater degree.

Local authorities in Britain are, as a result, heavily dependent on central government for their funding. Local taxation (the Council Tax) in 1996–7 in England accounted for only about 20% of total local authority income. The remainder of local authority income came from central government and other nationally distributed sources. In Wales only 14% of funding came from local sources. The figure for Scotland was 15%.

The bulk of the funding (about 40%) to local government comes in the form of a block grant to local authorities paid for from national taxes. A further substantial share (about 25%) comes from the redistribution of the national business rate. A smaller share comes through specific grants (about 10%) with the remainder provided from a variety of sources. The position in Northern Ireland is rather different. Local councils in the province are responsible for a smaller percentage of public spending. The bulk of their spending is met out of local taxation. Indeed Northern Ireland never suffered the imposition and then withdrawal of the Poll Tax and has sustained a system of local rates.

Funding is allocated to local authorities in Britain in a manner that is aimed at achieving full equalization. Central funding is distributed in a way that is intended to make the total flow of funds from central government adequate, with an assumed standard level of Council Tax to meet a standard level of spending. The standard level of spending contains elements which adjust it to local need. The block grant takes into account therefore both local taxable capacity and special local requirements.

The process starts from a figure – agreed at a national level – for total standard spending. This figure emerges in the course of annual discussions on central government expenditure. Once various specific grants are removed and other adjustments are made a net total standard spending figure is established which provides the basis for allocation through the system of spending assessments. Figures are developed in turn for each of the main service areas. For each of these areas a formula reflecting proxy measures of need and disadvantage is used to determine the allocation of funds to individual local authorities.

The equalization process is complex but not entirely convincing. The system is bound to fail to fully meet local views of need because it is a top-down process for determining how a predetermined amount of money should be distributed. Beyond this inherent problem there are various practical difficulties. Some of the data used in calculations are out of date, for example census data. Some of the proxy measures used are not adequate to the task. Yet the cost of developing more 'realistic' indicators could be prohibitive. Notwithstanding the complexity of the statistical results generated by computers, what emerges is a 'rough and ready' system of resource distribution.

The funding regime has been developed to provide central government with a considerable level of control over local spending. What has happened is that local authorities have found themselves constrained to spend at or close to their standard assessed spending figure by the holding of capping powers over local budgets to ensure that they do not rise above government approved levels. This system of tight supervision and the modest capacity of local taxation has created control for the centre but at the cost of a situation where it is all too easy for local authorities and others to blame central government for every deficiency of service and resources. Local accountability for local spending has been undermined.

The draconian measures taken by the government have delivered an increased degree of control over local spending. Indeed some authorities have had to make drastic cuts. Others have protected programmes through various measures and engaged in what is referred to as 'creative accounting'. They have become expert in juggling the books so that the figures for spending match government targets but resources continue to flow to local services. However over time the scope for creative accountancy has been greatly reduced through new controls and through the costs imposed by the past use of that practice. Many authorities have 'hived off' activities in order to reduce costs. Others have attempted to obtain extra resources by increasing charges for some services, improving treasury management or bidding for additional funds for special projects from central government or the European Union.

An Aston University team (Bovaird et al., 1997) have explored the viability of the different strategies and the practice of a range of local authorities in relation to the issues. These researchers argue that in general local authorities have managed to cope with cutbacks, that is budgets have been squeezed but services of an 'acceptable' level have in many cases continued to be delivered. Interestingly they also discovered that many budget processes involve an increased level of 'cutbacks' in order to find 'new monies' for local politicians to spend in each budget round on new priorities or schemes. The researchers also found that authorities tend to adopt a range of techniques for managing resources without much in the way of planning in the hope that some would deliver benefits. An overall finding is that authorities are rather more *ad hoc* than *strategic* in terms of planning within limited resources.

From the perspective of the advocates of public sector reform the changes in the financial regime for British local government are in many respects only a partial success. Local government spending has been held back, yet it still stands at a quarter of all public spending as it was in 1979 and has grown in real terms. The management of that spending does not match the aspirations of new management. Local spending is determined by national priorities. There is a lack of local responsibility and accountability. Local budget decisions are driven less by strategic objectives and more by *ad hoc* and increasingly desperate attempts to cope with imposed and somewhat arbitrary constraints guided by an inadequate spending allocation system.

Performance and best value

If a commitment to being strategic would seem axiomatic as part of the 'new management' for a local authority, then a willingness to manage performance can also be taken as read. To focus on performance means: a concern to secure and demonstrate value for money and an emphasis on outcomes, so that what is produced and with what effect are examined. Research indicates that local authority managers and councillors have some grounds for their belief that considerable progress has been made on both fronts in recent years.

The 'accumulated evidence of many managers is that changes can be achieved and benefits in terms of increased efficiency and sometimes improved service quality have been won' (Pollitt, 1996). There is case study evidence of organizational change, innovations in service delivery and improvements in performance (Leach et al., 1994). Using the somewhat crude measures provided by opinion surveys there is evidence of increased satisfaction with particular services (Young, 1997).

Research, however, also shows considerable variation in the impact of measures such as competitive tendering (Walsh and Davis, 1993). The intensity of competition varies between services and between different parts of Britain. Doogan (1998), in work for the ESRC Local Governance Programme, argues that there is a significant local dimension to the operation of contracting and marketization processes.

The impression is gained that marketization is a process which is constructed at local level within financial parameters established by central government. Market behaviour is therefore mediated by local agencies and conditioned by local and national bargaining capacities.

The British local government system is characterized by a spectrum of perspectives on competitive tendering, from enthusiasts to those that are relatively reluctant to develop contracting, externalization and performance measurement.

Local authority chief executives in England and Wales in 1994 gave 'remarkably upbeat' assessments of the benefits of competitive tendering in terms of their authority's approach to service delivery (Young, 1996). However they were more qualified in their judgement about the wider impact of competition in changing the culture and style of working of their authority. A SOLACE (1994) report by Scottish chief executives also argues that 'there have been benefits' from competitive tendering, although it rejects the compulsory framework and the frustrations of detailed regulations.

The introduction of performance measures and league tables seems to have also won endorsement among many in the local government community and other public services. However doubts remain about whether the measures promoted by central government do effectively measure outcomes or more generally are appropriate when attempting to assess the 'value added' in complex public services such as education or community care (Pollitt, 1995).

The purchaser–provider split is seen as instrumental in ensuring a focus on 'value for money' and 'performance'. The SOLACE report notes that 'the old fudge in most local government services clouded the issues of what was actually being provided and at what cost' (1994: 16). The purchaser–provider split has brought into sharper perspective the definition of service and the assessment of whether purposes have been fulfilled. Yet there is difficulty if the purchaser–provider split is interpreted too rigidly.

Research confirms that too narrow a view of purchaser–provider relations can undermine the development of more effective longer-term and partnership-oriented contractor relationships (Walsh, 1995). In part, the issue is to avoid another fallacy: that there is an easy divide between policy and implementation (Stewart, 1996). Establishing effective learning and matching approaches to a complex variety of services demand more than a simplistic purchaser–provider divide can provide. The reality of public expectations about there being a 'council' that they can hold responsible for public services (Miller and Dickson, 1996) makes too rigid an interpretation of the purchaser–provider split problematic.

What happens next in this arena will be affected by the outcome of the 1997 general election. The Labour Party is pledged to remove the compulsory nature of competitive tendering, but maximizing value and performance in public services is at the centre of its political and managerial agenda. What stimuli other than compulsion will be effective? Can local authorities be trusted to retain ownership of the value and performance agenda without the threat or reality of central government intervention?

Sustaining the customer revolution

Orientation towards the customer has been one of the strong themes of public service management since the early 1980s. As noted in the previous section there is considerable evidence to support the claim that local government 'has been making special efforts to re-define its service relationships and get close to its public' (SOLACE, 1994). There is a range of ways in which getting closer to the public can be pursued:

1 new ways of learning from the public
2 ensuring that organizational structures provide a focus on customer needs
3 enabling ease of access to council services
4 monitoring and measuring performance
5 motivating and equipping employees to serve the public.

All of these techniques are in common use throughout British local government.

What are the main lessons of the last decade or so? Stewart and Clarke (1996) identify a number of difficulties. The first issue reported by many local authorities is retaining the momentum to keep on going forward. The second is the danger that change is only surface deep. Attention is paid to customer care training, or reception and front-line staff, rather than the more challenging task of rethinking the nature and purpose of the service that is provided. Charter Marks or accreditation for British Standard 5750 indicate a formal level of achievement but may mean little to the public or lead to an air of complacency. Performance measures and associated charters are published but have little meaning for or impact on the public.

Another general concern that has been raised in a range of work is the ambiguity of using the language of the customer in public services (Prior et al., 1995). The public is both a citizen and a customer with respect to public services. As citizens, members of the public have a right to comment on services regardless of whether they directly use such services. The nature of some public services also marks them out from services normally provided in the private sector. Public services involve in some instances regulation, inspection and control. Public services can involve rationing by mechanisms other than price. The nature of that rationing process – which can be more or less explicit – needs to be explored as part of a commitment to public service. Finally a local authority has a responsibility to cope with the diversity of needs and communities within its area. It cannot simply identify a niche market. It has a responsibility to all of its publics. Issues of equity and fairness cannot be ducked.

Other issues have also been raised. What, for example, is the potential contribution of new information and communication technology? Have the opportunities to treat people 'in the round' (both across and beyond the local authority) been fully exploited? Is enough recognition given to the 'co-production' qualities of many services in order to extend service effectiveness? A 'litter-free' town or city is not simply the responsibility of the cleansing service. Is the public being made aware of needs and being encouraged to make its self-help contribution to meeting them?

In short, many commentators take the view that the challenge of reaching out to the public is more profound than originally understood and requires a deepening of commitment which gets beyond the basics of customer care and 'service with a smile'.

Some suggest (Barnes and Shardlow, 1996; Barnes and Prior, 1995) that the immediate challenge is for local government to think in terms of a far-reaching process of service design and redesign. Such an approach means starting with the public in terms of their definition of their needs and their concerns. It means developing performance measures and monitoring systems which have meaning to people. Within the authority, what is required is an across-the-board approach which is not constrained by artificial departmental boundaries. Service redesign requires a strategy of organizational change and the identification of change champions.

Another element in the debate about customer service is the role of further national legislation and exhortation to good practice by central government (Bynoe, 1996). Should there be codes of practice to promote fair treatment and effective methods for participation and consultation? How can monitoring, inspection and audit be made more effective? Should there be a quality standard for what constitutes a public service guarantee? How can methods of redress be enhanced? Should a clear-cut set of entitlements be laid out in relation to public services?

An embryonic community governance role

In what has been discussed thus far the assumption is that the local authority is defined by its role as service provider. Public sector reform has been about creating a leaner and more responsive service delivery system. However there is alongside such developments a growing vision and practice of local authorities which takes them beyond a role in service delivery. The term 'community governance' has been used to capture the embryonic conception of a shift in the purpose and rationale of British local government (Stewart and Clarke, 1996).

The starting point for this new vision involves setting a wider role for local authorities. The task is not the delivery of a discrete set of services but a concern with the well-being of the locality for which they are responsible. The key issue is not how to deliver services but rather how to maximize the well-being of the citizens of the area. A second feature of the new vision is its emphasis on working in partnership with other actors and agencies. The aim is to work with others in the formulation of shared strategic objectives but also to work with and through them to achieve implementation. A third feature of community governance is a concern with the outcomes of service delivery and policy initiatives and more broadly the impact of socio-economic change on the diverse interests within any community. Community governance asks: who gains, who loses?

A paradox in the developments of the last five years is that although local authorities have found many of their traditional service delivery tasks squeezed by financial constraints and challenged in their management by competitive tendering, opting out and performance targets, they have begun to develop a leadership role in some of the broader challenges of community governance. Economic development, urban regeneration, environmental protection, community safety and anti-crime measures, anti-poverty initiatives, preventive health care schemes and anti-domestic violence projects are among the areas where local authorities have sought to take forward the vision of community governance. Central government has encouraged such developments in part through giving local authorities particular responsibilities in areas such as environmental protection and in part through a series of funding schemes that enable local authorities to bid for monies to undertake initiatives in these areas in partnership with other stakeholders.

There have been problems. Developing a shared vision is challenging and it is even more demanding to find the capacity and resources to implement projects and get things done. Too many projects, because of the time-limited nature of their funding, have lacked the staying power and capacity to make a major long-term impact. Tensions have been identified in the relationships between key stakeholders. There remains a degree of uncertainty about the legitimacy and appropriateness of local authorities in the broader agenda of community governance.

What happens next will be influenced by the outcome of the 1997 general election. The Labour Party is committed to giving local authorities a new duty and powers in order to facilitate the community governance role. Even if the legislation takes time to come forward and be passed (the potential legislative agenda of Labour is vast), it is likely that through its pronouncements and its funding of other public sector agencies the Labour government will give strong support and encouragement to the emerging community governance role.

Conclusions

Local government in Britain has experienced a lot of change. A raft of legislation, a wholesale reorganization of its structure and the far-reaching impact of developments in the social and economic environment have contributed to a feeling for many in local government of being involved in a continuous revolution. Old certainties have been challenged and traditional ways of doing things have been questioned.

There is value in a healthy scepticism about some new management reforms and for that matter the extent of change that has occurred in the operations of local government. There is no doubt that fashion and glitzy marketing have played a part in the unfolding of the agenda of change. Hunch, guesswork and ill-considered promotion of 'best' practice from elsewhere have also played a role.

Yet it is unwise and mistaken to believe that there could be any easy return to the unquestioned and unchallenged traditional model of the local authority. The reform agendas of recent years are not wholly the idle product of fashion-driven politicians and management gurus. They are responses to changes in the environment: a public less trusting and more demanding of its public services; a sustained fiscal crisis created by expanding demand for public provision and an unwillingness to pay through taxation for that provision; a shifting pattern of work and community life creating new demands and decreasing support for services in some areas; and the emergence of a number of cross-cutting issues to do with training, economic development, environmental protection, drug abuse and crime prevention that call for new partnerships between agencies and with the public.

There are three main reasons for caution in assessing the impact of reforms (Pollitt, 1995). First, definitions of what is 'better' are inherently contestable. What constitutes better quality education, for example, is a matter of continuing debate. Secondly, the nature of a reform process means in many instances that the nature of the task and the associated categories of data that are collected change. Constructing reliable 'before' and 'after' measures in such circumstances is problematic. Finally there are major attribution problems. Given the complexity of the management and operation of local government, to single out a particular reform as responsible for a particular effect is difficult. The discourse is more in terms of a balance of probabilities.

Research from the Economic and Social Research Council Local Governance Programme has attempted to facilitate an understanding of the experience of change. If there is an underlying pattern to the themes emerging from that research it is to reinforce the message of one of the most well-worn proverbs of administration: 'most decisions about administration are true dilemmas in which the selection of either horn produces some undesirable results on the other' (Peters, 1993: 55). Remedies for solving one problem may indeed make other problems more difficult to solve.

The analysis offered in this chapter of four key agendas of change for local government is informed by the available research and supports the spirit of the argument thus far developed. There is no alternative but to carry on down the reforming path, but making progress may involve one step back as well as two steps forward. It is important to recognize what we may have lost by abandoning traditional structures. It is vital to develop a more reflective reform process. The first wave of management reform may have required revolutionary fervour. The second wave should be of a more pragmatic and analytical style.

Note

This chapter draws substantially on research from the ESRC Local Governance Programme. The Programme contained 27 projects. My role as Director of the Programme was to coordinate the research teams and synthesize the findings. For more information about the Programme, please contact me at: Department of Government, University of Strathclyde, Glasgow G1 1XQ (e-mail G.Stoker@strathclyde.ac.uk).

References

Audit Commission (1988) *The Competitive Council*. London: HMSO.

Barnes, M. and Prior, D. (1995) 'Spoilt for choice? How consumerism can disempower public service users', *Public Money and Management*, 15(3): 53–8.

Barnes, M. and Shardlow, P. (1996) 'Effective consumers and active citizens', *Research, Policy and Planning*, 14(1): 33–7.

Bovaird, T., Davis, P. and Green, J. (1997) *Managing within Limited Resources*. London: Local Government Management Board.

Bynoe, I. (1996) *Beyond the Citizen's Charter*. London: Institute for Public Policy Research.

Doogan, K. (1998) 'The contracting out of local government services', in G. Stoker (ed.), *Hierarchy, Markets and Networks. The New Management of Local Governance in Britain*. London: Macmillan.

Leach, S. and Stoker, G. (1997) 'Understanding the local government review: a retrospective analysis', *Public Administration*, 75(Spring): 1–20.

Leach, S., Stewart, J. and Walsh, K. (1994) *The Changing Organisation and Management of Local Government*. London: Macmillan.

Miller, W. and Dickson, M. (1996) *Local Governance and Local Citizenship: a Report on Public and Elite Attitudes*. Glasgow: Strathclyde University.

Peters, G. (1993) 'Managing the hollow state', in K. Eliassen and J. Kooiman (eds), *Managing Public Organisations*, 2nd edn. London: Sage.

Pollitt, C. (1995) 'Justification by works or by faith? Evaluating the new public management', *Evaluation*, 1(2): 135–57.

Pollitt, C. (1996) 'Managerialism revisited'. Paper presented to the Canadian Centre for Management Development 'Taking Stock' Project, May.

Prior, D., Stewart, J. and Walsh, K. (1995) *Citizenship: Rights, Community and Participation*. London: Pitman.

SOLACE (1994) *The New Management Agenda*. Stirling: Society of Local Authority Chief Executives, Scottish Branch.

Stewart, J. (1996) 'A dogma of our times: the separation of policy-making and implementation', *Public Money and Management*, July–September: 1–8.

Stewart, J. and Clarke, M. (1996) *Developments in Local Government*. Birmingham: INLOGOV.

Walsh, K. (1995) *Public Services and Market Mechanisms*. London: Macmillan.

Walsh, K. and Davis, H. (1993) *Competition and Service: the Impact of the Local Government Act 1988*. London: HMSO.

Young, K. (1996) *A Portrait of Change 1995*. Luton: Local Government Management Board.

Young, K. (1997) *Public Attitudes to Local Government*. York: Joseph Rowntree Foundation.

10

Fiscal and Financial Decentralization: a Comparative Analysis of Six West European Countries

Bernard Steunenberg and Nico Mol

One of the dimensions of reform in the public sector is the distribution of tasks between different levels of government. In most countries in Western Europe central government has become predominant, levying most of government revenues and providing a large number of goods and services. A reduction in the fiscal autonomy of local governments caused them to become increasingly dependent on central government grants for implementing their policies. In addition, a shift of political responsibility from the local to the central level caused local governments in some countries to fall increasingly under the control of central government. In the late 1970s a French governmental commission noted that central government had become too inflated, absorbing almost all administrative activities: 'Local public life is no longer local affairs by right. . . . Local authorities are woven into a resistant net of financial and technical supervision' (quoted in Norton, 1994: 124). Another example of local governments that were strongly constrained by central government is formed by Dutch municipalities in the late 1970s. These municipalities levied only a very small percentage of their revenues from local tax resources, relying for most of their revenues on central government grants.

These developments towards 'overcentralization' have led to a call for decentralization, which can be implemented for a variety of reasons. First, as the fiscal federalism literature suggests, it may lead to a more efficient allocation of resources in society. If groups of voters prefer different levels of local collective goods, then a centralized provision leads to an inefficient allocation, unless local provision carries with it disadvantages that outweigh this gain (Oates, 1972: 11–12). Secondly, decentralization may increase the legitimacy of government, since it allows voters to better select goods and services that match their preferences. Thirdly, as organization theory suggests, the extent to which an organization is able to control its operations becomes more difficult as its size increases. Centralization may therefore lead to an increase in the costs of bureaucratic control, reducing the effectiveness of central government policy-making. Decentralization can be a means to reduce these costs. Finally, and for rather pragmatic reasons, central government may favour decentralization to reduce its budget deficit. Shifting some tasks to local governments without transferring financial resources forms a rather effective cutback strategy at the central level.

While 'overcentralization' may induce a reform towards more decentralization, the interdependency of national economies has led to a conflicting tendency to shift tasks to a higher level of government. This can be most clearly perceived in the development of the European Union in relation to its member states. Nevertheless, similar tendencies may occur within these states. Central government may play a more dominant role in national economies because of external pressures, which are a result of 'global' competition. In addition, interregional mobility of goods, services, production factors and citizens may force central government to reduce unwanted local or regional diversity, which may lead to internal pressures to centralization.

Public sector reform, conceived as changes in the distribution of tasks between different levels of government, can be complicated and puzzling since centralization and decentralization tendencies may vary widely between countries. In this contribution we focus on these different and potentially conflicting developments, which determine the fiscal and financial relationships between central and local governments. This diversity is also reflected in empirical research on the relations between different levels of government. Differences between countries are not only limited to the range of tax bases for central and local governments; they also hold for expenditure levels, public goods offered, and transfer payments between levels of government (see Sharpe, 1981; Lotz, 1986; Gould and Zarkesh, 1986; Karan, 1988; Wallis and Oates, 1988; OECD, 1989). The question arises of whether relations between central and local governments should be regarded as stages of one uniform development, as the frequently mentioned 'centralization' thesis supposes. This thesis, ascribed to Bryce (Oates, 1972: 221–2) and Popitz (Hanusch, 1978: 131–2), states that relations between levels of government can be characterized as steps on a road towards unitary government. Some explanations of this tendency are economic growth-induced economies of scale (Peacock and Wiseman, 1961) and disparities between interlocal or interregional equity that also increase with economic development (Goedhart, 1973). However, the observed diversity of relations between central and local governments contrasts with these explanations, leading to growing doubt about the validity of the centralization thesis. This doubt is further increased by the fact that some of the fiscal indicators used in research show a tendency towards centralization, while other indicators point to decentralization. Departing from this fact, several contributions in the literature have narrowed the discussion of the dynamic of financial relations to the choice of the 'right' indicators (see Oates, 1972: 232–7; Pommerehne, 1977: 306–8).

Meanwhile, other factors have been proposed to deal with the development of financial relations between central and local governments within specific countries. For example, Inman (1988: 56–67) presented and tested a model for US congressional voting. Hanusch (1978) developed a political economic model for West Germany, while Goedhart (1973) stressed equity considerations in a model for The Netherlands (see further Shannon and Kee, 1989). However, these models only seem to provide interpretations of historical developments in specific countries and do not offer a general explanation. Therefore, the extent to which these models can be applied to other countries is rather limited.

In this chapter we investigate the developments in central–local fiscal and financial relations in six West European countries during the period 1950–90. Based on the shares of central government in total government expenditures and in total government taxation, which are traditionally used to measure centralization, these countries appear to have experienced substantially different developments. In view of this diversity we propose a different measure of centralization, which is based upon both government expenditures and taxation. Using this centralization measure, we find less divergent developments in the fiscal and financial relations between governments. Despite the reduction of diversity, a number of traditional hypotheses from the fiscal federalism literature cannot consistently explain the different developments in these countries on the basis of our centralization index. We therefore suggest an alternative explanation, which is based on a strong dependency between GDP and central taxation. We show that central government may play a central role in the allocation of additional tax revenues, which allows for a 'public choice' explanation of the developments in fiscal and financial relations between central and local governments.

The chapter is organized as follows. In the first section we describe the developments in the fiscal and financial relations between central and local governments of six West European countries and develop a new indicator for the degree of centralization. In the second section the differences in these developments are analysed based on explanations that are frequently mentioned in the fiscal federalism literature. In the third section we present an alternative explanation based on the 'public choice' literature. The chapter ends with our conclusions.

Developments in relations between central and local governments

Public production and taxation

Developments in the relations between central and local governments over time can be described in terms of different indicators. At the outset we should state, however, that it is difficult to develop a fully satisfactory measure that describes the amount of centralization in the relationships between central and local governments. Wallis and Oates (1988: 6–7) suggest two indicators, which they use in their study on centralization in the public sector. These indicators are the share of central government in central and local expenditures, and the share of central government in central and local revenues from its own sources. Following this distinction between revenues and expenditures, we propose to base a measurement of centralization on the

Table 10.1   *Fiscal and financial relations between central and local governments in six West European countries, 1950–90*

	1950–9	1960–9	1970–9	1980–9	Total 1950–90
(a) *Average share of central government expenditure in total public expenditure* (%)					
Germany (West)	49.0	46.0	42.9	43.8	45.4
The Netherlands	63.0	63.3	66.4	64.2	64.3
United Kingdom	76.1	70.4	67.5	73.0	71.8
Ireland	71.6	71.4	71.4	74.1	72.3
France	–	79.1	76.4	76.0	77.0
Belgium	79.9	80.2	82.4	84.1	81.7
(b) *Average share of central government taxation in total taxation* (%)					
Germany (West)	58.9	55.9	52.7	51.5	54.7
France	84.9	90.5	88.4	85.6	87.7
United Kingdom	90.0	87.0	87.3	86.9	87.8
Ireland	83.1	86.4	91.3	97.1	91.1
Belgium	95.3	93.8	93.4	93.0	93.9
The Netherlands	95.4	97.1	97.2	96.0	96.4

(relative) production of goods and services and the levying of taxes by central government. The first indicator points to the local government's dependence on central government in the provision of goods and services, while the second indicator focuses on its dependency in regard to financial resources.

The production indicator is measured in financial terms as the relative share of central government expenditure in total government expenditures. The taxation indicator is constructed as the relative share of centrally levied taxes in total government taxation.[1] With regard to the distinction between central and local government, we view local government as all levels of government other than central government. This implies, for instance, that we include expenditures of both provinces and municipalities in the expenditures of local government.

Developments in the fiscal and financial relations between central and local government, based on our indicators, are described in Table 10.1, which presents a summary for six West European countries during the period 1950–90.[2] Our data show rather different developments between these countries.

First, the country values on both dimensions of centralization are rather divergent. For the period 1950–90, Germany, as the only federal country, has the smallest share of total public expenditure (45%).[3] In addition, central government taxation in Germany is limited to 55% of total tax receipts. The other countries have higher shares of central government spending. A relatively small share is found for The Netherlands, where central government is responsible for 64% of the public expenditure. The largest share in this period is found for Belgium, where central government expenditure is about 82% of total expenditure.[4] A different ranking is found for central government taxation. Now The Netherlands ranks highest, with a share of central government in total taxation of 96%. The value of the production indicator is rather small in this case, which implies that local government expenditures are relatively substantial. As a consequence they must be mainly paid for by central government grants. France holds a relatively low value (88%), closely followed by the United Kingdom, which suggests that municipalities and provinces in these countries enjoy more fiscal autonomy.

Secondly, developments in the relative share of central government expenditure or central government taxation in these West European countries are very different. Ireland, for example, represents an example of a country in which both central expenditure and taxation increased during the period 1950–90. This suggests that government became more 'centralized' in Ireland over the years. In France, on the other hand, the relative share of central government in the production of goods and services decreased. This development is accompanied by a higher share of local taxation, especially in the 1980s. This development is in line with the decentralization policy of the French government in the 1980s, which aimed at strengthening the financial status of local authorities (see Norton, 1994: 166). Finally, Belgium represents a case in which both dimensions developed in opposite directions. The share of central government expenditure in Belgium increased over time, while the share of centrally imposed taxation decreased. This suggests that local government in Belgium became more independent in fiscal terms, while some local tasks were transferred to central government.

Based on both indicators, the countries analysed have experienced rather different developments in their fiscal and financial relations. These developments can be expressed as development paths, based on the relative share of centrally produced goods and services and centrally imposed taxes. Belgium, for instance, experienced an increase of central expenditure and a decline of central taxation over the years. In Ireland, on the other hand, the share of central expenditure stabilized at about 72% during the period 1950–80 and showed some increase during the 1980s. The share of centrally imposed taxation increased in the same period from 83% for the 1950s to 97% for the 1980s. These apparently different developments in Belgium and Ireland are illustrated in Figure 10.1. Based on both indicators, the developments in these countries can be conceived as paths in the two-dimensional production–taxation space. Belgium followed a 'north-westerly' path, while Ireland took an 'easterly' route. Based on these different development paths, the fiscal and financial relations between central and local governments in these countries do not seem to have much in common.

The analysis suggests that substantial differences exist between the countries analysed. This is in line with Sharpe's observation based on a survey of several West European countries.[5] He concluded 'that there is not a great deal in common between the six local government financial systems in the survey' (1981: 23). Based on the different developments of the expenditure and the revenue measure of centralization, Wallis and Oates (1988) report somewhat mixed empirical results in terms of potential

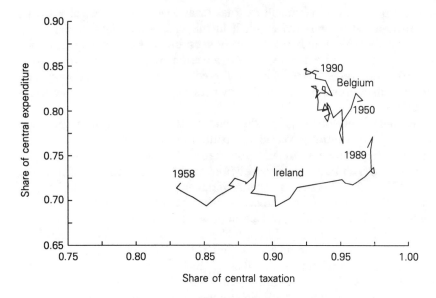

Figure 10.1   *Development paths for Belgium and Ireland in the production–taxation space*

explanations. A number of explanatory variables appears to correlate with only one of two centralization measures, raising the question of which is really the best measure of centralization. But can the degree of centralization only be measured in this way? Are the countries in our analysis really as different as the data suggest? And to what extent are there any similarities between the different development paths of fiscal and financial systems?

The degree of centralization

So far, our analysis has been based on two different, independent dimensions of centralization, which have been treated separately. Based on their independence, and weighting their values equally, these dimensions can also be used to construct a more general measure of centralization. This measure can be based on each country's values of the production indicator and the taxation indicator, which together form a production–taxation vector with values between zero and one.[6] Based on the values of this vector, the following four 'pure' types of central–local fiscal and financial relations can be distinguished:

1   *Completely decentralized government*: a state of affairs where the production–taxation vector has a value [0, 0], that is, there is no central expenditure and no central taxation. Local governments produce all public goods and levy their own taxes. In fact, fiscal and financial relations between local governments and the central government do not exist.

Table 10.2 *Average degree of centralization in central–local government relations in six West European countries, 1950–90*

	1950–9	1960–9	1970–9	1980–9	Total 1950–90
Germany (West)	0.54	0.51	0.48	0.48	0.50
Ireland	0.78	0.79	0.82	0.86	0.82
The Netherlands	0.81	0.82	0.83	0.82	0.82
United Kingdom	0.83	0.79	0.78	0.80	0.81
France	–	0.85	0.83	0.81	0.83
Belgium	0.88	0.87	0.88	0.89	0.88

2   *Central taxation with decentralized public production*: the production–taxation vector has a value [0, 1], that is, no central expenditure and only central taxation. Central government allocates all tax revenues to local governments for the production of public goods. Local governments produce all public goods, while the central government exploits the total tax base.

3   *Local taxation with centralized public production*: the production–taxation vector is [1, 0], that is, only central expenditure and no central taxation. Local governments levy all taxes, while the central government is responsible for the production of all public goods. In this case, and in contrast to type 2, the central government as a producer has local governments carry out the collection of tax revenues.

4   *Completely centralized government*: the production–taxation vector is [1, 1]. Central government produces all public goods and levies all taxes, while local governments do not exist.

These types can be used to define the *degree of centralization*. As indicated by type 1, decentralization is defined as the situation in which the production–taxation vector has the value [0, 0]; that is, local governments levy their own taxes for the production of local public goods. Moreover, there is no central production or taxation whatever. Centralization can now be regarded as any departure from this ideal situation of decentralization. More precisely, the degree of centralization will be conceived as the standardized Euclidean distance between a point in the two-dimensional production–taxation space and the origin.

Based on this measure, the degree of centralization can be computed for each of the countries in Table 10.1. The results are presented in Table 10.2, from which it appears that most countries experienced the same degree of centralization, while having different values according to the production and taxation measures. The average degree of centralization for the period 1950–90 in The Netherlands and Ireland, for example, is 82%, while both countries have rather divergent values on both underlying dimensions. Since our measure is based on a distance and not only on the values of the production–taxation vector, countries with rather different values on both

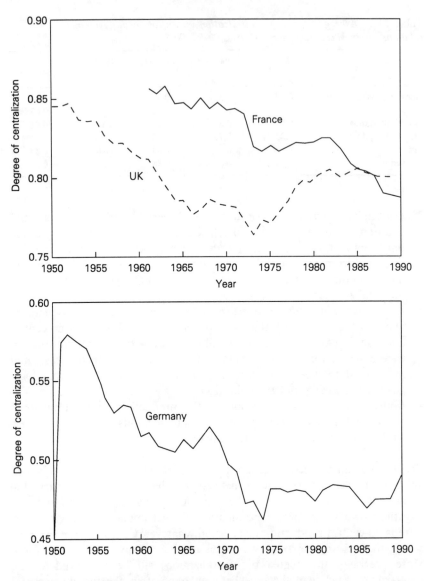

Figure 10.2   *Developments in the degree of centralization in six West European countries, 1950–90*

dimensions can be found on the same 'iso-centralization' curve, that is, the curve that connects all points with the same distance to the origin.

Despite these similarities in the degree of centralization, the six countries analysed experienced divergent developments in their central–local government relations. These developments are illustrated by Figure 10.2, which presents the annual centralization ratios. The average degree of centralization in Germany, for example, declined in the period 1950–89 from 58% in

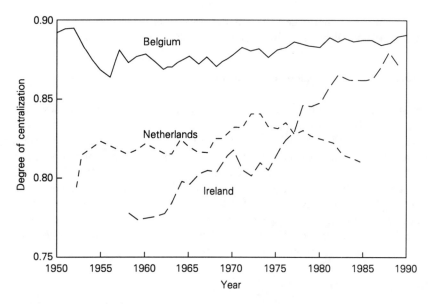

Figure 10.2 *(continued)*

1953 to 48% in 1989. A similar development is found in both France and the United Kingdom, although the development in the United Kingdom is less regular. As in the other two countries, the central–local government relations in the United Kingdom have become less centralized over the last 40 years. Nevertheless, the degree of centralization decreased in the 1950s and 1960s. According to Norton, this change in the development in the United Kingdom is the result of central government policy: 'The Conservative governments of the 1980s attempted to force this down in various ways. They appear, however, to have been much less successful than their Labour Party predecessors in 1974–79 who reduced local expenditure in real terms by ten per cent' (1994: 379).

The smaller countries in our sample experienced quite different developments. In Ireland, for instance, government became more centralized from 78% in 1958 to 87% in 1989. A similar development is found for Belgium, which gradually became more centralized after 1955, despite its different development path as illustrated in Figure 10.1. The Netherlands, finally, experienced a high degree of centralization in the early 1970s, which was reduced during the 1980s.

These different developments contrast with the traditional 'centralization' thesis of Bryce and Popitz, who suggest that central–local government relations become more centralized over time. Our data do not support the validity of this thesis. The countries in our sample experienced divergent developments in their fiscal and financial relations between central and local governments, some of which led to more centralization, others to less. These differences in these relations give rise to questions about its causes. Why do these countries experience different developments in central–local government relations? What are the reasons for this?

Traditional explanations of centralization

The fiscal federalism literature suggests several explanations for the development of relations between central and local governments (see, for instance, Lotz, 1986; Gould and Zarkesh, 1986; Karan, 1988; Wallis and Oates, 1988). So far, these explanations have led to mixed empirical results, partly because the degree of centralization was measured by different indicators. Using the centralization index derived in the previous section we will again test whether these explanations may account for the developments in Belgium, France, Germany, Ireland, The Netherlands, and the United Kingdom. The three factors which are expected to affect a country's degree of centralization are population density, income, and mobility.[7]

Land area and population

The size of a country in terms of land area and population may have important implications for the degree of centralization. Wallis and Oates (1988: 12–14) expect that the larger a country is in terms of both land area and population, the less centralized is its public sector. The main reason for this is that a large jurisdiction with a sizeable population offers more opportunities for decentralization. Land area may affect differences between countries. It is not a relevant factor in an analysis of developments within countries of a given size. We therefore restrict our attention to changes in the size of the population per square kilometre: it is expected that a higher population density will be associated with a less centralized public sector.[8]

The results of this analysis are presented in Table 10.3(a). Population per square kilometre does not have the expected negative impact on the degree of centralization. Its coefficient is not significant. The only significant variable in the analysis is last year's degree of centralization. This variable accounts for most variation in the dependent variable. The population density hypothesis, therefore, seems to be inadequate to explain the different developments in relations between central and local governments.[9]

Table 10.3(b) presents results for an analysis per country. It now appears that population per square kilometre has the expected negative impact on the degree of centralization only in France and Germany (bold face in table). For the other countries this variable is either insignificant or has the wrong sign. These results can easily be related to the developments in the relations between central and local governments described in the previous section. While population density increased over the last 40 years, the degree of centralization decreased in only France and Germany, leading to the expected negative coefficients in the table. However, in Ireland, and to a lesser extent in Belgium, the degree of centralization increased, which corresponds with the positive coefficients. The United Kingdom and The

Table 10.3 *The effect of population per square kilometre on centralization, 1950–90*

	Constant	Population per km^2	Last year's degree of centralization	Adjusted R^2 (N)
(a) *Linear regression for all countries*				
All countries	0.0078	−0.0000051	0.99[†]	0.99
	(1.56)	(−0.63)	(165.8)	(208)
(b) *Linear regression per country*				
France	0.37*	**−0.0012***	0.69[†]	0.93
	(2.12)	(−2.14)	(4.75)	(29)
Germany (West)	0.88[†]	**−0.0018[†]**	0.11	0.90
	(12.9)	(−11.5)	(1.52)	(40)
The Netherlands	0.21*	−0.000066	0.77[†]	0.61
	(2.23)	(1.57)	(6.40)	(29)
United Kingdom	−0.019	0.00017	0.98[†]	0.94
	(−0.25)	(1.12)	(16.2)	(39)
Ireland	0.093*	0.0019[†]	0.79[†]	0.97
	(2.44)	(2.89)	(10.4)	(31)
Belgium	0.21*	0.00012*	0.72[†]	0.62
	(2.37)	(2.09)	(7.13)	(40)

* Significant at the 5% level.
[†] Significant at the 1% level.
Bold face: see text

Netherlands experienced a less uniform development in their centralization ratios, which translates into insignificant results.

Income and wealth

A second explanation of the development of central–local government relations can be based on changes in the level of income and wealth. Since redistributional policies have a relatively high income elasticity, Wallis and Oates (1988: 14–15) suggest that only wealthier jurisdictions will provide more in the way of transfers to lower-income groups. Income redistribution is primarily regarded as a task of central government, because of the mobility of potential recipients across local government boundaries. This will lead to more centralization as income and wealth increase. Related explanations for this tendency are economic growth-induced economies of scale (Peacock and Wiseman, 1961), or disparities in interlocal or inter-regional equity, which also increase with economic development (Goedhart, 1973). Based on these explanations, it is therefore expected that the higher the level of per capita income, the more centralized will the public sector be. In our analysis income is measured in terms of gross domestic product (GDP).

The results of our analysis are presented in Table 10.4(a). GDP per capita does not have a significant effect on the degree of centralization. Its

Table 10.4 *The effect of GDP per capita on centralization, 1950–90*

	Constant	GDP per capita	Last year's degree of centralization	Adjusted R^2 (N)
(a) *Linear regression for all countries*				
All countries	0.0075	0.00084	0.99[†]	0.99
	(1.59)	(1.14)	(161.1)	(206)
(b) *Linear regression per country*				
Belgium	0.65[†]	**0.023**[†]	0.31[†]	0.71
	(5.75)	(4.88)	(2.54)	(38)
Ireland	0.013	−0.0000067	0.99[†]	0.96
	(0.17)	(−0.004)	(10.0)	(31)
United Kingdom	0.054*	0.46	0.93[†]	0.94
	(1.82)	(1.42)	(25.3)	(39)
France	0.20*	−0.14*	0.77[†]	0.92
	(1.90)	(−1.99)	(6.21)	(29)
Germany (West)	0.33[†]	−1.42[†]	0.40[†]	0.67
	(5.13)	(−3.86)	(3.33)	(40)
The Netherlands	0.23[†]	−0.20*	0.73[†]	0.62
	(2.62)	(−1.80)	(6.86)	(29)

* Significant at the 5% level.
[†] Significant at the 1% level.
Bold face: see text

coefficient is not significant. Again, only the last year's centralization ratio has a significant and positive effect on the dependent variable. In other words, the redistribution hypothesis is not able to explain the differences between countries in our analysis.[10]

The diversity among countries becomes clear from Table 10.4(b), which presents regression results per country. GDP per capita only has its expected positive effect on centralization in Belgium (bold face in table). For all other countries, GDP per capita either has the wrong sign (France, Germany, and The Netherlands), which means that it is negatively correlated with centralization, or is not significant (United Kingdom and Ireland). Since GDP per capita increased in all countries during the period 1950–90, these results are not very surprising. For France and Germany, which experienced a decline in the degree of centralization, negative coefficients have been found. For Belgium, which experienced a weak increase of centralization, we find a positive coefficient.

Mobility

The last explanation deals with mobility (that is, migration of inhabitants, flows of goods and services, and factors of production). An increase in mobility allows voters, firms and other actors to compare different local government systems and to use their option of 'voting with their feet'. This voting with the feet does not necessarily involve direct migration of citizens

Table 10.5 *The effect of mobility on centralization, 1950–90*

	Constant	Road mobility	Rail mobility	Last year's degree of centralization	Adjusted R^2 (N)
(a) *Linear regression for all countries*					
All countries	0.0076	−0.0012	−0.0014*	0.99[†]	0.99
	(1.55)	(−1.15)	(−1.88)	(158.1)	(194)
(b) *Linear regression per country*					
Ireland	0.27*	**0.029***	−0.003	0.69[†]	0.97
	(2.38)	(2.42)	(−0.25)	(5.18)	(30)
United Kingdom	0.039	**0.0051***	0.004	0.95	0.95
	(0.86)	(2.01)	(1.09)	(17.0)	(37)
Belgium	0.14	0.0033	0.0011	0.84[†]	0.74
	(1.12)	(1.43)	(0.28)	(5.80)	(35)
France	0.65[†]	−0.014[†]	−0.020[†]	0.27	0.90
	(4.14)	(−4.02)	(−3.02)	(1.53)	(24)
Germany (West)	0.35[†]	−0.025[†]	−0.046[†]	0.36[†]	0.79
	(6.82)	(−6.12)	(−3.48)	(3.60)	(39)
The Netherlands	0.22[†]	−0.0094[†]	−0.023*	0.71[†]	0.66
	(2.59)	(−2.70)	(−2.21)	(6.72)	(29)

* Significant at the 5% level.
[†] Significant at the 1% level.
Bold face: see text

themselves, as in the well-known Tiebout model; it may also involve the flow of capital, or the use of public goods and services provided by other municipalities, such as museums and theatres. This induces stronger demands for interlocal equity, leading to more centralization. It is therefore expected that the higher the mobility between local governments is, the more centralized are the central–local government relations.

Based on available time series data, mobility can be measured by the following five indicators: the per capita numbers of cars, of trucks and commercial vehicles, of telephone connections, and of passenger kilometres travelled by train, and the per capita total weight of freight transported by train. Based on factor analysis these indicators appear to represent two main underlying variables, which are interpreted as *traditional* or *rail mobility* (per capita passenger kilometres and railway freight) and *modern* or *road mobility* (per capita of telephones, cars and trucks).[11] Rail mobility and road mobility are used to explain the degree of centralization.

The results of our analysis are summarized in Table 10.5(a). The mobility hypothesis does not provide an adequate explanation for the developments in the relations between central and local governments for the countries analysed. Road mobility does not have a significant coefficient, while the coefficient for train mobility has the wrong sign. In addition, the lagged centralization ratio appears to be the most important explanatory variable. The mobility hypothesis has to be rejected as a general explanation for the diversity in the relations between different levels of government.[12]

Based on an analysis per country, only road mobility has the expected effect on the degree of centralization in Ireland and the United Kingdom (bold face in table). Rail mobility, however, is not significant in these two countries. For France, Germany, and The Netherlands, mobility, as measured by both variables, has a negative effect on centralization: it leads to less centralization rather than more, as hypothesized. In Belgium mobility does not play a role in explaining developments in central–local government relations. So the mobility hypothesis does not provide an explanation for the developments in these European countries either.

Evaluation

Based on our analysis, population density, income and mobility do not provide consistent explanations for the developments of central–local government relations. In some countries these variables have an impact on centralization, in other countries they do not. For some countries we find the predicted effect of these variables, for others the statistical relationship appears to be the reverse. In other words, the traditional explanations from the fiscal federalism literature are not adequate.

An alternative explanation

To explain the developments in central–local government relations we propose an alternative research strategy: we will show that taxation and public production are related and should therefore be explained simultaneously. In contrast to traditional efforts to establish trends in centralization based upon the *level* of any of these variable (that is, taxation and production indicators, or a centralization index), we focus on patterns in the *changes* of central government taxation and production. The reason for this is that central and local government taxation and public production are closely connected. The link between both levels of government is intergovernmental transfers. This can be illustrated with the following set of relations between central production P_C and central taxation T_C on the one hand, and local production P_L and local taxation T_L on the other. To keep our argument simple, we assume that governments have negligible non-tax revenues and no budget deficits or surpluses, so

$$P_C \equiv T_C - G \tag{1}$$

$$P_L \equiv T_L + G, \tag{2}$$

where G is the net transfer from central to local government. Note that only downward tax sharing is relevant for all the West European countries we analysed. As Table 10.1 indicates, the share of central government expenditure is smaller than the share of central government taxation in all countries. This means that all local governments depend heavily on central government transfers to fund local production.

Sharpe (1981: 23) also noted this imbalance between local expenditure and local taxation. To measure this effect, he proposes a 'resource squeeze' ratio, which is defined as the change of locally derived revenues divided by the change in total local expenditure. Except for rural municipalities in Norway, he finds ratios that are less than one: local taxation grows less than local expenditure, leading to a revenue shortfall at the local level.[13] This shortfall can only be compensated by an increase of central taxation and transfers, leading to centralization of the fiscal and financial relations between central and local governments. So changes in public production and taxation might be causally linked, affecting the degree of centralization.

In contrast to Sharpe, who presumes inflexible public expenditures, we assume that taxation is more fundamentally institutionalized than public production. This is in line with general observations about the rigidity of taxation. An important reason for this might be that voters want to avoid any excessive exploitation of their income and other taxable sources by government (see Brennan and Buchanan, 1980), which calls for all kinds of institutional safeguards. Consequently, public expenditure will be based on new opportunities created by changes in tax revenues and central–local government transfers, and not the other way around. A second observation from studies on the allocation of tax sources between central and local government is that central governments mostly levy income-elastic taxes, while local governments are restricted to levying inelastic taxes or they face constraints on tax rates or the proportion of taxes to be levied. As Sharpe notes: 'the centre takes the lion's share of the buoyant or income-elastic taxes, i.e. those that rise roughly *pari passu* with the general level of prices, and usually reserves for itself the progressive income tax that generates revenue at a faster rate than inflation, thus producing a "fiscal dividend" for the taxing authority' (1981: 7). Consequently, local governments usually depend on property (real estate) taxes and related sources of revenue, while central government has monopolized the control over income taxes.[14] Such an allocation of tax sources leads to divergent income elasticities for tax revenues in central and local governments, which implies an explicit relationship between economic growth and changes in central government taxation.

Hypothesis 1   Centralization of taxation as inferred from an increase in central tax revenues will vary positively with changes in GDP.

An increase of central tax revenues does not necessarily imply that these funds will only be allocated to central production. Some of the additional tax revenues can be allocated to local governments by increasing transfers. Now define

$$G \equiv \alpha \, T_C, \tag{3}$$

where α is the share of local government in central government taxes. Substituting (3) into (1) and (2) then yields:

$$P_C = (1 - \alpha)T_C$$

$$P_L \equiv \alpha T_C + T_L.$$

Note that $\alpha > 0$ for fiscal systems of downward tax sharing. Compensations for a (relative) resource squeeze that is introduced by economic growth, as noted by Sharpe, would then be reflected in an increase of α. In other words, political choice concerning the relative shares of central and local government in tax revenues is expected to be a determining factor in the degree of centralization of public production. Since left-wing or 'progressive' governments are much more concerned with equity considerations of publicly provided goods and services than 'conservative' governments, they generally favour 'state control' and therefore centralization of public production. Based on this argument, we derive a second hypothesis:

Hypothesis 2 Centralization of public production, as inferred from an increase in central government expenditure, will be larger under a 'progressive' central government than under a 'conservative' one.

Both hypotheses can be complemented by two additional hypotheses on the relationship between growth of GDP and public production (instead of taxation) and between political ideology and the change in tax revenues (instead of production). With respect to production we can deduce low values for α from Table 10.1 (substituting the measures for centralization in taxation and production in our equations). In most countries central government retains the additional tax revenues for itself. The dependence between economic growth and the centralization of taxation thus also holds for the centralization of production, although to a lesser extent. So we expect that:

Hypothesis 3 Changes in central production will vary positively with changes in GDP.

With respect to taxation, we assumed that taxes are rigidly institutionalized. If this assumption is valid, it should be reflected in a relative in variance between taxation and political change. We expect that:

Hypothesis 4 Changes in central government taxation do not vary with the political composition of central government.

Based on these hypotheses we thus expect a positive relationship between the growth of GDP and the change in central tax revenues and expenditure. Political ideology, however, is relevant to the explanation of the changes in central expenditure, for which we expect a positive relationship with the occurrence of 'progressive' governments. The expected signs for both explanatory variables are summarized in Table 10.6.

Table 10.6   *The expected effect of growth of GDP and political ideology on the change in central taxation and expenditure*

	Change in central taxation	Change in central expenditure
Growth of GDP	Positive	Positive
Progressive government	None	Positive

Table 10.7   *The effect of selected variables on change in central taxation: linear regression, 1950–90*

Groups of countries[‡]	Constant	Change in GDP	Progressive government	Last year's change in central taxation	Adjusted R^2 (N)
All countries except UK	−0.43	**1.09**[†]	−0.82	0.036	0.60
	(−0.54)	(14.0)	(−1.23)	(0.86)	(183)
United Kingdom	0.45	**0.63**[†]	4.24*	0.23	0.58
	(0.28)	(3.27)	(2.36)	(1.52)	(39)

* Significant at the 5% level.
[†] Significant at the 1% level.
[‡] Based on the Chow test, which indicates whether the coefficients are significantly different between countries. Using a 5% level of significance, the coefficients estimated for Belgium, France, Germany, Ireland and The Netherlands taken as one group differ from the coefficients found for the United Kingdom.
Bold face: see text

Table 10.8   *The effect of selected variables on change in central expenditure: linear regression, 1950–90*

Groups of countries[‡]	Constant	Change in GDP	Progressive government	Last year's change in central expenditure	Adjusted R^2 (N)
Belgium, France, Germany,	0.20	**0.75**[†]	**2.20**[†]	0.18[†]	0.36
United Kingdom	(0.18)	(5.96)	(2.60)	(2.73)	(154)
Ireland, The Netherlands	0.74	**0.88**[ǀ]	−1.63	0.26[ǀ]	0.40
	(0.40)	(4.56)	(−0.63)	(2.45)	(68)

* Significant at the 5% level.
[†] Significant at the 1% level.
[‡] Based on the Chow test. Using a 5% level of significance, the coefficients estimated for these countries differ from the coefficients found for Ireland and The Netherlands. In addition, the coefficients found for Ireland and The Netherlands do not significantly differ.
Bold face: see text

The results of our analysis are presented in Tables 10.7 and 10.8. A left-wing or 'progressive' government has been measured by a dummy variable. This dummy variable has a value of 1 if government is formed by a 'progressive' party, or is based upon a coalition of parties in which, at a maximum, one 'non-progressive' party participates. The labelling of parties as 'progressive' and 'non-progressive' is based on the orderings of national parties on a left–right dimension by Budge et al. (1987) and Laver and Budge (1992). A party is labelled as 'progressive' if it is found to the left of the median party on these scales.[15]

The results partly confirm our expectations. As hypothesis 1 predicts, the growth of GDP has a significant and positive impact on the change in central government taxation in all countries (bold face in Table 10.7). The coefficients for the United Kingdom have been estimated separately, since they differ significantly from the coefficients found for the other countries.[16] The United Kingdom appears to be the only country in which the political preferences of central government positively affect the change of central taxation. For the change in central government expenditure, we also find significant and positive coefficients for the growth in GDP, as hypothesis 3 predicts (bold face in Table 10.8). Ireland and The Netherlands appear to differ from the other countries in having a higher coefficient for the change of GDP. A 1% change in GDP leads to a 0.88% change in central expenditure in both countries, while this change is limited to 0.75% for the other countries.

The results in Table 10.8 also show a positive relationship between progressive governments and centralization in expenditures, as hypothesis 2 predicts. Progressive governments lead to a greater change in central expenditure than non-progressive governments in France, Germany, the United Kingdom, and Belgium (bold face in table). In Ireland and The Netherlands, the coefficients are not significant. The dummy variable measuring the political preferences of the governing coalition hardly varies for these two countries, where most governments are characterized as 'non-progressive'. This limited variation is a possible reason why this variable is not able to measure differences in political preferences, which might explain its insignificant effect.

The absence of any relation between the change in central taxation and the political composition of central government for all countries except the United Kingdom is in line with hypothesis 4 (see Table 10.7). Moreover, these results clearly show the (expected) differences between government taxation and production.

Conclusions

In this chapter we have analysed the fiscal and financial relations between central and local governments in six West European countries. We showed that these countries experienced different developments in this period, some leading to more centralization, others to less.

Based on our research, we may draw three main conclusions. First, the traditional hypotheses from the 'fiscal federalism' literature concerning uniform tendencies towards centralization in central–local government relations are not confirmed. The observed divergence between the analysed countries in the period 1950–90 does not justify any definite generalizations about the pattern of (de-)centralization. Popitz's 'law' or Bryce's 'centralization' thesis are not valid in view of our data.

Secondly, the construction of one centralization index, as suggested in this chapter, does not improve the intended explanation of the developments in the fiscal and financial relations between central and local governments. The construction of one centralization index reduces the ambiguities that are associated with the use of different indicators of centralization. Nevertheless, proposed explanations of the level of centralization in terms of population density or the level of income and wealth do not lead to consistent results. In some countries these variables appear to be correlated with the level of centralization, while in others they do not. These traditional hypotheses thus also failed to provide a *general* explanation of developments.

Finally, we have presented an alternative explanation from a 'public choice' perspective using a framework in which developments in central government expenditure are related to developments in central government taxation. We established that centralization tendencies in both variables depend on changes in economic growth. Moreover, we showed that politically induced variations in the centralization of public production can be explained in terms of differences in the political composition of government and thus in central government policies with regard to local government transfers.

This result may have important consequences for the development of the relations between central and local governments in the coming years. As current governments tend to favour more 'market-based activities' instead of 'state control', and thus can be characterized as having 'conservative' preferences, we expect a development towards more decentralization. This will lead to new public sector reforms that will strengthen the role of local governments in the public sector.

Appendix: data sources

Fiscal and financial data

For the period 1970–89 expenditure and tax revenue data are from *General Government Accounts and Statistics*, Luxembourg, Statistical Office of the EC (Eurostat), 1989, with the following exceptions and additions (data have been reconstructed to match the Eurostat data):

1 United Kingdom: various issues of *National Income and Expenditure* of the Central Statistical Office (period 1950–90). Central government expenditure without current grants to local authorities.
2 Germany (West Germany without the former DDR): *Der Staat in den Volkswirtschaftlichen gesamtrechnungen 1950 bis 1992* of the *Statistisches Bundesambt* (central taxation in the period 1960–9). Central government is only the Bund; local government are the various Länder and municipalities.
3 Belgium: *Het statistisch jaarboek van België* of the *Nationaal Instituut voor de Statistiek* (period 1950–69).
4 Ireland: *National Income and Expenditure* of the Central Statistical Office (period 1958–79).

5 The Netherlands: Centraal Bureau voor de Statistiek, *Negentig jaren statistiek in tijdreeksen, 1899–1989*, Den Haag, SDU, 1989 (period 1950–86). Supplemented with data from Eurostat for 1987–90.
6 France: central government expenditure and taxation from *Annuaire Retrospectif de la France 1948–1988*, Paris, INSEE (1950–87); local government expenditure from *Nationale rekeningen 1961–1971*, Luxembourg, Bureau voor de Statistiek der Europese Gemeen-schappen, 1972 (period 1961–9); and local government taxation from *Comptes nationaux des pays de l'OCDE 1953–1969*, Paris, OCDE (OECD), 1970 (period 1956–69).

Population and land area

From *Bevolkingsstatistiek*, Luxembourg, Bureau voor officiële publicaties van de Europese Gemeenschappen, 1989 (1960–1) and 1993. These data have been supplemented with data from B.R. Mitchell, *International Historical Statistics Europe 1750–1988*, London, Macmillan, 1992 (for 1951–5, 1956–7, 1959).

Passenger kilometres per train, freight per train numbers of cars and commercial vehicles, and number of telephone connections

From B.R. Mitchell, *International Historical Statistics Europe 1750–1988*, London, Macmillan, 1992 (for the period 1950–69). Supplemented with data from various issues of *Europa World Yearbook*, London, Europa Publications, and the *United Nations Statistical Yearbook* of the Statistical Office of the United Nations.

GDP

From Eurostat, *National Accounts ESA, 1970–1990*, Luxembourg, Bureau voor officiële publicaties van de Europese Gemeenschappen, 1991.

Progressive government

Based on the political parties and seats as listed in Woldendorp et al. (1993). Relevant left–right dimensions and the median party are based upon Budge et al. (1987) and Laver and Budge (1992).

Notes

The authors are at the University of Twente, Faculty of Public Administration and Public Policy, PO Box 217, 7500 AE Enschede, The Netherlands. We thank Leo Dieben and the participants in the 1996 ECPR Research Session on Public Sector Reform in Heidelberg for helpful comments and suggestions. Furthermore, we thank Vries Kool, Els Rommes, Janneke Schenk, and Erik Voeten for their research assistance.

1 Government expenditures are based on the Eurostat statistics and include subsidies, current transfers, and capital expenditures. Tax revenues are based on the revenues from direct and indirect taxation.
2 See the Appendix for a description of data sources.
3 Note that Belgium officially introduced a federal system in 1993, in which Brussels, Flanders and Wallonia are the main autonomous regions. Before 1993, Belgium can be regarded as a unitary system as for most other countries in our data set.
4 These differences *between* countries need to be approached with some care, since they also depend on the extent to which data are comparable between countries. For the period 1970–90 we checked our data from national statistical sources with data from Eurostat (*General*

Government Accounts and Statistics, Luxembourg, Statistical Office of the EC, 1989), which revealed only rather small difference, especially for tax revenues.

5 Note that Sharpe (1981) analysed the financial systems of Denmark, Italy, Norway, Sweden, the United Kingdom and West Germany.

6 Recall that the relative shares of central expenditure or central taxation also vary between zero (that is, no central expenditure or taxation) and one (that is, solely central expenditure or taxation).

7 The various factors are tested separately since strong bivariate correlations exist between their indicators.

8 Since land area is a constant, population and population per square kilometre are perfectly correlated. In the analysis we only use the second indicator.

9 We also did an analysis with the annual change in the degree of centralization as the dependent variable, which did not yield an insignificant result for population per square kilometre.

10 We also did an analysis with the annual change in the degree of centralization as the dependent variable. In this analysis GDP per person has a positive effect that is significant at the 5% level for some but not all countries.

11 Using Kaiser's criterion, two factors were extracted from the data using all countries. Applying varimax rotation, the indicators on cars (0.87), telephones (0.97) and trucks (0.80) strongly correlate with the first factor, while passenger kilometres (0.79) and rail freight (0.89) strongly correlate with the second.

12 We also did an analysis with the annual change in the degree of centralization as the dependent variable. Rail mobility now has a significant (1% level) but a negative coefficient, which is not expected. Road mobility has the expected positive and significant coefficient (5% level). However, since the mobility hypothesis predicts a positive impact of both variables, these results do not provide support in favour of this hypothesis.

13 Ratios are computed for Denmark (0.86), urban municipalities in Norway (0.91), Sweden (0.93), the United Kingdom (0.75) and West Germany (0.83).

14 An extreme example of this is the United Kingdom, where local government depends solely on a property tax.

15 The median party is defined as the party that holds the median position for a vote in Parliament.

16 Based on the Chow test of parameter stability (see Thomas, 1993: 62–4).

References

Brennan, G. and Buchanan, J.M. (1980) *The Power to Tax: Analytical Foundations of a Fiscal Constitution*. Cambridge: Cambridge University Press.

Budge, I., Robertson, D. and Hearl, D. (eds) (1987) *Ideology, Strategy and Party Change: Spatial Analyses of Post-War Election Programmes in 19 Democracies*. Cambridge: Cambridge University Press.

Goedhart, C. (1973) 'Local public finance in the theory of fiscal policy', in *Issues of Urban Public Finance: Proceedings of the 1972 Congress of the International Institute of Public Finance*. Saarbrücken. pp. 13–30.

Gould, F. and Zarkesh, F. (1986) 'Local government expenditures and revenues in Western democracies: 1960–1982', *Local Government Studies*, 12: 33–42.

Hanusch, H. (1978) 'Tendencies in fiscal federalism', in H.C. Recktenwald (ed.), *Secular Trends of the Public Sector: Proceedings of the 32nd Congress of the International Institute of Public Finance*. Paris: Editions Cujas. pp. 129–49.

Inman, R.P. (1988) 'Federal assistance and local services in the United States: the evolution of a new federalist fiscal order', in H.S. Rosen (ed.), *Fiscal Federalism: Quantitative Studies*. Chicago and London: University of Chicago Press. pp. 33–74.

Karan, T. (1988) 'Local taxing and local spending: international comparisons', in R. Paddison and S. Bailey (eds), *Local Government Finance: International Perspectives*. London and New York: Routledge. pp. 53–83.

Laver, M.J. and Budge, I. (1992) *Party Policy and Government Coalitions*. London: Macmillan.

Lotz, J. (1986) *Policies with Regard to Grants to Local Authorities*. Strasbourg: Council of Europe.

Norton, A. (1994) *International Handbook of Local and Regional Government: a Comparative Analysis of Advanced Democracies*. Hants: Edward Elgar.

Oates, W.E. (1972) *Fiscal Federalism*. New York: Harcourt Brace Jovanovich.

OECD (1989) *Revenue Statistics of OECD Member Countries 1965–1988*. Paris: OECD.

Peacock, A.T. and Wiseman, J. (1961) *The Growth of Public Expenditures in the United Kingdom*. Princeton, NJ: Princeton University Press.

Pommerehne, W.W. (1977) 'Quantitative aspects of federalism: a study of six countries', in W.E. Oates (ed.), *The Political Economy of Fiscal Federalism*. Lexington, MA: Lexington Books. pp. 275–355.

Shannon, J. and Kee, J.E. (1989) 'The rise of competitive federalism', *Public Budgeting and Finance*, 9: 5–20.

Sharpe, L.J. (1981) 'Is there a fiscal crisis in Western European local government? A first appraisal', in L.J. Sharpe (ed.), *The Local Fiscal Crisis in Western Europe: Myths and Realities*. London and Beverly Hills, CA: Sage. pp. 5–28.

Thomas, R.L. (1993) *Introductory Econometrics: Theory and Applications*, 2nd edn. London and New York: Longman.

Wallis, J.J. and Oates, W.E. (1988) 'Decentralization in the public sector: an empirical study of state and local government', in H.S. Rosen (ed.), *Fiscal Federalism: Quantitative Studies*. Chicago and London: University of Chicago Press. pp. 5–28.

Woldendorp, J., Keman, H. and Budge, I. (1993) 'Political data 1945–1990: party governments in 20 democracies', *European Journal of Political Research*, 24: 1–120.

11

Searching for Competitiveness: the Role of the Spanish Public Sector in the 1980s and 1990s

Carles Boix

Until the two oil shocks of the 1970s, rapid economic growth, full employment, an extensive welfare state and fiscal discipline went hand in hand in the advanced world. In the last two decades, however, the developed world has suffered broad structural changes in its economy and a growing deterioration of the public budget. Since 1973, the average OECD annual growth rate, which had fluctuated around 5% in the 1960s, has dropped to 2.6%. In Europe the unemployment rate has jumped from less than 3% before 1973 to over 10% in the mid 1990s. Finally, an ageing population and intense social demands have expanded the level of social spending on pensions and health. As a result, total public expenditure in the OECD has risen from around 30% in the mid 1960s to over 40% in the early 1990s. In addition, OECD government budgets have deteriorated sharply in a short period. From being balanced around 1970 they fell into an average deficit of more than 5% of GDP in 1982.

The combination of a sluggish economic performance, significant unemployment rates and a growing public sector has had substantial effects on the goals, nature and management of the public sector. In the first place, it has induced a generalized shift away from the Keynesian macroeconomic policies predominant in the 1960s and the 1970s in favour of an orthodox, anti-inflationary policy framework.[1] In the second place, promoting an intense debate on both the limits of redistributive policies and the long-term role that the state should play in fostering investment, growth and job creation, it has encouraged wide experimentation with opposing structural or supply-side economic policies, that is, policies to boost the productivity of input factors and maximize the long-run growth rate, across most advanced countries. Inaugurating what has become a growing movement to break away from the post-war consensus, the British Conservative Party, which came into office in 1979, launched a massive privatization programme, deregulated the labour market and overhauled the British tax system. On the other hand, in the early 1980s several socialist parties were elected in Southern Europe under a programmatic commitment to employ the state to modernize their countries, boost their economic competitiveness, and equalize social conditions. Social cohesion rather than deregulation took precedence there. Whereas the first strategy relied on reducing taxes to encourage private savings, boost private investment and accelerate the rate of growth, the second strategy, of a social democratic nature, consisted in raising the productivity of capital and labour through government intervention (through more expenditure on infrastructures and education and, sometimes, using the public business sector). Social democratic policy-makers expected that, by increasing the productivity of workers (particularly of those initially less endowed), productive sectors and regions, this sort of expenditure would boost, in the first place, the overall efficiency of the economy and its competitiveness, and would lead, in the second place, to higher wages and a more equal income distribution. Finally, besides altering the terms of the economic debate, the economic slowdown of the 1970s and 1980s triggered a process of internal structural change in the state and the progressive adoption of managerial techniques in the public sector.

The analysis of the evolution of the Spanish public sector in the 1980s and early 1990s, undertaken in this chapter, focuses on the set of policies, most of them of a social democratic nature, that the Spanish government developed in response to the growing dilemma – between efficiency and equity – that has gripped the advanced world. With this purpose in mind, the chapter is organized as follows. The first section depicts the general trends of Spanish public spending since the transition to democracy in order to show that, by the mid 1980s, the Spanish public sector had converged to OECD levels. The section concludes with a summary of the main traits of the evolution of the public sector in the 1980s and 1990s. The next two sections examine the core components of the supply-side economic strategy pursued by the Spanish government. The second section describes its initial strategy to reduce the public deficit, increase public savings, and expand expenditure on infrastructures and human capital. The third section explores the evolution of the public business sector: the rationalization plans of 1982–7, a strategy of internationalization in 1987–91, and a new wave of restructuring plans since 1992. The fourth section turns to discuss the political and institutional limits of the supply-side economic strategy pursued by the Spanish government. To complete the analysis of the Spanish public sector, the fifth section describes the (very limited) managerial reforms that have been undertaken.[2]

General trends

Until the early 1970s, public expenditure in Spain fluctuated at slightly over 20% of GDP, or around two-thirds of the OECD average. After the death of Carrero Blanco in 1974 and particularly with the beginning of the democratic transition, public spending underwent a clear change in its trend. During the following 20 years it grew by over 1% of GDP per year in real terms to reach 49.6% of GDP in 1993 (see Figure 11.1). The growth of

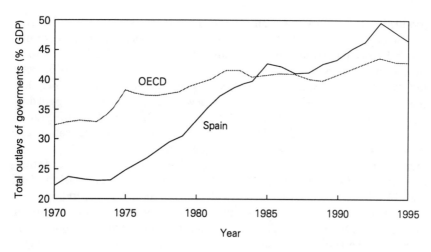

Figure 11.1 *General government total outlays, 1970–95*

public expenditure did not follow a uniform pattern, however. Public spending experienced an unprecedented expansion from less than 25% of GDP in 1974 to over 42% in 1985. The increase in public expenditure was generated by two sequential trends: a rapid growth in social expenditure (in the form of unemployment benefits and pensions) in the second half of the 1970s, caused by the transition to democracy and the economic crisis; and, in the first half of the 1980s, a significant rise in interest payments, resulting from a growing public deficit (to pay for the expansion of social spending). As a result of the expansion of public spending, by the mid 1980s Spain had closed what amounted to a historical gap with other advanced nations, building a public sector equal to the average OECD public sector – and only slightly below the European average.

The trend of public spending changed temporarily in the mid 1980s. After the accession of the Socialist Party (PSOE) to power in 1982 and mainly as a consequence of rapid economic growth in the second half of the 1980s, public spending stabilized as a proportion of GDP and then declined by 1.5% of GDP from 42.6% of GDP in 1986 to 41.1% in 1988. After 1988, however, public spending grew intensely again, reaching 45% of GDP in 1991. This should be considered its equilibrium rate today since, although the economic downturn of the early 1990s pushed public spending to 49.6% of GDP in 1993, two years later public expenditure has declined to its level before the crisis.

The evolution of public expenditure throughout the 1980s resulted from the operation of two fundamental forces. On the one hand, it reflected the effort of the Socialist government to employ the public sector to revamp the supply side of the Spanish economy and to boost the productivity of its input factors. As shown in Table 11.1, to develop an economic strategy in which the state would play a key role in the production and allocation of production factors, the government raised tax revenues systematically, from 32.4% of GDP in 1982 to 40.1% in 1991; contained social expenditure, which hardly increased until 1989; and cut subsidies and capital transfers substantially, by almost 2% of GDP between 1982 and 1989. To increase the level of public (and hence total) saving, which was at an extremely low point in the early 1980s, most of the new revenues were first applied to lower the public deficit, which fell by 3.2% of GDP from 5.6% of GDP in 1982 to 2.8% in 1989. Spending on infrastructures, general education and vocational training programmes was speeded up – even if that meant sacrificing the social component of the public budget. Fixed capital formation was steadily increased by 2.1% of GDP up to 5.2% of GDP in 1991; and 2% of GDP was allocated to both general education expenditure and new manpower programmes. A similar strategy was developed regarding the public business sector. After approving painful restructuring plans and minimal privatizations, in the mid and late 1980s the government engaged several key public firms in strong investment plans and in opening up new markets abroad.

On the other hand, the evolution of public expenditure was affected by intense social pressures to boost public transfers and expand the welfare state. In the wake of both a general strike in December 1988 to protest the strategy of fiscal discipline followed by the González government and of important electoral losses of the PSOE in favour of the radical left in 1989, the Socialist cabinet approved extensive social programmes in 1989 and 1990. In two years, social spending grew by 2%, putting total public expenditure at 45% of GDP (see Table 11.1). The economic downturn of the early 1990s would then trigger another increase in the volume of social transfers and unemployment benefits and push public spending close to half of GDP.

The public sector as an agent of growth

The failure of the French expansionary policies initially pursued by Mitterrand in 1981–3 and swelling public and trade deficits led the Spanish Socialist cabinet to reject the use of any counter-cyclical measures to expand the economy and fight unemployment. Except for the brief period of 1984–6, in which unions and governments concluded a nation-wide wage and social pact, throughout the decade the Spanish government embraced a strategy of macroeconomic discipline to attract capital and open Spain to the world economy. The plans for orthodox macroeconomic policies were complemented with a partial liberalization of the labour market in 1984 as well as the deregulation of financial and product markets.

Warmly embracing and even bolstering the logic of the market economy did not imply, however, either the reduction of social spending or the rejection of state-led strategies to foster economic growth and competitiveness. In the eyes of the González government, the increasing interdepen-

Table 11.1 *General government expenditure and public capital formation in Spain, 1982–91 (% GDP)*

	Level of expenditure				Change 1982–91
	1982	1986	1989	1991	
Total revenues	32.4	36.1	39.8	40.1	+7.7
Budget balance	−5.6	−6.0	−2.8	−4.9	+0.7
Total capital formation:	6.3	8.0	9.4	10.4	+4.1
Fixed capital	3.1	3.6	4.4	5.2	+2.1
Education	3.0	3.8	4.1	4.2	+1.2
Active labour policies	0.2	0.6	0.9	1.0	+0.8
Social expenditure:	18.4	18.6	18.7	20.4	+2.0
Pensions	9.2	10.4	10.2	10.8	+1.6
Unemployment benefits	2.6	2.6	2.4	2.9	+0.3
Other social benefits	2.3	1.0	1.3	1.6	−0.7
Health	4.3	4.6	4.8	5.1	+0.8
Public debt interests	1.0	4.0	3.5	4.0	+3.0
Subsidies and capital transfers	5.5	3.6	3.6	3.6	−1.9

Source: Statistical Annex in Lagares, 1992: 162–6, except data for active labour policies, derived from Table 5.4 in Boix, 1998

dence of Spain dictated granting the public sector an active role in the transformation of the structural conditions of the Spanish economy and in the expansion of its input factors. The sluggish performance of the Spanish economy, which was most apparent in the extremely high rate of unemployment, was attributed to the economy's weak structural conditions. Savings and fixed capital formation had declined by a third since the first oil shock. A sizeable part of the workforce was badly trained and could only take unskilled jobs. Moreover, the internationalization of the Spanish economy, furthered by the process of European integration, intensified the need for improving the country's productive factors. Increasingly open markets and growing capital mobility were undercutting the traditional resort to an exchange rate policy in order to increase competitiveness. As a result, the cost of production factors as well as their productivity were becoming the fundamental variables that determined the competitive edge of Spanish companies. The weakness of the Spanish input factors had straightforward redistributive consequences too – contributing decisively to the relative underdevelopment of most areas of the country in relation to Europe and producing wide income differentials. In 1984 per capita income in 16 out of 17 regions was less than 75% of the average per capita income in the EC. Moreover, the internal distribution of wealth was strongly unequal. The income level among all Spanish regions was widely divergent: the per capita income in the richest regions was more than twice the per capita income in the poorest areas. Finally, unless the growth rate, the productivity and the overall competitiveness of the Spanish economy were significantly boosted, the welfare state and the redistributive plans of the PSOE would be impossible to implement.

To revamp the supply side of the Spanish economy, the Spanish government developed a long-run fiscal policy in two steps. Gradual tax increases and moderate spending cuts in subsidies and social programmes were employed, in the first place, to reduce the public deficit and to raise the level of public (and therefore total) savings. Once the budget deficit was under control, public spending was geared to expand the formation of fixed and human capital.

A social democratic tax strategy

Although government revenues had increased strongly in the late 1970s, boosted by a comprehensive tax reform approved in 1977–8, they had not kept up with the rate of increase in spending, driven by a weak economy and the political pressures of the transition process. Since they had been insufficient to contain a deteriorating public deficit, tax revenues had to be raised to hold together the González economic strategy, which intended to combine a stable macroeconomic policy and the state's direct intervention in capital formation and economic growth.

Driven by its electoral commitments (PSOE, 1982: 18ff; Programa 2000, 1988: 162–3) and economic plans but constrained by a delicate economic situation, the González government designed a medium-term strategy to raise fiscal revenues over the decade. On the one hand, it developed a thorough campaign to combat pervasive fiscal fraud. As a result, by 1990 the number of tax returns being filed had jumped to almost 11 million – therefore nearly doubling the figures of 1981. Moreover, the total tax base had grown by 6.4% annually in real terms in 10 years. By 1990 the national tax base was almost twice that of 1981 measured in constant pesetas. In the same period, the Spanish GDP had grown by 40% in real terms.[3] On the other hand, the government raised revenue through fiscal drag,[4] which was then unequally corrected across tax brackets to enhance the overall progressivity of the tax system – a goal forcefully defended by the Socialist Party.[5]

After 10 years of incremental reform, the tax strategy of the government achieved the two fundamental goals that characterized the Socialist electoral manifesto of 1982. Revenues had surged markedly and the overall progressivity of the tax system had been strengthened markedly. In nine years revenues rose by 7.7% of GDP (or a relative increase of 24%) from 32.4% of GDP in 1982 to 40.1% in 1991 – therefore putting Spain on almost equal terms with other medium-sized European nations in relation to the size of fiscal revenues. Making good the promise to enhance the redistributive structure of the tax system, the increase was heavily concentrated on direct taxes. Almost two-thirds of the increase derived from higher personal and corporate income taxes (5.3% of GDP or a relative increase of 80%). Most of the rest came from consumption taxes as a consequence of the introduction of the VAT required by Spain's integration into the European Community.[6]

Overall progressivity deepened strikingly in less than a decade. In 1981, the effective tax rate on an income of pta 500,000 was 5.4%. For an income 10 times larger, the effective tax rate was 21%.[7] The effective tax rate reached 30% only when the income exceeded pta 9 million. Ten years later tax rates had gone up for all incomes over pta 700,000 (also in 1981 pesetas, which would be pta 1,478,000 in nominal terms in 1990) – that is, for more than 50% of all taxpayers. The real progressivity of the tax had increased substantially as well. For an income of pta 9 million (in 1981 pesetas) the effective tax rate was now around 42%.

Increasing public savings

Progress to reduce the public deficit and increase public savings was both slower and more volatile. During the first parliamentary term, the public deficit increased as a result of the expansionary measures approved in 1985. The government was able, however, to tackle some of the underlying structural causes of an excessive public deficit. The budgetary process was rationalized and the structure of personnel costs clarified. The government enacted a reform of the social security system, whose deficit had risen from 0.4% of GDP in 1977 to 2.5% in 1984, which slashed current benefits and shifted some contributions to employees. As a result, social benefits other than pensions fell 1.3% of GDP from 1982 to 1986. Finally, subsidies and capital transfers were cut by a third from 5.5% of GDP to 3.6% in the same period (see Table 11.1).

As soon as the economic climate improved and tax revenues grew accordingly, a considerable proportion of all new tax revenues was directly applied to reduce the deficit – even if that effort compromised the PSOE's political programme to enlarge public services and threatened to damage the electoral standing of the government among its supporters.[8] Between 1985 and 1990, 83% of all net tax increases (that is, tax increases minus new public transfers), which grew by 4.7% of GDP, were applied to reduce the public deficit (Zabalza, 1991). Public savings increased from -1.4% of GDP in 1985 to 2.9% in 1989. The government's capacity to raise the level of savings proved, however, short-lived. Competing political and social demands on the budget eventually led to higher expenditure in the late 1980s. As a result, the level of public savings then declined somewhat to 2.0% and 1.6% of GDP in 1990 and 1991 respectively.

Expanding the public stock of physical capital

Once the economic trough of the early 1980s was left behind and the budget deficit started to decrease, the government decided to press ahead with what would become the core of its supply-side strategy – building what was termed a 'national stock of public capital'.

Although the volume of public direct capital investment was increased in 1985 and 1986 to sustain a temporary expansionary policy, it was slightly curtailed in 1987 to accommodate a strong cut in the public deficit. It was from the 1988 budget onwards that public investment rose steadily – by almost 0.5% of GDP every year – to reach more than 5% of GDP in 1991. Although some of this increase was a result of decisions by the regional and local governments (around a fifth), most of it (more than two-thirds) was the result of the ambitious investment strategy approved by the central government.

Most of the public investment spending by the central government was allocated to build or ameliorate those basic infrastructures that were thought to play a key role in linking the country (and specially the less developed regions) to the European market, increasing overall productivity and therefore offering more incentives to private investment, and helping to overcome acute shortages and demand bottlenecks. Accordingly, the government developed a comprehensive set of plans to improve transport and communication networks. The construction and maintenance of roads, railways, ports, airports and urban networks represented more than half of the investment assumed by the central government. Another tenth of all the investment was directed to the extension of dams and irrigation systems. The rest was mainly employed in education and health infrastructure and, only secondarily, in culture, housing and environmental protection.[9]

Expenditure on roads and highways consistently attracted the largest portion of public capital – almost a third of all public investment incurred by the central government every year. From 1984 to 1991, an ambitious construction programme tripled the public highway network from 2,300 km to 6,000 km and repaired and improved another 15,000 km of existing roads (García-Blanch et al., 1990; MOPTMA, 1993). Total expenditures from 1985 to 1992 reached pta 1,680 billion (in 1990 pesetas) – close to 0.5% of GDP every year. The investment in the Spanish road transportation system was then strengthened with an overall plan for big cities and their metropolitan areas approved in 1990 that was to pour pta 445 billion in four years into Madrid, Barcelona, Valencia, Málaga and Seville. New plans (approved in 1987) to streamline the public railway company, modernize equipment and expand two-way railways represented pta 415 billion (in 1990 pesetas) or 10% of all investment by the central government (García-Blanch et al., 1990; Sánchez Revenga, 1990).[10] Completing the state effort to modernize the transportation system, pta 220 billion (in 1990 pesetas) were directed to expand the capacity of ports and to renew the Spanish coasts and pta 186 billion (also in 1990 pesetas) were spent to enhance both the capacity and the performance of airports from 1985 to 1992.

Public investment in the Spanish water system was equally strong. A total expenditure of pta 586 billion (in 1990 pesetas) was used to increase the capacity of dams from 43,540 hm^3 to 51,314 hm^3 from 1985 to 1992. Following the same redistributive concerns in the expansion of the communications system, 80% of all public spending was concentrated in the southern half of the country.[11]

Human capital formation

Most of the public effort on human capital formation took the form of increased expenditure on general education. Thus, public expenditure on education, which represented 3% of GDP in 1980, was steadily increased to 4.2% in 1991 and then to 4.7% in 1994 – an increase second only to public investment and higher than social expenditure in areas such as health and pensions (Maravall, 1992). Besides providing a strong boost in expenditure, the Socialist government decided both to reorganize primary and secondary education (through legislation in 1985 and 1990) and to extend free and compulsory education until the age of 16 (in 1990), and attempted to revamp the university system (through a new law in 1983). Combined with a decline in demographic growth, the rise in educational expenditure meant doubling the amount spent per student in real terms, a vast expansion in teachers' hirings and the extension of enrolments at the secondary and university levels (Puerto, 1991).[12] The proportion of students from 14 to 18 years attending school went up from 50% in 1980 to 70% in 1989 and from 19 to 23 years went up from 22% to 33.1%.[13] The volume of grants and scholarships was multiplied by six between 1982 and 1992, from pta 12 billion to pta 71 billion, and the number of beneficiaries went from close to 500,000 in 1987 to more than 800,000 in 1992 (Riviere and Rueda, 1993). Finally, the Socialist government attempted to strengthen the system of vocational education (*formación profesional*, FP) by adapting it to the demands of the market-place and by giving it more status within the overall education system. In 10 years, the number of students in FP doubled (CIDE, 1992).

Active labour market policies took off later. A first attempt came through the promotion of specific training contracts, approved with the assent of unions at the time of the social compact of 1984–6. From 1984 to 1992, around 10% of all hirings corresponded to training and apprenticeship contracts (or 20% of all hirings made under specific employment promotion schemes). Although timidly at first, the Socialist cabinet also embarked on active manpower policies, narrowly defined. In 1983 they totalled pta 53.4 billion, that is around 12% of all expenditure on labour market policies (the rest consisted of unemployment benefits) and 0.25% of GDP. Moreover, they were mostly focused on a rather disparate set of incentive schemes in the private sector. As a result of the social compact of 1984, their volume more than doubled in a single year and by 1986 they amounted to 0.64% of GDP. By 1991 they had reached 1.03% of GDP.[14] Their composition changed as well. Around a third still consisted in applying unemployment subsidies to finance workers' entrepreneurial projects (Espina, 1991). Yet by 1987–8 almost a third of the expenditure in manpower policies was directed to vocational training programmes. The so-called 'occupational vocational education' scheme (*formación profesional ocupacional*), created in 1985 to train workers in very specific jobs (compared with the general skills provided through FP), would multiply by four in a few years to reach almost 350,000 people in 1988 (Corugedo et al., 1991).

Capital formation and the Spanish public business sector

Public firms played an important yet, relative to fiscal policy, more subdued role in the PSOE's strategy. Aware of the dubious consequences of the French nationalizations programme, the González government focused on the rationalization of most of the public business sector until the mid 1980s. As the world economic cycle experienced an upturn, several key public corporations were then used to supplement direct public investment policies and to open up foreign markets for Spanish businesses.

Retrenchment and rationalization in the state-owned business sector, 1983–7

In 1982 the González government inherited what, by European standards, was a sizeable public enterprise sector, burdened, however, by a vast financial and managerial crisis. A product of nationalistic policies developed in the 1940s and the 1950s to grant the state a major role in promoting the industrialization of the country,[15] by the early 1980s the Spanish state-owned companies accounted for nearly 10% of both national value added and total compensation to employees, and for almost 15% of all gross fixed capital formation. The level of investment supplied by all public companies was only significantly higher in Austria, Greece, Norway and Portugal and was similar to Italy and the United Kingdom. Although overall rather diversified, the Spanish public enterprise sector played a key role in certain productive areas. As shown in Table 11.2, the state had a dominant stake in mining, heavy industries (such as steel, shipbuilding and aluminium), oil, electricity, telecommunications, railways, and maritime and air transport. In a fragmented industrial system such as the one prevailing in Spain, moreover, the average Spanish public enterprise was bigger than the average Spanish private enterprise,[16] and was significantly ahead in terms of exports.[17]

Both the economic shocks and the democratic transition of the 1970s left almost all state-run businesses in disarray. The historically high profits of the Spanish petroleum public sector (grouped within the Instituto Nacional de Hidrocarburos or INH since 1981) waned in just a few years. Entire sectors within the biggest public business group – the Instituto Nacional de Industria or INI – such as air transportation, mining or steel, which were extremely dependent on world-wide business cycles, registered massive deficits. Both the political uncertainty of the late 1970s and early 1980s, which translated into a lack of clear-cut managerial strategies, and the indiscriminate use of the public sector as a counter-cyclical instrument, further accelerated the deterioration of the INI's finances. To cushion the impact of the economic crisis during the democratic transition process, the centre-right coalition socialized a large string of loss-making enterprises – mostly in the automotive, steel and shipbuilding sectors. As a whole, INI lost pta 204 billion in 1983 – pta 131.7 billion coming from losses incurred by companies nationalized from 1971 to 1981 (García Hermoso, 1989).

Table 11.2 *Relative weight of the Spanish public business sector in the Spanish economy by selected production sectors, 1985*

Production sector	Production of public companies as % national total in 1985
Gas	100.0
Radioactive mineral	71.4
Coal	51.0*
Oil production and transformation	50.7
Electricity	24.8*
Aluminium	73.0
Iron and steel	28.6
Shipbuilding	65.0
Air and sea transportation	34.3*
Railways	100.0
Telephone	100.0
Banking	17.1†
Fertilizers	34.5
Potash	67.7
Paper pulp	65.7

* 1986.
† Only group ICO; proportion on total credit to the economy.

Sources: Fariñas et al., 1989; Rodríguez López, 1989; INI, several years

Meanwhile, the main railway company, RENFE, posted a deficit of pta 221 billion. Consequently, even when one adds up strongly lucrative enterprises, such as Telefónica, by 1983 the Spanish public enterprise sector turned out to be highly unprofitable (see Figure 11.2).

Until the mid 1980s the González government adopted a cautious strategy, and directed its efforts toward rationalizing the public business sector.[18] To turn around the critical situation of the public business sector, the Socialist cabinet engaged in a set of adjustment plans of different magnitude in several business sectors. Within the framework of global restructuring plans encompassing private and public companies alike, the government approved significant investment plans and set up generous programmes for layoffs (that reached 12,000 workers) in the steel, shipbuilding and fertilizer industries. Similarly, it approved specific plans to rationalize particular companies in the areas of military and capital equipment, aluminium, air transportation, coal and railways (García Hermoso, 1989; Rus, 1989). Throughout the public business sector, moreover, there was a notorious effort at reducing production costs. Hiring was almost frozen and, apart from the expenses incurred through the adjustment programmes, investment barely grew. Total fixed capital formation in public firms went down or remained constant in real terms through 1986 (see Figure 11.3).

Turning public companies into profit-makers also involved setting up a new managerial structure (through the creation of specific subholdings for

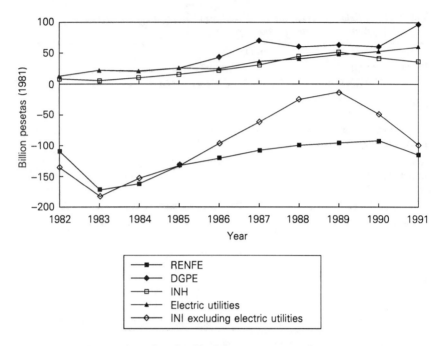

Figure 11.2   *Financial results of public business groups in Spain, 1981–90*

each business area) and trimming slightly the number of public firms through privatization. Until 1987, 30 companies (out of almost 500) were sold to the private sector. Those privatizations, however, resulted not from a political strategy aimed at devolving responsibilities to the private sector but, in the words of a former INI president, rather from 'criteria of industrial and financial rationality linked to the main goal of INI: the maximization of its assets' (Aranzadi, 1989: 258). Thus the state decided to sell either those businesses that were strongly internationalized but for which the public sector seemed to lack the material capacity to ensure their competitiveness in the medium run (such as SKF in the ball-bearing sector and SEAT in the automotive sector), or those that had no strategic interest for the public sector (such as textile industries or tourism operators) (Aranzadi, 1989; García Hermoso, 1989).[19] The extent of the privatization process was relatively limited. Apart from SEAT, which employed almost 23,000 people at the time of its sale, the privatized public companies had around 300 employees on average; in fact, a third of them employed fewer than 100 workers. Even after the privatization drive, the number of public companies kept on growing. According to IGAE, the Spanish government accounting office, in 1985 there were 479 state companies. Four years later, their number had increased to 553.[20]

Partly helped by the government strategy of cost containment and internal rationalization, but mostly driven by the economic upturn of the second half of the 1980s, the financial balance of public companies improved greatly (see Figure 11.2). The INI reduced its losses to pta 41 billion by 1987. Excluding the companies socialized in the 1970s, the industrial group obtained profits totalling pta 28 billion (García Hermoso, 1989). By 1988 the whole group would report pta 31 billion in profits. Similarly, the INH multiplied by 10 its profits from 1983 to 1988 in nominal terms – or seven times when profits are adjusted for inflation. As a result, public transfers and subsidies to public companies started to decline from over 3% of GDP in 1982 to less than 2% by the mid 1980s.

The mid and late 1980s: the supply of capital and the strategy of internationalization

Once the economic pressures on the public budget eased substantially and many state businesses began to report profits in the mid 1980s, the government's strategy towards the public business sector was altered in favour of granting public companies a more active, albeit still selective, role in the economy. On the one hand, capital investment was raised in several sectors controlled by public companies in order to supplement the current fiscal strategy aimed at ensuring high levels of fixed capital formation in Spain. On the other hand, the government decided to turn some public corporations into strong national champions capable of competing abroad, opening new markets for other Spanish businesses and supplying new technologies to Spain.

In line with the persistent determination of the Spanish economic policy-makers to substitute long-term supply-side strategies for discredited demand-management solutions, the public business sector was progressively granted a new function in the Spanish economy. Its role as a counter-cyclical tool and a means of providing employment was systematically abandoned. Employment in state-owned companies was cut over time – by more than a third in RENFE and INI. In turn, productivity gains were emphasized throughout the decade. The government strove to reduce the amount of public money being wasted in loss-making companies.[21] State transfers to public corporations were gradually reduced over time from 3% of GDP in 1983 to 1.1% in 1991.

In exchange, the Socialist cabinet openly used key public companies to complement the process of public capital formation that it was already promoting through the central government budget. Figure 11.3 shows, in a comparative manner, the annual change in real terms in the level of gross fixed capital formation by the general government, by all public enterprises and by the private sector *strictu senso* (that is, once public enterprises are excluded from the latter).

Capital formation in the public enterprise sector almost matched that of the private sector until 1986–7. This reflected a period in which public enterprises underwent a thorough process of rationalization in personnel and production systems. Yet from 1987 on, the rate of change in capital

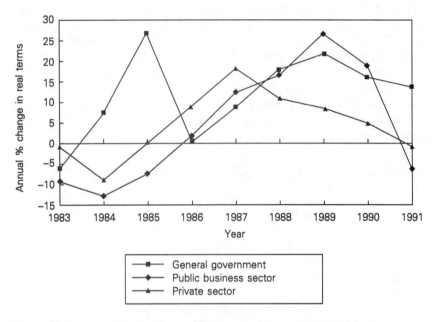

Figure 11.3 *Annual change in gross fixed capital formation by sectors in Spain, 1983–91*

investment by public firms accelerated steadily. It first closely followed the pace of growth in capital formation by the general government, only to outstrip it by 1989. In 1988 and 1989 investment by public companies increased over 20% in real terms. From 1988 on, the rate of change (in real terms) in capital formation in the public business sector doubled the rate in the private sector.

Responding to the general supply-side concerns of the government (jointly with its medium-term strategy of favouring the internationalization of some companies), the investment effort in the public business sector followed a distinctive pattern. Capital formation was directed towards the telecommunications sector (Telefónica tripled its investment in real terms from 1986 to 1990), internal transportation through railways (the state-owned railways company RENFE tripled its investment too in the same period),[22] oil and gas (INH's investment in 1990 was 2.5 times bigger than in 1986 in real terms) and air and sea transport (investment grew eight times from 1986 to 1990 in real terms). All other sectors, which included more traditional industries such as steel, mining, aluminium or shipbuilding, had their rates of investment unchanged or even curtailed (always in real terms). Besides increasing fixed investment, public companies made an important effort in human capital formation: INI doubled its expenditure on R & D to 2% of its total sales in those years – putting it above the European average and at levels similar to other big European industrial concerns.

The investment buildup was related in several cases to the cabinet's attempt to launch certain companies into leading positions in the world market. Apart from those enterprises owned by the state, all the big Spanish exporting companies were in international hands. Believing that Spanish medium and small private companies were unable to reap the benefits of economies of scale, paid no attention to human and technological investment, and lacked comprehensive commercial strategies in foreign markets, the government found it natural to employ the state to accomplish goals that private agents seemed unwilling or unable to achieve.[23]

To build something akin to a set of 'national champions', the government continued, on the one hand, to pursue a strategy of rationalization and concentration of business lines around strong companies. After buying shares in several private companies (Viesco, Fecsa, Sevillana, Saltos del Nansa), the electricity subholding company Endesa reinforced its predominant position in the domestic market and became one of the largest six electricity groups in Europe. In 1992 it agreed to exchange shares with RWE, a strong German electricity group, to open up new European markets. The electronics sector was organized around Inisel through several mergers and share exchanges; by the early 1990s Inisel and Ceselsa had become one of the biggest European subholding companies (Espina, 1992).[24] In the area of potash production, INI bought Potasas del Llobregat and ended up controlling 88% of total national output in this sector. In the area of oil and gas production and distribution, the Spanish government successfully maintained INH in a solid position after the process of European integration injected competition into the sector. The persistent process of heavy investment and managerial rationalization within INH was completed with new acquisitions at the end of the decade in the gas sector (Gas Madrid and 50% of Catalana de Gas) and in the chemical industry (to reinforce REPSOL vertically). Similarly, in 1991 all state banks were merged into CBE (Corporación Bancaria de España, later Argentaria CBE) to form the third largest banking group in the Spanish financial sector.

On the other hand, the state business sector followed a direct strategy of internationalization – through the purchase of foreign firms – to build up enough economies of scale to remain competitive in the world market. Still, the process of internationalization had a limited character. Although important, the Spanish public business sector lacked the size and the competitive edge of the French one. Even after the privatization drive of 1986–8, the French state controlled world leaders such as Péchiney, Rhône-Poulenc, Saint-Gobain, Thompson and Renault (Hall, 1990). Instead, the Spanish public industrial sector was formed by medium companies by world standards. Moreover, most of them pertained to declining sectors such as steel or aluminium that faced fierce competition from developing nations enjoying cheaper labour costs. Engaging in a long-term, aggressive industrial policy in those industries was out of the question. The public budget was constrained by the goals of deficit containment, direct capital formation and new social programmes. The EC laws on competition left scarce room for massive public aid. Thus, the Spanish strategy of internationalization had to rely upon a different set of companies, located in areas such as services or telecommunications, which seemed to offer bright prospects and in which the Spanish public business sector appeared to enjoy, by world standards, a set of medium companies. To become a strong international carrier, the airline company Iberia entered a joint venture with Lufthansa to develop Viva, an international charter company, participated in the international reservation system Amadeus, and launched an aggressive medium-term strategy to capture the Latin American market. A substantial investment was made to turn Miami into a vast air hub and Iberia bought stakes to control several South American companies – Viasa, Ladeco and Aerolíneas Argentinas. Telefónica, the telecommunications company, made similar strenuous efforts to penetrate new countries, such as Argentina, Chile and Venezuela in the late 1980s and Puerto Rico, Portugal and Romania in the early 1990s.[25] All these acquisitions led to a significant expansion in the volume of business managed by Telefónica.[26]

Shifting priorities, 1991–6

As the world business cycle worsened, however, the financial recovery of the state business sector proved to be short-lived. After a period of promising results, INI again posted losses of pta 86 billion in 1991 and pta 79 billion in 1992.[27] Excluding the electrical sector, which had been profitable throughout the decade, the industrial group's deficit climbed to more than pta 200 billion. Two-thirds of the losses originated in steel, aluminium, mining and air transport. In spite of a decade-long effort of rationalization, the economic costs of sustaining all public companies were high. Although state transfers (the sum of subsidies and capital transfers) had decreased over time to slightly over 1% of GDP in 1991, they still exercised a notorious pressure on the state budget.

The internationalization strategy was limited to a few firms and, even in those cases, the chance of success was waning; Iberia, for example, experienced big losses after the summer of 1990. Even there the costs and risks associated with opening new markets (normally by taking over huge loss-making companies) appeared to be daunting – and the benefits derived from them uncertain. Furthermore, technological shocks and Spain's membership in the European Union were eroding what previously were natural monopolies and pushing the government towards the creation of more competitive markets.

Following a political struggle within the governmental policy-making elite, the government favoured a partial reduction of the public business sector. On the one hand, at the end of 1991 the government decided to split INI into two holding companies. The first group (at first called Inisa, then Téneo), gathering all companies in competitive sectors, was to operate as a commercial company, completely detached from the state budget – a goal that had been previously planned to affect the whole of INI. The rest, called

Inise, would include unprofitable firms, such as steel and coal, which would endure significant restructuring programmes – in particular the steel sector, now under a specific subholding, Corporación de la Siderurgia Integral (Téneo, 1992). This reform was strengthened in 1995 with the reorganization of the entire public business sector into two groups. The State Corporation of Industrial Shares (Sociedad Estatal de Participaciones Industriales, SEPI) included all profit-making companies – Téneo and the energy sector – and was to receive no public subsidies. All loss-making industrial firms (mostly in the coal, steel and shipbuilding sectors) were to be managed by the State Industrial Agency (Agencial Industrial del Estado, AIE) through specific contracts in which the state offered financial aid in exchange for extensive restructuring plans.

On the other hand, the government decided to sell parts of the public business sector to raise revenue to reduce a swelling public deficit.[28] Accordingly, a small part of REPSOL was sold in 1992. The operation, repeated in 1993, reduced the public stake to less than 41.1%. In the spring of 1993, 24.5% of Argentaria – a recent merger of all financial public companies – was also sold to private agents. After the loss of the PSOE's parliamentary majority in June 1993 and the formation of a Socialist minority cabinet with the external support of the Catalan and Basque centrist parties, the privatization process speeded up. Between November 1993 and February 1996 the government sold 50% of Argentaria (reducing the publicly controlled share to 25.5%) and 30% of REPSOL (reducing the public stake to 11.1%). In 1994, the state approved a plan to fully liberalize telecommunications by 1998 and sold 10% of Endesa (to finance Iberia's restructuring plans). In 1995 the government sold 12% of Telefónica and 19% of Ence. As a result, between 1993 and 1995 the government raised over pta 900 billion or 1.4% of the average annual GDP (50% more than all the proceeds obtained between 1982 and 1992).

Progress towards privatization was, however, limited. Sales only affected the best performing companies. Public transfers and subsidies to public companies shot up again to around 1.5% of GDP. The state still attempted to shape the Spanish industrial sector. In 1995 it arranged the sale of 7.5% of Telefónica to three Spanish financial institutions (BBV, La Caixa and Argentaria) to secure Spanish control over the telecommunications sector. Finally, since the mid and late 1980s, regional and local governments have engaged in the creation of their own public business sector.[29]

Pressures for economic redistribution

The investment strategy undertaken by the Spanish Socialist government was based on the combination of strong public capital spending and fiscal consolidation. Strict electoral calculations underlay such a choice of policies in the following way. The Spanish Socialist government believed that an economic strategy focused on maximizing the investment rate in a way that combined growth and more equality would sustain a broad cross-class coalition based on the traditional working class and segments of the middle class. Higher expenditure on public capital formation would increase the productivity of regions, economic sectors and the workforce in general and therefore the competitiveness of the economy. It would attract private capital – always in search of high rates of return. And it would allow for higher wages across the board without threatening the performance of the economy. Higher wages would directly reduce inequality and bolster the support of blue-collar workers. But they would also imply an improvement among white-collar employees. With higher average productivity, taxes could be even higher without scaring away private investors – that is, as long as the latter's net return (after-tax profits) continued to be higher than in other countries. With increasing tax revenues, social transfers could be generous and not affect economic performance: a universalistic welfare state could then strengthen the cross-class coalition that initially voted for the Socialist Party.

Given the structure of the electoral support of the PSOE, the electoral success of such an investment strategy required two things: tax increases had to be moderate to avoid losing the support of centrist voters that had given the PSOE its parliamentary majority in 1982; and, since tax revenues were limited, social spending had to be contained in the short and medium run to provide room for capital spending. The González government achieved such a 'happy equilibrium' of low public deficits and high expenditure on fixed and human capital only until 1989. The general government deficit fell from 6.9% of GDP in 1985 to 2.8% four years later, partly as a result of restrictive fiscal measures in 1986 and 1987, but mostly driven by the spectacular improvement the Spanish economy experienced in the mid 1980s. Fiscal restraint waned, however, from 1988 on. Even in the presence of a booming economy, the size of the 'fiscal impulse' (that is, the change in the budget balance adjusting for the business cycle) oscillated around 1% of GDP for four years in a row (see Table 11.3, column 3). Still, until 1988 all expenditure overruns were comfortably absorbed by unexpectedly high revenues.

From 1989 on, however, the governmental fiscal strategy underwent considerable strain. The Spanish trade unions intensified the pressure to increase social spending. After participating in a national incomes pact in 1985–6, the labour movement rapidly radicalized its demands. Both the Socialist and the Communist unions joined in a one-day general strike in December 1988 to bring the government to its knees and to extract from it a set of social concessions that totalled pta 450 billion (more than 1% of the 1988 GDP) (Juliá, 1988). Given the extraordinary success of the strike, González promptly conceded the cabinet's defeat in Parliament, and agreed to part of the union's demands. The final cost of the governmental concessions in 1989 was put at pta 190 billion.

The intensifying pressure of trade unions to increase social spending could have been warded off had the PSOE kept its parliamentary majority

Table 11.3   *Fiscal policy in Spain 1988–95 (% GDP)*

	1 Total expenditure	2 General government financial balance	3 Change in overall government balance from previous year*	4 Change in structural government balance from previous year*† (fiscal impulse)
1988	41.1	−3.2	+0.1	+1.5
1989	42.6	−2.8	−0.4	+1.2
1990	43.3	−3.9	+1.1	+1.0
1991	45.1	−4.9	+1.0	+1.0
1992	46.3	−4.1	−0.8	n.a.
1993	49.6	−7.5	+3.4	n.a.
1994	48.0	−6.9	−0.6	n.a.
1995	46.5	−6.2	−0.8	n.a.

* In figures on deficit change, a positive sign means expansionary change and a negative sign represents a restrictive change.

† The change in the structural government balance corresponds to the change in the fiscal deficit that would have taken place if the GDP were to grow at its potential rate. The change in the structural balance therefore shows the net effect of governmental discretionary decisions concerning the budget.

Sources: for columns 1 and 2 until 1991, IGAE, 1993; after 1991, Bank of Spain, several years. For the column 4, data from González-Páramo and Roldán, 1992

intact. But in the general election of 1989 the PSOE vote declined by 3% – mostly to the advantage of the radical Left, depriving the González government from an outright majority in Parliament. This persuaded the cabinet to increase social transfers to avoid losing more popular support. Minimum pensions were raised to the minimum wage level in 1990. Increases on pensions were scaled to favour the lowest income levels. The government established non-contributive pensions. In addition, expenditure on unemployment benefits was sharply expanded from 2.7% to 3.8% of GDP in three years (Godé Sanchez, 1990; Jiménez Fernández, 1990; 1991; Ruiz Álvarez, 1992; García Perea and Gómez, 1993). Since this was done without reducing capital spending – which still constituted the core of the PSOE's economic strategy – higher taxes would have been necessary to avoid a fiscal deficit. Taxes were raised, however, in a limited way. The Socialist Party reckoned that an increase in taxes could endanger its grip on key centrist voters. As a result, the central government deficit rose to 2.9% of GDP and the general government deficit (that is, the sum of the central government and local government deficits) to almost 5% of GDP in 1991. A sharp decline in economic activity from 1992 on intensified the dilemmas of the government. In 1993 the general government deficit reached 7.5% of GDP.

The government's incapacity to either restrain social transfers or increase taxes had several important implications. First, it forced the Cabinet to engage in dramatic, unpopular and only mildly successful tightening measures during the course of the fiscal year to salvage its overall budget deficit goals. These cyclical patterns of extraordinary overruns followed by prompt cuts and *ad hoc* tax increases (all coming in a variety of forms) eroded the government's policy credibility and added indirect costs to the economic climate.[30] Secondly, it thwarted partially the long-run strategy of sustaining public investment: most of the cuts effected to compensate for increased social programmes were implemented on capital spending. Thirdly, it forced the Socialist government to rely on an extremely tight monetary policy to sustain the peseta within the European exchange rate, to reduce inflation and to stabilize the economy. Finally, it pushed public spending to 49.6% of GDP in 1993 – twice its level in 1975 – and led to a rise in the level of public debt from 20% of GDP in the late 1970s to 45% in 1991 and then to 64% in 1994.

The (limited) introduction of managerial reforms

In comparison to the historical experience of other advanced countries, the introduction of managerial techniques as well as the use of market mechanisms within the public sector have been fairly limited in Spain in the 1980s and 1990s. Several factors account for the lack of significant change in the operation and production processes of the Spanish state. On the one hand, whereas in countries like Britain and Sweden there was increasing popular concern about the inefficiencies of the public sector and mounting political resistance to higher taxes, in Spain a solid majority kept favouring the expansion of public services and the universal provision of welfare goods. In the mid 1980s, 70% of those surveyed thought that the state should ensure the welfare of all citizens. By contrast, the proportion was only 44% in France (Maravall, 1995: 187). On the other hand, the academic knowledge needed to inspire and sustain any managerial reforms has been extremely limited. Owing to the weight of the continental law tradition, most policy communities and expertise centres are controlled by legal scholars and practitioners, who, systematically insisting on the principles of (top-down) bureaucratic rationality and 'legal security' to organize the public sector, mistrust any managerial discourse.

Most reforms have been promoted by regional and local governments. As the pressure to contain expenditure grew in the early 1990s, they created quasi-public agencies, set up *ad hoc* committees to rationalize their administrations, and, in a few instances, introduced new units organized around the concept of service and client (Echebarría, 1995). To date, the most important reform to be implemented has consisted of the overhaul of the Catalan public health system: maintaining the principles of universal coverage and public finance, and tapping into a long tradition of private health organizations, the Catalan regional government has embraced a system of quasi-markets that encourages competition among suppliers and stresses the choice of patients.

The lack of internal reforms and the inability of the public sector to attend speedily and efficiently to all social demands has led to a growing disenchantment among Spanish citizens. In 1985, 55% of all surveyed thought that the government was wasting part or most of the tax money. In 1992 that proportion had increased to 83% (Wert et al., 1993). Indeed, in an interview by the end of 1992, Felipe González would acknowledge that the reform of the public administration had been one of the greatest failures of the decade (*El País*, 13 December 1992).

Conclusions

In 1982 the Spanish Socialist Party was elected to office with an impressive parliamentary majority. Acknowledging strong financial and international constraints, the González cabinet shunned demand-led expansionary policies and increasingly committed itself to a programme of macroeconomic stability. The Spanish Socialist government did not renounce, however, employing the public sector to enhance the competitiveness of the Spanish economy. Tax revenues were increased steadily. Total public revenues rose 7.7% of GDP to 40.1% of GDP in 1991. A remarkable effort was made to increase the level of public (and hence total) savings. Vast resources were directed to improve the Spanish physical and human capital stock. Fixed capital formation was doubled to an annual rate of 5% of GDP. Human capital formation jumped from 3% to over 5% of GDP as well. At the heart of these decisions lay the notion that only a strategy focused on enhancing the Spanish economy's productivity could reduce the level of unemployment, increase income levels and equalize social conditions. Only policies geared towards adding value to Spanish products could at the same time make them competitive enough in the world market and allow real wages to increase over time. With raising productivity, more resources could be then found to finance social transfers. As a matter of fact, supply-side economic policies of that kind have always constituted the core element of all social democratic strategies.[31]

The González government encountered, however, several important obstacles, which are directly related to the growing efficiency–equity trade-off that advanced economies are experiencing, in the implementation of its investment policies. First, a divided and radicalized union movement made the reproduction of a corporatist pact impossible after 1986. In the context of a very rigid labour market, which the PSOE was unwilling to reform, González was forced to embrace extremely tight policies to quell inflation. Above all, the Spanish Socialist government faced a strong political dilemma between increasing social spending to meet the demands of workers and leftist voters, and stabilizing taxes to keep the support of centrist voters. Governing in a country with a relatively unskilled workforce – the levels of educational attainment in Spain are low relative to other European countries – it probably made economic sense to intensify all capital formation efforts to avoid the trap of excessively high levels of social protection and spending. Yet the almost exclusive focus on public investment until 1989 (to the detriment of public transfers) had important political costs for the Socialist Party. Spanish voters expected the state to build up a complete, universalistic welfare system in a short period. After several years of fiscal consolidation, the Socialist government had to face a severe general strike in 1988 demanding more social spending. The combative strategies of the trade union movement threatened to ruin the macroeconomic strategy pursued by the government and to alienate important parts of the industrial working class from the PSOE. In the 1989 parliamentary elections the PSOE's share of the vote dropped from 43.4% to 40.3%. The radical Left more than doubled its vote from 4.6% to 9.2%. González responded by increasing social spending along with public capital formation. Since taxes could not be substantially increased without losing centrist voters, the public deficit began to rise rapidly. The resulting expansionary fiscal policy had several damaging effects: it reinforced the need to tighten monetary policy to stabilize the economy and sustain the peseta in the European exchange rate mechanism; it pushed public spending close to 50% of GDP and the level of public debt to 64% of GDP in 1994; and it probably accounted for much of the defeat of the Socialist Party at the polls in the mid 1990s.

Notes

1 See Hall (1986; 1995) and Scharpf (1987; 1991).

2 As a result of the 1978 constitution, the Spanish state has undergone a gradual process of political decentralization through the creation of autonomous regions. In 1995, regional governments accounted for 25.5% of total public spending and over a third of total public investment. Although this has changed the structure of the Spanish public sector quite substantially, this chapter does not examine either the nature or the consequences of this decentralization process. A first analysis can be found in OECD (1993).

3 All data are for Spain excluding the Basque Country and Navarra.

4 Fiscal drag accounted for 80% of all new revenue through 1985 (Argimón and González-Páramo, 1987; Valdés et al., 1989) and for 80% of the new revenue from 1986 on (Jiménez and Salas, 1992).

5 See PSOE (1982: 18), Programa 2000 (1988: 163). See also Solchaga (1986a: 214ff), Borrell (1987; 1988; 1989).

6 The implementation of a value-added tax in 1986 led to a temporary upsurge in revenue from indirect taxes. For a strong statement that this situation was merely provisional and that the Socialist cabinet was committed to rely mostly on direct taxes over the long run, see the declarations of the Minister of Economy before Parliament in October 1986 (Solchaga, 1986b: 35–7).

7 Less than 1% of all taxpayers were in that category.

8 The fact that those calculations were explicitly taken into account by the government can be seen in Borrell (1990: 47).

9 All these proportions refer to central government non-military investment and they include investment by all autonomous institutes (*organismos autónomos*) and the social security. Military investment, which declined over time, represented 0.8% of GDP in 1987 and 0.5% in 1990 (IGAE, 1990). Besides direct public investment, the central government financed investment by private and public enterprises through capital transfers – which fluctuated around 2% of GDP. Most of them will be examined in the section on public companies.

10 This figure, however, does not include strong capital transfers from the central government to the two public companies, RENFE and FEVE, totalling pta 535 billion (in 1990 pesetas) from 1985 to 1992. This represented 56% of all the investment effort made by RENFE and FEVE the same period (pta 947 billion in 1990 pesetas).

11 All figures on central government investment are own estimates based on MOPTMA (1993) and MOPT (several years).

12 Around 80% of the new expenditure in education was directed to secondary and university education, according to data collected by Bandrés (1993) comparing 1980 to 1990.

13 All children between 6 and 12 years were already attending school in 1980.

14 These programmes were also spurred by European funds, which financed 52% of all of them (Espina, 1991).

15 For a history of the public enterprise sector in Spain before the 1980s, see Martín and Comín (1990) and, more generally, Comín and Martín (1991).

16 In 1986, for example, the average public enterprise had 1,600 employees, sold pta 15,500 million and had assets amounting to pta 26,000 million. The average private enterprise figures were 200 employees, pta 2,900 million in sales and pta 3,000 million in assets (Cuervo, 1989).

17 In 1985, manufacturing public enterprises exported 28.9% of their product while all manufacturing enterprises sold abroad 21% of their production.

18 The Socialist cabinet only nationalized the high-tension electric network. Moreover, in 1983 it took over RUMASA – a financial and industrial holding the government judged was heading towards immediate collapse. The companies included in RUMASA were devolved to the private sector over the following years.

19 A third of the companies that were sold corresponded to companies nationalized in the 1970s.

20 These numbers fall to 402 and 484 respectively when we exclude all commercial services as well as the *organismos autónomos*.

21 It is true, however, that the government continued to sustain some heavy loss-making sectors. This was, for example, the case in the coal mining industry (Servén, 1989), heavily concentrated in one region, Asturias, in which employment in the public holding amounted to 44% of all industrial employment (the data correspond to 1976 and are reproduced in Martín and Comín, 1990).

22 This excludes capital transfers from the state.

23 See declarations by M. Cuenca, Vice-President of INI, on 26 August 1992 (*El País*, 27 August 1992) and Espina (1992), Secretary of State for Industry since April 1991. See also Eguiagaray (1995).

24 This consolidation process implied the integration of Entel and Eria in Eritel (in 1991), mainly controlled by Inisel; an accord between Inisel and Ceselsa; and a share exchange between Sainco and Inisel (INI, several years).

25 Telefónica bought 20% of Entel and 43.6% of CTC (both of them serving the Chilean market), shares in Telefónica de Argentina and CANTV (in Venezuela), 79% of the Puerto Rican TLD, and part of two telephone mobile services in Portugal (Contactel) and Romania (Telefonica Romania) (Telefónica, several years).

26 In 1992 Telefónica managed close to 14 million telephone lines in the Spanish domestic market and another 5 million through all the foreign companies in which it participated (Telefónica, 1992). Thus, the international strategy pursued by Telefónica increased its business volume by 40% in just three years.

27 Notice that Figure 11.2, which reports the financial balance of key public corporations, shows results in constant 1981 pesetas.

28 In order to finance large investment plans, already in 1988 the government had sold shares in three electricity companies – totalling pta 101 billion. The following year 24% of the oil company of INH, REPSOL, was also sold to the public.

29 See *El País*, 29 September 1996.

30 See Pérez Campanero (1992) and González-Páramo (1992).

31 For a longer, more detailed exposition of this idea, see Boix (1998).

References

Aranzadi, Claudio (1989) 'La política de desinversiones en el INI', *Papeles de Economía Española*, 38: 258–61.

Argimón, Isabel and González-Páramo, José Manuel (1987) 'Una medición de la rémora inflacionista del IRPF, 1979–1985', *Investigaciones Económicas. Segunda Epoca*, 11: 345–66.

Bandrés Eduardo (1993) 'La eficacia redistributiva de los gastos sociales. Una aplicación al caso español (1980–1990)', in *I Simposio sobre Igualdad y Distribución de la Renta y la Riqueza, Fundación Argentaria*. Madrid: Fundación Argentaria. Vol. VII, pp. 123–71.

Bank of Spain (several years) *Informe anual*. Madrid: Banco de España.

Boix, Carles (1998) *Political Parties, Growth and Equality: Conservative and Social Democratic Strategies in the World Economy*. Cambridge: Cambridge University Press.

Borrell, José (1987) 'Balance del sistema tributario', *Papeles de Economía Española*, 30–1: 56–63.

Borrell, José (1988) 'Evolución y tendencias del gasto público', *Papeles de Economía Española*, 37: 174–93.

Borrell, José (1989) 'Economía y fiscalidad en Europa', *Papeles de Economía Española*, 41: 91–101.

Borrell, José (1990) 'De la Constitución a Europa: una década de política fiscal', *Información Comercial Española*, 680: 9–37.

CIDE (1992) *El Sistema Educativo Español, 1991*. Madrid: Ministerio de Educación y Ciencia, Centro de Investigación, Documentación y Evaluación.

Comín, Francisco and Martín, Pablo (eds) (1991) *Historia de la empresa pública en España*. Madrid: Espasa-Calpe.

Corugedo, Indalecio, García, Enrique and Martínez, Jorge (1991) *Un análisis coste-beneficio de la Enseñanza Media en España*. Madrid: Ministerio de Educación y Ciencia, Centro de Investigación, Documentación y Evaluación.

Cuervo García, Alvaro (1989) 'La empresa pública: estructura financiera, rentabilidad y costes financieros', *Papeles de Economía Española*, 38: 177–98.

Echebarría, Koldo (1995) 'La paradoja de la reforma administrativa de las comunidades autónomas', *Papers ESADE 135*, ESADE, Barcelona.

Eguiagaray, Juan Manuel (1995) 'Editorial: Empresa pública y sectores estratégicos', *Presupuesto y Gasto Público*, 16: 5–8.

Espina, Alvaro (1991) *Empleo, democracia y relaciones industriales*. Madrid: Ministerio de Trabajo y Seguridad Social.

Espina, Alvaro (1992) *Recursos humanos y política industrial: España ante la Unión Europea*. Madrid: Fundesco.

Fariñas, José Carlos, Jaumandreu, Jordi and Mato, Gonzalo (1989) 'La empresa pública industrial española: 1981–1986', *Papeles de Economía Española*, 38: 199–216.

García-Blanch, José, Garrido, Andrés and Rubio, Alberto (1990) 'Política de infraestructuras de transporte', *Presupuesto y Gasto Público*, 28: 139–53.

García Hermoso, José Manuel (1989) 'El INI como grupo de negocios: presente y futuro', *Papeles de Economía Española*, 38: 262–76.

García Perea, Pilar and Gómez, Ramón (1993) 'Aspectos institucionales del mercado de trabajo español, en comparación con otros países comunitarios', *Banco de España. Boletín Económico*, September: 29–47.

Godé Sánchez, José Antonio (1990) 'Los gastos sociales en el Presupuesto de 1990', *Presupuesto y Gasto Público*, 2: 131–44.

González-Páramo, José Manuel (1992) 'Presupuestos Generales del Estado para 1993: el reto de la credibilidad', *Cuadernos de Información Económica de Papeles de Economía Española*, 67: 11–20.

González-Páramo, José Manuel and Roldán J.M. (1992) 'La orientación de la política presupuestaria en España: evolución reciente y perspectivas de convergencia', *Papeles de Economía Española*, 52–3: 167–79.

Hall, Peter A. (1986) *Governing the Economy: the Politics of State Intervention in Britain and France*. Oxford: Oxford University Press.

Hall, Peter A. (1990) 'The state and the market', in Peter A. Hall, Jack Hayward and Howard Machin (eds), *Developments in French Politics*. London: Macmillan. pp. 171–87.

Hall, Peter A. (1995) 'The political economy of Europe in an era of interdependence'. Unpublished manuscript, Center for European Studies, Harvard University.

IGAE (1990) *Actuación económica y financiera de las Administraciones Públicas*. Madrid: Intervención General de la Administración del Estado.

IGAE (1993) *Boletín de información estadística del sector público 1991*. Madrid: Intervención General de la Administración del Estado.

INI (several years) *Informe Anual*. Madrid: Instituto Nacional de Industria.

Jiménez Fernández, Adolfo (1990) 'La Seguridad Social en 1990: El presupuesto del consenso social', *Presupuesto y Gasto Público*, 2: 75–96.

Jiménez Fernández, Adolfo (1991) 'La política de prestaciones que informa el contenido del presupuesto de la Seguridad Social para 1991 y breve descripción de este último', *Presupuesto y Gasto Público*, 4: 97–126.

Jiménez, Miguel and Salas, Rafael (1992) 'Causas del incremento en la recaudación del IRPF, 1982–1987', in Instituto de Estudios Fiscales, *La reforma del IRPF*. Número monográfico de Hacienda Pública Española. Madrid: Instituto de Estudios Fiscales.

Juliá Díaz, Santos (ed.) (1988) *La desavenencia: partido, sindicato y huelga general*. Madrid: El País/Aguilar.

Lagares, Manuel J. (1992) 'Comportamiento del sector público: perspectiva de una década y planteamientos de futuro', *Papeles de Economía Española*, 52–3: 132–66.

Maravall, José María (1992) 'From opposition to government: the politics and policies of the PSOE', in J.M. Maravall et al., *Socialist Parties in Europe*. Barcelona: Institut de Ciències Polítiques i Socials. pp. 7–34.

Maravall, José María (1995) *Los resultados de la democracia*. Madrid: Alianza Editorial.

Martín, Pablo and Comín, Francisco (1990) 'La acción regional del Instituto Nacional de Industria, 1941–1976', in Jordi Nadal and Albert Carreras (eds), *Pautas regionales de la industrialización española (siglos XIX y XX)*. Barcelona: Ariel. pp. 379–419.

MOPT (several years) *Los transportes y las comunicaciones*. Madrid: Instituto de Estudios del Transporte y las Comunicaciones.

MOPTMA (1993) *Anuario Estadístico 1992*. Madrid: Ministerio de Obras Públicas, Transporte y Medio Ambiente. Dirección General de Programación Económica y Presupuestaria.

OECD (1993) *OECD Economic Surveys of 1992–93: Spain*. Paris: OECD.

Pérez Campanero, J. (1992) *La pérdida de credibilidad de la economía española*. FEDEA informe técnico 92–19, FEDEA, Madrid.

Programa 2000 (1988) *La economía española a debate*. Madrid: Siglo XXI.

PSOE (1982) *Programa Electoral*. Madrid: Partido Socialista Obrero Español.

Puerto, Mariano (1991) 'La reforma de la enseñanza no universitaria: aspectos económicos y presupuestarios', *Presupuesto y Gasto Público*, 4: 153–70.

Riviere, Angel and Rueda Fernando (1993) 'Igualdad social y política educativa', *I Simposio sobre Igualdad y Distribución de la Renta y la Riqueza, Fundación Argentaria*. Madrid: Fundación Argentaria. Vol. VIII, pp. 8–34.

Rodrígnez López, Julio (1989) 'Credito oficial: la transición', *Papales de Economía Española*, 38: 340–8.

Ruiz Alvarez, José Luis (1992) 'Un análisis económico de las recientes políticas presupuestarias del mercado de trabajo', *Presupuesto y Gasto Público*, 7: 7–17.

Rus, Ginés de (1989) 'Las empresas públicas del transporte en España', *Papeles de Economía Española*, 38: 349–82.

Sánchez Revenga, Jaime (1990) 'La inversión en infraestructuras públicas en el Presupuesto para 1990', *Presupuesto y Gasto Público*, 2: 97–130.

Scharpf, Fritz W. (1987) 'A game-theoretical interpretation of inflation and unemployment in Western Europe', *Journal of Public Policy*, 7: 227–57.

Scharpf, Fritz W. (1991) *Crisis and Choice in European Social Democracy*. Ithaca, NY: Cornell University Press.

Servén, Luis (1989) 'La empresa pública en un sector estratégico: HUNOSA', *Papeles de Economía Española*, 38: 383–9.

Solchaga, Carlos (1986a) 'Discurso parlamentario sobre la reforma del IRPF', *Hacienda Pública Española*, 99: 205–20.

Solchaga, Carlos (1986b) 'Discurso en la presentación de la Ley de Presupuestos Generales del Estado para 1987 ante el Congreso de Diputados', *Hacienda Pública Española*, 102–3: 17–46.

Telefónica (several years) *Informe Anual*. Madrid: Telefónica.

Téneo (1992) *Informe Anual*. Madrid: Teneo.

Valdés, T., Argimón, Isabel and Raymond, José Luis (1989) 'Evolución de la recaudación del IRPF: determinación de las causas y estimación de los efectos', *Investigaciones Económicas*, 13: 14–44.

Wert, José Ignacio, Toharia, José Juan and Pintor, Rafael López (1993) 'El regreso de la política. Una primera interpretación de las elecciones del 6-J', *Claves de Razón Práctica*, 34: 32–42.

Zabalza, Antoni (1991) 'La reforma de l'IRPF i la política fiscal', *Revista Econòmica de Catalunya*, 15: 51–7.

12

Incorporation as Public Sector Reform

Jan-Erik Lane

Public sector reform comes under the DPM framework – deregulation, privatization and marketization – which terms stand for a variety of strategies. These strategies, inspired by Chicago School economics, will be analysed here from a theoretical point of view, namely in relation to the question: what are the pros and cons of the increased employment of the public joint stock company in allocative and regulatory schemes? This institutional mechanism is chosen today because it is considered superior to the alternative mechanisms of the bureau and the traditional public enterprise, but does the public joint stock company resolve the principal–agent difficulties? Who are the stakeholders surrounding this new mechanism, which involves privatization and deregulation to some degree but not completely?

Public sector reform is very much on the political agenda in the 1990s. In an OECD survey all countries reported various ongoing efforts at public sector restructuring. Some countries have embarked on fundamental changes, such as the Commonwealth countries, whereas others seem to work more incrementally, revising bits and pieces here and there. Only in France have far-reaching reform proposals met with fierce resistance. The purpose of this chapter is to pinpoint one main difficulty in public sector reform, that is the principal–agent problem in relation to the major new mechanism in public sector reform – the use of public joint stock companies (Thynne, 1994). Does incorporation solve the principal–agent difficulties typical of public enterprises or even bureaux?

Background

The welfare state in the countries with an advanced economy may be decomposed into allocative and redistributive programmes. But the latter one refers to transfer payments in the social security system compensating individuals by maintaining income at a certain level. Although public sector reform includes changes in both the allocative and the redistributive programmes, these types of programmes are entirely different, calling for separate treatment. Whereas allocative programmes aim at efficiency, redistributive programmes are based upon considerations about social justice. Public resource allocation makes up about 50% of the entire public sector expenditures on average for the OECD countries. Public regulation comes close to the concern of public resource allocation – namely efficiency, especially when it is a matter of economic regulations whereby an organization is presented with a legal concession by government to provide certain goods and services.

The use of public joint stock companies raises questions about how public allocation and public regulation may be combined in public sector reform. Would not the spread of public joint stock companies replacing bureaux and public enterprises require a new kind of regulation or some kind of regulatory boards? In the aftermath of the processes of privatization and deregulation, initiated during the 1980s, we see today that governments in the countries with an advanced economy introduce more and more a new governance mechanism, the public joint stock company. It not only takes the place of the traditional public enterprises within infrastructure, but is also employed under the internal market schemes that have made a huge inroad into the core of the public sector, especially in countries which adhere to the compulsory competitive tendering framework.

Does the public joint stock company really solve the principal–agent difficulties that characterized traditional public administration? If governments pursue deregulation policies favouring competition and levelling the playing field, then why would they want to operate huge and risky firms, where managerial discretion is large? For politicians the joint stock company poses new challenges, but perhaps politicians may simply turn to the joint stock model because it takes away their responsibility for painful decisions.

When the firm institution has received much attention in public sector reform, then it is not a question of the traditional public enterprise. This type of institution is considered outdated. What is at stake now is the increasing use of joint stock companies for the provision of goods and services by the political community, although the joint stock company operates under private law conceptions. The political community may often wish to transform bureaux or public enterprises into joint stock companies where, as the principal, it owns the shares or the majority of the equity. Before we discuss whether this move resolves the typical principal–agent problems involved in bureau supply, we point out that the traditional public enterprises constituted an institution that has been little appreciated, mainly owing to the misuse of it in the form of so-called parastatals, which typically run losses most of the time.

The public enterprise used to be an institutional compromise between the bureau and the firm as a joint stock company. It was legally part of the public sector but enjoyed more discretion than an ordinary bureau. Thus, it possessed legal personality but had to operate under a public fiscal regime involving user fees set at cost pricing where rates would be decided by the community following deliberations about what quantities of goods and services the enterprise should supply, possibly at some level of subsidization. Typically, running costs would be determined at the level of the public enterprise whereas large capital expenditures would be decided by government.

The distinction between bureaux in public administration and public firms is made in different ways in various countries, reflecting historical legacies and legal practices. English practice has used the following institutional distinction between three different bodies: (1) departments of the central civil/public service, or of local governments; (2) statutory/public/crown/ government corporations, created by special statutes (there are a few unincorporated boards, commissions, etc., but most of those operating business enterprises are incorporated); (3) state-owned companies, which are also corporations but are created by registration under general companies Acts. In America there are the public utilities.

This is not the place to examine various country practices. Let us introduce a conceptual framework for discussing the trend towards incorporation proper, that is the introduction of public joint stock companies instead of traditional public enterprises in general or even bureaux in some cases.

Principal–agent notions

In present public sector reforms the emphasis is on privatization and deregulation. Although we face here a number of different strategies they have a common core in so far as they restructure the relationship between the political community as the principal and the agents to whom the principal may turn. The two main changes involve first that bidding is favoured ahead of hierarchy, and secondly that private agents are given precedence before public agents, or that traditional types of public agents such as the bureau and the public enterprise are to be restructured in such a manner that they acquire the typical features of private agents although they remain in public ownership. There are two different aspects of the principal–agent interaction when governments constitute the principal.

On the one hand, there is the question of the nature of the agent which a government may turn to. The government as principal may employ either a public or a private agent, a choice with institutional implications. Thus, the agent may be a bureau, a public enterprise, a joint stock company or simply a private entrepreneur. On the other hand, there is the question of how government as the principal interacts with the agent it employs, the two fundamental alternatives being either hierarchy (long-term contracting) or tendering/bidding (short-term contracting).

Typical of hierarchy is the command–obedience relationship, whereas characteristic of bidding/tendering is contractual negotiation (Alchian and Demsetz, 1972). In organizational economics, the key question is what are the pros and cons of these two institutional alternatives (Williamson, 1973; 1986). Adding the principal–agent distinction to the Alchian and Demsetz interaction distinction, we arrive at the typology outlined in Table 12.1 which combines the nature of the agent with the interaction pattern in a 2×2 table where government is the principal.

Table 12.1   *Principal–agent relationships in government*

| | | Type of agent | |
		Public	Private
Interaction pattern	Hierarchy	I	II
	Tendering/bidding	III	IV

Classical public administration based upon the bureau is an example of type I, whereas traditional public utilities regulation used to be of type II (Stigler, 1988). Type III occurs in the public sector reform endeavours under the purchaser–provider model. Type IV, finally, has for a long time been characteristic of contracting-out schemes in the public sector, although not taken to the extremes of the now widespread so-called compulsory competitive tendering (CCT) or 'internal markets'. Type IV would be characteristic of Walrasian markets.

Privatization and deregulation are definitely the concern of types III and IV, as privatization and deregulation can be regarded as calls for institutional reforms of types I and II. In type III one tends to favour the employment of the joint stock company, while under type IV one often observes competition between private and public joint stock companies when governments deregulate a sector.

One may interpret the search for new arrangements in the provision of goods and services by government as a struggle to come to grips with a basic problem involved in all kinds of principal–agent interaction (Ricketts, 1987). We are referring to the difficulty on the part of the principal of monitoring the agent so as to check whether the agent's team production is efficient (Tirole, 1993). What is a public principal?

Public principals

A political community that has been set up in order to accomplish certain tasks constitutes a public principal. This community may be a government at any level, such as a central, regional or local government. It may be part of a unitary or a federal state. The community has been set up in order to deliver certain goods or services which the members of the community cannot provide themselves by means of the voluntary exchange mechanism. Markets may not exist for the type of goods or services which the community needs or the market mechanism may not deliver an efficient solution to the allocation of these goods.

There is a large literature on the problems involved when political communities move to specify their objectives. We will not enter this debate about how public policies are decided upon, as we simply assume that the community has decided by some democratic procedure or another on a set of social objectives and that it then moves on the search for institutions that will engage in the production of goods and services which further these objectives. Likewise we will not enter into the debate about the implementation deficit. There is an entire literature which questions whether objectives can ever be fully accomplished. However severe the implementation deficit is, the political community has to look for some implementation mechanism to further its objectives (Pressman and Wildavsky, 1984).

Typically, the community looks for an agent that will assist it in the accomplishment of social objectives. Thus arise the principal–agent relationships in the public sector. Structuring these principal–agent relationships involves deliberations about institutional arrangements through which the principal attempts to handle the possibility of opportunistic behaviour on the part of the agent.

In traditional public administration one started from the politics/administration distinction, which is still entrenched in public administration in different ways in various countries (Aberbach et al., 1981). The political community is to decide upon the goals whereas the public bureaux are to identify and implement the means. Yet, a number of criticisms have been launched against the traditional public administration scheme. First, it has not proved possible to make the separation between politics and administration in any acceptable manner. Various suggestions have been tried, identifying values or goals with politics and means or technology with administration, but these conceptual pairs do not coincide with the politics/administration separation in real life.

Secondly, if political communities are interwoven in intergovernmental mechanisms, then complexity will arise due to so-called *Politikverflechtung* blurring the division of labour between politicians and bureaucrats. The range of players involved in the making and implementation of policy cannot be restricted to two neatly separate sets of politicians and bureaucrats but may be expanded to include anyone who is a member of a policy network, blurring also the public–private sector distinction. Policy networks may involve so much reciprocity between players that any separation of roles becomes impossible.

Thirdly, processes of policy-making and implementation may enter a phase of garbage-can processes where ends are ambiguous, technology is uncertain, participation is fluid and players have a solution but lack a problem. In such circumstances the traditional separation between politics and administration cannot be applied. No attempt will be made to reinstate the relevance of the distinction between politics and administration. The long-standing critique of the politics/administration distinction still appears valid.

At the same time, one may look also at the policy networks approach from the principal–agent perspective: to whom is the political community going to entrust the task of providing goods and services whose allocation enhances the achievement of the social objectives of the community? This is a question about choosing an agent and deciding about the institutions that will structure the interaction between the political community as a principal and the agent selected. The political community as a principal may pick either a public or a private agent or a combination. The key question is that of efficiency, meaning how the principal can get value for the resources handed over to the agent for the accomplishments of the objectives of the principal. This is at heart a matter of institutional arrangements such as various forms of regulation, contracting and monitoring.

To get things done the principal must not only contact an agent but also provide the agent with resources that cover the costs of the agent's operations. How is a contract between the principal and the agent to be agreed upon and how is it to be monitored? This is the classical problem in public administration as far as resource allocation is concerned. How is the agent to be paid and how much money should be allocated to the agent? The principal and the agent have mutual interests in getting things done but opposing interests in relation to how high the costs may go, especially concerning the remuneration of the agent.

Given this starting point we now proceed to spell out the consequences of alternative institutional arrangements for the interaction between the principal and the agent, of which there exist only a few conceivable ones. The bureau mechanism and the public enterprise constitute such institutional arrangements, the public joint stock company too.

Public agents

The political community, whether a simple or a complex one, must turn to a public agent. There exist three institutionally defined public agents: the bureau, the public enterprise and the joint stock company owned by a public principal. Each of these institutions involves monitoring problems, whether the principal employs hierarchy or bidding/tendering.

The bureau: hierarchy versus tendering/bidding

The standard type of public agent is the bureau. It is an institution which may be employed by the political community at any level of government. Ministries are bureaux just as much as national public agencies or boards. Regional and local governments operate a number of bureaux or authorities. The political community interacts with the bureau on the basis of hierarchy, through which it specifies that the bureau concentrates upon the delivery of services in a certain area as the sole provider. The political community entrusts the bureau with certain tasks on the condition that the community pays the costs of operating the bureau over the public budget by means of an appropriation. The critical question is whether the bureau delivers a performance that matches the appropriation that the community puts up – a typical principal–agent relationship problem.

Much public sector reform has focused on the writing of the contract between the community and the bureau, how it should be framed, monitored and evaluated. The problem is that of asymmetric information, as the bureau knows more about the activities it engages in than the community. The bureau has information about the costs of producing various amounts of goods or services which it will not willingly reveal, at least not automatically. It also knows more about the relationship between its own efforts and the actual services it provides than what the community is able to disclose by looking at information made available by the bureau. Finally, the bureau has a strategic information advantage also in the sense that it knows more about the links between the activities it provides and the objectives that the community has set up for the bureau. The combination of asymmetric information and opportunistic behaviour on the part of the bureau results in X-inefficiency, or the generation of slack within the bureau as well as a risk for excessive supply in the Niskanen sense.

What can the political community do? The only way is to reduce the amount of asymmetry between the information that the community has and the information that the bureau possesses. In public sector reform the community may try to do that by monitoring the bureau more closely, for example by using a third agency which specializes in the collection and analysis of productivity and effectiveness. However, monitoring involves costs which rise as a function of the amount of monitoring activities whereas the benefits of each additional monitoring activity decrease. If the community were to monitor the bureau closely, it would soon run up staggering monitoring costs.

Each bureau is instructed to deliver certain goods and services, but why would the bureau have any incentive not to run slacks, thus reducing X-inefficiency? What would be the gain for the bureau in servicing all its potential client's so minimizing the risk of Y-inefficiency? The bureau receives an appropriation in relation to its requests in the budgetary process. They are based upon cost calculations concerning what inputs the bureau needs to deliver its outputs. The bureau is basically a team, meaning that it faces all the difficulties in team production in calculating correctly the contribution of each input to its output of goods and services. The bureau will tend to inflate its cost estimates in order to protect itself against miscalculations, especially if it can pass the slack on to the overall budget where its appropriation may be fairly small and thus not receive special attention.

Public sector reform has been conducted in several countries for a number of years in order to improve the monitoring of the principal of its agent, the public bureau. This involves the introduction of evaluation techniques, of management tools and changes in the budgetary process in order to reduce the role of opportunistic behaviour. Special bureaux for performance assessment may be employed, but then the principal simply faces another principal–agent question: who controls the controllers? Special monitoring bureaux may provide governments with poor policy analysis or governments may lack the power to use the knowledge provided by evaluation bureaux in order to curb the opportunistic behaviour of their agencies. Thus, despite the fact that evaluation has been emphasized heavily in public sector reform, there has still been a search for an entirely new mechanism for handling the bureaux, namely bidding instead of hierarchy.

Under tendering/bidding schemes the traditional Weberian bureau is radically transformed. Instead of receiving an appropriation out of taxation and being the sole provider of some goods or services, the bureau now becomes a production unit which has to enter a bidding process in which it competes with other production units, public or private. Under the new internal market model the most cost effective bidder receives the contract for a specified period only. Thus, competition in supply among several bidders will replace hierarchy in internal organization, according to the Williamson (1986) framework. The bureau may go on doing what it used to do under traditional public administration, but it will no longer be immortal, because it may lose out in the recurrent bidding process to any suppliers that contest the position of the bureau.

The increased employment of bidding calls for a number of extensive institutional changes in public administration, when competition is going to replace hierarchy. The legal framework comprising the rules of competition has to be reformulated in order to make it real in relation to goods and services provided by government. Perhaps CCT schemes can only work if there is a regulatory scheme with a powerful board of competition, but does public regulation work? And will the transfer to tendering/bidding help solve the principal–agent problems involved in any public provision?

The employment of bidding has a dramatic impact upon the position of the bureau with regard to asymmetric information. The only way for the bureau to get the contract that is up for tendering is to come in with the best bid, which entails that it has to cut excessive costs given that there is real competition with at least one more supplier that contests the bureau. By comparing alternative bids the principal moves towards a position of symmetry in information in relation to the agent, especially if the principal can start making comparisons between marginal utility and marginal costs in relation to different quantities of the goods or services that may be supplied. The reduction in information asymmetry also narrows the scope for opportunistic behaviour on the part of the agent.

The critical question is, however, whether bidding really works in relation to the kinds of tasks that bureaux have been entrusted with in an advanced economy. The problem has two sides: internal and external competition. Internal competition refers to whether the principal really can get access to more than one bid from the bureau, whereas external competition stands for the opportunity for the bureau to engage in competition not only in relation to its given principal but also elsewhere. The experiences from public sector reforms in various countries indicate that internal competition is not easily achieved and that external competition creates institutional problems.

On the one hand, some tasks that the principal wants done seem to be of such a nature that no agents wish to come up with bids. On the other hand, when a bureau is instructed to deliver a bid instead of a request for an appropriation, then it becomes impossible to restrict the bureau from entering other competitions, even those where there is no public principal involved at all. What we are talking about here is the distinction between the public and the private sectors. There may exist no private agents that wish to contest the position of the bureau in a bidding process, meaning that competition fails. And bureaux may start entering all kinds of bidding processes, taking contracts from private agents within the private sector, meaning that competition in the private sector could become precarious if the bureau has a strategic advantage owing to its established position in the public sector.

Thus, the move to bidding in relation to bureaux may have the paradoxical effect that no real competition is achieved in the public sector but competition in the private sector is increased. The introduction of bidding in public sector reforms has called for a revision of the established rules of competition as well as the creation of agencies or tribunals which police these rules. What we are talking about here is the introduction and implementation of *anti-trust* policies, possibly with an anti-trust regulatory agency.

Now, contracting out has always been used in the public sector in relation to services where a tendering process is easy to administer. But in the new schemes, under the label of the purchaser/provider split, contracting out takes on an entirely different scale. When the principal refrains from setting up bureaux but is content to establish a so-called enabling authority, then tendering becomes the chief mechanism for the provision of goods and services. Such a development makes heavy demands upon the making and application of anti-trust policies, especially if the political community decides that bidding should prevail over hierarchy. Under a CCT scheme an institutional structure may be laid down which requires that the provision of almost any kind of service in the public sector be subjected to a bidding process. Such institutions require not only their own implementation organs but also congruence with the general norms of competitive and anti-competitive behaviour in the market economy.

Once one changes the interaction between government and bureaux from hierarchy to bidding, then one may raise the question of whether the principal should resort to a different type of agent altogether, the joint stock company. In many countries the political community has changed bureaux into 'production units' for the supply of goods and services to be provided for by government. Perhaps the production unit should be a private law entity although owned by government: the public joint stock company (Thynne, 1994). Before we discuss the implications for resource allocation we point out that in many countries there has existed a hybrid institution combining characteristics of public bureaux and firms, the public enterprise.

The traditional public enterprise

The public enterprise institution was often used in various regulatory schemes, where the principal was not content to use only regulation of private firms in order to accomplish social objectives. If the principal could set up its own agent, the public enterprise, then public regulation could work even more effectively, it was believed. Thus, the public regulation of infrastructure involved not only the setting up of regulatory bodies overlooking private firms but also the running of huge public enterprises.

However, the critique of public regulation entailed that the public enterprise institution did not resolve the fundamental problems in principal–agent interaction (Stigler, 1988). Even if the regulated firm was a public enterprise the political community as the principal could not be sure that the agent would try hard to reduce X-inefficiency. On the contrary, the comparative evidence about public enterprises revealed that they were often less cost effective than private firms. The public enterprise as an agent could count upon investing in opportunistic strategies, not only because under public regulatory schemes there is bound to exist asymmetric information but also because of the bail-out option under which government would have to cover any losses made by the public enterprise.

The combined attraction of deregulation and privatization created an enormous strain upon the public enterprise as a distinct institution. Strictly speaking, 'privatization' means the hiving off of activities from the public sector to the private sector, for instance by selling public enterprises to private entrepreneurs. Deregulation policies have concerned the status of not only public enterprises but also private ones, but their general impact is to favour another institutional mechanism for the production of goods and services, the firm according to private law definition. Deregulation is part of the general process away from hierarchy towards bidding and tendering. Yet, the combination of privatization and deregulation has in public sector reform not simply meant a reduction of the public sector in favour of private ownership and market allocation. Often, public enterprises were transformed into public joint stock companies and deregulation was replaced by anti-trust policies.

The adherents of the firm institution for delivering services in the public sector emphasize that they do not wish to go back to the subsidized public enterprise. What they have in mind is the joint stock company model, where the political community owns the majority of the shares. Joint stock companies, it is claimed, can even take on a large number of the tasks which bureaux have been entrusted with. Thus, governments at various levels now restructure their service provision by setting up joint stock companies within not only infrastructure but also the health care and education sectors. We ask now: is the public joint stock company an institutional device for strengthening the principal *vis-à-vis* the agent?

The public joint stock company

The joint stock company is basically a private sector institutional mechanism. It does not operate according to public law. When it is employed by the political community, then there immediately arise questions about how its institutions can be accommodated with the requirements of public law concerning openness, fairness and procedural accountability. One may tackle these difficulties either by somehow extending public law notions to apply also to joint stock companies owned by public principals or by setting up special tribunals instructed to check the operations of these new joint stock companies. The strengthening of anti-trust policies offers one route for checking public joint stock companies, but do anti-trust policies work?

It is, though, difficult to see why the transfer from one institution, the bureau or the public enterprise, to another, the joint stock company, in itself would solve the difficulties in principal–agent reciprocities. Actually, the monitoring problems become much more severe under the private sector institutional mechanism, because of the vast gulf between owners and managers that tends to be characteristic of limited liability firms. The transaction costs involved in checking the public joint stock company will simply increase owing to the loss in hierarchical supervision. More is needed in order for joint stock companies to work better than the bureau and the public enterprise than simply introducing a firm, where the shares are owned by the political community. Such a firm would actually be more capable of opportunistic behaviour than the traditional bureau or public enterprise, unless it is checked by the fundamental private sector mechanism of competition. A publicly owned joint stock company could be just as X-inefficient as a bureau or a public enterprise, whether the joint stock company is financed on a contract basis with government or has the right to raise its own revenues by user fees.

The institutional reform of putting publicly owned joint stock companies in the place of the bureau or the public enterprise will only strengthen the position of the political community as the principal if it is combined with a move towards bidding when the public joint stock company is paid for by means of a contract with the principal, or the introduction of full-scale competition if the joint stock company has the right to levy user fees. The danger is the same in both cases, namely that the joint stock company engages in opportunistic behaviour which the principal cannot counter if the position of the joint stock company is not contestable.

One may actually question the whole idea of having publicly owned joint stock companies, because what is their rationale? If they can only work to the benefit of their principals under competitive schemes, then why not privatize them completely, that is sell out the equity to private investors? The principal would then face private agents entirely, with which it would interact by introducing various schemes of bidding and competition. One may actually regard the new institutions in the public sector, the competitive production unit or the joint stock company, as private agents. Some bureaux have been reformed into independent production units in which the employees may have ownership stakes while others retain their public status at the same time as they are allowed to make a profit from their operations.

Private agents

The political community may turn to private agents in order to get tasks accomplished. These private agents may be of different types: privately owned joint stock companies, small private firms or simply individual entrepreneurs. The community may wish to set up a public–private partnership, finding an institution which combines public and private ownership according to some formula. The critical question, though, is again whether the principal can monitor the agent and establish a quid pro quo equating the costs of the agent's operations with corresponding benefits.

The standard institution for monitoring a private agent has been that of public regulation. The principal enacts regulatory schemes which introduce a legal framework for the operations of a private agent, be it a firm or an entrepreneur. Public regulation may also cover a public agent, be it an enterprise or a publicly owned joint stock company. Public regulation may focus upon the goods and services which the agent delivers: this is product regulation. Or it may concern itself with the conditions under which the agent operates: that is entry regulation. The basic problem in public regulation is that of asymmetric information. The agent knows more than the principal about the production processes, which in combination with opportunistic behaviour results in an economic rent for the agent, meaning higher than necessary costs for the principal (Tirole, 1993).

In the public sector reform movement it has been demanded that extensive processes of deregulation be initiated. Public regulation is not an institutional tool for monitoring an agent effectively, as it may actually become a strategic instrument for the agent in order to capture the principal. Under regulatory schemes the agent may have a better chance of securing its self-interests by capturing the monitoring mechanism with the principal. Rent-seeking is the tactic of the agent in order to get regulatory frameworks enacted, and enacted in such a manner that the agent can generate a slack.

Deregulation could constitute the tool of the principal in order to tame the agent only if it is combined with a strategy of competition. Deregulation may only result in a monopoly for the entrepreneur if there is no other agent willing to contest the entrepreneur. If contestation is not forthcoming owing to so-called natural circumstances, then the principal will not be better off by deregulation. It will simply face an agent over which it has no monitoring capacity at all. Thus, deregulation will not automatically work in order to solve principal–agent problems. What is decisive is contestability. Can the principal contrive contestability on a grand scale? Perhaps it should use a special agent in order to implement a detailed and strict anti-trust policy?

Anti-trust policy-making and transaction costs

Whether the principal faces a public or a private agent, the principal will need to use the new tools of tendering in order to check the agent, once hierarchy is not going to be used. There are two scenarios. In the first, the principal engages itself in processes of tendering, asking a set of bidders to come up with bids for contracts offered by as well as paid for by the principal. In the second, the principal makes arrangements to the effect that various agents are allowed to compete for the right to provide goods and services to be paid for by the consumer directly through user fees. In both cases the principal faces an agent that it cannot approach benevolently owing to the risk of opportunistic behaviour on the part of the agent.

What is the capacity of a public principal to set up and monitor schemes for bidding and competition? The main theory about anti-trust policy-making delivers a negative answer to this question. It is argued in the Demsetz interpretation that anti-trust policies are ineffective, as contestability is forthcoming spontaneously whenever an entrepreneur judges that there is a profit opportunity. The only thing that government can do to enhance competition is to see that there are no legal barriers to entry which it has enacted itself (Demsetz, 1991). Actually, in relation to a bureau which takes care of anti-trust policy, government faces the same principal–agent problem: how is government to know that the anti-trust bureau takes the right steps to promote the interests of the principal?

The warning that there are limits to the power of anti-trust policies to enhance competition entails that the principal, when resorting to tendering and contracting out, must pay much attention to institutional matters, making rules of competition transparent as well as seeing that they are implemented in an impartial manner by tribunals. What will matter more than anti-trust policy-making and implementation is the establishment of a uniform and clear framework of rules that can be tested in courts.

A public principal can handle an agent, whether public or private, by means of two interaction mechanisms, hierarchy or bidding. In the public sector reform movement in the early 1990s the latter was given precedence over the former. In order to handle a variety of forms of bidding the principal will have to accept increasing transaction costs.

Transaction costs involve a number of different items such as the costs of opening up and managing a bidding process, the costs of negotiating with potential suppliers as well as the costs of implementing a contract once it has been struck. Sometimes transaction costs are measured broadly to include all kinds of effort to reach and implement an agreement.

Obviously, the principal is prepared to incur a certain amount of transaction costs in order to reduce its production costs. There is a limit, however, to how much can be gained in incurring transaction costs. There is a risk in the new tendering schemes that the principal simply invests a lot in transaction costs but receives little reduction in production costs. The danger is again the possibility of opportunistic behaviour which does not go away when agents are transformed institutionally or bidding replaces hierarchy.

An agent may use various strategies under a bidding process to promote his/her interests which the principal may find it difficult to counter. It is not just a matter of the availability of numerous bidders. Opportunistic strategies may enter also at the stage when a final contract has been written but it is not clear how it is to be interpreted. The principal may not be enthusiastic about going to another supplier owing to extensive switching costs.

The scope of opportunistic behaviour for the agent depends upon his/her command of asset specific knowledge (Williamson, 1973). One must raise the question of whether or not many of the goods and services that governments provide in an advanced economy involve agents with asset specific knowledge. If this is so, then the principal may gain less than is hoped for by abandoning hierarchy and transforming the institutional status of the agent in public sector provision.

Why public joint stock companies?

If, as the Chicago message runs, contestation is naturally forthcoming – because if government was the only actor that would restrict contestability through either public provision or public regulation – and if contestation secures first-best solutions in allocation, meaning efficiency, then why should governments do anything else than further competition through the installation of schemes for tendering/bidding? Why in such a world of privatization and deregulation would the political community set up public joint stock companies that have to enter into competition with private firms to which they may very well lose out?

There is a paradox involved here. If the drive to introduce competition is successful, then public joint stock companies lack a purpose. Even worse, they will only constitute a government liability, because they cannot run huge profits when there is contestability. And if they constitute an asset, then government can cash that value by selling them immediately, meaning that it does not have to take on the risks involved in continued operation in a competitive market. Why, then, do governments favour the public joint stock company at the same time as they engage in aggressive deregulation?

If public joint stock companies are needed in a deregulated world where all players demand that the playing field be levelled, then perhaps when deregulation has been achieved government should sell off its shares in the joint stock companies? The deregulation, privatization and marketization framework, inspiring much public sector reform, really entails the final step of hiving off public enterprises once and for all from the public sector. Why should governments own firms that operate in a market environment? Immediately when a public joint stock company begins to operate in a deregulated environment facing contestability, the government assumes two contradictory roles: owner of the firm by means of property rights to the equity of the joint stock company, and representative of the consumers asking for the implementation of rules about competition and free entry. As owner, the government wants huge profits in order to safeguard the capital invested in the company, but as consumer agent it aims for competition, which could eliminate the company.

If one looks for a rationale for the incorporation process that occurs in most advanced countries, then one should search much more narrowly in the management structure, comparing the traditional public enterprise with the public joint stock company, where managerial discretion is much larger. The new autonomy of managers may be employed for the making of decisions that were politically impossible under the traditional governance structure.

When governments transform bureaux or public enterprises into public joint stock companies, then they may improve their bargaining position in relation to the other stakeholders surrounding the unit. The managers and not the politicians will then be responsible for any costs in staff. Private company law or the rules regulating the operations of joint stock companies offer an institutional setting under which efficiency promoting measures may be taken without too much political trouble, since private law requires that joint stock companies maintain their capital, punishing loss-making activities and instead accepting lay-offs.

In relation to the citizen-consumer, the public joint stock company can raise prices much more easily than the other two institutional mechanisms. Public joint stock companies operate under the same profit maximization restriction as any private firm, as politicians may argue when facing protests against higher user fees. But why is there a need for consumers to pay higher prices in relation to companies which they basically own themselves? In the last resort, the public principal is the set of citizens. If one accepts profit maximization in public joint stock companies, how can the citizen-consumer protect him/herself against monopoly behaviour on the part of the new agent, the public joint stock company?

The introduction of the joint stock company not only in infrastructure but also in the welfare state entails that people are no longer citizens with rights in relation to their authorities but merely consumers shopping around to see if they can get a good bargain even from public joint stock companies, of which they are the real owners. If public enterprises as joint stock companies are to make a profit on their activities beyond covering all kinds of costs, including capital expenditures, then to whom does the profit belong? If public joint stock companies really can operate in a market environment, then why are they not partially or completely privatized? Is there any better mechanism for the evaluation of public joint stock companies than bourses?

Conclusion

The provision of goods and services in the public sector has been the target of intensive reform activities, aimed at increasing efficiency in allocation. Why is efficiency such a major problem in the public sector? A simple principal–agent model (Laffont and Tirole, 1993) is suggested below that helps us locate where the critical problems arise in the public sector with regard to allocation. The key problem of efficiency may be approached in terms of a principal–agent framework, a public principal hiring an agent to do something for the political community.

The abandoning of the bureau model for the purpose of public resource allocation may be interpreted as a result of the realization that it involved difficulties on the side of the principal to monitor the agent and reach a quid pro quo. The same difficulties occurred also in public regulation of the entry type in relation to either a private firm or a public enterprise. From this realization comes the drive to employ bidding and to transform the nature of the agent with which the principal would interact.

The critical question is, however, whether the principal is in a stronger position in relation to the new agents under tendering schemes. What the principal must be able to handle are the complexities in processes of bidding and competition. The public principal may actually have a whole set of new problems when bidding replaces hierarchy and the principal faces agents other than the bureau and the public enterprise. The putting into place of competition on a massive scale calls for the clarification of the rules of competition as well as the existence of legal adjudication of such trans-parent rules. Even if such a set of institutions could be devised and made to operate smoothly, the principal may still not be pleased. There are two dangers: either that no real competition is forthcoming as public sector services are not attracting enough bidders, or that the transaction costs in handling the tendering processes become staggering.

The public joint stock company is supposed to operate under market conditions, bringing a profit for its owners, the government. But why should government run businesses and make profits from consumers in a deregu-lated world where there is free entry? The government becomes both the umpire and a player. If government can use taxation in order to pay for its standard operations, then why should it be involved in risk-taking in the market economy?

There are several rational arguments for incorporation. I do not wish to deny that moving a traditional public enterprise out of its status as a kind of government authority or quasi-bureau to the private sector in the form of a limited liability firm involves efficiency gains. In many countries the tradi-tional public enterprises occupied a grey zone between the ordinary Weberian bureaux and the other joint stock companies owned by govern-ment, which really operated under market conditions. Thus, public enter-prises were firms and bureaux at the same time, reflected in a special regime under which managers could run the enterprise on a day-to-day basis with much discretion, but had to consult with government on any major decision about investments or charges. In a deregulated economy public firms also have to operate in an international environment, in which slow decisions may hurt firms. Thus, transforming a public enterprise into an ordinary joint stock company, while at the time deregulating it, would make the firm operate more smoothly and certainly more effectively. In a world domi-nated by international capital markets and the mondialization of demand, it does not make sense to conduct the state enterprises as they used to be managed.

Changing the regime for the state firms, from the old state enterprise format to the joint stock company format or the limited liability company where government owns the equity, offers several efficiency gains. First, managers can act quicker, which is often important in an international economy. Second, there is a clearer distinction between the owners and the managers, as managers' responsibility is increased at the same time as their autonomy is widened. Third, it becomes more transparent what the objectives of the firm are, as strictly economic goals can be distinguished from social ones. Finally, managers have to take the responsibility for unpleasant decisions such as downsizing or raising charges, which politicians would have immense difficulties in facing without bringing in other kinds of considerations. In one sentence, state joint stock companies would have a better chance of being run solely on the basis of economic deliberations than the traditional state enterprise. It may even turn profitable, giving government a reasonable rate of return on its invested capital, which is often immense in state enterprises.

However, why should not governments also take the next step and place their equity on the stock market? If governments run companies and deregulate at the same time, then they will be both player and umpire. If governments want to develop their own enterprises, which is what owners do, then how can they at the same time insist upon a Ricardian regime of full competitivity and neutrality in processes of bidding and tendering where its own enterprises participate? Governments may wish to retain their firms because they run profits, but selling the shares at their market value will allow governments to cash in all known future profits. State joint stock companies do not make sense in a deregulated international economic system. Incorporation is a first step, but privatization is the next logical one under a Ricardian regime of competition.

Few governments have, however, pursued a straightforward policy of privatization. Most governments hesitate to sell off their leading public enterprises, considering that they remain in the public interest even after incorporation in a deregulated world. Even full-scale incorporation may be too much for governments who aspire to control parts of the economy by means of their ownership of large firms, like the Norwegian government. Norway has been identified as a regime somewhere in between full incorporation and the traditional administrative firm. Governments in Germany and France have been very slow to sell out their huge infrastructural firms, even partially, although their profitability has not been impressive with the possible exception of the energy sector.

I would argue in any case that under a Ricardian regime state ownership of equity in huge firms should be diminished in order to minimize the risks that government should take in private sector ventures. The control that governments seek through their ownership of these incorporated firms could be achieved by means of new forms of regulation. The state cannot be simultaneously a player in a market and the umpire of the market without creating confusion. Let us look more closely at the new Ricardian regime for the public sector, which is in line with the theory of David Ricardo that markets tend to operate effectively when left alone to do what they are supposed to do, i.e. allocate resources under competitive forms of inter-action between demand and supply.

References

Aberbach, J.D., Putnam, R.D. and Rockman, B.A. (1981) *Bureaucrats and Politicians in Western Democracies.* Cambridge, MA: Harvard University Press.

Alchian, A. and Demsetz, H. (1972) 'Production, information costs, and economic organization', *American Economic Review,* 62: 777–95.

Demsetz, H. (1991) *Efficiency, Competition and Policy.* Oxford: Blackwell.

Laffont, J.-J. and Tirole, J. (1993) *A Theory of Incentives in Procurement and Regulation.* Cambridge, MA: MIT Press.

Pressman, J. and Wildavsky, A. (1984) *Implementation.* Berkeley: University of California Press.

Ricketts, M. (1987) *The Economics of Business Enterprise.* Hemel Hempstead: Harvester Wheatsheaf.

Stigler, G. (ed.) (1988) *Chicago Studies in Political Economy.* Chicago: Chicago University Press.

Thynne, I. (1994) 'The incorporated company as an instrument of government: a quest for a comparative understanding', *Governance,* 7: 59–82.

Tirole, J. (1993) *The Theory of Industrial Organization.* Cambridge, MA: MIT Press.

Williamson, O. (1973) *Markets and Hierarchies.* New York: Free Press.

Williamson, O. (1986) *Economic Organization.* New York: Free Press.

13

Conclusion

Jan-Erik Lane

Public sector reform is omnipresent in the countries with an advanced economy and democratic political institutions. What varies is the amplitude of the reform drive putting into place a new type of public management that we will call 'Ricardian'. How can we identify some of the main differences in public sector reform? One way to approach the considerable country differences is to focus upon a couple of salient distinctions along which public sector reform vary.

Public sector reform can have two objectives, or only two fundamental purposes: efficiency or justice. Raising the outputs in relation to the inputs or achieving more and better outcomes for a given set of government outputs are the efficiency goals, which have loomed very large in all countries studied in this book. The second major goal of public sector reform is to enhance social justice. All too often these two objectives collide, which forces governments to find trade-off solutions, combining a certain amount of each. How that balance between efficiency and justice is found and established varies from one country to another, reflecting to a large extent whether a country not only reforms its public sector but also makes an overhaul of its welfare state.

Thus, one source of variation concerns the nature of welfare state reform. Much of public sector reform has implications for the welfare state, but not all reforms change the welfare state. Public sector reform may focus upon the public enterprises or change the mode of service provision without any considerable retrenchment of welfare state programmes. Yet, public sector reform may be closely connected with an overhaul of the welfare state, or even a complete restructuring of welfare state programmes. In the case of New Zealand there is the simultaneity of two processes, both extensive public sector reforms as well as welfare state dismantling. In Western Europe, only the United Kingdom would come close to New Zealand. The aim of public sector reform may even be to protect and consolidate the welfare state, as in the Nordic cases. Or these reforms may rather be independent, meaning that public sector reform is one thing and welfare state reform another, as in Germany and the Netherlands. When public enterprises are turned into public joint stock companies – incorporation – then the ambition may simply be to generate a surplus that can actually be useful in paying for welfare state programmes, which tend to remain gratuitous to a large extent in Western Europe.

Another source of variation is the extent to which public sector reform is merely trimming or cut-back management or whether it involves the move to a different regime, or set of principles for structuring the public sector. Trimming a public programme is different from putting into place a different regime. There have been many forms of retrenchment in public sector reform, especially when generous welfare state programmes have been made less so, either in terms of handouts or in terms of eligibility. But retrenchment need not imply a different regime.

Thus, many governments have cut back on various transfer payments or introduced or raised user fees for several services that used to be gratis. But some governments have started to experiment with an entirely different regime for public sector programmes. Take the example of unemployment benefits or poverty relief programmes. Whereas these handouts used to be almost unconditional in Denmark, the Danish government has moved these programmes towards a 'workfare' conception, demanding that the clients in these programmes take steps to enter the ordinary labour market. In 1993 a new labour market law demanded much more from the unemployed, not only cutting the length of time that a person could receive unemployment benefits but also requiring an individual contract by which the client commits him/herself to take steps to leave the predicament of being unemployed. A similar regime was introduced in the area of social or poverty relief in 1997, called 'active social policy'.

Thus, still another source of variation is the nature of the regime changes enacted in different countries. Regime changes in the governance of the public sector may be either economical or social, reflecting whether public sector reform is based upon a new economic regime or a new social contract. And both kinds of regime changes, enacted by means of a new economic regime or social contract, may remodel the public sector or replace public sector programmes with market supplied services.

Much of public sector reform is no doubt driven by the search for a new economic regime for public service provision. It is not merely a matter of increasing efficiency, whether internal efficiency or productivity, or external efficiency or goal attainment. Efficiency has been a standard objective in many reform waves over the past decades. It is the means that are different this time, and they point to the search for a different regime – the DPM-framework. This Ricardian regime for the public sector is not merely a new fad to be added to the long series of novelties of how to provide for public services, often labelled 'public management' or recently 'new public management'. It involves a real break with the entire approach that looks upon the public sector as a necessary correction of market failures. Instead of focusing upon public sector programmes as vital complements to weaknesses in the way in which markets operate, the public sector must learn from the basic insights of the market mechanism, using this Ricardian wisdom both when it structures an answer to the macro problem of the overall size of the public sector and when it provides micro solutions to public sector provision. Ricardo argued, of course, that the private sector with its market mechanism increases economic efficiency, or total output, if left to operate according to its logic – the laizzez-faire philosophy.

The call for deregulation is based upon the perception that state intervention in the form of economic entry regulations does not result in better outcomes than the use of markets, especially competitive ones. Governments must learn how to stimulate competition, not legislate it away in the form of licences. If regulation is resorted to, then governments must learn how to operate an entirely different form of regulatory scheme under which a regime of competition is nourished as well as implemented in judicial forms. Take the example of the French reform of its railroad system in 1997. In an attempt to restructure the debt ridden railroad company – SNCF – the French socialist government will place the track in a new RFF (Le reseau ferre de France), which will lease its track to operators like the SNCF under competitive bidding and tendering. Such a Ricardian regime is far away from the old regime for state enterprises, operating not only as a regulated monopoly but also with government as the principal in order to reduce even more the scope for opportunistic behaviour on the part of the agent – at least so it was believed before the advent of the deregulation philosophy. The risk is that transaction costs rise.

There is some truth to the claim that successful deregulation requires not only the dismantling of old regulatory regimes of state intervention but also the putting into place of new forms of state activities which agree with Ricardian notions. The European Union appears to have been successful in choosing regulatory schemes that enhance competition while at the same time calling for limitation of national regulation that restricts competition.

The search for privatization implies that public enterprises will lose their rationale. Operating in the business sector of the public sector, these firms used to motivate their existence with the standard arguments about economies of scale and the risk for monopolies. However, in a deregulated economic system facing a more or less open world economy – mondialization – there seems to be little need for the traditional public enterprises. Governments have responded to the changed environment for these often giant firms by engaging in the strategy of incorporation. Yet, we ask why governments should stop ahead of full-scale privatization, if in a Ricardian world of free competition the only forms of monopolies that survive are those backed by government legislation, i.e. market restriction. Consequently, governments should list their joint stock companies at the bourse.

Marketization is the final step in the Ricardian regime, as it concerns basically the core public sector functions, or the so-called soft sector. When public programmes cannot simply be shifted over to the private sector, because they make up the soft parts of the public sector which – it is considered – should remain public, then their provision could be marketized in the sense that contracting and bidding is used instead of hierarchy. The move to so-called internal markets can be done more or less comprehensively, which constitutes a major source of variation in the punch of public sector reform among countries.

Here, the new Ricardian regime for the public sector is based upon a fundamental reassessment of the role of the Weberian bureaucracy. Competition in supply is considered vital not only in relation to the first major institution in the public sector, the state enterprise or the local government firm, but is also considered relevant for the second major institution, the bureau. Under the new economic regime for the public sector, Ricardian mechanisms such as contracting out, bidding and tendering replace the Weberian bureau characteristics of monopoly, authority and longevity. If one believes more in short-term contracting than long-term contracting, which is distinctive of Ricardian marketers, then marketization of the core or soft public sector is the correct reform. But why is there to be only competition in supply under the new economic regime? Why not also choice on the demand side meaning that citizens send signals about preferences through a system of user fees?

The new economic regime also has implications for the redistributive part of the public sector, which is today as large as the allocative part. The new economic regime reforms the transfer programmes that constitute often more than half of the cost for the entire public sector. While the new Ricardian regime for the allocative part of the public sector focuses strictly on micro efficiency, the same economic regime about the redistributive side of the public sector delivers macro efficiency considerations. Transfer programmes have been trimmed or cut back as well as changed structurally in order to recognize the problems of incentive compatibility in income maintenance programmes and of excess burden in taxation.

In relation to bureaux and state enterprises the Ricardian regime equates schemes involving bidding and tendering with efficiency. This is the allocative side of the public sector. With regard to the redistributive side the Ricardian regime warns of committing two kinds of errors in policy-making for income maintenance, one of which hurts efficiency by the incentive system whereas the other is detrimental to the full utilization of a qualified labour force, i.e., a type I error versus a type II error.

In providing for income maintenance governments may choose too high a replacement rate, which is not strictly necessary from the point of view of poverty relief and which may hurt the incentives in the economy. Governments choosing a very high replacement rate may erroneously believe that only such a high rate prevents the client falling back into deterimental poverty – a type II error involving the failure to reject a false hypothesis. However, governments may also accept a false hypothesis, setting the replacement rates too low meaning that clients will never be able to come back into the economy or maintain a tolerable standard of living – a type I error. When governments try to steer clear of making a type I error or a type II error in redistribution policies, they probably end up somewhere around 60–70% as a general replacement rate in most transfer programmes, which has been a target in some recent transfer payments reforms.

Yet, we also have here a source of variation in public sector reform, as some governments have been more reluctant than others to cut income maintenance programmes, partly for tactical reasons and partly for justice considerations. Some governments have adopted harsh means-tested criteria for income support whereas other governments have kept very high replacements rates at about 90% – with risks for type I or type II errors. When governments cut the transfer programmes, then it is considered as threatening the welfare state much more than when it introduced bidding into the allocative programmes. Most governments have introduces more user fees for public services, but to a varying extent from one country to another as well as from one service sector to another. With regard to the core welfare state services, user fees, if existent, never fully cover programme costs.

Avoiding the two kinds of errors in the making of redistributive policies, governments have come to rely more and more upon actuarial principles, connecting transfer payments with individual contribution schemes, thus moving away from the pay-as-you-go schemes, at least to some extent. If a government is not sure about how to avoid a type I or type II error, then perhaps it should trust the clients to take the necessary decisions about replacement rates by planning their futures and pre-empting their risks in relation to their predicted opportunities.

The Ricardian regime is basically about the economic relation between government and the individual, attempting to increase the benefits for the individual in relation to his/her costs for the public sector – i.e., proportionality. The new social contract for the public sector emphasizes impartiality, both with regard to public administration and in relation to the private sector. Whereas the Ricardian regime for the public sector calls for less public expenditure, the demand for impartiality involves increasing public outlays. Under the impartiality norm enters a vast variety of measures to protect the rights of individuals and groups by means of the establishment of institutions – legal as well as non-legal – for complaint and correction. The reform of the public sector in order to enhance impartiality is not only a major feature of the new state structures in Eastern Europe, they also loom very large in public sector reform in OECD countries.

In the advanced capitalist democracies there is a powerful search for a new civic morality, including a better protection of human rights for all men and women including minorities of various kinds. On the one hand, human rights are interpreted in a much broader sense and on the other hand human rights begin to cover also group rights, referring not only to historical minorities but also to newly identified groups in the welfare state. One observes legislation to protect not only language minorities or groups with a special historical culture, but also numerous new legislative measures in relation to women, homosexuals and immigrants. In Western Europe, much of the judicial efforts have focused upon the incorporation of the European Convention for the Protection of Human Rights and Fundamental Freedoms from 1950, including additional protocols from 1952 and 1963, into national legislation.

Although many European states have signed the Convention making it binding upon the state in question, several countries do not recognize these rights as genuine municipal law until the Convention has been incorporated into national law by means of a legal instrument enacted in the national assembly. In the last decade several West European states have moved to either transform the European Convention into municipal law or to incorporate the whole Charter and the additions into their legal system. Thus, the following countries have pursued the full incorporation strategy: Finland (1990) and Denmark (1992), whereas Sweden and Norway have done so most recently. In 1952 West Germany incorporated the Convention with Austria following in 1958 and France in 1974. In the latter two countries the Convention has a higher status than ordinary law. The United Kingdom is now considering incorporation in the form of a bill of rights.

The incorporation of the European Convention entails the judicialization of politics in the country in question. Not only can matters be referred to the European Court of Human Rights in Strasbourg, whose judgements the states have bound themselves to respect, but the various national courts can also refer to this human rights framework when examining national administration or legislation. Although several countries have not accepted full-scale legal review, the general trend is towards more and more powers for judges or courts to examine the public sector from the point of view of human rights interpreted in an increasingly broader sense. The now relevant human rights framework covers the rights to life, to never being subjected to degrading treatment, to liberty and security, to lawful arrest and treatment under due process of law, to having respect for private and family life, to the classical negative freedoms of thought, religion and expression, to association and to engage in trade practices including property rights, to marry and found a family as well as to be protected against discrimination in whatever form that may take.

Human rights tend to be interpreted in an even wider sense as including group rights, involving numerous immunities of minorities, which may restrict the operation of the principle of majority rule so fundamental in a democracy. The judicialization of politics involves not only rights of cultural minorities but also various forms of positive discrimination or affirmative action.

The requirement of impartiality is not raised only in relation to public administration but also with regard to private sector activities. Thus, governments have taken steps to counteract various forms of discrimination not only in the public sector but also in the private sector.

The demand for more impartiality necessitates a strengthening of the implementation mechanisms. Thus, governments have not only taken steps to legislate about human or group rights, but various institutions have been empowered to deal with grievances and seek redress. Thus, the institution of the ombudsman has spread more and more, either in its Swedish or its Danish version, which is a first step for expressing a complaint. However, the judicial institutions have also been empowered to seek redress for individuals or groups.

Let us end this volume by quoting the master champion of markets, David Ricardo. In his *Principles of Political Economy and Taxation* we find the following lines:

> It is only in consequence of such variations that capital is apportioned precisely, in the requisite abundance and no more, to the production of the different commodities which happen to be in demand. With the rise or fall of price, profits are elevated above, or depressed below, their general level; and capital is either encouraged to enter into, or is warned to depart from, the particular employment in which the variation has taken place. (1965: 48)

Replacing the old Weberian framework for state operations with a Ricardian regime of tendering/bidding and incorporation would be conducive to removing the efficiency problems connected with the two traditional public sector institutions, the bureau and the public enterprise, reflecting the typical cost-benefit incentives system in these institutions (Alchian, 1977: 127–49).

Modern government in the advanced capitalist democracies operate two kinds of activity: (a) soft sector activities such as education, health care and social care, besides public goods; and (b) business activities such as infrastructure and housing. The Ricardian regime is highly suitable for (b) whereas the Weberian framework remains attractive for (a). The closer one gets to a legal manner of approaching the provision of public services – *rights* – the more relevant Max Weber becomes (Weber, 1978). This justice reforms should be handled by Weberian hierarchies.

References

Alchian, A.A. (1977) *Economic Forces at Work*. Indianapolis: Liberty Press.

Ricardo, D. (1965) *The Principles of Political Economy and Taxation*. 1817. London: Everyman's Library.

Weber, M. (1978) *Economy and Society. I*. Berkeley: University of California Press.

Index